PROJECT PLANNING AND MANAGEMENT

An Integrated System for Improving Productivity

Louis J. Goodman, P.E.

Project Management Consultant and Lecturer
Visiting Scholar, UCLA

CBS

CBS Publishers & Distributors Pvt. Ltd.

New Delhi • Bengaluru • Chennai • Kochi • Kolkata • Mumbai
Hyderabad • Nagpur • Patna • Pune • Vijayawada

CBS Pubs ISBN: 81-239-0473-8
Chapman ISBN: 0-442-22762-0

First Indian Edition: 1996
Reprint: 2001

This edition has been published in India by arrangement with Chapman & Hall Inc., New York

Published by **Satish Kumar Jain** and produced by **Varun Jain** for
CBS Publishers & Distributors Pvt. Ltd.,
4819/XI Prahlad Street, 24 Ansari Road, Daryaganj, New Delhi - 110002
delhi@cbspd.com, cbspubs@airtelmail.in • www.cbspd.com
Ph.: 23289259, 23266861, 23266867 • Fax: 011-23243014

Corporate Office: 204 FIE, Industrial Area, Patparganj, Delhi - 110 092
Ph: 49344934 • Fax: 011-49344935
E-mail: publishing@cbspd.com • publicity@cbspd.com

Branches:

- ***Bengaluru:*** 2975, 17th Cross, K.R. Road, Bansankari 2nd Stage, Bengaluru - 70 • Ph: +91-80-26771678/79 • Fax: +91-80-26771680 E-mail: cbsbng@gmail.com, bangalore@cbspd.com
- ***Chennai:*** No. 7, Subbaraya Street, Shenoy Nagar, Chennai - 600030 Ph: +91-44-26681266, 26680620 • Fax: +91-44-42032115 E-mail: chennai@cbspd.com
- ***Kochi:*** Ashana House, 39/1904, A.M. Thomas Road, Valanjambalam, Ernakulum, Kochi • Ph: +91-484-4059061-65 Fax: +91-484-4059065 • E-mail: cochin@cbspd.com
- ***Kolkata:*** 6-B, Ground Floor, Rameshwar Shaw Road, Kolkata - 700014 Ph: +91-33-22891126/7/8 • E-mail: kolkata@cbspd.com
- ***Mumbai:*** 83-C, Dr. E. Moses Road, Worli, Mumbai - 400018 Ph: +91-9833017933, 022-24902340/41 • E-mail: mumbai@cbspd.com

Representatives:

• Bhubaneswar	0-9911037372	• Hyderabad	0-9885175004	• Jharkhand	0-9811541605
• Nagpur	0-9021734563	• Patna	0-9334159340	• Pune	0-9623451994
• Uttarakhand	0-9716462459	• Dhaka (Bangladesh)	01912-003485		

Printed at:
J.S. Offset Printers, Delhi (India)

Preface and Acknowledgments

This book is based on nine years of experience with an international, interdisciplinary project team committed to the task of developing and testing a new approach to project planning and management in the dual interests of productivity and safety. The model designed and developed is based on the conceptual framework of an integrated project planning and management cycle (IPPMC). Experience with the IPPMC demonstrates its effectiveness in planning and managing projects from inception through completion as a unified process with continuous evaluation to ensure proper attention to each phase/task of the integrated project cycle. This includes additional emphasis on environmental feasibility—a sorely neglected area—along with a detailed checklist to prevent waste (costly overruns), project failures (not meeting objectives), and structural failures and to analyze the impact of all projects on the environment.

The book is intended to meet the needs of both educators and practitioners, who must understand the integrated project cycle from inception through completion and the broad range of factors that contribute to a project's success or failure. The process of decision making in anticipating problems that might arise during design and implementation is enhanced by the use of IPPMC case histories. The lessons derived from these cases have also been found to be useful in many fields other than public works, such as agriculture, industry, and social areas (education, public health, etc). A brief description of each chapter will illustrate the diverse groups and interests served by this book.

Chapter 1 introduces the concept of the IPPMC and its four phases, ranging from project identification to completion, evaluation, and refinement. It highlights the need for a new project management team to assume responsibility for all tasks in the integrated project cycle in order to provide unified control. This new approach is reinforced by experience with many projects in many countries which shows that the majority of projects in all sectors follow a similar process from inception to completion *and* that the process is a function of the integrated project cycle.

Chapter 2 introduces the IPPMC and case history materials. It summarizes a three-year search by members of the project team for resource materials on the various tasks in the IPPMC. This exhaustive search demonstrated many gaps in the literature, in education, and in practice. A major conclusion was the need for carefully researched and published case histories of a wide variety of projects from all sectors to establish badly needed data bases that would provide useful lessons and insights for future projects. A review of available case studies from different disciplines is included to demonstrate the need for case histories in the IPPMC framework. The chapter also discusses critical gaps in the literature, which are covered in this book.

Chapter 3 discusses feasibility and appraisal. Based on preliminary formulation and design work, feasibility studies must be conducted and analyzed to determine if the project is justified from economic, social, and technological points of view. If so, can the necessary human, financial, and organizational resources be provided to implement it? Will the project offer sufficient benefits to justify the use of scarce resources, with due regard given to possible long-term environmental changes (both material and cultural)? These are critical questions that must be answered by competent professionals. This chapter represents the critical juncture in the project cycle in all sectors. It provides baseline data for subsequent tasks in the IPPMC.

Chapter 4 addresses project evaluation, an area not covered in the classroom and only recently (1970s) emerging in practice, especially in international funding agencies. Various models are examined and related to the IPPMC to emphasize the need for both ongoing and postproject evaluation.

Chapter 5 presents and discusses guidelines for researchers and writers of case histories of public works projects. The guidelines also serve as a checklist for project control, evaluation, and troubleshooting.

Chapters 6, 7, and 8 cover three case histories of projects with environmental problems and issues. Chapter 8 also demonstrates the large number of serious problems that emerge when a fragmented approach is used to plan, design, and implement a complex project. Each case is written in the IPPMC framework.

Chapter 9 discusses the all-important and often neglected factors of how best to analyse and incorporate the lessons learned from evaluation of the project into future project planning, design, and management.

Chapter 10 presents a brief summary followed by conclusions for both educators and practitioners in a variety of engineering and scientific fields.

Appendix A contains a syllabus of the IPPMC prototype curriculum. Appendix B consists of executive summaries of six IPPMC case histories, including a small hydroelectric power project in China.

Appendices C and D briefly cover geothermal energy and biomass energy, respectively. Appendix E presents a sample checklist of guidelines and questions in the IPPMC framework for the necessary quality control of each task.

The IPPMC curriculum and supporting materials were developed, tested, and refined over a nine-year period (1975–1984) by senior scholars and practitioners from 10 countries in Asia, the Pacific, and the United States. The motivation for this intensive team effort was the ongoing waste and mismanagement in their respective countries by both national government agencies and international funding organizations.

The initial international team comprised 18 scholars and practitioners from seven countries, increasing to 30 persons from ten countries. The author is indebted to each of them and their cooperating institutions for their commitment, dedication, and many contributions. Special thanks are conveyed to Dr. John Hawkins, University of California, Los Angeles, who remains active with the author in expanding the applications of the IPPMC to various aspects of society, including education. As friend and colleague, he wrote Chapter 4 and prepared one of the executive summaries. Then I wish to acknowledge my co-authors for the Hawaii bagasse and geothermal cases, Dr. Tetsuo Miyabara and Barbara Yount; and the co-authors of the Trans-Alaska Pipeline case, Drs. George Geistauts and Vern Hauck. I am also indebted to Dr. Takeshi Yoshihara, Energy Program Administrator, State of Hawaii, for his assistance in updating the two Hawaii case histories for the Epilogues.

Thanks are also due the East-West Center for its financial and moral support from 1975 to 1983 and to the Exxon Education Foundation for its significant grant in 1978, which enabled the researching and writing of 30 case histories of development projects in the IPPMC framework as integral components of the curriculum. Finally, much credit is due to my secretaries, Maggie Hurwitz in San Diego, California, for her endless typing and retyping of the initial chapters and Jane Reeves in Clemson, South Carolina, for her preparation of the final chapters.

LOUIS J. GOODMAN
ORLANDO, FLORIDA

Abbreviations

bbl	barrel	kWh	kilowatt-hour
Btu	British thermal unit	l	liter
°C	degrees Celsius	lb	pound
cm	centimeter	m	meter
dB	decibel	m^2	square meter
°F	degrees Fahrenheit	m^3	cubic meter
ft	foot	μ	micron
ft^2	square foot	μg	microgram
ft^3	cubic foot	mg	milligram
g	gram	mV	millivolt
gal	gallon	MW	megawatt
hp	horsepower	MWe	megawatt electrical
hr	hour	ohm-cm	ohm-centimeter
Hz	Hertz	ohm-m	ohm-meter
in.	inch	ppb	parts per billion
kcal	kilocalorie	ppm	parts per million
kg	kilogram	psig	pounds per square inch, gauge
km	kilometer		
klb	kilopound	W	watt
kW	kilowatt	Wh	watt-hour
kWe	kilowatt electrical	Whe	watt-hour electrical

Contents

Contents

PROJECT PLANNING AND MANAGEMENT

CHAPTER 1

Introduction to the Integrated Project Planning and Management Cycle (IPPMC)

A BRIEF OVERVIEW OF MANAGEMENT PROBLEMS

The key to economic and social growth in all countries—developed or developing—is better management in all sectors: agriculture, industry, public works, education, public health, government. In the U.S. in recent years, investigators have studied waste and mismanagement on a wide range of construction projects, including nuclear power plants, in the federal government itself, and in numerous other situations.[1,2,3]

Remedial actions are being attempted in both education and practice. There is a growing awareness of the need to improve both the productivity and quality of projects. For example, in 1969 a report by the American Society for Engineering Education (ASEE) indicated only 10 bachelor's level programs in engineering management.[4] Yet, according to the Engineers Joint Council, two-thirds of all engineers are likely to spend the last two-thirds of their careers as managers.[5] With schools of engineering becoming more aware of the need to include management in the curriculum, the number offering engineering management programs had risen by 1979 to 25.[6] In 1979 Kocaoglu surveyed the status of graduate programs in engineering management and found 70 with some offered jointly with a school of business.[7] In 1980 Bennett reviewed the history of engineering management programs, including a survey of related activities by national professional engineering societies.[8]

Engineering management programs are mostly in civil and industrial engineering departments, with some interaction with business administration. Surprisingly, management receives little or no attention in one of the newer engineering disciplines—environmental. The need to better understand the impacts of various projects on the environment and public health is intimately related to project planning and management. The National Environmental Protection Act (NEPA), signed into law on January 1, 1970, encourages harmony between man and his environment. The Act imposes environmental impact statement requirements on all agencies and departments, requiring identification of adverse environmental impacts, consideration of alternatives, and public distribution of these documents.

Internationally, the environment emerged as an important public issue during the 1960's. At that time it was perceived almost exclusively as a concern of the industrialized countries. For urbanization and industrialization, which had created great benefits for these societies, were also producing unexpected costs in: (1) pollution of air, soil and water; (2) destruction of natural resources; and (3) deterioration in the quality of urban life. In June 1972 the United Nations held a conference on the human environment in Stockholm. The conference had two significant results: (1) establishing the environment as an important item on the agenda of governments throughout the world; and (2) creating the United Nations Environment Program to assist developing countries.

Yet, in spite of the widely acknowledged idea that man needs to *understand and manage* the relationship between the environment and economic and social projects, there remains a major gap: We still deal with pollution problems in compartments neatly related to single parts of the environment—air, land, and water. This fragmentation is compounded by the even more serious fragmentation of project planning, design, implementation, and management. Indeed, my experience with over 700 public works projects in the United States, Ecuador, Egypt and Asia confirms the outstanding need for more *unified* control of all projects, both public and private, from inception to completion.

Unfortunately, engineering management education and practice have not fully addressed this need for a unified approach. On many projects we continue to encounter serious problems of waste and mismanagement of financial, human, and natural resources. On most projects, this waste stems from the aforementioned fragmented approach. Beyond the waste and reduced productivity is the adverse impact of mismanagement of the environment itself—pollution of air, soil, and water with resulting degradation of vegetation, water supply systems, and public health.

EXAMPLES OF PROJECT* PROBLEMS

Since its completion in 1977, much has been written about the Trans-Alaska Pipeline System (TAPS).[9] While originally budgeted at $900 million in 1968, by the time of its completion, the project actually cost over $8 billion (later

*By definition, a project achieves a given objective within a set time frame. Projects should be a response to a readily apparent need for economic and social growth in any sector in both developing and developed societies. Therefore, the terms "development project" and "project" have the same meaning.

studies show over $9 billion), making it the most expensive privately financed project in history. In the process, TAPS transformed the economy of Alaska, caused a boom-bust cycle in some communities, endangered its environment, and restructured its society.

Another classic example of project complexity and cost overruns is the Washington Public Power Supply System's (WPPSS) nuclear power plant projects. The 1973 $4.1 billion cost estimate ballooned to an estimated $25 billion in 1983. Even more serious are the facts that (1) the State of Washington defaulted on $2.25 billion in municipal bonds, the largest such default in U.S. history, and that (2) three of the five plants under simultaneous construction were abandoned.

In the field of hazardous waste disposal and subsequent consequences, the United States is still struggling, through the Environmental Protection Agency (EPA) and Congress (for policies and funding), to accomplish two top-priority needs. First, toxic waste cleanup has barely begun, in spite of the so-called Superfund of $1.6 billion established in 1980. In 1984, according to EPA staff members, only six toxic dumps were eliminated, with well over 1200 (1800 according to some estimates) to go. Second, a mechanism has yet to be designed and tested for monitoring soil and groundwater contamination from toxic waste disposal. Few site-specific data are available on the performance and costs of remedial measures. The lessons of Love Canal and Times Beach have *not* been fully learned.

Internationally, there have been project problems similar to, or more severe than, the three briefly mentioned. However, experience clearly demonstrates a common thread running through the majority of the problem areas experienced in most projects, and in all sectors and all countries. The common thread is lack of teamwork among planners, designers, implementers, and managers of projects, compounded by a lack of adequate *and* accurate information. This relates directly to the priority needs of the construction industry, as reported by The Business Roundtable's Construction Industry Cost Effectiveness study.[1] The 1983 Summary Report places high priority on (1) the need for teamwork among planners, designers, contractors, and owners and (2) the need for accurate information.

These identical conclusions were reached by an international, interdisciplinary project team at the East-West Center* in 1975, with the author as project director. In addition, the project team recommended a new approach to project planning and management that would focus on the con-

*The East-West Center is an educational institution established in Hawaii in 1960 by the United States Congress. The center's mandate is "to promote better relations and understanding among the nations of Asia, the Pacific, and the United States through cooperative study, training, and research."

cept of an integrated project cycle as the basis of a new curriculum and related resource materials.

THE PROBLEM: THE NEED TO IMPROVE PROJECT PLANNING AND MANAGEMENT

The East-West Center and its partner institutions in the Asian-Pacific region had for many years recognized problems in the area of public policy implementation and project management (PPIPM). Specific aspects of the problem were studied at the Center during 1971–1974 in a series of annual conferences and workshops on public leadership, project feasibility and evaluation, and manpower development for project management. The experiences and recommendations of the scholars and practitioners in 18 countries who participated in these meetings indicated the need for research and development of a systems methodology to solve the overall problem of project management. This need was emphasized by many international assistance agencies such as the World Bank, the Asian Development Bank, the United Nations Development Program, the U.S. Agency for International Development, the Inter-American Bank, and the Canadian International Development Agency.

It was deemed advisable to convene a Planning Workshop on Project Management in June 1975. This workshop provided a forum for a group of resource persons representing 10 countries in Asia, the Pacific, and the United States to articulate what was needed to achieve better project management and to recommend a strategy for follow-up activities to meet these needs. A two-day joint session was held with participants of a complementary Workshop on Public Leadership Strategies. This provided an opportunity to gain mutual understanding and support from leaders representing various ministries, universities, and private organizations from these same countries. Thus the PPIPM project team was created, and agreement was reached on the curriculum research activities over the next year. The project team would convene at the East-West Center in August or September 1976 for progress reports and critiques. It was also agreed that a curriculum would be developed in the context of an integrated project cycle, from project identification to completion and evaluation.

The rationale for the concept of an integrated project cycle as the basis for curriculum research and development was reinforced by a series of meetings with senior officials in both public and private institutions in Japan, Korea, the Philippines, and the United States in 1973 and 1974.[10] Indeed, support for the need to improve project management training and education emerged rapidly in the late 1960s with postmortems and analyses of what went wrong with development strategies and projects in the first two decades after World War II.[11-13]

THE INTEGRATED PROJECT PLANNING AND MANAGEMENT CYCLE (IPPMC)

Studies of costly overruns and failures of development projects by the PPIPM project teams in their respective countries pointed to the need for more effective coordination *and* control of the various tasks throughout the project cycle. The project cycle is not a new concept. It has been used by the World Bank and other international funding agencies for a number of years as a basis for their lending programs. There is general agreement that each project passes through a cycle which, with some variations, is common to all.[14] The PPIPM project team developed the IPPMC as its conceptual framework for the new curriculum because of the need to systematically integrate the many tasks and procedures to ensure better control and productivity.

The IPPMC is a conceptual tool for observing and analyzing the process of a development project (Figure 1.1). This integrated matrix has been developed to clarify the major phases and tasks that constitute the project, from planning through implementation, evaluation, and refinement, with the central function of policymaking providing focus and direction throughout.

The IPPMC may be divided into four phases:

- Planning, appraisal, and design
- Selection, approval, and activation
- Operation, control, and handover
- Evaluation and refinement

Specific tasks may be further identified within these four phases.

Figure 1.1 illustrates the relationship among the phases of the project cycle, the tasks within each phase, and the overall dependency on central policy issues. It must be emphasized that the project cycle is an ideal model; not every project will conform exactly to it. However, as mentioned earlier, each project does pass through a cycle consisting of a sequence of phases, and the last phase should produce new project ideas and approaches. Thus, the project cycle is self-renewing, as shown in Figure 1.1. Continual feedback and dependency do exist among the tasks, however. Each task is dependent upon and influenced by the others.

There is a two-way flow of information between those responsible for policy and those responsible for managing each of the project tasks. This

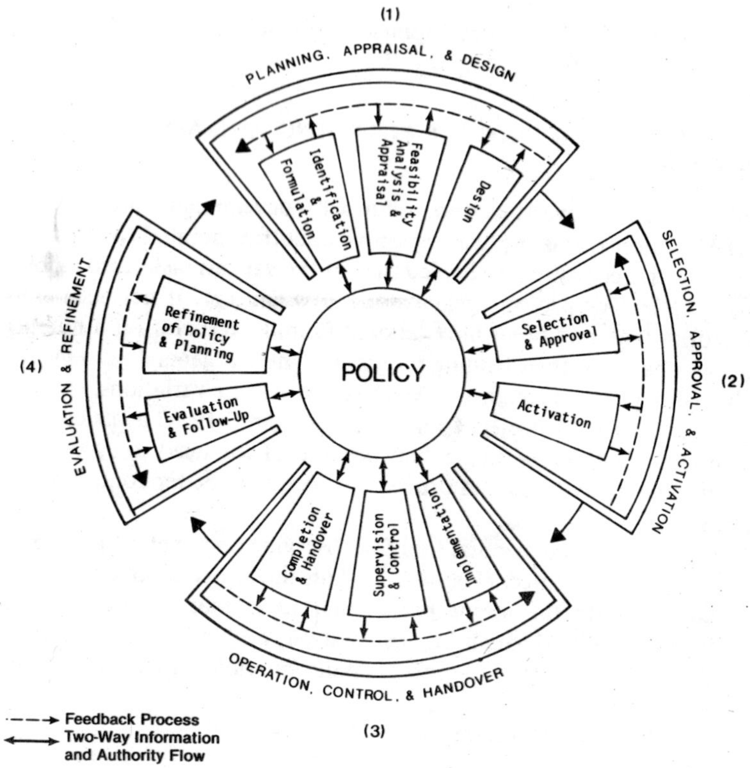

Figure 1.1. Integrated project planning and management cycle: The four phases.

feedback to policymakers and management's response is an important part of the integrated project cycle. Decisions on project implementation, although in the hands of the manager on a day-to-day basis, are closely linked to the policy framework within which the project operates. Thus, all tasks within the four phases of the IPPMC are tied together by policies emanating from the various authorities concerned with the project.[15*]

The IPPMC framework emphasizes the interdependent and cyclical nature of projects. However, because each task within the four phases of the cycle is distinct and must be examined as an individual entity, proceeding in an orderly time sequence, the cycle must also reflect this linear progression.

The IPPMC is intended to be a flexible model for analysis and observation. The bond between the myriad activities it encompasses is the authority relationship of all of the decision makers involved, from top government policymakers down to project foremen. By analyzing these changing power relationships within the framework of the integrated project cycle, a cohesive and readily intelligible overview of the project can be provided. The IPPMC conceptual framework provides the basis for the syllabus of the prototype curriculum.

With this overview of the IPPMC, we can proceed to examine each of the four phases and their tasks.*

Phase 1: Planning, Appraisal, and Design

The first phase of the project is planning, appraisal, and design. There are three basic tasks in this phase: (1) identification and formulation of the project, (2) feasibility analysis and appraisal, and (3) design of the project. The first joint task, *identification and formulation*, involves the actual conception or identification of a project, which may occur in several ways. Basic requirements of a country indicate the need for projects to satisfy them. The planning process often identifies a variety of project possibilities for each sector of society. Identification of an agricultural project may first require irrigation and transportation projects.

The major sources of projects in developing countries, however, are the government departments or ministries, including central planning agencies. Projects may be identified by political parties or government officials. In this case, the motivation to undertake a project may be political, such as an attempt to gain the support of particular constituents. In some countries, private entrepreneurs or multinational corporations will identify projects that meet the criteria established by the government.

International agencies have their own procedures for identifying projects. The identification process, then, must take into account various needs, preconditions, and policies if the project idea is to proceed to operational reality.

After a project has been identified, its parameters must be defined. This is part of the *formulation* task. The formulation of a project involves the development of a statement in broad terms which shows the objectives and expected results of the project and provides an estimate of the various resources required to achieve them.

The second set of tasks in the first phase, feasibility analysis and appraisal, are critical ones which involve two distinct operations. A prerequisite for this set of tasks is the development of preliminary designs for the project. These early designs must be detailed enough so that cost estimates and decisions on various aspects of the project can be made.

Feasibility analysis is the process of determining if the project can be implemented. *Appraisal* is the evaluation of the ability of the project to

*Source: Reference 15.

succeed. Projects will proceed to the feasibility stage only if decision makers find them desirable.

While feasibility analysis and appraisal are being conducted, several critical decisions need to be made. These decisions will determine, first, if the project is capable of achieving its objective within the limits imposed by the decision makers and, second, whether it will proceed. Preliminary estimates of the resources required, and basic decisions about size, location, technology, and administrative needs, must be made.

Feasibility and appraisal should be approached systematically and deliberately. Time spent in researching the feasibility of a project is usually time well spent. Moreover, the findings at this point in the project will be useful during other phases of the project, particularly phase 3.

Determining the feasibility of the project depends on the accuracy of the information received. Even though the final detailed design of the project can be undertaken only after approval has been given, the preliminary designs form the basis of future decisions. Most developing countries have to contend with a shortage of both design and research-development capabilities. The result may be a lack of attention to critical aspects of the project. When decisions have been made on the overall project concept, its dimensions and parameters, it is then possible to determine its feasibility in the terms required by the policymakers and funding agencies.

Some projects may require a pilot study as part of the feasibility process. Pilot studies provide data that enable more meaningful decisions to be made about larger projects. The appraisal process may require a comparative study to determine the merits of one project over another. Although the project identified may be feasible to implement, a comparative study determines whether the resources will be best used in this project or in some other form.

Many governments and international agencies have developed rigid procedures to be followed when their funds are required. While the actual details vary from project to project and from organization to organization, the trend in recent years has been toward more sophisticated and more systematic project-related studies. For example, to receive a recommendation from the United Nations Development Program (UNDP) for industrial projects, prospective borrowers must undertake market analyses that include national trends in production, foreign trade, consumption, and consumer prices, together with details about output type and use, cost of production, and estimated sales. Other agencies have added new dimensions to their studies, such as the impact on the social and cultural life of the community and the environmental and ecological impact of the project.

Numerous components of the project must be dealt with in the feasibility report. Studies can relate to the feasibility of the technical, economic, commercial, financial, administrative/managerial, and organizational aspects.

Additional political, social, environmental, and cultural factors that affect the project may also be included. Of great importance here is the need to make an inventory of the present environment in order to assess and manage the impact of the project on change in any of the environmental baseline factors such as groundwater contamination and/or air pollution. Various technical alternatives must also be studied to ensure that the suggested approach fulfills project requirements.

Economic studies examine the overall sector into which the project falls and consider how the project fits into this sector and the national planning framework. Related to economic feasibility studies are commercial studies, which may be necessary to determine the competitiveness of the proposed project. These studies examine the market demand for the output of the project, consider the costs of production, and look at all aspects of the project to determine if it is viable.

Financial studies determine how much capital is required to complete the project. These studies focus on whether the project can sustain its financial obligations, have adequate working capital, and generate enough funds to ensure adequate cash flow to keep the project operational.

Administrative/managerial studies determine the adequacy of procedures to control and direct the project. Studies in this area are not always undertaken, even though all projects would benefit from them. Their objective is to determine whether a project that is economically, financially, and commercially sound can be properly implemented by available managerial and administrative procedures. Many countries suffer from a lack of management and administrative capacity to direct projects. Related to this problem is a lack of ability to ensure that a project can be administered effectively by an appropriate agency or organization. Because administration of a project differs from normal departmental procedures, a careful assessment of the operational methods of existing units is necessary to ensure that a project's unique features can be catered to. Even though a project may be conceived and sponsored by an existing department, the department itself may not be the appropriate body to administer it. This is especially true when the involvement of a large group of outside personnel and agencies is necessary, since existing departmental procedures are often unable to provide the required flexibility.

Once the feasibility studies have have completed, a meaningful appraisal of the project is possible. Policy and decision makers and lending institutions may carry out the appraisal. They satisfy themselves that the project meets the conditions that enable it to proceed. Their concern is to determine whether or not the project is the best means of reaching the objectives they have set. In addition to viewing the project itself, they may consider alternative means of reaching the objective.

Potential lending institutions may undertake their appraisal with a healthy skepticism toward all phases of the project. They attempt to determine if the project is intrinsically sound and if all the circumstances that surround it are favorable.

The last task within this phase of the integrated project cycle is *design*. As mentioned earlier, preliminary design criteria must be established before project feasibility and appraisal begin. Once it has been determined that the project will continue, the design proceeds. Design is a critical function. It establishes the basic programs, allocates responsibilities, determines activities and resources, and sets down in operational form the areas of priority and functions to be carried out. All inputs relating to projects, including personnel, skills, technical requirements, and so on, must be determined at this point. Environmental factors, social criteria, and procedures must be assessed and included.

The design task also includes the preparation of blueprints and specifications for construction, facilities, and equipment. Operating plans and work schedules are prepared and brought together in a formal implementation plan; contingency plans may also be prepared. Designers must bring together the views of policy and decision makers and technical experts in such a way that the design reflects the inputs of all persons contributing to the project.

Phase 2: Selection, Approval, and Activation

This phase of the project has two major tasks: (1) selection and approval and (2) activation. *Selection* takes place after the project has been accepted by policy makers and funding organizations as meeting the feasibility criteria. At this point, the design function, including the formal implementation plan, has been completed. The project has been well defined, with key elements and inputs clearly identified. The selection of one project over another is made on the basis of several criteria. Policy makers consider the feasibility of the project and the priority of the project area. If a project fulfills a major need or contributes to national or sector goals and is politically desirable, it may be selected over a competing project that is not politically important. Funding agencies, however, have a variety of techniques for determining whether resources will be allocated to a particular project. These techniques may range from cost-benefit to other complex forms of analysis. Overall, however, the policy makers and the funding agency must conclude that the project itself has a priority claim for the resources it requires. Therefore, the selection process is normally competitive.

Project selection requires negotiations to obtain formal *approval* from national authorities, funding agencies, and other contributors. This requires the finalization of funding proposals, agreements, and contract documents, including tenders and other contracts and the introduction by the government or some other organization of appropriate regulations.

Activation of the program involves the coordination and allocation of resources to make the project operational. This is a complex process in which the project manager brings together a project team, which may include professionals, technicians, and resource personnel. Other contributions to the project may come from other groups, such as consultants, contractors, suppliers, and policy makers in other agencies. The outside inputs must be coordinated with the work of the project team. Responsibility and authority for executing the project must be assigned at this point. This includes the granting of authority to make decisions in areas relating to personnel, legal, financial, organizational, procurement, and administrative matters.

The activation task must ensure that planning for all phases is undertaken so that delays in vital inputs do not occur. Organizational and administrative procedures, together with feedback and responses to policy makers' decisions, will have an important bearing on implementation. Concern for detail and proper planning during activation can save a great deal of time and resources during later phases of the project. At this point, the actual work of the project is about to begin.

Phase 3: Operation, Control, and Handover

Looking at the development project from the outside, the uninitiated observer might mistake this most visible phase for the entire project. As has been indicated, phase 3 in fact makes up only a small part of the integrated project cycle. This phase has three sets of tasks: (1) implementation, (2) supervision, and (3) completion and handover.

Implementation involves the allocation of tasks to groups within the project organization. It is based on procedures set down during the two earlier phases. At this point, a final review of the project design and timetable is undertaken, and any necessary changes or adjustments are included. Decisions about the procurement of equipment, resources, and manpower also need to be made. Schedules and time frames need to be established, and efficient feedback, communication, and other management information systems must be set up. The responsibility for implementation rests with the project manager. This person must work with policy makers, authorities, and organizations related to the project, as well as with the policy makers controlling it. His task is a complex one, requiring him to steer the project through many obstacles.

The second set of tasks in phase 3 is *supervision and control.* Appropriate procedures must be activated to provide feedback to both the policy makers and the project manager. Control procedures must identify and isolate problem areas; because of the limited time span of a project, fast action is necessary if costly delays are to be avoided. At this point, specific management tools, such as the critical path method (CPM), program review and evaluation techniques (PERT), and other forms of network analysis are particularly useful. These control and supervision techniques break down a project into detailed activities and establish the interrelationships between and among them. This allows the project manager to organize the project into manageable components, to coordinate all activities, and to set a time-sequence schedule for project implementation. Although using such techniques means taking more time prior to implementation, it is time well spent. Not only will these techniques give the project internal coherence, they will also save implementation time by isolating any problems to the appropriate project component.

In addition to providing internal control, those funding the project maintain an independent monitoring and control system. The project manager must therefore meet control criteria established by either the government or another controlling agency, or perhaps by the funding institution. This may involve using specified procedures, such as international competitive bidding, for supply contracts. Formal procedures are established by many international organizations for the procurement and control of resources.

Whatever supervision and control techniques are used, they must take into account the changing patterns that occur during the life of the project. These may include changes in policymaking and political organizations, difficulties with procurement, and poor performance by project team members and contractors. In many cases, the overall project design will need to be reviewed. Many technicians are involved in the supervision and control processes, and adequate information flow in all directions—from the project manager and from those within his organization with special responsibilities—is essential if these procedures are to be effective. As part of supervision and control, any problems relating to environmental factors must also be identified and appropriate action taken.

Control procedures are useful only if action is taken to correct any deviation. It should also be noted that both personnel and input patterns change as the project proceeds through its four phases. As work on some tasks is completed, other personnel, experts, and contractors move in to begin new tasks. Personnel must adjust to their new environment, and procedures need to be reviewed and updated to meet the changing situation.

Project *completion* prepares the project for phasing out and *handover* to another form of administration. These are the third set of tasks in this phase. Project completion consists of scaling down and dismantling the project organization. It also involves the transfer of project personnel to other areas of operation. Assets and other facilities, including equipment and technology, may not be required by the operational project. Provisions for their transfer must be made, since it is not always possible to have an automatic transition from the development to the operational stage.

Completion may take place over a considerable period. As various parts of a project are completed, however, they may be taken over by a new organization, and handover may therefore be accomplished piecemeal. It is essential that development resource linkages between scaled-down projects and projects in the elementary stages of implementation be planned systematically to ensure optimal use of limited resources, particularly in broad development programs. The new project, when operational, will have an effect on other aspects within the sector. As the project becomes operational, the new controlling organization must have the skills, personnel, and technical backup required. Key personnel working in the development stage will often transfer over to the new controlling organization.

In cases where technical, financial, political, or other factors prevent projects from being completed according to the original terms, handover and termination procedures may have to be implemented at an earlier stage. This may involve considerable loss as far as the project is concerned. In this situation, the objective should be to liquidate the project in a way that will obtain the most benefit.

As a project nears completion, special reporting systems should be set up so that full information on the project is available. Completion reports should be prepared for various authorities, including funding organizations and policy makers.

The actual handover of the project's operation involves finalization of contracts, termination of loan facilities, and so on. It also includes the transfer of the project's activity and resources to the new administration. This is a critical task. While the development of the project can be viewed initially as a creative task, once the project is completed, it must be viewed as a long-term operational program.

Phase 4: Evaluation and Refinement

The final phase of the project is the evaluation and refinement of policy and planning factors. The first task is *evaluation and follow-up*. While it is possible to evaluate project results immediately, actual benefits—both anticipated and unanticipated—together with their side effects, may not become apparent until the project has been operating for some time. Evaluation thus needs to cover several time periods. Evaluation normally includes a retrospective examination of the project in attaining its intended goals within both the timetable and the budget. However, experience clearly demonstrates that it is necessary to consider evaluation as an ongoing process integrated with each phase of IPPMC. For example, evaluation procedures must be designed to analyze and propose solutions to problems that may arise during the tasks of activation, implementation, supervision, and control. Ongoing evaluation, which includes retrospective evaluation, should result in a careful documentation of experiences which can provide both insights and lessons for improving project planning and project management in the near future.

Evaluation of a project can take several forms. These include evaluation by those responsible for implementation and by others with an interest in the project, including funding organizations and contractors. Those who are funding the project will undertake a thorough investigation of its financial aspects, including an effectiveness study of goal attainment. The agency responsible for the project will determine whether its goals have been attained and whether the expected impact on a sector or on national development will be achieved. The studies should consider, in addition to the project's impact on the target group, its influence on the political, social, cultural, and environmental factors relating to the project. An exhaustive evaluation of each phase, to determine its contribution to the project in terms of the budget, timetable, and other factors, is most desirable. In most cases, however, the project is evaluated as a whole, with little effort made to analyze each phase or each task separately.

International agencies, such as the World Bank and the United Nations, have their own procedures for evaluating projects. These may be useful to policy makers, since they provide the opportunity for comparative analysis with similar projects.

Related to and often arising from the evaluation of a project is the need for follow-up. Follow-up activities may vary from determining how unmet needs can be satisfied to action on project tasks not properly fulfilled. The piggyback or follow-up projects mentioned earlier may come into play at this point. For a project to achieve its full objective, smaller or related projects may need to be implemented almost immediately. There is then a clear need to relate follow-up action closely to project evaluation. Follow-up action is one aspect of the project manager's role which may involve considerably more commitment than he initially envisages. If follow-up action makes the difference between the project's being fully or only partially operational, it is wise to undertake these activities as quickly as possible. Aspects arising from the follow-up procedures may be useful in the future. If the project is successful, guidelines can be set down for the project to be repeated in another setting.

The second and last task is *refinement* of policy and planning. Policy makers and managers will need to refine their procedures in the light of each completed project. Experiences and lessons learned should be the basis on which planning and policy tasks are reviewed. As the essential controlling force, policy procedures must be continually updated to meet future challenges. Planning must also be able to meet new demands and situations. Refinement of these procedures is an important contribution that the project can make to future development programs.

The IPPMC is a flexible model for all phases of projects from conception to completion. The force unifying all of the phases and tasks of the IPPMC is the power and authority vested in various policy makers, ranging from top government and political decision makers to those in charge of one aspect of the project. The project manager, the staff, and outside contributors such as consultants or contractors are bound by and exist within the framework of policy decisions. Analysis of these changing relationships through the IPPMC model can provide a comprehensive overview of a development project. It is also useful for policy makers in providing guidelines for addressing policy issues as a basis for more viable policy formulation and related decision making.

It is significant that the IPPMC conceptual framework was developed as the basis of a new and dynamic approach to planning and management because of past experience with the problems of poor planning and management, resulting in the waste of enormous human and capital resources in projects from all sectors. The viability and effectiveness of the IPPMC in designing and implementing new curriculum materials for educating and training project planners and project managers have been established. In addition, the IPPMC has been shown to provide an effective conceptual framework in four sorely neglected areas: (1) encouraging long overdue teamwork among planners, designers, contractors, and owners of projects; (2) satisfying the need for accurate information flows between and among these groups to ensure safe, cost-effective projects; (3) creation of data bases in each sector through carefully documented case histories of projects; and (4) the most difficult task of all—application of lessons learned from the case histories to refinement of policies and planning to improve productivity and quality of new projects.

These four areas are covered in detail in subsequent chapters.

REFERENCES

1. "More Construction for the Money," *Summary Report of the Construction Industry Cost Effectiveness Project*, New York: Business Roundtable, 1983.
2. Goodman, Louis J. "Integrated Project Planning and Management: A New Approach." Drexel Hill, PA: Project Management Institute, Vol. 15, No. 4, 1984.
3. Summary Report of the President's Private Sector Survey on Cost Control. *War on Waste.* New York: Macmillan Publishing Co., 1984.
4. "Management Programs in Engineering Colleges," *Engineering Education*, ASEE, Vol. 59, No. 8, April 1969, pp. 967–971.

5. Babcock, D. L. "Engineering Management: Origins and Growth," *Engineering Education*, ASEE, Vol. 70, No. 4, January 1980, p. 349.
6. Easter, William T. and Sarchet, Bernard R. "B.S. Engineering Management Education: A Status Report," *Engineering Education*, ASEE, Vol. 70, No. 4, January 1980, pp. 356–362.
7. Kocaoglu, Dundar R. "Master's Degree Programs in Engineering Management," *Engineering Education*, ASEE, Vol. 70, No. 4, January 1980, pp. 350–352.
8. Bennett, F. Lawrence. "Engineering Management Education." Paper presented at the Engineering Education Breakfast, American Society of Civil Engineers, Annual Convention and Exposition, Hollywood, Florida, October 28, 1980.
9. Geistauts, George and Hauck, Vern. *The Trans-Alaska Pipeline*. Hawaii: East-West Center, Resource Systems Institute, August 1979.
10. Goodman, Louis J. "Project Management: The Need for Innovation," TECHNOS 5, No. 4. Fort Collins: Colorado State University, 1976.
11. United Nations, "Second United Nations Development Decade: A System of Overall Review and Appraisal of the Objectives and Policies of the International Development Strategy." New York: United Nations, 1971.
12. See, for example, "What Now: Another Development—The Dag Hammarskjold Report," *Development Dialogue*, Special Issue. The Netherlands: Dag Hammarskjold Foundation, July 1975.
13. Waterson, Albert. *Development Planning: Lessons of Experience*. Baltimore: John Hopkins University Press, 1968, pp 249–267.
14. Baum, Warren C. "The World Bank Project Cycle," *Finance and Development*. Washington, D.C., December 1978.
15. Goodman, Louis J. and Love, Ralph N., eds., *Project Planning and Management: An Integrated Approach*. New York: Pergamon Press, 1980.

CHAPTER 2

The IPPMC and Case Materials

IPPMC PROTOTYPE CURRICULUM

The IPPMC prototype curriculum was designed and developed by the PPIPM project team during the period 1975–1977 as part of an overall strategy to develop, test, and refine both the curriculum and supporting resource materials. A primary objective of the strategy was to design a curriculum that would view planning, design, and implementation as parts of a total process.[1] In addition, the outstanding problems in project management training was believed to be a lack of innovative instructional programs that increase the capacity for both analytical thinking and practical implementation skills.[2] Clearly, the PPIPM project team was committed to the task of closely examining the managerial role in projects.

In September 1976, the PPIPM project team convened at the East-West Center to present and discuss curriculum development progress reports. It was agreed that the concept of a *prototype curriculum* was necessary—a curriculum that could be adapted to both training and educational programs. It was further agreed that the curriculum would include policy issues related to development projects. A timetable of nine months was established to complete the following materials: (1) a syllabus and course outline for a 15- or 16-week training program; (2) identification of selected readings on each task of the integrated project cycle; (3) a portfolio of five or six case studies of development projects to be researched and written in the context of the integrated project cyle; (4) an annotated bibliography; and (5) a Teacher's Guide on the use of these case studies.

The project team reached a consensus on the prototype curriculum in June 1977[3] at its next meeting at the East-West Center. At that time, it was agreed to implement the curriculum for testing and refinement during the 1977–1978 academic year, provided that the East-West Center could package all the materials into a 16-week (six hours per day, five days per week) curriculum and deliver it to the participating institutions by September 1977. It was also agreed to develop the curriculum and supporting materials within the IPPMC framework. A final request called for additional case studies of projects from four sectors: agriculture, public works, industry, and social services. The management plan for the various activities within this intensive effort is summarized in Table 2.1.

TABLE 2.1. MANAGEMENT PLAN: INTERNATIONAL PROJECT TEAM ACTIVITIES (1975–1983) FOR IPPMC.

ACTIVITY	LOCATION	TIME PERIOD
1. Initial research planning workshop	East-West Center (EWC)	June 1975
2. Curriculum research and development[a]	Participating countries	July 1975–June 1977
a. Interim workshop for progress reports and critiques	EWC	September 1976
b. Travel to participating countries by project director (three trips per year)	Participating countries	October 1975–March 1977
3. Exxon Education Foundation Grant Proposal: To research and write 30 case histories of development projects	EWC	June 1977
4. Initiate case history component of the curriculum	Participating countries	July 1977
5. Initial implementation/ prototype curriculum	Participating countries	September 1977
6. Case history research and publication	Participating countries and EWC	September 1977–May 1982
a. Exxon grant approved June 1978		
b. Travel by project director to meet with case writers and officials responsible for necessary permissions (three trips per year)		
7. Comparative evaluation of initial implementation/ prototype curriculum workshop	EWC	August 1978
8. Exxon Grant International Steering Committee meetings	EWC Manila	August 1978 May 1979
9. Thirty case histories completed and published	EWC	June 1979–October 1982
a. Five case books/ Pergamon Press (22 cases)	Pergamon Press	
b. EWC Publications (8 cases)	EWC	
10. Basic textbook on IPPMC (published by Pergamon Press; this replaces selected readings in the prototype curriculum)	Pergamon Press	August 1978–June 1980
11. Planning conference on management training for public works projects[b]	EWC	September 1982
12. Seminar for trainers of public works project managers (from eight countries)[b]	EWC	February 28–March 11, 1983

[a]Project team agreed that the curriculum would consist of a detailed syllabus, drafts of the first five cases, selected readings (1,000 pages), and a Teacher's Guide on the Use of Case Histories.
[b]Not part of the original management plan.

The syllabus for the prototype curriculum designed in the IPPMC conceptual framework is shown in Appendix A. It reflects the results of the initial testing in 1977–1978 (Tables 2.2, 2.3, and 2.4), as well as further refinement resulting from a Training of Trainers Seminar in 1983.[4,5] The initial selected readings to be used with the curriculum resulted from an intensive global literature search in 1976–1977. One thousand pages were finally identified, representing 25 book chapters and/or journal articles from 23 publishers throughout the world. Twenty copies of these readings were reproduced and packaged in 1977 for initial testing purposes. Selected references for these readings are shown for each phase of the IPPMC,[6–9] In addition, Goodman and Love packaged a case book containing drafts of five cases researched and written in the IPPMC conceptual framework.[10]

TABLE 2.2. COURSES IN PROJECT MANAGEMENT IN DIFFERENT COUNTRIES.[a]

COUNTRY	ACADEMIC COURSE	TRAINING COURSE
New Zealand	X	X
Malaysia		X
United States	X	
Philippines	X	X
Indonesia	X	X
Taiwan	X	
Iran		X

[a]Courses offered at the institutions represented by the workshop participants.

TABLE 2.3. COMPARISON OF TRAINING COURSES OFFERED.

	NEW ZEALAND	MALAYSIA	PHILIPPINES	INDONESIA
Agency	University	Government planning	University	University
Duration	12 weeks	8 weeks	7 weeks (2 weeks in plant)	32 weeks
Number of participants	18	24	39 (15 in plant)	45

TABLE 2.4. COMPARISON OF ACADEMIC COURSES OFFERED.

	NEW ZEALAND	UNITED STATES	PHILIPPINES
Name of university	Massey university	University of Arizona	University of the Philippines De La Salle University
Type of university	Public	Public	Public/private
Program/college	MBA	MPA/Ph.D	MPA/ME/MBA

The evaluation of the initial implementation of the curriculum[4] concluded that the most important component is a series of IPPMC case histories covering projects from agricultural, industrial, public works, and social sectors. It was also concluded that the case histories must come from a representative cross section of socioeconomic settings.

Case study research has been used throughout the world for over 100 years in teaching law and medicine. It has also been successfully used for about half a century in teaching business administration. The use of engineering cases is reported to have originated at Stanford University in 1964.[11] More recently, schools of public affairs and administration have become interested in developing cases for use in strengthening both administration and program management capabilities in developing countries.[12]

However, the IPPMC approach is innovative in that it represents the first attempt to write a series of case histories based on a shared conceptualization of the project cycle as an integrated process. Carefully documented and readable cases covering the entire project cycle are proving extremely useful in both training programs and formal education. Indeed, the use of the IPPMC in researching and writing a case history of a project is analogous to conducting an autopsy or postmortem of the project. More than 1000 abstracts of cases from the Harvard Graduate School of Business Administration, the Philippine Case Clearing House, and the American Society for Engineering Education (ASEE) were examined by team members in 1975–1977 and 1982 in arriving at this conclusion.

Business school cases utilize studies of actual business situations and decisions faced by real corporations, large and small. The ASEE maintains an Engineering Case Library (ECL) which included some 258 cases as of May 1985.[13] For the most part, the cases deal with specific problem situations such as "Failure of a Rotating Mirror" (ECL 30),[11] "Development of a Flowmeter" (ECL 33),[11] "Mechanical Hayhook Design (ECL 176),[8] and "Difficulties with Modular Housing" (ECL 219).[11] These cases range from 6 to 100 pages in length, and some include Instructor's Notes (usually 1–4 pages).

In 1980, the ASEE introduced a creative program, the Washington Internship for Students of Engineering (WISE). This program is sponsored by a number of engineering societies such as the American Society of Civil Engineers (ASCE) and the American Society of Mechanical Engineers (ASME), in addition to ASEE. The focus of the 10–15 WISE students each year is the development of public policy-related engineering cases. As of May 1985, two of these cases had been added to the engineering cases from ASEE.[13] These cases are "Double Alkali Flue Gas" (ECL 256) and "The Magnetic Fusion Energy Engineering Act of 1980" (ECL 258). ECL 256 examines the engineering, legal, and regulatory conflicts surrounding a utility company's efforts to change the way it controls emissions. ECL 258 contains information and provides insights on how a major national research effort is defined and managed.

The IPPMC framework allows the examination of a broad range of factors that contribute to a project's success or failure. Each case examines and analyzes the entire spectrum of a particular project, from inception through completion, showing how the interrelationships (or lack thereof) among policy makers, planners, designers, implementers, and managers contributed to the success (or failure) of the project. The variety and range of projects documented by the cases further ensure that where one case focuses on technical factors or managerial policy, for example, other cases will complement it with an emphasis in other areas.

The cases are a record of events and issues that actually have been faced by managers: events interwoven with facts, opinions, prejudices, and data upon which the manager's decisions depended. They contain the experience and influence of government officials, consultants, international assistance officials, designers, contractors (especially in public works projects), and project managers so that others can learn from these successes and mistakes. The projects presented vary in country, sector, form of management, and funding.

The foregoing illustrates the need and potential for educating and training a more effective project manager. This effort requires a curriculum and supporting materials that focus on unified control of all projects. The IPPMC and related cases represent such an approach.

Thirty IPPMC cases have been researched and published as of this writing. Eash case is analogous to an autopsy or postmortem of a project in a similar framework, which is essential to establishing a data base in a given field such as public works.[14]

Seven of these cases were selected for executive summaries as a result of a conference at the East-West Center in 1982 comprising senior scholars and practitioners in public works. Appendix B contains six executive summaries (the seventh concerns the Trans-Alaska Pipeline project, which is covered in Chapter 8). Executive summaries provide brief coverage of a project's background, objectives, results, impact, and conclusions.

Abstracts of five ECL cases follow.

ABSTRACTS OF ECL CASES

1. *ECL 175*[11]

    The Case of the Methodist Chapel Failure, P.F. Sanders, 1971.

    Human errors caused the collapse of this beautiful $83,000 chapel. These errors were made by the architect, engineer, general contractor, and subcontractor, all of whom suffered financial loss as a result. Study of this case is especially appropriate for courses in civil engineering structural analysis and design. An Instructor's Note is available.

Total: 18 pages. Instructor's Note: 3 pages.

2. *ECL 219*[11]

Difficulties with Modular Housing, G. Kardos, 1975.

This case deals with the problems of introducing an innovative form of residential housing. The problems are both technical and managerial. The housing system discussed was conceived and developed as a complete system which provides attractive housing, yet offers cost advantages in production, transportation, and erection. But technical competence is not enough. The principal problem becomes one of convincing the various regulatory bodies that the innovative methods of construction are as good as the more traditional methods.

(Parts A, B, C) Total: 30 pages. Instructor's Note: 2 pages.

3. *ECL 238*[11]

The Sinking Floor, B. Dennehy, 1978.

Jim Smith felt that he had been chosen as the fall guy. As a soil engineer, he had been consulted when Black & Associates had designed a building for Universal Packaging. When the president of Universal Packaging noticed that the floor of his office was tilting and sinking, Jim was called by Black & Associates to discuss the problem. This case shows the background of the problem: Bill's efforts to retain the goodwill of his clients without admitting any liability and the eventual outcome. It consists of two parts. Part A states the situation, gives the technical background, and lists several questions for discussion. Part B covers Bill's actions and the outcome.

Total: 11 pages.

4. *ECL 256*[13]

Double Alkali Flue Gas Desulfurization: The CIPS Experience, Richard Myhre, 1984.

This case examines the engineering, legal, and regulatory conflicts surrounding a utility company's attempt to change the way it controls emissions.

Total: 49 pages. Instructor's Note: 6 pages.

5. *ECL 258*[13]

The Magnetic Fusion Energy Engineering of 1980, Anthony Flores, 1984.

An exploration of the key technical and political decisions affecting federal funding for the development of fusion technology. The role of technical experts in the decision-making process is highlighted. Total: 44 pages. Instructor's Note: 4 pages.

ECL 256 and 258 are the first two engineering cases that have been published as part of ASEE's WISE program.

Chapter 5 contains a detailed checklist of questions in the IPPMC. Both the instructor and the student will find it useful in developing a better understanding of the complex nature of a project's life cycle. This chapter also provides a supplementary set of guidelines for the instructor in preparing class assignments.

CONCLUSIONS

There is agreement among many project planners, designers, contractors, and managers[14] regarding the need to provide unified control of all projects in all sectors in order to ensure both safety and cost effectiveness. This new approach must start in the classroom because education and training are basic to future philosophies, methodologies, and professional growth of the various groups responsible for different aspects of projects from inception through completion. The IPPMC provides a useful model for this necessary integration and teamwork to improve policy making and the planning/management process for future projects.

The IPPMC has been demonstrated to be a powerful tool for unified project control. However, it is embryonic, and there is need for data banks of case histories of public works projects to provide the necessary scientific and engineering data to strengthen project planning and management capabilities. This situation is true of all sectors, but it is especially crucial in hazardous waste disposal systems because of its direct impact on public health.[15] IPPMC cases must include more attention to the problems of project feasibility and evaluation. These needs are reinforced by the intensive worldwide literature search noted earlier in the chapter. The literature is filled with reference materials on project implementation.[8,16–19] Unfortunately, there is a paucity of reference materials in project planning for engineering projects (including feasibility studies) and project evaluation.

As noted earlier, this book places heavy emphasis on project feasibility, project evaluation, and the use of IPPMC cases. Regarding the last factor, there is urgent need for case histories of public works projects, especially in areas of hazardous waste disposal and water supply systems. There are 259 engineering cases which were produced over a 21-year period (1964–1985). These are useful for classroom exercises on specific problems such as a sinking floor or a contaminated water supply. The great need is for more comprehensive cases that conduct autopsies or postmortems of projects in a conceptual framework developed from the integrated project cycle. Chapter 5 covers this methodology for researching and writing IPPMC case histories.

REFERENCES

1. United Nations. "Second United Nations Development Decade: A System of Overall Review and Appraisal of the Objectives and Policies of the International Development Strategy." New York: 1971.
2. Yip, Yat Hoong. "Role of the Universities in National Development Planning in Southeast Asia." Singapore: Regional Institute of Higher Education and Development, 1971, p. 35.
3. Goodman, Louis J., et al., "Summary Report of the Workshop to Critique and Refine Prototype Curriculum Package." Hawaii: East-West Center, Technology and Development Institute, June 1977.
4. Aquino, Rosemary, Goodman, Louis J., and Hawkins, John N. "Summary Report: Workshop for Comparative Evaluation of Prototype Curriculum for Project Management." Honolulu: East-West Center, Resource Systems Institute, 1978.
5. Aquino, Rosemary, Goodman, Louis J., and Hawkins, John N. "Summary Report: Training of Trainers Seminar, Management of Public Works Projects." Honolulu: East-West Center, Centerwide Programs, 1983.
6. Solomon, Morris J. *Analysis of Projects for Economic Growth: An Operational System for Their Formulation, Evaluation and Implementation*. New York: Praeger Publishers, 1970.
7. Frankwicz, Michael J. "A Study of Project Management Techniques," *Journal of Systems Management*. Vol. 24, No. 10, October 1973; pp. 18–22.
8. Ahuja, H. N. *Construction Performance Control by Networks*. New York: John Wiley & Sons, Inc., 1976.
9. Harberger, Arnold C. *Project Evaluation: Collected Papers*. London: MacMillan Co., 1972.
10. Goodman, Louis J., and Love, Ralph N., eds. *Management of Development Projects: An International Case Study Approach*. New York: Pergamon Press, 1979.
11. American Society for Engineering Education, "Engineering Cases." Washington, D.C., 1976.
12 Milakovich, Michael E. "International Project Planning and Management." Summer course, University of Miami, Florida, 1983, 1984, 1985.
13. American Society for Engineering Education (ASEE), "Engineering Education," Washington, D.C., 1985.
14. Goodman Louis J., et al. "Summary Report: Planning Conference for Training of Trainers Seminar on Use of IPPMC in Public Works Projects." Honolulu: East-West Center, Centerwide Programs, 1982.

15. Ruckelshaus, William. "Science, Risk, and Public Policy." Washington, D.C.: Environmental Protection Agency, 1983.
16. Burman P. J. *Precedence Networks for Project Planning and Control.* New York: McGraw-Hill Book Co., 1972.
17. Cleland, David I. and King, William R. *Systems Analysis and Project Management,* 3rd ed. New York: McGraw-Hill Book Co., 1983.
18. Heyel, Carl, ed. *The Encyclopedia of Management*, 2nd. ed. New York: Van Nostrand Reinhold Co., 1973.
19. O'Brien, James J. *CPM in Construction Management—Project Management with CPM*, 3rd ed. New York: McGraw-Hill Book Co., 1984.

CHAPTER 3

Feasibility Analysis and Appraisal of Projects

Figure 1.1 shows the formulation of a project is the second task in the planning process and involves the articulation of objectives or goals and outputs. It must also provide an estimate of the various resources required to achieve the objectives. This makes it possible to develop a preliminary design as the basis for conducting feasibility studies to determine if the project can be implemented according to the standards and criteria set forth in the preliminary design. Appraisal consists of an evaluation of all of the feasibility studies to determine the ability of the project to succeed. Thus, feasibility analysis and appraisal form the critical juncture in the integrated project cycle.

FEASIBILITY ANALYSIS

The major portion of this chapter presents a step-by-step approach to the preparation of project feasibility studies. A complete feasibility analysis of a project must cover six important study areas: (1) technical, including manpower and technological requirements; (2) economic justification, such as the costs and benefits; (3) administrative/managerial, including external linkages and internal organization; (4) environmental, including present baseline data and the impact of those data; (5) social/political, including demographic data and social needs; and (6) financial for funding needs and sources. Each of these six studies should answer five interrelated questions:

- Is the proposed project responsive to urgent present or anticipated social and economic needs?
- Will the project as planned adequately serve or fulfill the intended purpose without harming the environment?
- Will the benefits of the project to both society and the economy be justified by the costs?
- Should various technical alternatives be studied to optimize or maximize the cost effectiveness of the project without sacrificing its quality or function?

- Do the feasibility studies provide sufficient baseline criteria and measures to establish a checklist for subsequent project implementation and evaluation?

Well-prepared feasibility studies and analyses examine and question every aspect of the preliminary design within the actual project environment. They determine whether a project can be satisfactorily carried out with the financial, technical, human, material, and organizational resources available. Thus, together with design, feasibility and appraisal function as the interface between conception and reality. They link the planning set of project tasks—identification, formulation, and preliminary design—with the action-oriented set of tasks—selection and approval, activation, implementation, handover, and evaluation.

In providing this link, feasibility and appraisal serve several other crucial functions. First, by examining project goals and by questioning all assumptions, they provide a framework within which to reformulate the preliminary design into its most appropriate form. Second, feasibility and appraisal help guide the implementation of the project. Not only do they point out potential trouble spots, they discuss the use of possible contingency plans. Finally, a complete feasibility study includes criteria and baseline measures to evaluate the project, providing the framework both for monitoring the project during implementation and for evaluating its overall success and completion.

In the field of project management, the bulk of the literature on feasibility and appraisal deals almost exclusively with economic analysis (including market studies, which are not always applicable to development projects) and technical studies, with particular emphasis on engineering criteria. In practice, however, feasibility analysis and appraisal incorporate a much wider range of factors—including such areas as management and personnel considerations, environmental impact, and sociopolitical repercussions—together with their often complex and overlapping relationships.

Although feasibility studies have been divided for convenience here into six major types, it is important to remember that these categories are interdependent and, in the case of closely related areas, often present the same information within different analytical frameworks. After these feasibility reports are completed, the appraisal must provide the generalist overview that interprets and reconciles the specific analyses undertaken in each of these areas. The sequence in which these studies are examined here, however, does not necessarily reflect the real-life situation; often such reports are conducted simultaneously, unless (as in the case of technical studies that provide vital information for economic analyses) the data provided by one study are needed before the second study can begin.

Table 3.1 outlines the major areas of concern covered by the six types of feasibility studies, showing in matrix form significant factors that each study should undertake in projects drawn from the agricultural, industrial, public works and social sectors. Within this matrix, the general terms of each feasibility study listed are translated in each project into specific questions that the study must ask and answer. Not all projects, it should be noted, require all aspects of the six types of feasibility analysis; a public works project, for example, does not always need a marketing program. A survey of Table 3.1, moreover, shows that particular issues within these general guidelines are determined by the nature of individual projects.

With the broad guidelines of Table 3.1 as a starting point, and bearing in mind the difference between an ideal model and reality, the six types of feasibility studies can be examined separately in greater detail.

Technical Feasibility

Technical feasibility studies remain the foundation of all other feasibility reports. A careful and thorough investigation of the technical and physical parameters is essential for an accurate assessment of a project's capabilities. This is especially true of projects in developing countries, where a common error of foreign consultants brought in at the planning stage of a project is to lay down technical specifications that cannot be met by the country's own resources. Projects in developed countries, it should be noted, flounder just as readily when technical feasibility has not been adequately determined.

Leading directly from the specifications of the preliminary design, a technical study establishes further design criteria, conducts engineering studies to determine the physical and technological alternatives to meet budgetary and sociopolitical requirements, outlines the form that activation and implementation will take, and estimates the scheduling of project inputs and outputs to satisfy both immediate and long-term development goals. As the foundation of the project, this technical analysis must therefore anticipate the broader problems to be considered in the economic feasibility study by addressing three interrelated questions:

1. Is there an adequate choice of available technologies for alternative design purposes, considering the physical layout, engineering design, and availability of raw materials?
2. What are the costs of constructing and operating project facilities (and services), including machinery, equipment, and spare parts?
3. What are the manpower requirements, from professional to labor, and are they locally available?

TABLE 3.1. FEASIBILITY STUDY CHECKLIST.

STUDY AREA	INFORMATION NEEDED
1. Technical	a. Site data • Geology • Soil conditions • Drainage characteristics • Climatic conditions • Water supply • Waste disposal • Power • Transportation b. Choice of available technologies • Equipment and machinery • Manufacturing process • Spare parts c. Design • Layout • Engineering requirements • Construction materials (local versus imported) d. Manpower • Professional • Technical • Labor
2. Economic	a. Demand • Domestic • Export b. Supply • Domestic • Import c. Marketing program d. Employment impact e. Raw material needs • Domestic • Import f. Costs and benefits
3. Administrative/managerial	a. Internal organization • Structure • Authority • Lines of communication • Flexibility b. External linkages • Government support • Government regulations • Funding (appropriations) c. Personnel • Needs/capabilities • Position descriptions • Local versus foreign • Policies

(Continued)

TABLE 3.1. (continued)

STUDY AREA	INFORMATION NEEDED
	d. Management • Management of the project • Control techniques • Scheduling techniques
4. Environmental	a. Physical/chemical • Water • Land • Air • Noise b. Ecological • Species and population • Habitats and communities • Ecosystems c. Aesthetic • Land • Air • Water • Biota • Man-made objects • Overall composition d. Social • Individual well-being • Social interactions • Community well-being
5. Social/political	a. Social impact • Culture and lifestyle • Demography b. Political impact • Equity • Social justice • Political organization c. Community resistance d. Institutional resistance • Legal constraints • Stability of political support
6. Financial	a. Project design and implementation b. Cash flow studies, profitability • External • Domestic c. Source of funding d. Adequacy of funds

The responses to these questions will vary according to the sector, as noted in Table 3.1.

Besides its primary task of blueprinting the manpower needs, resources, and design, the technical study must provide design alternatives, a choice of available technologies, and cost estimates for each alternative. In a water improvement project in Thailand,[1] for example, pumps can be selected from a wide array of equipment, with the availability of spare parts for the pumps in Thailand itself being an important consideration. The results of the technical analysis are also the basis for cost estimates and implementation schedules, necessary inputs for both economic and financial feasibility analysis.

Technical investigators compiling a project feasibility report must fully understand the concept of *alternative ways* of solving potential problems. Technical solutions may differ in their (1) technical or production process, (2) size or scale, (3) location, and (4) timing. Because these factors are interdependent, a sound knowledge of their relationships is necessary to ensure consistency in the analysis; a labor-intensive production process, for example, is appropriate only for a certain scale of production. The degree to which these factors are interdependent, moreover, depends on the type of project.

The importance of this aspect of feasibility analysis can be demonstrated by a closer look at specific factors to be considered in, for example, infrastructure projects, where technical considerations are critical. What technical feasibility factors, for example, might be relevant to transportation projects? Projects for the construction of roads or bridges would have to consider such factors as need (including the project's relationships to the existing transport network); location; nature of subsurface conditions; alignment; width (traffic capacity, present and future); drainage, earthwork (cuts and fills, including selection and availability of both local materials and equipment); pavement selection, design, and construction; and the costs and benefits to the user, which will also be analyzed in the economic feasibility study.

Suppose, however, that the project is a waterworks project for domestic consumption. In this case, feasibility experts might examine the relative benefits of two types of water storage: earth dams and deep wells. Determining the feasibility of an earth dam would require analysis of such factors as demand or capacity; dam location (including quality of the water, stream flow and other pertinent hydrologic data, rainfall and runoff, and water losses through seepage and evaporation); availability of local materials for construction; foundation selection, design, and construction; reservoir design and construction; and purification system. Factors determining the feasibility of a deep well, on the other hand, would likewise include demand, location, pumping system/equipment, and purification system.

As the foregoing demonstrates, the detailed data generated by the technical feasibility study will almost always result in modification of preliminary design specifications, a process that will continue throughout the project's lifetime. The technical feasibility study, however, provides the first systematic investigation of project design viability.

Economic Study

An economic study examines a proposed project in terms of its net contribution to the economy and to society. The study should address three interrelated questions:

1. Is the project responsive to an urgent present or anticipated economic or social need?
2. Will the project's planned economic outputs adequately serve the intended purpose?
3. Will the services proposed to be performed by the project, and will the benefits produced by the project justify its cost?

The response to these questions requires a detailed study of all of the economic implications of the project, such as the demand for and supply of all project outputs; the project's ability to increase employment with "multiplier" effects on increased purchases of goods and services; its effect on increasing public sector revenue (such as through income tax, property tax, sales tax, and so forth); and its use of locally available resources. Upon completion of these studies, it is possible to assess the project's net contribution to the economic and social welfare of the community (town, city, state, national). This is done through a comparison of the economic and social benefits expected to be generated from the project with the costs of its construction and operation. If the benefits exceed the costs, the project is considered economically feasible.

There are various techniques for assessing economic feasibility, depending upon the sector (private or public) and the nature of the project. In general, a profitability analysis is conducted. For commercial projects this is referred to as "commercial profitability" and for government or public works as "social profitability." This discussion will focus on the latter, or the project's contribution to the economy, and therefore society. An example of benefit-cost analysis will be given from a case in India.

To obtain a comprehensive assessment of social profitability, a benefit-cost analysis is normally made. An in-depth benefit-cost analysis must include a complete study of all costs and benefits of the project. The study should be made for each technical alternative. It is important that the listed costs and benefits be valid and quantifiable.

There are various indicators of social cost-benefit or profitability analysis. The three most commonly used are (1) benefit-cost ratio (B/C), (2) net present value (NPV), and (3) internal rate of return (IRR).[2,3] These three techniques take into account the relative timing of cost and revenue (benefit) flows by translating future values into their present worth by applying discount factors that reflect the diminishing value of a given amount of money in the future.[4] The use of discount factors is illustrated in each of the three most commonly used indicators of social profitability. For example, the benefit-cost ratio (B/C) is the ratio of the present value of gross benefits to the present value of gross costs.

In equation form, the B/C ratio is expressed as follows:

$$\frac{B}{C} = \frac{\sum_{t=0}^{n} \frac{b_t}{(1 + r)\,t}}{\sum_{t=0}^{n} \frac{c_t}{(1 + r)\,t}} \qquad \text{(Eq. 3.1)}$$

where

b_t = benefits in time t
c_t = costs in time t
r = discount rate
n = discounting period (usually the estimated life of the project in years)

The rate of the discount is critical because it reduces future costs and benefits sequentially in an annual time series. Thus, if a 10 percent discount rate is used, then one year from now \$100 in project benefits will be reduced to \$90. Two years from now, \$100 in benefits will be reduced by the \$10 lost during the first year *plus* an additional 10 percent lost during the second year. This means that two years from now \$100 in project benefits will be valued at only \$81. The discount rate thus drastically reduces a project's social profitability. Moreover, the higher the discount rate, the greater the magnitude of the reduction.

It is readily apparent that the formula for discounting is derived from the formula for compounding any amount of investment. To illustrate, the formula for compounding is:

$$P_N = P_0\,(1 + r)^n \qquad \text{(Eq. 3.2)}$$

where

P_0 = the value of the investment at year zero
P_N = the value of P_0 at some future year, n
r = interest rate
n = number of years between year zero and year N, i.e., the *compounding* period

and the formula for discounting is:

$$R_N = R_n \frac{1}{(1 + r)^n} \qquad \text{(Eq. 3.3)}$$

where

R_N = expected revenue at year n
R_0 = present value of R_n
r = discount rate
n = number of years between year zero and year N, i.e., the *discounting* period

The preceding discussion shows how the techniques of benefit-cost analysis provide a clear and convenient presentation of a project's contribution to the economy, and therefore the society. The value of this decision tool is highly dependent upon a comprehensive understanding of all of the costs of the project, which must be estimated from the preliminary design, and all of the anticipated benefits. The importance of valid and quantifiable measurements of costs and benefits cannot be overstated. This includes the rate of discount selection and the estimated project life. In developing countries, economic feasibility studies must consider the possibility of drastic changes in cost data because of uncertainties in the price of foreign exchange, wages and salaries, the discount rate, and the timing of implementation. In fact, the timing of implementation can have drastic impact on the cost of construction in developed countries as well.

An interesting illustration of social cost-benefit or profitability analyses is the case study of the Ratnigiri Fisheries project in India.[5] The Maharashtra government wishes to promote the well-being of the people in the Ratnigiri District by:

1. Building 30 fishing trawlers and financing their sale.
2. Building a freezing plant to package the catch of shrimp and fish.
3. Constructing an ice plant.
4. Constructing a service station for the trawlers.

The Ratnigiri District Fisheries Federation is to be the implementing group. It will be responsible for selling the trawlers to local fishermen and for operating the plants and the service station. Operations based on the project are expected to continue for 22 years, with 1970 as the base year.

To prepare the analysis, the first step is to estimate the project costs for each of its 22 years. These estimates must include all capital costs, such as the price of trawlers, freezers, and plant construction; they must also include all operating costs, such as wages and salaries, taxes, and loan repayments.

The next step is to estimate the benefits generated by the project. In this case, the benefits include revenue from the sale of frozen fish and shrimp, money earned from the sale of ice, and, in the final years, money from the sale of scrap machinery. The costs and benefits are then listed year by year. Table 3.2 illustrates the costs and benefits for 5 of the project's 22 years.

Columns 1 and 2 reflect the costs and benefits to the project sponsor, not the project's actual contribution to society. To determine the contribution to society, changes must be made in calculating the costs and benefits. First, in determining the costs, only those payments that reflect the actual use of a societal resource must be charged against the project. Those payments which simply represent the transfer of control over resources from one segment of society to another should be deducted. These economic transfers include project costs such as taxes, loan repayments, and interest payments on loans.

Second, since the project contributes to society in addition to earning a profit, this contribution should be added to the calculation of benefits. In this respect, the project will contribute to society by (1) promoting India's self-sufficiency through the import earning of foreign exchange and (2) promoting development by employing unskilled workers in the Ratnigiri District. To reflect these social contributions, the project's net earnings of foreign exchange and its wage payments to unskilled laborers must be weighed more heavily than their actual market value. In economic terms, this would signify the project's contribution to society.

In this case, foreign exchange is valued 40 percent more highly than the official market price. This percentage reflects the scarcity of foreign exchange in India, as well as its value in promoting self-sufficiency. The project's wages to unskilled workers are valued 20 percent more highly than

TABLE 3.2. A PARTIAL LIST OF PROJECT COSTS AND BENEFITS. (In Thousands of Rupees)

	TO PROJECT SPONSORS		TO SOCIETY	
FOR YEAR	BENEFITS	COSTS	BENEFITS	COSTS
1	289	2,273	289	1,742
5	2,388	3,105	3,051	1,503
10	2,585	2,862	3,327	1,503
15	2,470	2,544	3,182	1,479
22	1,464	818	1,678	536
Total all years[a]	47,258	58,972	59,601	36,340

[a]Includes totals from all 22 years.

their actual price. This percentage weighs the project's contribution to the national development goal of employing low-status groups. It must be noted that wages are counted as project costs. Therefore, in charging costs to the project, the wages payed to unskilled laborers are reduced by 20 percent. Table 3.2 demonstrates how the stream of costs and benefits is altered by evaluating the project's contribution to society.

As noted earlier in the chapter, it is necessary to express future costs and benefits in terms of their present worth (1970 in this case). Table 3.3 demonstrates what happens to the Ratnigiri project's costs and benefits when discounted at 0 percent, 10 percent, and 30 percent.

Needless to say, an appropriate rate of discount must be chosen to make the NPV meaningful. In this instance, the discount rate is 10 percent; it was chosen because it reflected the Indian level of consumption, population growth, time preference for consumption, and several other variables. From Table 3.3, the B/C is 20,979,000/15,277,000 = 1.37, showing a contribution to society. As this example demonstrated, however, there are limits to cost-benefit analysis.[6-8] First, only those project impacts that can be quantified in economic terms can be incorporated into the analysis. Thus, social projects, which may produce benefits such as teaching a village how to organize or instilling in the villagers a sense of pride and self-worth, cannot be adequately assessed by using cost-benefit analyses. Second, the definition of certain benefits must be conceived very narrowly. For example, in this case, self-sufficiency was defined as earning foreign exchange, and this is an extremely narrow definition. Finally, in determining weights by which to value a project's contribution to society or in determining the social rate of discount, there is too much room for discretion and arbitrariness. Given this flexibility, a cost-benefit analysis can be manipulated to show a social profit.

TABLE 3.3. RATNIGIRI PROJECT: DISCOUNTED PROJECT COSTS AND BENEFITS. (Thousands of Rupees)

	DISCOUNTED 0%		DISCOUNTED 10%		DISCOUNTED 30%	
FOR YEAR	COSTS	BENEFITS	COSTS	BENEFITS	COSTS	BENEFITS
1	1,716	406	1,583	263	1,340	222
5	1,399	2,798	933	1,895	404	820
10	1,399	2,798	579	1,281	108	239
15	1,399	2,798	353	760	28	60
22	515	1,477	66	206	2	5
Total all years[a]	34,179	54,642	15,277	20,979	6,673	6,661

[a]Includes totals from all 22 years.

Put in perspective, then, cost-benefit analysis allows one to compare competing projects and alternative approaches to the same project. In all countries, this analysis should attempt to quantify the multiplier effects noted earlier. With increased employment, there will be increased purchasing power for goods and services, and thus increased benefits. Then, as experienced in the Ratnigiri case, there are intangible benefits and costs that should be considered in the analysis. These benefits may include education, training, recreation, and reduction of accidents, in addition to those discussed in the previous paragraph. On the cost side, one should consider air pollution, water pollution, soil erosion (loss of fertile soil), and other project outputs detrimental to the environment. The treatment of intangibles should result in a concise description as a minimum, and, if possible, should include some quantitative indicators.

A checklist of costs and benefits should be prepared for each technical alternative developed in the preliminary design. Following is such a checklist for a proposed highway.

Direct Costs

1. Inventory of present road conditions
    a) Geometric features
    b) Condition of bridges
    c) Condition of pavement
    d) Condition of drainage
2. Preliminary design*
    a) Geometric features
    b) Nature of subsoil conditions
    c) Earthwork (cut and fill)
    d) Drainage requirements
    e) Bridge and pavement loads
    f) Availability of local resources (people and materials)
3. Construction (unit cost of each item)†
    a) Materials
    b) Equipment
    c) Quality control
4. Maintenance

*For each alternative route, including design standards (and timing of implementation).
†For each alternative route, including design standards (and timing of implementation).

Direct Benefits (for Each Technical Alternative)

1. Savings in transport costs
   a) People
   b) Goods
   c) Vehicle operation
2. Stimulation of new economic growth
   a) New industries
   b) New housing and shopping facilities
3. Reductions in accidents
4. Other tangible and intangible benefits, quantified to the extent possible

Economic Feasibility

1. Summary of the economic benefits and costs of the project
2. The extent to which savings are passed on to shippers or users, and the effect on transport tariff levels
3. Economic feasibility calculations using accepted indicators, such as NPV, B/C, and IRR
4. Optimum timing of the project
5. Sensitivity analysis, considering the influence on feasibility results of variations in construction costs, traffic forecasts, vehicle operating costs, discount rate, and other critical parameters
6. Conclusions as to the economic feasibility of the project

Administrative/Managerial Study

The administrative/managerial study evaluates the strategy of the implementing agency in carrying out project activities. Although the analysis is intended to assess the feasibility of this strategy, it should concentrate on providing information and guidelines that can be used to improve overall project administration. Since the effectiveness of the management plan depends upon experience and practice in applying management techniques, it is desirable to include a project manager in the investigating team. The study examines four separate components: external linkages, internal organization, personnel, and management plan.[9]

External linkages refer to the structure of government and private organizations which directly or indirectly condition the project's environment. These include the administrative funding agency, the regulating agency, and the numerous advisory organizations that provide political, technical, and other types of support. Although the feasibility analysis can suggest little to alter the institutional relationships of the project, it should be able to determine the kinds of barriers and supports that the project will encounter.

Especially vital is information on whether the implementing agencies are capable of providing adequate support, particularly for large, complex projects. With this knowledge, project planners can prepare for contingencies and cultivate appropriate linkages to mediate possible adverse impacts of the institutional environment. One decision about the project's environment that will deeply affect the organizational course of the project is the choice (if available) between increasing the ability of existing institutions to implement the project or creating a new organization.

Internal organization is the actual organization of the implementing unit. While all kinds of possibilities exist, ranging from matrix to hierarchical, the study should determine whether the proposed organization can implement the project satisfactorily. Some relevant questions to be asked about the proposed organization are: Is it comprehensive enough? Is it appropriate for carrying out project goals? Is it flexible enough? Is internal communication well established and are lines of authority clearly defined?[10] Although the most appropriate type of internal organization depends upon the project's goals and requirements, in general a project requiring individual initiative, flexibility, and accountability should be organized in matrix fashion. A project requiring a high degree of coordination, authority, and supervision should be organized in more hierarchical fashion. Thus, the feasibility study should discriminate between the advantages and disadvantages of each in evaluating the project organization needed to accomplish the objectives.

Management is the specified management plan of the project. Basic questions to be asked include: Are schedules and networks sufficiently worked out? What are the control techniques and the methods of supervision? Is the entire management plan integrated so that the project manager can control all aspects of the project? Is the management of the project formulated well enough to ensure that the project will be well coordinated and controlled? Does the plan provide for contingencies? A key issue here is whether the plans are realistic, given the actual project environment. For example, procurement of certain equipment often requires a long lead time in many countries. If adequate lead time is not scheduled, it can cripple the manager's ability to coordinate activities.

Personnel is perhaps the key issue in administrative feasibility. Without competent and appropriate personnel, a project has a difficult time in succeeding. The analysis of the proposed personnel plans should evaluate several key items. First, it should ensure that the job descriptions and qualifications are appropriate and that they are written out completely. Next, it should examine whether or not the necessary personnel are available. Then the impact on every area of a project made by the choice of foreign or local personnel—not only in activation and implementation but also in preliminary design, technical analysis, and general consulting—should be examined. Finally, the analysis should question whether there is adequate provision for hiring expert consultants in crisis situations.

The four components of administrative feasibility—external linkages, internal organization, management, and personnel—are often referred to collectively as "operational feasibility."[11] In this sense, operational feasibility focuses on the point when the project has been approved and is ready for activation and implementation. This study must therefore include such factors as whether or not project implementation will generate the expected budgets. The project's operational feasibility will depend on how well it meets estimates in terms of (1) political acceptability and/or legality of the activities; (2) organization or administrative structure and management aspects; and (3) availability of resources and operating costs.

These considerations must also be dealt with, in varying degrees, by the financial and social/political feasibility studies, demonstrating the overlapping boundaries of all of these analyses. In the operational feasibility report, however, the emphasis is usually on organization and management. The soundness of a project is often determined by the thoroughness of its management and organization planning. With competent management, a project may be successful even when there are inadequacies in the original concept. But it is doubtful whether any project, however well conceived, can overcome the handicap of poor management. Equally, it is difficult for managers, no matter how competent and experienced, to succeed without the necessary personnel, equipment, materials, and other resources required for effective operation and maintenance.

In sum, major areas that must be explored in the operational feasibility study are:

1. The political acceptability and legality of project operation.
2. The organization that will manage the project and supervise its operations; to be accompanied by organization charts, initial and projected, together with the staffing pattern and functional statements of the organizational units.
3. Experience records of available key management and technical personnel.
4. Number, qualifications, and availability of required operating employees.
5. Plans for recruiting and training required personnel.
6. Projections for competent management and maintenance throughout the project's life.
7. Availability of necessary supplies, materials, equipment, and so on.

Examined in turn, these areas add up to a comprehensive picture of the organizational capacities and limitations of a proposed project, a perspective that is vital to both project planners and policy makers. The significance of this perspective is demonstrated in the Trans-Alaska Pipeline project, where poor management supervision and coordination, inadequate geotechnical planning, inadequate inventory and cost control systems, and poor project policies were responsible for at least $1.5 billion in wastage.[12]

Environmental Feasibility

The environmental feasibility studies address two separate questions:

1. Is the environment suitable for the success of the project?
2. What will be the project's impact on the environment?

In determining environmental suitability, the feasibility study must ask whether or not a given environment can support a given project. The environmental analysis of an agricultural project, for example, must raise and answer such questions as: Is the soil quality appropriate for the proposed crops? Is there sufficient water? Is there adequate drainage? Is there adequate sunlight? Is the climate right?

Industrial and infrastructure projects pose other questions, some of which were raised earlier in the context of technical feasibility in site and location studies. In this context, there is a natural overlap between technical and environmental analyses; and, where appropriate, the studies should be combined. A separate environmental study, however, adds an extra dimension to the technical study by ensuring that the technical analysis includes two important considerations: (1) the project's present environmental needs and (2) its long-term environmental needs. Environmental suitability involves determining whether or not the ecosystem of a region can support a project over the long term. And this introduces the concept of *resource management* for the project.

The practical importance of examining long-term as well as short-term environmental needs can be illustrated by a fairly common example of project shortsightedness. Suppose a pulp and paper plant is built in a heavily forested area of a country. The project planners know that the forests have a projected life expectancy of 20 years but do not take into account what might happen to the pulp and paper plant after that time. Within several years, with vast tracts of the forest severely depleted, it becomes evident that the environment's long-term ability to support the plant has not been considered, with the result that the plant will face a shutdown in the near future, with a corresponding waste of manpower and material resources.

Although such obvious factors that concern the environment's impact on the project are usually taken into account, with the project's environmental needs studied and systematically examined either in feasibility studies or in the project design, the reverse is not always true, which leads us to our second main consideration. Environmental studies must also ensure that systematic assessment is made of the *project's impact on the environment*, for, as the previous example demonstrates, this is clearly a two-way street. The studies must therefore examine a project's likely effect upon soil erosion, water supplies, wildlife, and plants.[13] They must also examine the project's potential to deplete nonrenewable resources, to create adverse microclimatic changes, and to pollute the water, air, or land.

Several methods can be used to assess these environmental impacts. Mapping, computer simulation, social B/C analysis, various scoring techniques, and matrix methods all provide systematic evaluation.[14] The choice of the best method in each case, however, depends upon the data available, the type of project, and the level of analysis desired. All of these studies begin by collecting baseline data on the environment. With these data, the project's environmental impact can be analyzed in a systematic and comprehensive manner, and its impact can be projected.

Probably the most practical and straightforward of these methods is the matrix, which is used in Table 3.1 to illustrate the major concerns of an environmental study.

The Environmental Protection Agency (EPA) has published guidelines for environmental assessment for a number of industrial projects.[15] These guidelines complement Table 3.1 and are outlined in Figure 3.1. The EPA has also set forth the feasibility studies and analyses required for a variety of projects ranging from a complex refinery to a relatively straightforward water storage reservoir. Figure 3.2 illustrates the procedures involved.

The impact of a project is determined by examination of all of its atmospheric, aquatic, and terrestrial wastes. Compliance with governmental regulations must be shown. All pollution control techniques and devices must be reviewed, as must applicable process modifications. Water and waste recycling is encouraged, and such processes should be described. New technology should be employed when feasible, with an explanation when necessary.

The impact identification must show the relationship between each process waste stream and governmental regulations. Table 3.4 is an example of the type of information required. Any doubts concerning a waste stream's content, quantity, and concentration must be stated. All social and economic factors which can become environmental impact sources must be assessed.

The most important task in the environmental impact statement (EIS), however, remains the collection of the baseline data. This includes lists of the types and numbers of plants and animals (see Table 3.1) and a macroanalysis of the total ecologic system. Periodic checks of the baseline data

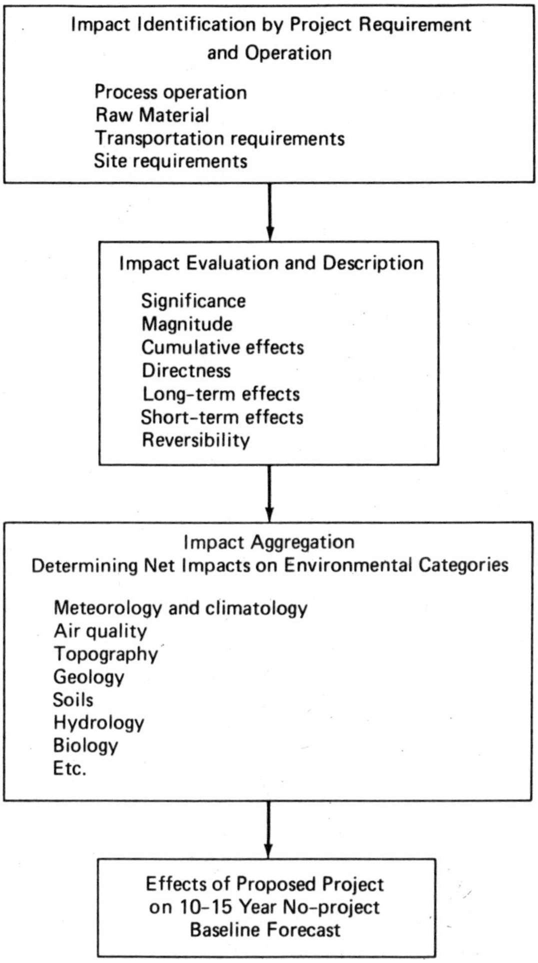

Figure 3.1. Environmental impact assessment outline.[15]

can be made as the project progresses; these checks will monitor the actual impact of the project upon the environment.

EISs are costly (for example, those for the Trans-Alaska Pipeline totaled $9 million), and their findings in certain industrialized nations have delayed or even halted projects. Developed nations can generally afford to make choices which safeguard the environment; developing nations may have harder decisions to make. Regardless of the decisions that confront each

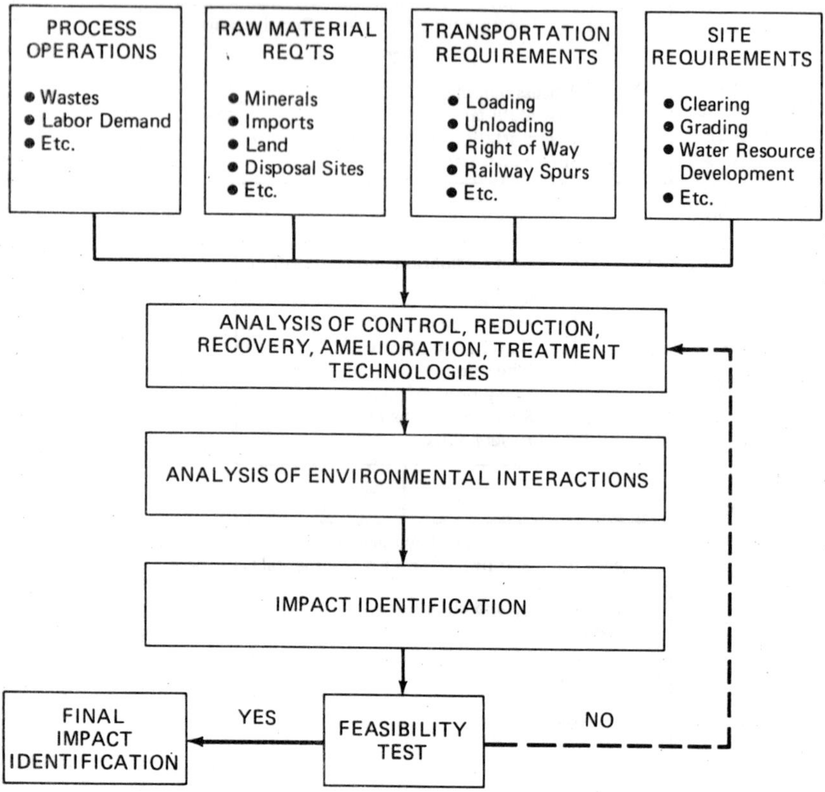

Figure 3.2. Environmental impact identification procedures.[15]

municipality (or state or country), however, an EIS informs policy makers of the environmental consequences of their decisions. With this information, a project can be planned to meet the critical needs of economic and social growth and, at the same time, to include adjustments to ensure future resource needs.

Social/Political Study

A social/political study is seldom undertaken when project feasibility studies are being conducted. Even when one is made, it is infrequently given adequate weight in assessing the project. Yet social and political factors can often be the primary reason a project fails to achieve its ultimate objectives. This is particularly true of projects in the social sector, where success cannot be measured in economic or directly quantifiable terms.

TABLE 3.4. TABULAR SUMMARY OF STANDARDS AND REGULATIONS.

SOURCE IDENTIFICATION	CONCENTRATION (AVG. AND MAX.)	QUANTITY (FLOW RATE: AVG. AND MAX.)	METHOD OF DISPOSAL	STANDARD OR REGULATION		RESPONSIBLE REGULATORY AGENCY	OTHER
				REQUIREMENT	PROPOSED		

The social/political study attempts to answer four basic questions:

1. What is the project's likely social impact?
2. What is the project's likely political impact?
3. What social factors in the project's environment will hinder or aid the project in achieving its goals?
4. What political factors in the project's environment will hinder or aid the project in achieving its goals?

The first step in conducting the social/political study is to collect baseline economic and sociological data on the community for which the project is intended. These data are intended to provide a general profile of the area's residents and should include demographic information such as population level and distribution, employment pattern, level and distribution of income, education, and housing and health situations. Also vital to the analysis is information about the social fabric of the area. This information includes the degree of community solidarity and integration, the lifestyle of the residents, important customs, and the residents' recreational habits, values, and family structure.

Then the political structure must be detailed. Focusing on the decision-making process, this section of the analysis describes the area's political relationship to regional and national governments and assesses its political autonomy. It also describes the area's informal and formal political organizations and specifies the local ordinances, zoning requirements, and statutes that will affect the project. Finally, information must be gathered on the opinions and attitudes of residents and leaders toward the project. Particularly important is the residents' opinion about how the project will affect the area, how it can be improved, and how it can be made acceptable.[16] While this aspect of the study is intended for future planning, it is also used to provide avenues for local participation in planning the project. Thus, the ideal technique to use is the open community meeting. Often, however, such meetings are not practical, and other less direct techniques, such as questionnaires, interviews, panel discussions, and expert judgments, must be used to obtain community input.

Once the basic data are collected, they must be synthesized in a report which systematically describes the total political and social environment. This is the point where most social/political analyses end, but it is actually just where the study should begin. Still to be examined are how the project will affect the area, socially and politically, and how the area's social and political reality will affect the project.

Although various methods, such as scoring techniques, social assessment, social accounting, and ecologic analysis, are used to address these questions, no broadly accepted framework exists.[17] Each has limitations, particularly in its reduction of sensitive social and political factors to quantitative indicators. Moreover, any framework imposes the limitations set by the questions it is designed to answer. Thus, in conducting the analysis, it is wise to deemphasize the use of a specific framework and instead to pose questions about the project which are sensitive to the social and political concerns of the area. This emphasis puts extreme importance on the individuals who are to prepare the study. Ideally, they should be very familiar with the social, cultural, and political aspects of the area. In many instances, residents qualified to conduct the study are the ideal choice.

Let us amplify this discussion by turning to a specific example: a Pacific island livestock project.[18] Most appropriately, the investigators selected to conduct the study were local residents with experience in livestock management and production. First, they comprehensively outlined the social and political setting of the area. Once this task was completed, they examined the setting in relationship to the project and noted that two social/political factors were relevant to project plans. First, the land tenure system was traditional, meaning that the land was collectively owned by entire villages. Second, there were no local residents trained in livestock production. In analyzing the first factor, they noted that the project might be hindered because an entire village must collectively agree to let its land be used for cattle raising; they recommended that the project employ someone familiar with appropriate ways of negotiating. The lack of indigenous skilled manpower meant that the project would have to rely heavily on foreign personnel and foreign techniques. Since these techniques might be inappropriate to the Pacific, it was recommended that the project either establish a local training program or operate first as a pilot experiment. Finally, in concluding the study, the investigators noted that the traditional lifestyle and autonomy of the villages would be disrupted by the building of roads to transport the beef, the operation of processing facilities, and the intrusion upon the tenure system. Thus, in opening the area and making it more accessible, the project would strain the governing capacities of the local villages and make them more vulnerable to disruption.

This example shows how a social/political study, conducted by researchers knowledgeable about local settings, can reveal a possibly serious conflict of interest between project goals and the underlying social fabric of a region. Failure to consider such factors can undermine the success of an otherwise well-planned and executed project. A perceptive social/political feasibility report anticipates these types of conflicts and proposes modifications or alternative procedures to avert them. In cases where the project, by its very nature, runs counter to the social pattern of its region of operation, its chances of achieving viability in the long term should be reassessed.

Financial Study

The financial study addresses five basic questions:

1. What are the capital and operating costs of the project?
2. What are the sources of funds and draw-down schedules, and are they sufficient to cover the costs of activities and implementation? What are the alternative financing schemes from other funding sources?
3. What is the projected cash flow of the project? To what extent are necessary borrowings scheduled to meet running deficits at activation? How soon will initial revenues cover part or all of operating costs?
4. Is there an adequate accounting system to provide regular balance sheets, cash flow statements, debt servicing schedules, and other financial reports?
5. What are the provisions for project completion investment and other means of recovery investment and operating costs?

An important feature of the financial study is that it totals up the costs of project implementation and design, which were broken down separately in the other feasibility studies. In many projects, therefore, economic and financial feasibility considerations overlap, and in some cases there may be good reason to conduct these two analyses simultaneously.

The two facts to be determined in a financial analysis are (1) whether the project can succeed with the amount of money stated in the proposal and (2) whether the project is expected (if it is in the private sector) to show a profit. In private sector projects, financial analysis must also determine the rate of return on the investment.

Assessing financial profitability and debt service capacity during the project's lifetime involves a projection of all revenues and expenses, receipts and expenditures, defined as follows:

1. *Revenues:* transactions that generate income, whether or not cash inflows are involved.
2. *Expenses:* transactions that reduce income, also irrespective of cash flows.
3. *Receipts:* transactions that involve cash inflows, whether or not income is generated.
4. *Expenditures:* transactions that involve cash outflows, whether or not income is reduced.

Simply stated, revenues and expenses affect *project income*, and receipts and expenditures affect *cash position*. Thus, revenues and expenses determine the project's profitability, and receipts and expenditures determine its debt-servicing capacity, which is more directly dependent on cash position.

To determine the project's profitability and debt-servicing capacity, projections of the following financial statements are made:

1. Profit-and-loss statement (income statement)
2. Balance sheet
3. Cash flow statement

The periods covered by the project statements may vary from the first few years of normal operation to the entire lifetime of the project, depending on the purpose of the statements and the reliability of the estimates for later years.

Many projects, it should be noted, are financed by loans from development banks such as the World Bank, the Asian Development Bank, and others. The World Bank normally follows a policy of balancing the need to use scarce resources efficiently, considerations of equity, and the need to generate additional funds to replicate the project so that it may reach the largest number of potential beneficiaries. The World Bank also scrutinizes each project to ensure that the funds requested will be sufficient to implement it. In the long run, this examination facilitates a successful project, which in turn helps to ensure that the loans will be repaid.

Completing the Feasibility Studies

Once the feasibility studies have been completed, they must be packaged together as a single document. The individual studies form the heart of the document, while an introductory and a concluding chapter provide organization and coherence. The introductory chapter summarizes the major findings of the studies. Since these findings are intended for the decision maker, who may not have time to read the entire report, each finding should be brief and precise and should reference the page numbers where the detailed information can be found. The introductory chapter should also include a description of the project, as well as its relationship to a larger program and to other related projects. Finally, the introductory chapter should clearly and explicitly list the goals and objectives of the project.

The feasibility study should conclude with a final chapter evaluating the project. Included in this chapter should be the data required for the evaluation. Generally, these data should measure the extent to which the project has achieved the goals and objectives specified in the introductory chapter. For example, in the Ratnigiri Fisheries project discussed earlier, the goals and objectives included increasing self-sufficiency and promoting the development of low-status groups. Thus, relevant measures of goal achievement could include the amount of foreign exchange earned by the project, the extent to which the project generated income for the Ratnigiri District, the project's impact in generating new subsidiary businesses, the number of unskilled laborers employed, the number of these workers advancing to skilled positions, and the number of people learning a new trade or skill. Usually project goals also specify that the project has acceptable environmental and social impacts. Thus, in the Ratnigiri Fisheries project, the concluding chapter would also stipulate the collection of environmental baseline measures, such as the number of fish and shrimp in the fishing ground. Periodic checks against the baseline would monitor the depletion of the resource. Finally, the concluding chapter should discuss who will collect the data and when, and who will conduct the evaluation.

APPRAISAL

After the individual feasibility studies have been assembled, an appraisal report must tie together these diverse findings, attempting to reconcile conflicting results and providing an assessment of the project's likelihood for success.

Project appraisal must address two questions:

1. Will the project meet its own objectives, as well as the larger needs of the local area and the country?
2. How does the project compare with other projects it may be competing with for funding?

Although the competitive factor is not always present in project selection, it can be important in situations where a number of project proposals have been put forward to fill a particular need or where there is not enough funding to cover all areas of development. In such cases, comparison of projects to assess, for example, which one provides the most jobs becomes an important task.

The primary function of appraisal, however, is to evaluate a project's ability to meet its stated objectives and to provide long-term economic growth in the larger framework of local and national needs. Some debate has been focused on the scope of the appraisal function: whether it consists merely of a social cost-benefit analysis within a larger framework or whether, in fact, some of the issues involved at this level of decision making—disruption or strengthening of cultural values, for example, or an increase or decrease in life expectancy—can even be quantifiable.[19] While social cost-benefit factors at this level are interpreted in strictly economic terms, such as benefits to the country's economy, consumer surplus, and income, social cost also includes intangible factors such as equity and social justice.

No matter how these larger issues are approached, there is no substitute for sound, thoroughly researched feasibility studies as the groundwork for decision making. In this respect, all aspects of feasibility must be examined, from technical to social-political. All too often, a project fails to achieve its ultimate goals because the social and political impacts were not addressed. And equally, all too often, an ambitious project design proved too sophisticated for an environment with limited resources, making it impossible to sustain without continued reliance on outside aid. Such mismatings of plan with reality would be less likely to occur if all feasibility studies had been thoroughly executed and intelligently appraised. If a project is to be *feasible* in the true sense of the word, it must be viable within the environment it has been designed to improve; all long-term projections of benefit are undermined if the most basic capabilities and limitations of site and country have not been carefully considered.

Assessment Factors

How is the integration of feasibility studies and outside policy factors into a comprehensive appraisal to be accomplished? As mentioned earlier, all data provided by the feasibility reports, including conflicting findings, must be taken into account without compromising the main factors involved. Thus, appraisal involves more than simply adding up projected gains and losses as quantified in the feasibility studies. If, for example, a highway project between two market towns will provide employment for unskilled laborers and will bolster the small-farm economy, how should these two pluses be weighed against the minus that the highway may produce more rapid central growth, disrupting the rural social structure?

Such decisions frequently have a political dimension that varies widely with the situation, and this political aspect is crucial because it goes beyond feasibility. It addresses the question of whether or not a project *should* be undertaken. It also defines alternatives, providing a basis for identifying and selecting a design for final approval.

To illustrate appraisal, let us consider an infrastructure project to build a highway. The first step in writing the appraisal report might be to provide an overview of this highway project within the larger transport system of the country. Such an overview would include a description of the existing highway system, a description of existing transport systems other than highways, and an assessment of ways in which lack of highway transport has been slowing the country's economic growth; a description of any national program for highway development, together with this project's priority in the program and reasons for assigning it this priority; and, finally, the development plan for the region this highway project will tranverse and how the project fits into this plan.

Next, an appraisal would compare the project to other transport systems currently in use. It would describe the existing distribution of traffic among the various types of transport in the project area. It would estimate the effect of the highway project on the present distribution and on the economics of the other transport systems. It would list the comparative availability of various types of vehicles, operating personnel, and other components among the various types of transport systems, together with their relative costs of operation.

From this overview, the appraisal would move to an analysis of specific components based on information provided by the various feasibility studies. Under technical analysis, the appraisal would summarize findings of the technical feasibility report, including such engineering aspects as existing road conditions, alternative technical solutions, preliminary surveys and plans, construction standards, availability of local resources, anticipation of special construction problems, and preliminary design for project implementation.

The appraisal's administrative/managerial section would outline the important features of construction organization, as provided by the administrative/managerial feasibility study, and—a second important factor—the organization of the maintenance and operation of the highway after it has been completed. Turning to the environmental impact, the appraisal would note what effect, if any, the alignment or location of the highway would have on natural resources. If the effect appears detrimental, the appraisal would select the best alternative route from among the choices given in either the technical or the environmental feasibility study. It should be noted, however, that even if the original route is shown to have an adverse impact, this negative factor must still be weighed against all of the other positive factors the project may possess, with final selection of the route to be used presented in the wrap-up of the appraisal report, after all pros and cons have been carefully weighed. Similarly, in assessing the social/political impact of the highway, the appraisal would pinpoint its benefits to users, such as providing them with ready access to work and recreation areas, and whether or not the local community would be likely to resist or support such a highway. Finally, since political considerations can often override technical and other feasibility studies, the appraisal should take note of the political climate as it bears on construction of the highway.

In assessing economic feasibility, the appraisal would first summarize the findings on *each technical alternative* listed in the technical feasibility report, listing such benefits as savings in transport costs provided by the project, savings in time costs, stimulation of economic development of the location and the country, other miscellaneous project benefits, such as reductions in accidents, and, finally, overall economic feasibility—the summary of project costs and benefits as given in the economic study, using such accepted indicators as NPV, B/C ratio, IRR, and others.

In tying the financial analysis to the economic analysis, the appraisal would again summarize the costs of each alternative listed in the technical feasibility study. In each case, total costs would include the construction cost, the cost of maintenance and operation, revenues (if any), and financial profitability (if any).

Last and most important, on the basis of all of the information previously obtained, the appraisal would present its choice of, and reasons for, the most feasible alternative. All the pluses and minuses of the different feasibility sectors must be weighed, both against each other and against the larger economic and political concerns that are frequently outside the scope of any of these reports. Since both the individual factors involved and the policy-making climate vary so widely from situation to situation and from country to country, guidelines are difficult to set for this delicate final task. But if it has conscientiously absorbed and integrated the contents of all of the feasibility studies, the appraisal should not contain any startling new information; rather, it should simply represent the next logical step, based on the feasibility studies.

FINAL DESIGN

After the feasibility studies have been conducted and the appraisal written, and before the project is formally selected and approved, some design modification will occur. In fact, the project's preliminary design must almost always be modified to a greater or lesser degree, based on the findings of the feasibility studies. The modification, it should be emphasized, is an ongoing process that continues past appraisal through approval and activation. For convenience, we distinguish the preliminary design, occurring before feasibility studies have been conducted, from the final design, the cumulative result of the modification that has been taking place throughout the feasibility and appraisal processes. (It must be noted that before work can begin on the detailed final design, initial approval must be given to the project. This approval must be obtained because the costs of completing the final design are approximately 10 percent of the total project budget.)

This modified design becomes the basis of final specifications, contract drawings, and the myriad details of the technical design that must be finalized before project activation and implementation begin. Such detailed specifications include not only technical design but also the blueprint of the tasks and activities required in the next phase of the project cycle. Design is therefore not an isolated task occurring at one point in time, but rather an ongoing process that tends to overlap and merge with many of the other tasks in the integrated project cycle.

In sum, the final design must be specific and detailed to provide a sound basis for receiving bids on the implementation of the project. This includes

(1) final technical design, (2) preparation of specifications and cost estimates, (3) preparation of listings of all project tasks/activities and time estimates to complete each, and (4) preparation of contract documents. To accomplish this effectively, a set of guidelines and checklists should be developed from the feasibility studies to assure the final design and implementation result in both environmental quality and project quality. The value of this approach is multi-fold as discussed earlier in the chapter. In particular, such a set of guidelines and checklists guide implementation of the project, identifying potential trouble spots and providing contingency plans. In addition, they provide a viable framework for both monitoring and evaluating. These points are discussed further in Chapters 9 and 10.

REFERENCES

1. Noranitipadungkarn, Chakrit. *Bangkok Metropolitan Immediate Water Improvement Program*, in Louis J. Goodman and Ralph N. Love, eds., *Management of Development Projects: An International Case Study Approach.* Elmsford, N.Y.: Pergamon Press, 1979.
2. Ward, William. "Competing Evaluation Systems: A Survey of Project Appraisal Methods." Washington, D.C.: Economic Development Institute, World Bank, August 1975.
3. Ray, Andar Andarup and van der Tak, Herman G. "A New Approach to the Economic Analysis of Projects," *Finance and Development*, Washington, D.C., March 1979.
4. Mishra, S.N. and Beyer, John. *Cost-Benefit Analysis: A Case Study of the Ratnigiri Fisheries Project*. Delhi, India: Hindustan Publishing Company, 1976.
5. Ibid.
6. Baum, Warren C. "The World Bank Project Cycle," *Finance and Development*, Washington, D.C., December 1978.
7. Mishan, E.J. *Economics for Social Decisions: Elements of Cost-Benefit Analysis*. New York: Praeger Publishers, 1975.
8. United Nations Industrial Development Organization, *Guidelines for Project Evaluation*. New York: United Nations, 1972.
9. Muro, Vincente. *Preparing Feasibility Studies*. Manila, the Philippines: Systems Publishing Co., 1975.
10. Whang, In-Joung. "Administrative Feasibility Analysis for Development Projects: Concept and Approach." Occasional Papers, Series No. 4. Kuala Lumpur, Malaysia: Asian and Pacific Development Administration Centre, 1978.
11. Republic of the Philippines: National Economic and Development Authority. "A Guide to Project Development." Manila, 1978.
12. Lenzner, Terry F. *The Management, Planning and Construction of the Trans-Alaska Pipeline System*. Washington, D.C.: Wald, Harkrader and Ross, August 1977.
13. A complete list of all environmental factors is included in: Chermisinoff, Paul N. and Morresi, Angelo C. *Environmental Assessment and Impact Statement Handbook*. Ann Arbor, Mich.: Ann Arbor Publishers, 1977.

14. Seader, David. "Evaluations and Planning Techniques," in David Hendricks et al., eds., *Environmental Design for Public Projects*. Fort Collins, Colo.: Water Resources Publications, 1975.
15. U.S. Environmental Protection Agency, "Environmental Impact Assessment Guidelines for Selected New Source Industries." Washington, D.C.: Office of Federal Activities, October 1975.
16. Connor, Desmond M. "Public Participation," in David Hendricks et al., eds., *Environmental Design for Public Projects*. Fort Collins, Colo.: Water Resources Publications, 1975.
17. Koppel, Bruce and Schlegel, Charles. "Sociological Perspectives on Energy and Rural Development: A Review of Major Frameworks for Research on Developing Countries." Paper presented to the Annual Meeting on the Rural Sociological Society, Burlington, Vermont, August 24–26, 1969.
18. Walsh, John E. *Preparing Feasibility Studies in Asia*. Tokyo: Asian Productivity Organization, 1971.
19. Solomon, Morris J. *Analysis of Projects for Economic Growth: An Operational System for Their Formulation, Evaluation and Implementation*. New York: Praeger Publishers, 1970.

CHAPTER 4

Project Evaluation*

Evaluation is an analytical process to determine, as systematically and objectively as possible, the effectiveness, efficiency, and significance or relevance of projects. In Chapter 1, evaluation is presented as the first task in the final phase of the IPPMC. However, Chapter 1 demonstrates that evaluation must be an ongoing process throughout the project cycle. Evaluation should critically examine and analyze the results of each task in the integrated project cycle to provide the necessary feedback to project management, ensuring cost effectiveness and safety in fulfilling project goals. This process will also accomplish three additional needs: (1) provide rapid solutions to unexpected problems that might emerge during implementation; (2) provide a sound basis for postproject assessment and evaluation; and (3) provide useful lessons to improve policies, plans, and management for future projects. The lessons drawn from an evaluation of four IPPMC case histories are presented and discussed in Chapter 9.

Brief Overview of the Status of Project Evaluation

Unfortunately, until recently, evaluation has been either neglected or given low priority. There are many reasons for this neglect. The most outstanding one has been the lack of attention in both higher education and training programs until the late 1970s. Training programs are now partially addressing this need, but higher education still gives the problem low priority.

In practice, failure to provide adequate evaluation has been primarily due to the sociopolitical nature of projects. Thus, accountability for funds that have been spent or blame for project failures are not actively sought. In some cases, given the scanty economic resources of a country or state, it is considered better to spend funds on new and necessary projects than to review old ones. In other cases, reasons have included loss of interest in past projects; no agency directly responsible for evaluation and follow-up; no team or agency responsible for the entire project; lack of appreciation for evaluation; and lack of adequate planning for the whole project—meaning that standards or objectives were never comprehensively determined and that the project, like Topsy, just grew.

---

*By John N. Hawkins, Professor of Comparative Education and Interim Director, International Studies and Overseas Programs, University of California, Los Angeles.

Some of these reasons do not exist only in developing countries. They are found everywhere, a circumstance that accounts for the recent emergence of literature on techniques and procedures in project evaluation.[1,2] Even less literature is available on related aspects such as the scaling down, termination, and reallocation of project resources when a project is completed.[3]

The importance of ongoing and postproject evaluation must not be underemphasized. The limited resources of many countries and states demand that their administrators ensure that projects are well planned and efficiently initiated. But even more, administrators must see that these projects are effective and efficient in (1) implementation, (2) completion and handover, and (3) postcompletion maintenance. At the same time, the administrators must be aware of the need to achieve the objectives of individual projects, which contribute to the economic and social growth of the state or country as a whole. While this may seem obvious in theory, all too often the dictates and pressures of short-term performance indicators shift the allocation of priorities away from evaluation toward new, more activity-oriented areas.

In an attempt to provide a formal mechanism for project evaluation, two handbooks have been published by international funding agencies. These are the *Evaluation Handbook*[4] and *Procedures for the Design and Evaluation of ILO Projects*.[5]

The *Evaluation Handbook* distinguishes between different levels of activity—multicountry-level studies, program-level studies, sector-level studies, and project-level studies. Obviously, there will be a significant difference in evaluation scope and emphasis, depending on the level of activity and the degree of complexity being reviewed. In addition, the focus is on postproject evaluation, which may not take place for at least 1 or 2 years after completion, and, in some cases, over 10 years.[6] There is no formal mechanism for analyzing the lessons learned in order to improve policies, plans, and management of future projects.

The United Nations International Labor Organization (ILO) defines evaluation as "the act of discovering how successful we are in achieving our objectives." It is an analytical process of comparing plans with accomplishments, attempting to explain significant differences between the two. The process looks upon design and evaluation in an integrated framework, where design establishes the goals or objectives of the project and formulates the work plan for implementation. Design also stipulates the means of measuring progress. Evaluation asks questions such as "Whom is this project intended to help?" and "Did it?"

The evaluation process is normally divided into three phases: (1) preparation for evaluation, (2) conduct of evaluation, and (3) preparation of the report and recommendations. As with the United States Agency for International Development, the World Bank, and other funding agencies, there was no evidence of useful output for future projects as of 1986.

A basic guideline in project evaluation that will optimize the results for both implementation and lessons learned is comprehensiveness and consistency. In this regard, it is useful to examine the evaluation process in the context of the IPPMC. This is particularly important because of the thoroughness of the feasibility studies (Chapter 3) and the guidelines for IPPMC case writers (Chapter 5). These chapters provide necessary baseline data and a comprehensive checklist.

EVALUATION IN VARIOUS PHASES OF THE PROJECT CYCLE

It is important to note that postproject evaluation is distinct from, but assumes as necessary for project success, both *ex ante* and ongoing project evaluation. Because postproject evaluation is linked to different types of project evaluations in earlier phases of the project cycle, the following section briefly examines the activities involving evaluation at each point in the history of the project.

Evaluation During Planning and Appraisal

In the early days of a project, evaluation is conducted when project proposals, prefeasibility studies, and feasibility studies are considered. In effect, these evaluation processes involve different sets of documents and different evaluating bodies at each point, and can be summarized as follows:

Project Stage	*Documents Evaluated*	*Evaluating Body*
Project identification	Interagency memoranda or preliminary project proposals	Internal to agency
Initial feasibility analysis and appraisal	Prefeasibility study	Internal to agency
Project selection and approval	Feasibility study	Top management of agency Financial institution National planning agency Other national agencies • Pollution commission • Energy commission • Regional council • Regulatory industry commission

The criteria used by each evaluating body may be different. For the agency involved, the yardstick may be return on investment, whereas for the national planning agency, it may be national security or net social benefits.

Evaluation During Operation and Control

Ongoing evaluation can and should be conducted while a project is being implemented. This allows corrective measures to be taken while the project is active.

During implementation, the project manager concentrates on effective utilization of resources—completing the project at the right time, at the lowest cost, and at an acceptable level of quality. The project manager needs to be informed on the progress of the project as measured against performance, cost, and schedule standards. This level of evaluation for efficiency is often referred to as the "control" function. Usually, however, it is higher management that conducts a running evaluation of the impact of the project—i.e., changes in the environment that affect the project's objectives.

Evaluation documents at this stage include (1) progress and status reports, (2) contractor's reports, (3) project engineer's reports, (4) budget reports, (5) year-end reports of all projects in process, and (6) funding agency's project status reports.

Evaluation During Completion and Handover

Once a project is completed, a project completion report may be required of the project manager. Again, this is an evaluation tool which can be used to determine whether expected project output levels are actually attainable and whether problems were incurred in resource input conversions.

The project completion reports are submitted to the top management of the agency; they may also be submitted to the national planning agency and the funding agency for further evaluation.

Postproject Evaluation

This evaluation, coming at the end of the project, reviews all previous evaluations made. The culmination of postproject evaluation is a formal report analyzing the project itself, as well as recommendations for future projects. The main components of the post-project evaluation report are (1) A study of the project objectives; (2) A study of the resources available and utilized for the project; (3) Alternatives, opportunities, and constraints at each decision point; (4) An analysis of the overall project with regard to its outputs and impact; and (5) Implications for future project planning.

The postproject evaluation is intended to produce recommendations that will benefit the agency not only in handling similar projects but also in future project planning and management in general. The overall benefits of both ongoing and postproject evaluation are covered in Chapter 1 and are demonstrated in the IPPMC case histories.

Models for evaluation will now be examined and their applications to the IPPMC discussed.

EVALUATION MODELS AND THEIR APPLICATION

Models for evaluation proliferate; it is estimated that as many as 20 different models may be applied. However, it has been suggested that these models can be grouped into six main types, each of which is more or less useful to the various stages of a project.[7]

First, it is possible to consider evaluation as an applied science. Thus, the evaluator uses the experimental method: operationalizing his models, measuring the results quantitatively, and exercising control over the entire process. Inspired by the social sciences, this method of evaluation appeals to those seeking causes, measuring the differences an intervention can make, and then adjusting the project to avoid mistakes and problems.

Second, evaluation can be viewed as systems management. Here the emphasis is on ensuring that the project runs well, smoothly, and efficiently. All data received from the evaluation process are interpreted with these goals in mind. In this sense, the evaluator is similar to an engineer who understands the complexities of a project and realizes that each phase must be watched and evaluated to ensure that it runs smoothly into the next phase.

A third manner in which to view evaluation is as decision theory. At each stage of the project (but more in some stages than in others), decisions must be made on whether and how to proceed next. Decision theories are statistically applied according to certain criteria, and a go–no go decision is reached. Decisions are viewed as being logically connected to evaluation data. Therefore, once the decision is made, everyone concerned is convinced that it is the right decision based on the data gathered.

A fourth model is goal oriented and treats evaluation as the assessment of progress toward goals. Great care is taken to identify goals clearly and to define a method of evaluating various stages on the way to meeting the goal. The success or failure of each stage of the project is determined by how well progress toward the goal was maintained.

A more recent evaluation method utilizes judicial procedures to assess a project. Using the legal profession's model of evaluation as jurisprudence, project evaluators identify advocates for differing views of the project's value and success. Cases are argued in a debate, a judicial decision is reached, and a verdict is handed down. Only after all sides of an issue have been heard does the project move ahead.

Finally, evaluation can be viewed as description or portrayal. This more comprehensive manner of evaluation attempts to view a project in all of its complexity, through a complete description or portrayal of each stage. This process approaches the anthropological method as the evaluators attempt to respond to the people and events surrounding a project. This method may be more useful for the project manager who wants information quickly and is less interested in statistical data than in perceptions of trusted evaluators.

These six evaluation models have in common several aspects of the evaluation process. Each attempts to determine progress in some way. Each also attempts to analyze progress with respect to effectiveness, efficiency, relevance, continuing validity of the design, unanticipated effects, possible alternatives, and causality. Each also involves the participation of interested parties, ranging from a minimal number (project management team, funding representatives, local government officials, etc.) to a broader group (employer or worker association representatives, other technical experts, representatives of consumer groups, etc.).

The context in which each of the six models of evaluation is applied is equally important and must be taken into consideration. For each of these models, three typical issues emerge: how evaluation is applied, when it is applied, and who typically participates. Although the literature on each of these issues is substantial, space allows only a short summary.

With respect to the how evaluation is applied, the process can be summarized in three phases as follows. Phase 1 determines the progress of the project. It consists of preparing evaluation worksheets, detailing plans, and listing accomplishments to date.

Phase 2 provides an analysis of the progress. This phase represents the heart of the process. Several aspects of a project's progress must be analyzed. Typical of these aspects are project effectiveness, efficiency, relevance, design validity, unintended outcomes, alternative scenarios, and causality. The answers to these questions lead to the thrid and final phase of the process of evaluation: action/decisions and preparation of the summary report. Taken together, these three phases provide the context in which project evaluation takes place.

Equally important is when evaluation takes place. Typically, this occurs at the end of the project cycle. However, experience shows that the timing of project evaluation is more complex.

In terms of timing, there are three categories of evaluation. The first is interim (or ongoing) evaluation—sometimes referred to as "formative" evaluation. This form of evaluation analyzes project outputs, likely effects, and impact while the project is being implemented. This form of project evaluation allows management and decision makers to adjust policies, objectives, and institutional arrangements based on periodic analytical data supplied by the evaluation team.

There is also terminal or "summative" evaluation, which is provided at the end of a project or at a distinct phase of an undertaking embedded in a project. It provides decision makers and planners with information for future project planning and evaluation.

Finally, there is "ex-post" evaluation, which is a retrospective examination of a project some time after its completion. Each of these timing models is valuable, and project managers must decide which to emphasize based on the nature of each project.

The last issue—who participates in the evaluation process— provides the most variability and is best determined by the nature and complexity of the project. However, some general guidelines can be utilized. In addition to the typically subcontracted external evaluation team, it is advisable to include, at a minimum, the representatives of the project management team, along with relevant governmental officials (local EPA, county, or city representatives, etc.), and representatives of extramural funding agencies. Additional participants may include regional or local employer or worker associations, other technical experts, and representatives of the local consumer group.

If these three questions—how evaluation is applied, when it is applied, and who participates—can at least be explored, the probable success of the project evaluation will be enhanced. It is not possible to judge one form of evaluation as superior to another. Rather, due to the complexity of each project, as illustrated by the IPPMC, one or another form of evaluation is more relevant. This concept is summarized in Table 4.1:

As the chart shows, different models of evaluation are more appropriate for different stages and phases of the project cycle. It is important to remember that evaluation is an ongoing aspect of project planning and management, that it occurs during and after the project is completed, and that there is no one best model to follow. Creative project managers will judiciously choose the most appropriate form of evaluation. Those discussed in this chapter are illustrative and are not meant to be inclusive, but they do demonstrate that a variety of approaches are possible.

Finally, case histories written in the IPPMC framework are useful evaluation devices, particularly for (1) education and training programs and (2) practitioners. When one is able to view a project in its entirety, it is possible to learn a great deal about its strengths and weaknesses. This process allows project managers to avoid mistakes by utilizing the evaluation data from previous projects. As a whole, then, project evaluation is not a simple exercise; it involves a complex web of interrelationships. These interrela-

TABLE 4.1. EVALUATION MODEL.

TASK	APP. SCI.	SYST. MGT.	DEC. TH.	GOALS	JURSP.	DESC.
1a		X	X	X		X
1b		X		X	X	X
1c	X	X		X		X
2a			X	X	X	X
2b				X		X
3a				X	X	X
3b			X	X		X
3c				X		X
4a	X			X		X
4b	X			X		X

Code:
1a: identification and formulation
1b: feasibility analysis
1c: design
2a: selection and approval
2b: activation
3a: implementation
3b: supervision and control
3c: completion and handover
4a: evaluation and follow-up
4b: refinement of policy and planning

tionships, when integrated, provide the project manager with the kind of information needed to assess each aspect of each project correctly.

CONCLUSIONS

Each project should be evaluated in the context of (1) its goals or objectives in meeting economic and social needs, (2) performance of each task in the integrated project cycle, (3) budget and time factors, and (4) short- and long-term effects on the environment. Such a comprehensive evaluation program requires the establishment of adequate evaluative systems or models and policies at the outset of the project to ensure the necessary studies, data gathering, and measurements. The parameters are prepared as part of the project formulation task, and are augmented by critical baseline data and criteria from the feasibility studies (see Chapter 3).

The advantages of using the IPPMC conceptual framework in project evaluation are threefold: (1) the many tasks in the project cycle are intimately linked; (2) baseline parameters are obtained in phase 1; and (3) phase 4 provides for evaluation of all three previous phases, resulting in a baseline for improving the policies, planning, design, and management of future projects.

REFERENCES

1. *Evaluating Development Assistance*. Paris: Organization for Economic Cooperation and Development, 1975.
2. Freeman, H.E., Rossi, P., and Wright, S. *Evaluating Social Projects*. Paris: Organization for Economic Cooperation and Development, 1975.
3. Goodman, Louis J. and Love, Ralph N., eds. *Management of Development Projects: An International Case Study Approach*. New York: Pergamon Press, 1979.
4. *Evaluation Handbook*. Washington, D.C.: U.S. Agency for International Development (USAID), 1976.
5. *Procedures for the Design and Evaluation of ILO Projects*. Geneva: United Nations International Labor Organization, 1981.
6. Meetings with USAID officials, Washington, D.C., 1984, 1985.
7. Glass, Gene Ve. and Elliot, Frederick S., Jr. "Evaluation Research," *Annual Review of Psychology*, Vol. 31, pp. 211–228, 1980.

CHAPTER 5

Guidelines for Writing IPPMC Case Histories

PURPOSE AND USE OF THE CASE HISTORIES

Chapter 2 clearly demonstrated the significance of a series of carefully documented case histories that describe and analyze the process of managing projects within various sectors and diverse economic and social settings. The case histories provide a direct and intimate view of the role and activities of the project manager. They also focus on the many techniques, relationships, and other factors that contribute to the success or failure of particular projects. For education and training purposes, they provide a realistic context for analyzing the management of projects. As a reference, they provide both scholars and practitioners with useful insights in (1) planning and managing new projects and (2) troubleshooting for ongoing projects. Written in the IPPMC framework, case histories provide firsthand accounts of management difficulties that occur within each phase of the project cycle and the methods used to analyze these interrelated problems. This framework helps to create an awareness of a project's integrated, cohesive nature.

The case histories are an integral part of the curriculum for the education and training of project managers. Thus, they will be used to provide realistic contexts in studying the special difficulties inherent in sound project management. To accomplish this purpose, the cases must be written in a prescribed format with detailed guidelines to ensure that all factual data relevant to each case are obtained.

The essence of teaching by the case method is that students carry the main load. Simply passing on the accumulated wisdom of others by lectures will neither assist students nor improve their performance in real situations. The students must approach each of these cases as a new learning situation in which they must examine the data; untangle the web of facts, prejudices, and opinions; determine the available courses of action; and decide what action they would take.

These exercises, however, are not done in isolation. Students must interact with one another, discussing their evaluations and defending their recommendations based on the facts presented in each case. Such participation is vital. It allows students to become dynamically involved in realistic situations, where they must use the important project management skills of perception, judgment, decision making, and communication.

To make possible such meaningful interaction, the cases must be written so that readers can examine the entire project situation. Not only must cases provide an intimate view of the manager's activities, they must also focus on the many techniques, relationships, and other factors that contributed to the project's success or failure. In this respect, case writers must detail the facts, opinions, prejudices, and forces upon which the manager's decisions were based, as well as include the raw data of the project situation. This gives the students the opportunity to analyze the project manager's effectiveness and to decide what they would have done under the same circumstances. Here it must be emphasized that project management is not an exact science. There is no single right answer; there are always alternatives and the expectation that the best solution has not yet been found. Thus, the cases must provide sufficient detail to allow the students to devise their own solution; and they must be carefully documented so that students can follow up on any unanswered questions.

There must, however, be some internal order to the cases; the massive amount of information on each project must be organized using a common format. The IPPMC provides this common format. Through the IPPMC, each project history focuses on the inextricably related set of activities—ranging from planning and identification to evaluation with feedback to policy—that constitutes the life cycle of the majority of projects in each sector.

GENERAL OUTLINE OF THE CASES

The form of the case histories should generally follow the framework of the IPPMC and should be organized in the following manner:

Chapter 1 Project Background
Chapter 2 Planning, Appraisal, and Design
Chapter 3 Selection, Appraisal, and Activation
Chapter 4 Operation, Control, and Handover
Chapter 5 Evaluation and Refinement
Chapter 6 Conclusion

Suggested Discussion Questions

Although the case writers should generally follow this sequence of chapters, they may not be able to adhere exactly to the sequence of tasks within each chapter. The tasks may run together, or be out of sequence, or possibly omitted in one of the phases. Thus, the writers should exercise imagination and flexibility in organizing a project's activities and interactions.

Moreover, since each project is a new situation set in a new environment, the writers must highlight the factors significant to their case. Thus, the writers must emphasize or deëmphasize phases according to the individual requirements of the case history. This means that some chapters of a case history will be more detailed than others. Above all, the case writers must focus on the special lessons to be learned from their project, describing fully the different sets of issues, problems, interrelationships, and tasks.

The IPPMC is thus a focal point—not a rigid framework—from which writers can elucidate the many variables and interrelationships that make their case an excellent learning device.

CHECKLIST OF QUESTIONS IN THE IPPMC

All of the questions and issues inherent in the IPPMC cannot be covered in this chapter because of the complex nature of the life cycle of most projects. The 248 questions presented here represent the composite experience of 18 senior scholars and practitioners involved in policy making, planning, design, implementation, management, and evaluation of large numbers of projects in their home countries.

Thus, the questions serve a variety of purposes in addition to providing a uniform framework for researching and writing case histories. First, they give the reader an appreciation of the number and complexity of the factors and issues affecting project management. Second, the questions are useful in the analysis of other projects for either evaluation or troubleshooting purposes. Third, they are extremely useful for the instructor in planning and guiding student assignments for term papers, group reports, and class discussions. Fourth, questions in the final phase of the IPPMC are useful for both policy makers and planners in refining policies and plans for new projects.

The questions are systematically arranged according to the IPPMC. Each phase is presented with a synoptic discussion of the process, which is covered in detail in Chapter 1.

Phase 1: Planning, Appraisal and Design

In the first phase of the IPPMC, projects ideally originate from the identification, definition, and analysis of problems and needs within the context of larger program plans and policies. In most countries and states, this process is carried out through centralized government planning, the private sector, and mixed systems of private investment and government-sponsored activities, including unstructured entrepreneurial investments. A project can be pinpointed from outside a country, as well as from inside it, by an international funding agency such as the World Bank or a multinational corporation. To translate a project idea into reality, the identification and formulation tasks must take into account community needs and preconditions, as well as the social and political environment. Strong agricultural lobbies, for example, may place pressure on government to favor projects in the rural sector.

Once the broad outline of a project idea has been formulated, planners must conduct a feasibility analysis to determine if available resources are sufficient to handle the many dimensions of implementation. In addition to this systematic analysis of parts and details, an overall appraisal of the project as an entity is necessary. Both feasibility analysis and appraisal must focus on the project's likelihood of success; at this stage, therefore, planners must define goals and assess whether or not they can be achieved.

If proper planning is an important prerequisite for a successfully executed project, then design is certainly a critical task. The success or failure of a project often depends upon the comprehensiveness of its design, which must strive to consider all pertinent factors. Project design establishes in detail the responsibilities, activities, and resources necessary to operate the project.

Important questions during phase 1 of the project include:

Identification and Formulation

1. Was the project identified in the course of the national (or state) development planning process?
   a) If so, what was the policymaking characteristic of this process?
2. Can the national (or state) planning process ensure that policies and programs for economic and social development at that level are translated into or integrated with counterpart plans at regional and local levels?
3. Did the original project idea relate to problems identified in the national, sectoral, or regional plan?
4. What were the major environmental factors—political, economic, social, cultural, technical, or others—that led to the project?
5. What was the primary source of the project idea?
6. Who were the individuals or groups that first proposed the project?
7. Did other organizations become involved in defining the project?
8. What was the role of external donors or international funding agencies in project identification?
9. Who, other than the earliest proposers, supported the project idea? Who opposed it?
10. Were other groups or individuals involved in the preparation, such

as clients, users, beneficiaries, political supporters or opponents, resource suppliers, and potential project implementors?

11. How and by whom was the initial idea justified in order to be included in the country's investment program?
    a) Should it be in the program at this stage?
    b) If so, how?
12. Were prefeasibility studies done?
13. How clearly and explicitly were the purposes and goals of the project stated or defined?
    a) Were the major potential problems also identified at this time?
    b) Were the time constraints taken into consideration?
14. Was there a general commitment to the goals of the project by all of the constituencies in its design?
    a) Whose political and administrative support could be initially counted upon?
    b) What recourse did these supporters have?
    c) What conflicts arose and how were they settled?

Feasibility Analysis and Appraisal

1. How extensive was the preliminary design?
    a) Who prepared it?
    b) How reliable were the assumptions and supporting documents?
2. Was a formal feasibility analysis conducted?
3. Who conducted it?
    a) Was it a national organization, an international assistance agency, a consulting team, or a combination?
    b) What were the qualifications of the key persons involved?
4. How comprehensive and detailed were:
    a) The technical feasibility studies (project location and layout, subsurface conditions and problem areas, technology needs, availability of construction materials, training of technical personnel)?
    b) The financial feasibility analysis (investment analysis, projected capital needs at various stages)?
    c) The economic feasibility analyses (national economic benefits, cost-benefit studies of alternative designs, effect on employment)?
    d) The market and commercial feasibility studies (as appropriate)?
    e) The administrative, organizational, and managerial studies?
    f) The environmental baseline studies?
    g) The environmental impact studies (estimated impact of the proposed project)?
    h) The social and political impact studies?

5. Did the studies reveal any weaknesses in the project that might affect future operations?
   a) If so, what were these weaknesses?
   b) How were the weaknesses addressed?
6. What appraisal criteria were used?
   a) Who had the authority for the appraisal?
   b) Was the appraiser(s) trained?
7. What procedures were used during the appraisal process?
   a) How many stages did it go through?
8. Did the appraisers and reviewers make an on-site inspection?
9. Were there any reservations about the overall ability of the project to succeed?
   a) If so, what were these reservations?
   b) Were there any problems that other appraisers foresaw that were not included in the final appraisal?
   c) If so, what were the problems and why not included?
10. How were uncertainties and gaps in the reliable estimates or projections affecting project appraisal dealt with?

Design

1. What were the major sources of data or information used in designing the principal components of the project?
2. How well did the project design reflect the initial objectives and targets of the project idea?
3. How clearly and explicitly were the purposes and goals of the project defined and stated?
   a) Were immediate goals distinguished from longer-range goals?
   b) Were project objectives related to broader development policies?
4. Did the proposal include measurable targets for attaining objectives and specifications for the project's outputs?
5. Did the source of the project's identification influence how it was prepared and designed?
6. Was an attempt made to identify the potential project manager and to involve him in reviewing both project planning and project design?
   a) Did the project manager have the necessary capabilities?
7. Were the project's activities, functions, tasks, and components clearly identified and defined?
8. How many and what kind of design alternatives were considered and analyzed?
   a) How were these alternatives evaluated and chosen?
   b) Were relevant building and other codes satisfied?
   c) Were environmental impact assessments made for each alternative?

9. Were preconditions or prerequisites of success considered during the design task?
   a) Were potential problems or bottlenecks to successful implementation identified?
10. Were potential social and cultural impacts of the project taken into consideration in its design?
    a) Were adverse effects identified?
    b) If so, how was the design modified?
11. Did the project design indicate an adequate mechanism for internal and external communication requirements?
12. Were links and relationships with complementary or competing projects examined?
13. In how much detail were plans, budgets, specifications, job descriptions, and work schedules prepared?
14. Were alternative organizational arrangements for project execution and operation considered?
    a) Were plans made for expanding the administrative capacity of the potential project implementation unit?
15. Did the project organization maintain a balance—appropriate to the project task—between technical and managerial persons and functions?
16. Were the different elements of the project design integrated into a coherent whole?
    a) Was there one person who was responsible for this integration?
    b) If so, what were his qualifications?
17. Was a postevaluation plan prepared, and were arrangements made for collecting baseline data for the various tasks?
    a) If so, what method was selected for the evaluation?
    b) Did it include checks on project goals, costs, and quality?

Phase 2: Selection, Approval, and Activation

Preliminary work on a project is well underway long before it is actually selected and approved for operation. For this reason, the analysis and preparation that have gone into designing the project should also provide sufficient information for policy makers to use in making a final decision about its funding. A project must compete for selection on the basis of extremely diverse factors: sophisticated forms of cost analysis, political and economical priorities, competition between pressure groups, and many other considerations. Even within government, departments are often competing for scarce resources for their own ministries, with top officials, including ministers, pressing their case for particular projects. Thus, for example, educators may consider that their claims for more funds for schools outweigh those of defense experts concerned with expanding defense capabilities. To provide convincing evidence of their project's priority, development project administrators must be able to perform such varied tasks as preparing loan documents, assessing public reactions, obtaining necessary ministry approvals, negotiating agreements with international assistance agencies on the content and scope of their project, and resolving proposed loan covenants.

In activating a project that has been selected and approved, the project manager faces the complex task of coordination. The commitment of professionals, technicians, resource suppliers, and policy makers to the project must be formalized. The project manager must decide on the type and location of the organization that will be responsible for executing the project, and must determine what work structure best translates operating plans into project activities. The project manager must coordinate a number of outside resource persons, delegate responsibilities within the project, and make a wide range of related administrative decisions.

Critical questions during phase 2 include:

Selection and Approval

1. What appraisal and selection criteria were used?
2. How many stages of review were necessary before final selection and approval?
   a) Who participated in the review, selection, and approval processes?
3. Did these stages involve:
   a) Obtaining legislative authorization?
   b) Obtaining executive approval?
   c) Confirming procedures for budget operation, personnel management, and interagency operation?
4. Did any changes occur in the project environment since the time of the feasibility study that affected project approval?
5. How long did the appraisal, selection, negotiation, and approval processes take?
   a) What were major sources of delay, if any?
6. What major factors—political, social, technical, economic, administrative, environmental, or other—influenced decisions at each stage of the review?
7. How were uncertainties and gaps in the reliable estimates of projections affecting project appraisal and selection dealt with?
8. Was the proposal in competition with others?
   a) If so, was the project appraised and evaluated comparatively with these others?

9. Which of the following criteria were used in the selection?
   a) Linkage with national or local development programs
   b) Accelerating the pace of economic and social progress in the area
   c) Availability of natural resources and raw materials
   d) Priorities dictated by political pressures
   e) Cost and duration
   f) Other criteria
10. From what sources was the project to be funded?
   a) Which organizations—national or international—provided other basic resources or inputs?
11. Who was involved in the negotiation of loans, grants, or other forms of funding for the project?
   a) What were the major issues of negotiation?
   b) What were the positions of the negotiators?
   c) How were differences resolved?
12. Were constraints and conditions placed on the project's design or operation by the selection, approval, or funding authorities?
   a) Was the plan modified to conform to those conditions?

Activation

1. What criteria were used in choosing a project implementation unit or executing agency?
2. What variables influenced the choice of organizational structure?
3. What was the relationship between the project implementation unit and higher organizational authorities in terms of responsibilities and support?
4. Who was included in the project team?
   a) Were they relieved of their previous responsibilities temporarily or permanently?
   b) Were they included on a part-time or a full-time basis?
   c) What were their qualifications?
5. What criteria were used in selecting personnel for the project team? In selecting the project manager?
   a) What recruitment methods were used?
6. Were the project leader and the project team given their job responsibilities clearly?
   a) Were they given an orientation or a period of retraining?
7. What working contracts and activation documents were used?
   a) Who prepared them?
8. Were adequate information and control systems provided at the activation phase?
   a) If not, why not?

9. How was the project organized internally with regard to:
   a) Work and task division?
   b) Authority, responsibility, and supervision?
   c) Communication channels among divisions and supporting organizations?
   d) Relationships between technical and administrative divisions?
   e) Resource procurement and allocation?
   f) Monitoring and reporting?
10. What types of systems or procedures were established for bidding and contracting?
11. What were the major sources of the following project inputs?
   a) Financial resources
   b) Materials, supplies, equipment, and facilities
   c) Manpower
   d) Political support
   e) Technology
   f) Public participation
12. Were detailed and realistic project operation plans formulated for:
   a) Budgeting?
   b) Recruitment and training of personnel?
   c) Data collection?
   d) Work and activity scheduling?

Phase 3: Operation, Control, and Handover

The start-up of the project results in intense activity as the various tasks and functions become operational. The project manager must coordinate and control the many diverse operations and resources that may be working together for the first time. After basic administrative blueprints have been established, the project manager allocates tasks to groups within the project organization, making sure that the flow of necessary resources is properly scheduled. The initial implementation task requires close coordination and control. While equipment, resources, and manpower are being procured, timetables and communication, information, and feedback systems must be set up.

As implementation continues, good supervision, control, and information dissemination procedures must provide the project manager with rapid feedback which highlights problems and bottlenecks as quickly as possible. A good control system not only pinpoints problems that arise during the project cycle but also measures progress by evaluating both the quality of the performance and the extent to which outputs adhere to preliminary plans and specifications. Control procedures provide the basis for guiding project operations and redirecting them, where necessary, to achieve the goals that have been set. Setting up an adequate supervision and control system means that the project manager must coordinate activities that occur both inside and outside the formal limits of the project organization.

Ending a project properly is just as important as beginning it. Project completion in this sense means that the project is prepared for its inevitable termination and handover to a different type of administration. Completion involves scaling down project activities, transforming experimental, pilot, and demonstration projects into institutionalized programs and production units, transferring outputs to beneficiaries, and diffusing project results. This task also includes the reallocation of unused or excess resources. Generally, the project manager must closely supervise the slowing down of the project and the transfer of personnel and equipment in such a way that assets are liquidated with maximum benefit.

Important questions during phase 3 of the project include:

Implementation

1. How were work activities and project tasks scheduled?
   a) Did the project management team make use of such techniques as CPM and PERT analysis?
   b) What other techniques were used, and why were they selected?
2. Was there an adequate management information system?
3. Did it define:
   a) Information requirements?
   b) Sources of information?
   c) Systematic procedures and organizations for collecting data?
   d) A coordinated design to integrate internal and external project activities?
4. Were feedback channels and feedback elements identified?
   a) Was adequate use made of these channels?
   b) Was adequate use made of the information received from these channels?
5. Were formal problem-solving or troubleshooting procedures established?
6. What arrangements were made for coordination of project activities with supporters, suppliers, and clients?
7. What was the leadership style of the project manager during the implementation phase?
8. Could it be characterized as:
   a) Management by control?*

*Management by control is a management approach involving authority and responsibility to oversee and coordinate all phases in the project cycle in order to ensure that project goals are met on both budget and schedule.

b) Management by objectives?*
c) Management by exception?†
9. Was the project redesigned or modified to meet unanticipated problems during implementation?

Supervision and Control

1. Were formal systems or procedures created to:
   a) Procure, inspect, and inventory at optimum levels raw materials and other resources?
   b) Ensure vigorous recruitment and optimum utilization of manpower and output?
   c) Monitor budget performance and cash flows; forecast changes in funding requirements?
   d) Test and adapt transferred technology?
2. What methods were used to report progress and problems to higher authorities?
   a) What type of information was reported?
   b) How frequently were reports made?
   c) To whom were they addressed?
3. How were remedial actions initiated and performed when monitoring and control procedures indicated problems?
4. Did conflicts occur:
   a) Between technicians from different disciplines or specializations?
   b) Between administrators and technicians?
   c) Between project managers within the parent organization?
   d) Between the project implementation unit and other organizations?

Completion and Handover

1. Were project completion reports prepared and reviewed?
2. Was a plan prepared either for replication or for the transition of a successful experimental, pilot, or demonstration project to full-scale operation?
3. What arrangements were made for diffusion of project outputs and results?
4. Were replicable components of the project identified?
5. Were arrangements made for follow-up investment or multiphase funding?

*Management by objectives is a management approach according to which performance is monitored by comparing actual outputs with initial goals or objectives.

†Management by exception is a management approach that focuses on problems in scheduling and actual progress (progress of the project is of primary concern).

6. Were extension or technical assistance services created to assist clients or users in adapting project outputs and results?
7. Were the procedures and methods of handover to an ongoing organization well established?
   a) Were they complied with?
   b) If not, why not?
8. What kinds of arrangements were made to transfer unutilized or excess resources—human, financial, physical, and technical—from the project at completion to other projects or organizations?
9. What arrangements were made for the transfer or disposition of the capital assets of the project?
10. What arrangements were made for credit or loan repayment?
11. Would levels of outside funding change considerably upon handover to an ongoing organization?
12. Were project personnel reassigned to new duties at the project's completion?
    a) Were they prepared and trained for this?
13. Did the handover mean that new persons took over the project activities, or were the same persons transferred to a different setting within the organization?
14. What restructuring or modification was required of the receiving agency or institution?
15. What difficulties arose as a result of the transfer and handover:
    a) To the project team?
    b) To the receiving institutions?
    c) To the beneficiaries?
    d) To the funding agencies?

Phase 4: Evaluation and Refinement

Evaluation, an often neglected task of project management, is in fact the means by which the entire success or failure of the project is measured and the only means by which useful information about its impact can be transmitted. More than simply an after-the-event examination, evaluation should be an ongoing process during each phase of the integrated project cycle. Project evaluation includes both financial auditing, to ensure that the funds were used for the specified purposes, and postassessment of the project results. Postassessment consists of examining the following factors: the effectiveness of the project in attaining its goals; the impact of the project in attaining its goals; the impact of the project on sectoral, regional, and national development; and the degree to which the goods and services provided by the project have been made available on a continuing basis through normal administrative channels.

Follow-up is the action taken on the basis of evaluation and can include both corrective action on unmet needs arising from the project and implementation of smaller, related "piggyback" projects.

Refinement of procedures is the last necessary task in the life of a project, because this modification, based on lessons learned from the old project, will be the foundation of future projects. It is the function of refinement both to pass on the project experience to new projects and to improve national policy. This refinement of procedures, as much as the actual work accomplished, constitutes the project's contribution to the well-being of a country.

Important questions during phase 4 include:

Evaluation and Follow-Up

1. Was the need for the evaluation adequately perceived?
2. Were the objectives of the evaluation sufficiently clear?
3. What type of evaluation was decided upon?
   a) Was the focus to be on short-, medium-, or long-term effects/benefits of the project?
4. Were formal evaluation procedures established?
   a) Was an evaluation timetable set up?
5. What techniques were used in the evaluation (cost-benefit analysis, baseline measures, etc.)?
6. Who did the evaluation?
   a) Was it an individual or a team?
   b) If a team, was it composed of individuals independent and outside of the parent institution, or of individuals from within, or both?
   c) Why was this choice made?
7. What level of seniority did the evaluator(s) have?
   a) Was the evaluator(s) trained?
8. Were adequate background information and data provided for evaluation purposes?
9. Was the evaluation team provided with adequate administrative support?
10. What were the results of the evaluation?
    a) Were the intended benefits realized?
    b) If not, why not?
11. Was project efficiency measured using time schedule, budget, and performance output considerations?
    a) What were the major factors causing delay, cost overruns, and failure to meet project performance criteria?
12. Was variance analysis used to measure the difference between projected and actual results?

13. Did the evaluation consider the appropriateness of the following aspects of the project
    a) Management information system
    b) Level of technology
    c) Operating design
    d) Manpower capabilities
    e) Organizational structures and flexibility
14. Did the outcome of the project support the programmatic and national policy goals for which the project was intended?
15. What was the overall impact of the project on the locality, sector, or nation?
16. What was the prevailing attitude and reaction of the end users at the start of the project?
    a) What was it at the end?
    b) Did they perceive the project objectives in the same way?
17. Did the evaluation identify unmet needs?
    a) Did the evaluation identify piggyback or follow-up projects?
18. Did the evaluation identify replicable components of the project?
    a) Did it identify the need for follow-up investment or multiphase funding?
    b) Did it detect unforeseen side effects of the project, whether fortunate or unfortunate?
19. Were formal evaluation reports prepared and presented?
    a) To which individuals or agencies were they given?
    b) When?
    c) How were they used?
20. Did the project team see the reports or participate in their formulation or preparation?
    a) If so, what was the response?
    b) If not, why not?

Refinement of Policy and Planning

1. Were the results of the evaluation followed up?
    a) If so, by whom and how soon afterward?
    b) What were the results?
    c) If there was no follow-up, why not?
2. Did the evaluation results lead to the formulation of proposals for further projects?
    a) Did they lead to improvements or modifications of national policy?

3. What lessons and insights were gained from the project?
   a) Was there an analysis of the reasons for deviations in implementation from the operating plan?
   b) Did the analysis reveal both long- and short-term lessons?
4. How can these lessons be applied to refine the project or future similar projects?
5. How can these lessons be applied to future policy decisions on project management?

As the foregoing list of questions demonstrates, the issues and factors affecting development project management are numerous and complex. To bring order out of this maze of diverse factors, the IPPMC organizes management tasks and issues into an integrated scheme which views development projects in their entirety—from identification to follow-up—and places them in a cohesive framework. This conceptual framework provides a comprehensive and balanced approach to project management.

To date, 30 case histories using the IPPMC conceptual framework have been researched and published. Three such cases involving energy projects are presented in Chapters 6, 7, and 8.

A sample of the form developed for IPPMC case proposals follows.

PROPOSAL FOR CASE HISTORY

1. *Proposed Title of Case History:* ______________________________

____

2. *Author:* ______________________________________
   (Family) (First) (Title)

Address: ______________________________________

____

____

Present Position: ______________________________

____

Qualifications: ________________________________

____

Curriculum Vitae: Please attach C.V. to proposal, giving further details, particularly regarding positions held, list of publications, etc.

3. *About the Case*

Description of the case: Please attach a two- to four-page description of the case, covering the various stages as outlined in the integrated project planning and management cycle. Include in your description:

a) The dates of the project: commencement and completion.

b) Details of the stages of the case that you consider especially important in teaching particular aspects of project management.

c) The key organizational or management activities in the project which impressed you as being particularly significant.

d) *Organizational setting:* Attach a one- to two-page description of the organizational setting of the case, including details of the project organization and project management personnel.

e) *Personnel involvement:* State briefly any personal involvement you had in the case.

4. *Source Materials*

a) Are the materials, documents, etc. needed for the case available for your use?

____

b) What organizations have the materials?

____

____

____

____

c) Is special permission required to use the materials? If so, please list those materials and state how permission should be obtained.

____

____

____

____

5. *Work Plan*

a) How long will it take you to write the first draft?

____

b) When are you able to start writing the case?

____

c) If your proposal is accepted, when can you visit the East-West Center to finalize the case?

(continued)

6. *Illustrations—Photos*
   a) Do you propose to use illustrations (e.g., graphics, photos)?

   ____

   b) If you do, please estimate the number to be used.

   Line drawings: ______________________________________

   Photos (black and white): ____________________________

CHAPTER 6

Hawaii Geothermal Project

This case history was researched during the period 1978–1979 and published in 1980.* The pilot or demonstration power plant was put on line in 1981, supplying 3.0 MW of electricity to the residents of the island of Hawaii. The Epilogue discusses increased geothermal explorations and updates the economic, environmental, and social impact analyses to 1984. Two additional factors from 1979 to 1984 are of interest: (1) the population of the state increased to slightly over 1 million, with 780,000 persons on Oahu, and (2) dependence on imported petroleum for energy in the state decreased from 99 percent to 90 percent.

A brief overview of geothermal energy is presented in Appendix C.

PROJECT BACKGROUND

Hawaii, one of the 50 states of the United States, is an island chain located in the central Pacific Ocean, approximately 2,500 mi (4,000 km) west of the continental United States. It is composed of numerous islands extending across 2000 mi (3218 km) of the Pacific and is dominated by five major islands (see Figure 6.1). At the northern end of the chain lies the capital and population center of the state, the island of Oahu. Oahu has a population of 718,400, while the state of Hawaii as a whole has a total population of 886,400. Approximately 200 mi (320 km) south of Oahu is the island of Hawaii, which is the youngest and the only volcanically active of the major islands. It has a population of 76,400.

The state as a whole is blessed with magnificent mountains, beautiful beaches, cool valleys, lush vegetation, fertile plains, abundant sunshine, and plentiful rainfall, all of which have made it possible to develop both a thriving tourist industry and a profitable agro-industry in sugar and pineapples. Ironically, the same geography and geologic characteristics that have helped these industries to thrive have also deprived Hawaii of the conventional sources of fuel needed to power them. Because of the islands' recent volcanic origin, no indigenous fossil fuel reserves exist. In addition, geog-

*Louis J. Goodman, Tetsuo Miyabara, and Barbara Yount, in Louis J. Goodman and Ralph N. Love, eds., *Geothermal Energy Projects: Planning and Management*. New York: Pergamon Press, 1980.

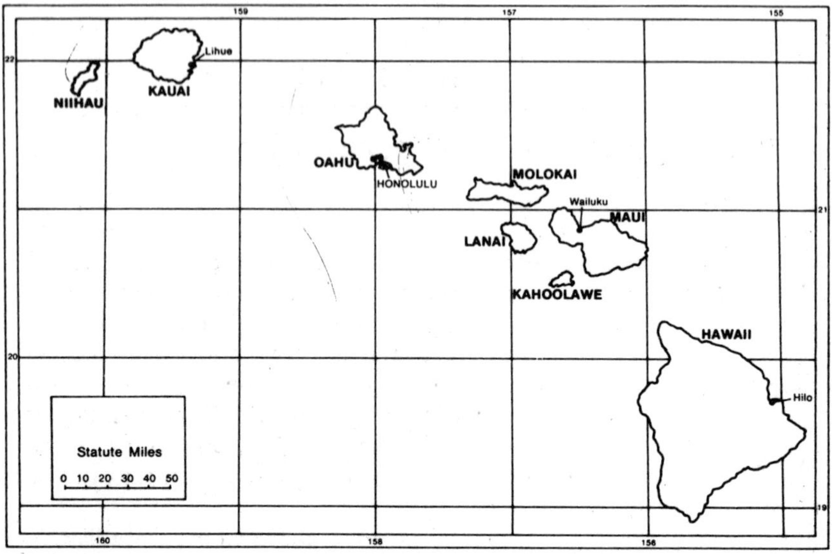

Figure 6.1. Map of Hawaii.

raphy has isolated Hawaii from potential energy sources. Unlike the rest of the United States, no coal comes into the state by rail; no natural gas is received by pipeline; and no regional grid of electricity serves Hawaii. The only presently feasible source of fuel is oil, shipped in by large tankers. In short, Hawaii is almost totally dependent upon outside oil, and is thus vulnerable both to disruptions in delivery and to fluctuations in the global market. Its vulnerability was succinctly summarized by the opening statement from the Mayor's Energy Resources Committee: "In Hawaii, 'Energy is Oil.' We are totally dependent on oil and gas for our energy consumption needs."[1]

This vulnerability is underscored by several statistics. From 1960 to 1974, over 99 percent of Hawaii's power was generated from crude oil which was shipped to the state.[2] Approximately 25 percent of all petroleum products was used to generate electricity, 25 percent was used for air transportation, 28 percent was used by gasoline service stations, 14 percent was used for industrial and commercial purposes, and 8 percent was used for a variety of other pupposes.[3] Several trends have also increased Hawaii's vulnerability. The cost of oil has risen dramatically; in 1970 it was US$2.50 a barrel, and by 1974 it was US$10. Between 1958 and 1975 consumption of petroleum rose 300 percent, from 12 million to about 38 million barrels per year.[4]

Yet this dependence and vulnerability upon imported oil is a paradox because Hawaii possesses abundant alternative energy sources—solar, wind, wave, biomass, ocean thermal, and geothermal. Unfortunately, until recently, these sources have not been developed. A significant factor in this lack of development was the lack of an overall U.S. energy policy. In its absence, the responsibility for developing alternative energy sources fell to the private utility companies, which generate most of the power in the United States, and to the individual state and county governments. For the utility companies, however, there was little incentive to risk their capital in research and development. Fossil fuel sources, particularly oil, were abundant and cheap, and therefore cost effective; nonconventional power sources could not compete with oil. Thus, the initiative for developing energy alternatives rested primarily with state and local organizations, such as universities and planning boards. For the most part, these organizations did not have the resources to conduct the research and development necessary to make the various energy alternatives feasible. Nor did they receive the necessary support from the state governments, since energy development was not seen as a high priority.

In contrast, the government of the State of Hawaii and county governments of each island placed a high priority on the development of energy alternatives. Hawaii's vulnerability to oil shortages and dependence on oil had made state and county officials keenly aware of the urgent need to develop Hawaii's indigenous sources of energy. As early as 1970, three years before the Arab oil embargo, the Hawaii state legislature passed a resolution requesting the University of Hawaii's Center for Engineering Research to submit a study on the potential for new energy sources for Hawaii. The report, completed in 1971, listed a number of alternatives.[5]

Geothermal energy was considered one of the more exciting new possibilities. The concept itself—that of using the heat of the earth to generate electricity—could be applied in Hawaii by harnessing and controlling the sometimes destructive heat of the volcanoes. Since the island of Hawaii was formed by the largest volcanic mass in the world (see Figure 6.2), geothermal energy had great potential. And this potential captured the imagination of many of the state legislators and helped gain local momentum for geothermal research.

Additionally, the county government of the island of Hawaii was enthusiastic about using its untapped resource. In this regard, several early experiments had been conducted on the island. In the 1920s someone had attempted to use volcanic heat directly to generate electricity. More recently, in the 1960s explorations for geothermal reservoirs had been conducted. These explorations resulted in the drilling of four wells in the Puna region, the deepest of which was about 700 ft (213 m). However, no reservoirs were found and the drilling projects were abandoned as economically unfeasible. If any reservoirs existed, they existed at considerably greater depths and could be exploited only at great cost.

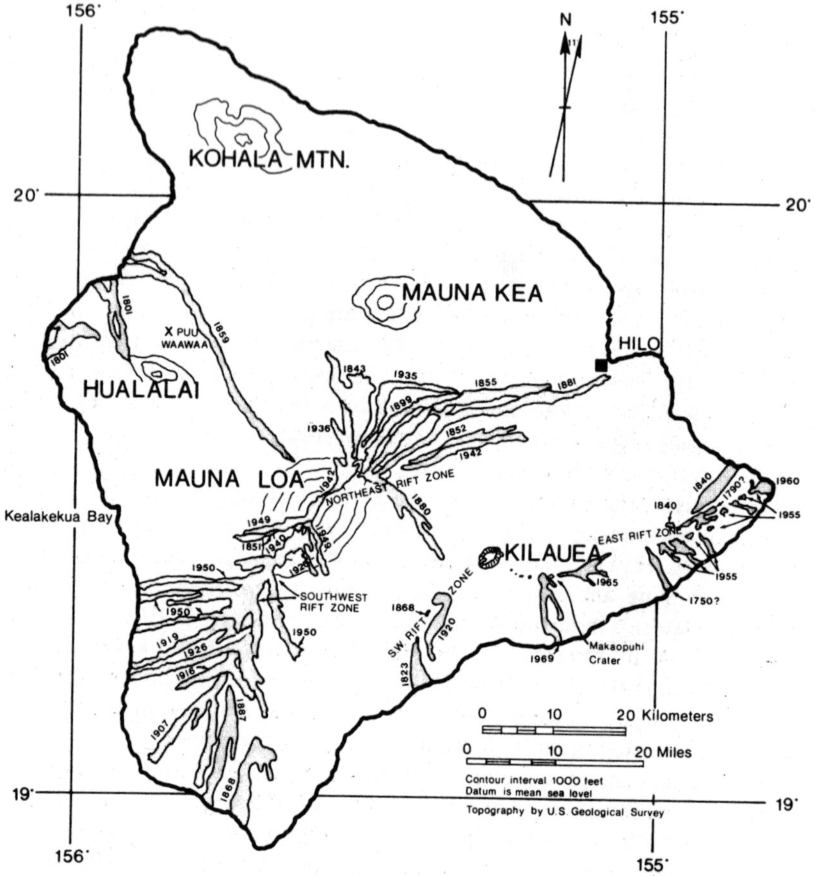

Figure 6.2. The island of Hawaii with volcanoes.

PLANNING, APPRAISAL, AND DESIGN

Identification

In 1972, with the encouragement of state and county governments, Howard Harrenstein, director of the University of Hawaii's Center for Engineering Research and a long-time believer in Hawaii's geothermal potential, submitted a US$2.7 million research proposal to the National Science Foundation (NSF). The proposal outlined a two-year project, called Project Pele. It was essentially a multidisciplinary effort that would include:

1. Geophysical program: geophysical explorations on the island of Hawaii. These would include surface studies, as well as the test drilling of a series of shallow wells and a deep well, possibly to depths of 10,000 ft (3048 m).
2. Engineering program: engineering research on problems associated with geothermal generation of electricity.
3. Environmental/socioeconomic program: investigations on geothermal energy's socioeconomic and environmental implications.

The project appeared to have one major drawback: Although it outlined a very ambitious plan that would result in potentially useful scientific information, it was a pure research project. No plans were made to actually convert geothermal energy into electricity. Nonetheless, the Hawaii state legislature and the county government of the island of Hawaii strongly supported the proposal, each giving the project US$100,000 contingent upon its receiving NSF matching funds. However, the project was not immediately funded.

Instead, in June 1972, the NSF awarded a smaller geothermal research grant of about US$400,000 to George Keller, a professor of geophysics at the Colorado School of Mines. Keller intended to drill a well about 3500 ft (1067 m) deep in the Hawaii Volcanoes National Park at a site where the U.S. Geological Survey indicated there might be underground steam. Even if Keller discovered no reservoir of steam, he would take core samples and conduct geophysical tests. Since these tests would indicate the potential of usable geothermal energy in Hawaii, they would have a strong bearing on the more elaborate Project Pele proposed by Harrenstein. Positive findings would add justification for funding the multi-million-dollar research project.

Keller's project was eventually successful in obtaining research data and in drilling to its target depth of 3500 ft (1067 m). The project also encountered certain problems.

One significant problem arose just prior to the drilling. The Congress of Hawaiian People, a group representing the interests of indigenous Hawaiians, asked Hawaii Volcanoes National Park officials to delay the project. A co-chairman of the Congress said that his group had two objections. First, the drilling might violate religious and spiritual beliefs of the Hawaiian people: "Hawaiians should have been consulted before the drilling was approved because it will take place on the sacred religious grounds of our ancestors."[6] The co-chairman argued that Keller should have prepared an EIS that detailed the site's religious and historical value. Second, he claimed that if the drilling found any commercially usable steam, Hawaiians should profit from it because the state constitution declared that indigenous natural resources should be used for the betterment of the Hawaiian people.

Both problems were eventually resolved. Keller met with the Congress and ensured them that the project site was not located in an area of historical or religious significance. He also obtained a ruling from the Hawaii Volcanoes Park superintendent stating that any geothermal steam from the site would never be exploited commercially. The park was a public reservation, and therefore none of its resources could be bought or sold.

Formulation: The Initial Proposal

While Keller's project was being implemented, the proposed Project Pele suffered a setback when Harrenstein resigned his University of Hawaii post to accept another position at the University of Miami. Since Harrenstein was listed as the project's principal investigator, the proposal had to be revised and then resubmitted to the NSF. Initial planning meetings were held, and the first decision made was to name a management team to replace Harrenstein. The management team was to consist of John Shupe, dean of the University of Hawaii's College of Engineering; George Woollard, director of the University of Hawaii's Institute of Geophysics; and John Craven, the State of Hawaii Marine Affairs Coordinator and the dean of the University of Hawaii's Marine Program. The project was also renamed the Hawaii Geothermal Project (HGP).

In August 1972, an NSF official advised the HGP management team that a single person should be assigned to manage the project. The failure to name one well-qualified person to assume overall leadership would endanger potential funding. It was then decided to appoint John Shupe as the principal investigator. He would be the project director, responsible for the project's overall administration and management and, in essence, for the success or failure of the project. Sharing responsibility with him were to be three co-principal investigators: Augustine Furumoto, a professor of geophysics at the University of Hawaii; Paul Yuen, associate dean and professor of the University of Hawaii College of Engineering; and Robert Kamins, a professor of economics at the University of Hawaii. They were to be the coordinators, respectively, of the geophysics program, the engineering program, and the environmental/socioeconomic program. Each would devote half of his time to the project and the other half to his normal university duties.

An HGP Executive Committee was also established. The Executive Committee was composed of Shupe, the coordinators of each research program, George Woollard, and John Craven. Although this committee would make no direct decisions, it would play a policymaking and planning role. Figure 6.3 illustrates the 1972 organizational chart of the HGP.

By late 1972, the Executive Committee realized that the proposed project would have a better chance of being funded if it included research and de-

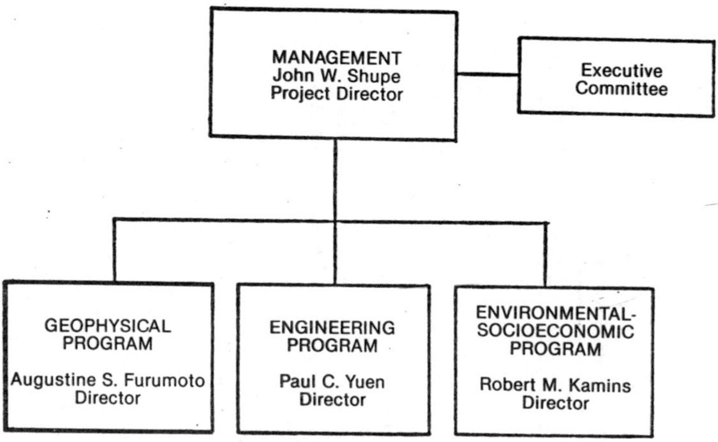

Figure 6.3. Hawaii Geothermal Project: Organization Chart (1972).

velopment that led directly to the conversion of geothermal energy to electricity. This would demonstrate the practical value of the research, as well as provide tangible results for such a costly research.

Consequently, the HGP Executive Committee expanded the scope of the project to include the planning and construction of a 10-MW prototype geothermal power plant. As in the originally proposed Project Pele, research under HGP was divided into three areas: geophysics, engineering, and environmental/socioeconomic. A total of 37 separate tasks were identified in these three areas (see Table 6.1) and a team of 54 researchers was named to conduct the investigations.

Requiring US$5 million over a two-year period, the HGP proposal was conceived in the following three stages:

Stage I was to be the initial, short-range exploratory and applied technology research that would assist in the early development of geothermal power. This stage was intended to acquire scientific information and to help locate possible drill sites for geothermal steam.

During Stage II, the geophysical data collected in Stage I would be used to establish an exploratory drilling program. This stage would culminate in the drilling of one deep hole that would, hopefully, tap a steam or hot water reservoir.

Stage III was envisioned as a planning stage for the actual construction of a geothermal power plant. The well would be analyzed and the tests necessary to design the power plant would be conducted. The actual generator design would then be prepared. In May 1973, approximately a year after the submission of the project proposal, the NSF announced that it was

TABLE 6.1. HAWAII GEOTHERMAL PROJECT: PROPOSED RESEARCH.

GEOPHYSICAL SURVEYS	ENGINEERING STUDIES	ENVIRONMENTAL/SOCIOECONOMIC STUDIES
Photogeologic survey	Well test analyses	Environmental impact
Aeromagnetic survey	Ghyben-Herzberg lens dynamics	Geotoxicology of thermal areas
Electrical resistivity survey	Geothermal plant optimum design	Land use and land law
Electromagnetic induction survey	Corrosion and wear reduction	Legislation and regulation
Microseismic survey	Electrical energy transmission	Planning
Offshore seismology	Energy extraction from high-temperature brine	Economic analysis
Thermal (300 ft) survey	Materials for use with magma and hot rock	Phytoplankton by-product research
Shallow seismic survey	Direct extraction of magma energy	Agriculture research
Petrology, structural, geology, and geochemistry	Direct energy conversion	Trace metal recovery
Geochemistry of fluids	Alternative modes of energy transmission and storage	
Physical properties of rock	Pilot plant steam production	
Groundwater	Mechanical design and layout for pilot plant	
Deep drill	Pilot plant electrical generation and transmission	
Model study		
Evaluation		

Source: *Hawaii Geothermal Project Quarterly Progress Report No. 1*, June 1, 1973–August 31, 1973, pp. 1–3.

awarding the HGP a one-year budget of US$252,000. Although numerous other geothermal projects had requested funding, it had been decided that the U.S. energy programs required more information on geothermal potential in island volcanic regions. This amount, added to the initial grant of US$200,000 which had been given to the project in 1972 by the state and county government, provided the HGP with a first-year budget of US$452,000. Although this was far less than the originally requested US$5 million, it was viewed as the beginning of a long-term commitment to develop geothermal power in Hawaii. The budget was also sufficient to enable Stage I, the early exploratory research, to get underway.

Feasibility and Appraisal: 1973–1975

The initial research activities of the HGP were, in a sense, the formal feasibility studies, determining the chance of the project to eventually generate electricity from Hawaiian geothermal sources. The exploratory geophysical surveys would help determine if and where reservoirs of steam or hot water existed and thus allow the NSF to assess the HGP's scientific feasibility. The engineering and environmental/socioeconomic studies would identify and clarify the technological, environmental, legal, regulatory, and economic problems that could hinder the eventual development of geothermal power in Hawaii—provided, of course, that a usable source of geothermal energy existed.

Upon word of the NSF's allocation to the HGP, the state government and the county government of Hawaii island, which both strongly supported the development of alternative energy sources, released funds to the HGP to begin planning activities. Shupe then convened a meeting of the Executive Committee, and each of the program coordinators was given a separate budget. This provided each coordinator with the independence and flexibility needed to administer the research in his area and, at the same time, made each accountable for his program. Shupe was responsible for the overall management and coordination of the project. He was also responsible for maintaining project cohesiveness and for ensuring that each research program developed consistently with the overall project goals.

The Executive Committee also had to make important budgetary decisions. The separate budgets initially proposed by each program coordinator had to be reduced because the initial level of funding was considerably less than anticipated. Thus, it was decided that each program would receive only enough funds to initiate crucial tasks. The bulk of the money, however, would be allocated to the geophysics program because it was conducting the exploratory surveys crucial to the project's continued progress. Despite the reduced funding, it was anticipated that the NSF or some other government agency would provide the HGP with additional funds if the geophysical surveys indicated the existence of a reservoir of steam.

With these decisions made, the directors of the geophysics, engineering, and environmental/socioeconomic programs began organizing their respective activities.

Geophysics Program. The geophysics program director, Augustine Furumoto, had requested about US$800,000 for the 1973–1974 activities but received only about US$250,000. He decided to limit the geophysical surveys to those which could begin immediately; the remaining surveys depended upon the data from the initial surveys and would be undertaken if additional funds were received. The chosen surveys were those crucial in identifying a potential reservoir of steam or hot water. Providing clues to subsurface conditions, they would be like pieces of a large jigsaw puzzle, which, when put together properly, would serve as a geophysical model of the volcanic area. Included were photogeologic, geoelectrical, microseismic, and geochemical surveys. Other surveys, such as gravity and magnetic surveys, were planned for 1974 if funds were available. The photogeological survey, contracted out to a commercial firm with the necessary equipment and experience, involved flying over the volcanoes at approximately 2100 ft (640 m) and taking infrared photographs of the rift zones—zones of innumerable fissures that served as underground pathways for the rise of magma. When developed, the photographs would expose gradations of surface heat and would locate volcanic vents and other "hot spots" along the rifts. Any surface temperatures that exceeded the highest range of the film would be exposed as spots of white. Flights were conducted during August 1973, and the photos were developed soon afterward. The photographs revealed a concentration of white dots along the east rift of Kilauea volcano, in an area named Puna. The temperature range indicated by the film was 61–77°F (16–25°C).

The initial electrical resistivity survey was subcontracted to George Keller, who already had equipment in the field from his earlier project. These surveys, called "dipole-bipole mapping," checked the earth's electrical resistance by passing an electrical current between two poles set in the ground; low resistivity readings indicated conductive foundations, such as hot saline water or highly conductive soils. Since low resistivity readings could also indicate pipes or electrical wires, several surveys had to be conducted to help determine the true sources of the readings. The survey indicated two areas of low resistivity that could be attributed to thermal sources—the Opihikao anomaly and the Pahoa anomaly—both located in the area of Puna. The Opihikao anomaly had resistivities of about 5 ohms/m from 1969 to 6890 ft (600 to 2100 m), whereas between the same depths, Pahao had resistivities of about 8 ohms/m.

The microseismic surveys were to have measured the velocity of sound passing through the ground, thus providing indications about the area's subsurface structure. These surveys were postponed because of delays in receiving the necessary equipment. The geophysics coordinator agreed, however, to begin a ground noise survey, which would indicate the variance in subsurface noise. Since, in Hawaii, sites of volcanic activity produce intense sound, these surveys would help to locate sources of geothermal heat. Like the initial surveys, the ground noise survey discovered intense sound.

The geophysical surveys progressed steadily through early 1974, with the geophysics coordinator assigning tasks to appropriate geophysicists on the project team. Often the assigned individual would subcontract the survey to a specially equipped commercial firm and then analyze the data himself. This arrangement proved satisfactory for many of the tasks. However, when no commercial firm could undertake the surveys, the geophysicist had to order special equipment or redesign existing equipment and then conduct the survey. This led to some delays, and the surveys fell behind schedule.

Engineering Program. The engineering program, like the other two research programs, had to reduce the number and scope of its initially proposed research tasks. The engineering director, Paul Yuen, thus decided to concentrate on (1) geothermal reservoir engineering and (2) optimal geothermal plant design. These two tasks dealt directly with applied research crucial to the production of geothermal energy in Hawaii.

Geothermal reservoir engineering was initially two separate tasks, but because of their close linkage, these were later collapsed into one task with two related components. These components included (1) numerical modeling and (2) well testing and analysis. The engineers working on numerical modeling attempted to do a computer simulation of the operational dynamics of a geothermal system under different conditions. To derive the mathematical relationships, they first had to investigate several issues. How, for example, would pumping, reinjecting, and recharging the geothermal well affect the Ghyben-Herzberg lens? The Ghyben-Herzberg lens is a pool of fresh water trapped in porous rocks beneath the island's surface. Sea water also permeated the island's subsurface, but the fresh water was lighter and thus floated on the sea water, forming a lens which supplied much of the island's water. When the engineers completed these investigations, they would construct a model that would generate computer answers to questions such as: How deep must the well be drilled to avoid destruction of the Ghyben-Herzberg lens? What is the life span of the well? What is the capacity of the geothermal reservoir?

Well testing and analysis would culminate in field measurement of the geothermal well—assuming, of course, that a successful well was drilled. The task would proceed in several stages. Initially, the engineering team would evaluate the existing equipment and the methods used by the geothermal engineers in other areas of the world; this involved a literature search. Then they would examine the techniques used by petroleum reservoir engineers to measure oil wells. However, since the volume and capacity of a geothermal reservoir depended on temperature but a petroleum reservoir did not, many analytic techniques of petroleum reservoir engineering were inadequate. Thus, during the next stage of research, engineers would modify and adapt both the geothermal and the petroleum methods to develop a comprehensive geothermal testing program. The completed program would be appropriate for a geothermal well and would include a complete array of geological and reservoir engineering tests, as well as recommendations for the purchase of equipment. After the researchers developed the well testing program, they would conduct the tests on the well itself. Ultimately, the data collected would help predict the life span and capacity of the geothermal well.

The engineering program's second research task was to study power plant designs that could be used if a geothermal well was discovered. Since the optimal power plant design depended upon the form of energy produced by the well (it might be dry steam, wet steam, hot water, gases, dissolved solids, or vapor), the engineering team might have to study many options. The team decided, however, to limit their investigations to two basic types of geothermal power plants: the vapor flashing plant and the binary fluid plant.

The vapor flashing plant would be practical if the well produced geothermal steam. In this system, the geothermal well would contain hot water under intense pressure. As the water rose from the bottom of the well, the pressure on it would decrease and some of it would flash to steam. The well would thus emit a mixture of hot water and steam. The steam would be separated from the hot water by a separator and piped directly to a turbine generator. The hot water could be discarded or piped to another separator, which would further reduce the atmospheric pressure on it, causing it to flash to steam. This steam would then be piped to the generator (see Figure 6.4).

The binary fluid plant would be efficient if the well produced hot water. In this system, the hot water would be used to heat a secondary liquid, such as isobutane. When the isobutane became vaporized, it would power a turbine that would then produce electricity (see Figure 6.5).

To design the optimal plant, the engineers would have to answer questions such as: What would be the most efficient steam pressure to power plants of different sizes? What plant configuration would be most feasible given different well conditions? What kind of turbine generator should be used if the well produced wet steam or dry steam? How should the plant's discharge system be designed to make it environmentally sound?

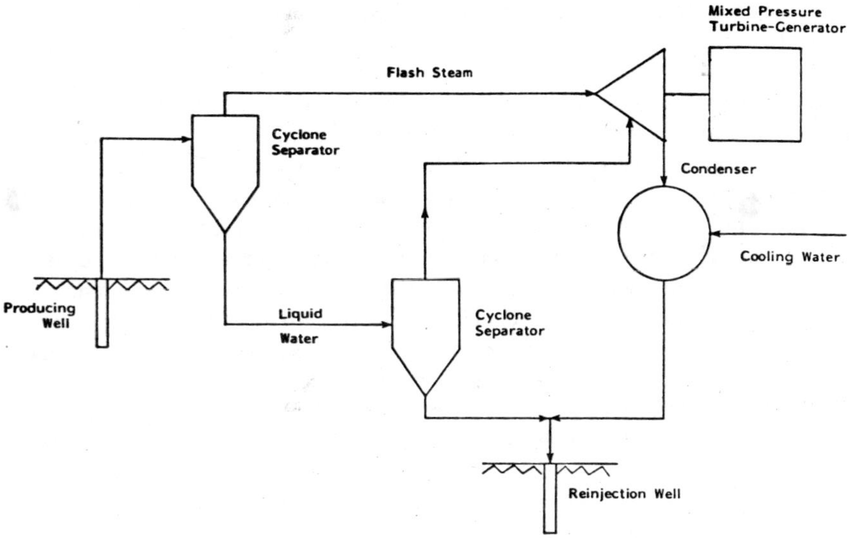

Figure 6.4. Vapor flashing plant.

The engineering team began work on each of these tasks in late 1973, and the research proceeded smoothly through 1974. However, much of the research was intended to be applied to the actual production of geothermal energy in Hawaii. Thus, the engineering program could succeed only if

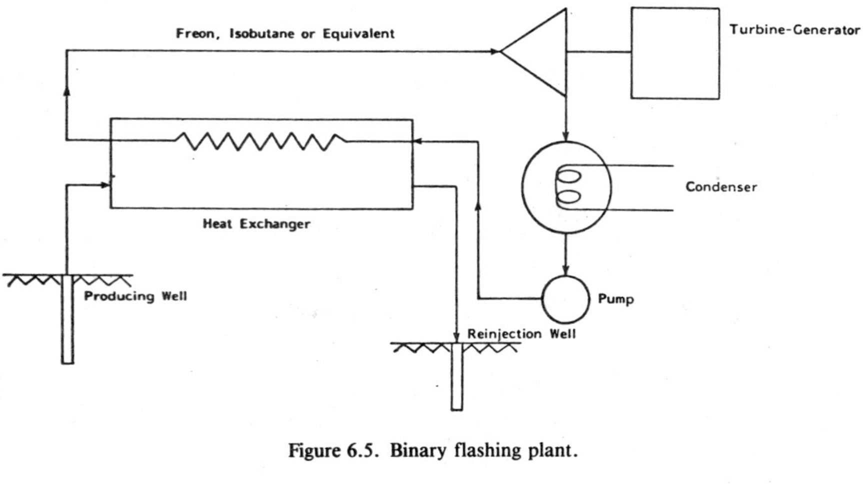

Figure 6.5. Binary flashing plant.

money was obtained to continue the overall project and only if a successful geothermal well was drilled.

Environmental/Socioeconomic Program. With only limited funding available for environmental and socioeconomic studies, the coordinator of the program, Robert Kamins, decided to focus on the following three aspects of geothermal development: (1) legal and regulatory aspects, (2) economic implications, and (3) environmental impacts. These topics had a direct bearing on the social, economic, and political factors that would help or hinder the implementation of geothermal energy projects in Hawaii.

The first aspect, the legal-regulatory research, involved the complex questions of ownership and government regulation. Because Hawaii's public law did not cover geothermal resources, it was uncertain whether geothermal steam was publicly or privately owned. In order to clarify this issue, the research team would first have to examine how other U.S. states settled the ownership question. These approaches would then have to be compared to the relevant statutes in Hawaii and alternative solutions proposed that were consistent with Hawaiian law. Of particular importance in this regard was whether geothermal resources could be classified as mineral, water, or a substance unique in nature. If geothermal resources were classified as mineral, some would be owned by the state under mineral rights clauses; if they were classified as water, they would be owned by private landowners through legal precedence; and if they were classified as unique in nature, their ownership would be uncertain. This situation was further complicated by two issues. First, some of the land deeds issued during the early 1900s did not reserve to the State of Hawaii the exclusive ownership of any subsurface minerals. Since it was not known how many of these deeds existed or where the land pertaining to them was located, ownership could be determined only by reviewing individual land deeds. Second, several Hawaiian rights groups claimed that the geothermal resources belonged to indigenous Hawaiians. They claimed that their ownership was upheld by Hawaii's constitution.

In examining the regulatory issues, the environmental/socioeconomic team would have to address questions such as: Which government agencies, if any, should possess authority over the drilling, land use, and development of geothermal energy? What safety requirements should be adopted for drilling and for geothermal power plants? What environmental safeguards should be imposed upon geothermal development? How should the public interest be protected?

A fundamental issue regarding these questions was the multiplicity of government agencies potentially involved in answering these questions. On the federal level, these included the Environmental Protection Agency and the Energy Research and Development Administration. On the state level, they included the Department of Health, the Department of Transportation, the Department of Planning and Economic Development, the Department of Land and Natural Resources, the State Energy Resources Coordinator, the Department of the Attorney General, the Office of Environmental Quality Control, the Hawaii state legislature, the Public Utilities Commission, and the Department of Regulatory Agencies. On the county level they included the Department of Public Works, the Department of Research and Development, the Department of Water Supply, and the Planning Department.

The second research topic, the economic impact of geothermal development, involved building an econometric model that would provide projections to the year 1980. To begin this task, the researchers would collect data on the cost, source, amount, and distribution of Hawaii's present energy use. Data would also be collected on the cost and production of geothermal energy around the world. From these data, the researchers would make certain assumptions about energy prices. Then, after building a dynamic model, they would estimate the demand for geothermal energy under varying supplies. Projections could then be made of the resulting impact upon employment, population dispersion, industrial growth, public revenue, and economic growth.

The third research task, environmental analysis, would monitor the ecologic impact of any geothermal well or power plant developed by the HGP. Initial studies would involve the collection of baseline data on the vegetation and wildlife in the drilling area. Of particular concern, however, was the Ghyben-Herzberg lens, which supplied much of the island of Hawaii's fresh water. A medium or deep geothermal well might penetrate the lens, endangering the water supply. To provide information about the impact of drilling, researchers would initially measure nearby springs for salinity, temperature, and chemical characteristics. Then they would establish a program to monitor the springs for any deviations from the baseline measures. Eventually the environmental program would complete a comprehensive environmental impact statement.

In late 1973, the program team began working on the legal/regulatory aspects and the economic implications of the project. The environmental analysis, however, could not be initiated until a potential drilling area was designated, and in late 1973 it was uncertain if the HGP would receive drilling funds. Nonetheless, there was an urgent need for the study on legal implications because the Hawaii state legislature was considering legislation to clarify the ownership of geothermal resources.

To assist the legislators, in February 1974, the research team completed a preliminary analysis of all geothermal ownership options and their consequences. Aided by this study, the legislature passed the state's first geothermal law. It classified geothermal resources as mineral, thus reserving them to the state under mineral rights provisions. Work on the regulatory aspects and the economic impact continued through 1974.

Overall Coordination and Management of HGP, 1973–1974

While each program's research was being conducted, John Shupe attempted to ensure continued support for the HGP and to maintain the project's overall cohesion. He conferred regularly with federal, state, and county agencies, made presentations of the envisioned HGP program at public symposiums and international conferences, and formed contacts with a widespread network of geothermal experts, who would provide HGP with advice, information, and assistance. In August 1973, Shupe also formed the Hawaii Advisory Committee (HAC) and the National Liaison Board (NLB).

The HAC was composed of Hawaii's business, political, and community leaders such as the president of Hawaii's major electric company, the director of the State Office of Environmental Quality, the director of the State Department of Planning and Economic Development, the director of a leading environmental group, the president of the Congress of Hawaiian People, and officials from the County of Hawaii. Since these individuals represented the groups that formulated Hawaii's energy policy, their support was critical for the successful development of geothermal energy. Moreover, many of the groups, particularly the state and county officials, strongly supported the development of indigenous alternative energy sources. Therefore, it was natural that the project include them in an overall cooperative effort. The first HAC meeting was held in October 1973, and the group decided to meet semiannually.

The NLB was composed of geologists, geophysicists, and engineers from the U.S. mainland. Experts on geothermal power development, they would monitor and advise the HGP on its progress and direction. Since they also represented a core of the nation's geothermal experts, as well as working for key agencies such as the NSF and the U.S. Geological Survey, they would be extremely influential in ensuring continued federal funding for the project. The first NLB meeting was scheduled for early 1974.

Maintaining the overall cohesion of the HGP was the project director's most difficult but most important task. He realized that the project was, to a certain extent, naturally segmented because each program conducted very different kinds of research. Moreover, some separation was necessary to give each program the flexibility and independence required to accomplish its own goals. At the same time, however, the ultimate goal of each research program was to support the generation of geothermal power in Hawaii. This goal provided the driving force for the HGP and integrated the research programs with one another. Thus, the project director had to encourage all program coordinators to keep the ultimate goal in mind and to avoid concentrating on research that was not relevant to the project's overall goals.

At the beginning of 1974, the HGP was increasingly embroiled in the major policy question of whether or not to establish and proceed with an experimental drilling program. The project director felt that the project had to make progress by drilling an experimental well. He thus advocated the establishment of a drilling program. The geophysics program coördinator felt that further research had to be conducted before the HGP could even consider a drilling program. However, the engineering and socioeconomic program coordinators supported the establishment of a drilling program. Other HGP team members, particularly Agatin Abbott, professor and chairman of the Department of Geology and Geophysics at the University of Hawaii, supported a drilling program because it was the only way to actually determine if a usable geothermal source existed. However, a final decision could not be made immediately.

Against the background of this unresolved policy issue, Shupe convened the first meeting of the NLB. The meeting was held in February 1974 on the island of Hawaii, where any potential drilling would occur. The meeting was intensive. The director of the NSF's Advanced Energy Research program outlined the foundation's interest in HGP, emphasized the crucial role of the NLB in evaluating the HGP's progress, and pointed out that the NSF could not fund commercial exploratory drilling but could fund a research drilling program.

Then, each HGP program coordinator presented a progress report. The engineering coordinator described the reservoir engineering and mathematical work to date; the environmental/socioeconomic coordinator described the Hawaii state legislature's efforts to establish a legal framework for the ownership of geothermal resources. Most of the meeting was spent, however, on the progress of the geophysical program. Initially, the geophysics coordinator described the infrared air photo survey and the electrical resistivity surveys, and also presented data from his deep (4000 ft) (1257 m) drill. A review of surveys conducted prior to the formation of the HGP was also presented, and a lively discussion ensued. Board members, HGP personnel, and persons in the audience asked probing questions and offered interpretations of the geophysical data.

At the end of the meeting, the NLB could reach no consensus on which sites had the greatest geothermal potential. But it did agree on recommended courses of action for the HGP. The NLB felt that the HGP should move rapidly to establish a research drilling program. There was no other way to test the theories and interpretations. The NLB further recommended that the coordinator of the drilling program be Agatin Abbott. Abbott was the senior geologist on the research team and had conducted the aerial infrared surveys. He was also an advocate of an early drilling program and had vigorously supported its establishment. The NLB also advised that a Site Selection Committee be formed. This committee should be composed of senior geologists and geophysicists, who would collectively make decisions about all aspects of the drilling program, including the number of research wells and the location of all drill sites. Abbott was recommended to chair the Site Selection Committee. After reaching a consensus on these recommendations, the board members concluded the first NLB meeting.

Shupe informed the HAC about the NLB's recommendations, and the HAC likewise encouraged the organization of a drilling program. The HAC also told Shupe that they would aid the HGP in securing state government funds to support the drilling. With the pledge of HAC's support, it was decided to request funds from the state legislature, which was just beginning its 1974 session. In this process, a lawyer first drafted an appropriations bill requesting $500,000 from the state government. The bill was then introduced to the legislature, and each program coordinator testified before the legislature's appropriations committees about his program's progress and about its relationship to the development of geothermal energy in Hawaii. The keystone of the testimonies was a discussion of geothermal drilling by Abbott. Since a drilling program had not yet been formulated, he could provide only a general overview. Nonetheless, the overview was sufficiently detailed to capture the legislators' interest. At the conclusion of the formal testimony, Shupe was assured that the HGP would receive support. But he would have to wait until the legislature formally approved the funds and until the governor released them.

In late February 1974, the project director determined that it was time for the HGP to establish a formal drilling program. Thus, the HGP Executive Committee was convened to discuss the issue and reach a decision. At the meeting, Augustine Furumoto, the geophysics coordinator, stated that establishing a drilling program was premature; HGP funds could be most usefully spent on further geophysical surveys and data interpretation. In response, Shupe argued that both the NLB and the HAC, the two advisory groups, had strongly recommended the formulation of a drilling program. Moreover, it was an appropriate time to establish and proceed with such a program because the project had to progress toward its long-range goal of generating geothermal power.

Paul Yuen, coordinator of the engineering program, Robert Kamins, coordinator of the environmental/socioeconomic program, and other members of the Executive Committee also pointed out that the geophysical surveys had generated a large quantity of data. The data had been interpreted and varying predictions of the subsurface conditions had been made. But the only way to check the interpretations and to verify the accuracy of predictions was to actually drill. Finally, the drilling proponents argued, the area in which the drilling would occur was one of the most thoroughly studied geological regions in the world. The HGP, the University of Hawaii, the U.S. Geological Survey, the state and the county governments, and other universities had conducted geological and other survey expeditions in the area. Surveys such as geodetic, gravity, deformation, seismic refraction, magnetic, and thermal surveys had already been conducted. An experimental drilling program was thus long overdue.

After discussing the issue a while longer, the Executive Committee voted to establish a drilling program. Abbott was appointed the program coordinator, and Shupe provided him with a small budget to initiate planning activities. Abbott's first act as coordinator was to form a Site Selection Committee, which would assist in planning and making decisions for the program. By March 1974, then, the HGP consisted of four research programs with several advisory and policy boards. (The HGP's organizational structure as of April 1974 is illustrated in Figure 6.6.)

Following these actions, the project director turned his attention to fiscal management. He realized that the HGP would require more time and money to complete the research programs presently underway. Additionally, a large grant was required to support the research drilling program. It was therefore decided that each program coordinator would assist in the preparation of (1) an eight-month budget extension to fund their current activities and (2) a new proposal to fund an experimental drilling program, including related activities.

Design: Completing the Proposals and the Drilling Program

From March to June 1974, each research team continued to make progress on its scheduled research tasks. The engineering program's researchers con-

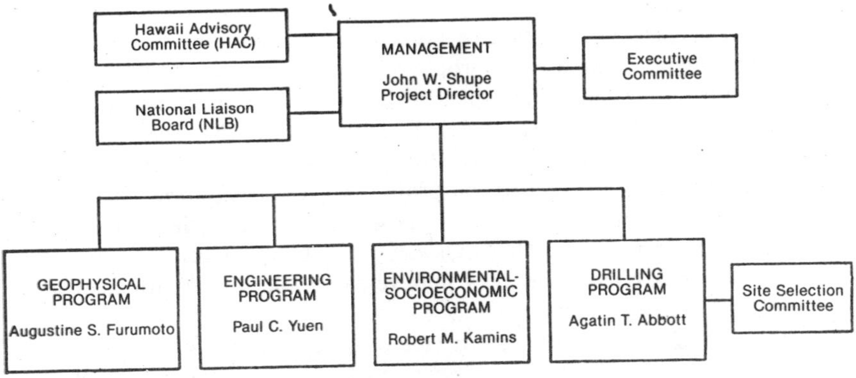

Figure 6.6. Hawaii Geothermal Project: Organization Chart (1974).

tinued working on the numerical modeling and the well testing program. Additionally, they continued designing the optimal geothermal plant. In the environmental/socioeconomic program, research continued on the legal-regulatory issues and the economic analysis.

Finally, in the pivotal geophysics program, work was being done on a wide variety of exploratory surveys. The geophysics researchers completed the building of a wire loop magnetic induction system and implanted 12 pairs of electrodes deep into the earth by air dropping them in inert missiles. This system was designed to follow up on the initial electrical surveys and would help to determine whether or not geothermal resources existed at depths of 1.24 mi (2 km). Other surveys that continued under the auspices of the geophysics program included a microseismic survey, a magnetic survey, and geochemical surveys of groundwater. Also, during this period, Donald Zablocki of the U.S. Geological Survey, with the assistance of HGP team members, began an electrical self-potential survey of the Puna area. In the past, these surveys had proved extremely useful in helping to locate potential geothermal sites.

Important as the geophysical research was, however, the top priority of the HGP increasingly shifted to completing the budget extension and the experimental drilling proposal. Preparing the budget extension was relatively simple but time-consuming. Each program coordinator wrote a progress report elaborating on his program's research results, on the problems encountered, and on the funding necessary to complete the research. The project director reported on the overall status of the project and justified the requests for a time extension and for additional funds. When completed, the 108-page budget extension requested an additional US$340,000 over an eight-month period ending in December 1974. It was submitted to the NSF in April 1974.

The Executive Committee then met to discuss the preparation of the experimental drilling proposal. The geophysics coordinator emphasized that the tone of the proposal should stress the project's continuing experimental focus. The intent of the drilling program would thus be to check the geophysical predictions and interpretations, not to discover a usable geothermal resource. In response, the project director and the other program coordinators acknowledged the experimental nature of the drilling but added that the ultimate goal of the project was to develop the capability for generating geothermal power. This meant that it was crucial to discover a usable geothermal source. They thus emphasized that the proposal should retain a judicious balance between pure research and the development of practical applied techniques.

After discussing this issue, they decided that a sharp restatement of the overall goals of the HGP was necessary to keep the drilling proposal in perspective. These goals included:

1. Improvement of geophysical survey techniques for locating underground heat resources.
2. Identification of potential geothermal resources, initially on the Big Island.
3. Experimentation with deep-drilling techniques for subsurface heat.
4. Development of efficient, environmentally clean systems for conversion of underground heat resources to useful energy.
5. Completion of socio-economic and legal studies for conversion of underground heat resources to useful energy.
6. Establishment of environmental baselines with which to monitor subsequent geothermal development.
7. Development of a geothermal production field and prototype power plant on the Big Island . . . [7]

With these goals in mind, all agreed that the proposal would request funds for each program to continue its research tasks. However, the priority research tasks would be those that directly supported or related to the drilling program. Finally, they agreed that the proposal would give highest priority to the drilling program itself.

The task of writing the proposal was divided among the program coordinators; each coordinator would be responsible for his program's plans. The project director would coordinate work on the proposal, assemble it, make it cohesive, and compile all of its financial and administrative sections. The program coordinators completed the plans for their programs in May, and by late June 1974, the proposal was finished. It was divided into four sections; a brief description of each section follows:

Geophysics Program. During the time period of the proposal, work would continue on all geophysical surveys that were not yet completed; these would probably be the microseismic studies, the magnetic studies, and the geochemical surveys. Additionally, follow-up studies would begin; these would include a geochemical survey, thermal surveys of well water, and mathematical modeling. Also, in early 1975, the geophysics team would make a preliminary analysis and interpretation of the data to help the drilling program determine the most useful sites for drilling. Finally, two new tasks would be undertaken: (1) a hydrology study of the Puna area and (2) a study of the physical property of rocks in the same area. The hydrology study would analyze geochemical data to determine the source of geothermal water, the way it circulated beneath the earth, and the process by which it recharged the geothermal reservoir. The physical property of rocks study would measure the thermal conductivity of the drilling area.

Engineering Program. During the grant period, research would continue on the optimal geothermal plant design and the numerical modeling. However, the priority task would be the well testing program, which the engineering team had designed. The testing program was composed of three sections: (1) bore hole tests, (2) well completion methods, and (3) well tests.

1. Bore hole tests would be conducted during the drilling. Researchers would continuously monitor the temperature and composition of geothermal fluid; and at regular intervals, as well as periods of sharp temperature increases, they would take formation logs. Formation logs would include information such as the temperature, pressure, and composition of the fluid in the drill hole, as well as the type, density, and porosity of the rock surrounding the drill hole. The engineering researchers would obtain this information by drawing core samples of the earth and by lowering a probe into the drill hole. The bore hole tests would not only provide valuable data but would also help determine how deep to drill and when to stop.
2. Well completion involved deciding how to complete the drill hole and what kind of equipment to use to build the well head. If the well tapped a favorable geothermal reservoir, the drill hole would be prepared for further testing by installing a slotted liner or a gravel pack. After the hole was completed, the well head would be assembled. The specific equipment to complete the well head would be chosen after further study. But the well head design required (a) a valve assembly to control the flow of steam from the well, (b) a silencer to reduce the roar of the steam as it flashed from the well, and (c) a centrifugal cyclone separator to separate the well's steam and hot water. The final task of well completion would be starting the well. If the well did not flow naturally, the engineering team planned to force the geothermal fluid to the surface by injecting compressed air into the hole; thereafter the natural pressure and heat of the geothermal reservoir would force the steam and water up the drill hole to the well head.
3. Well testing would occur in two stages: a downhole fluid measurement stage and a well flow stage. In the downhole stage, the engineering team would lower measuring probes into the well and record the temperature, pressure, and flow rate of the geothermal fluid. This information would help the engineers to estimate the life span and generating capacity of the geothermal reservoir. After allowing the subsurface conditions to stabilize for at least one month, the engineers would initiate the flow testing. The steam would then be allowed to flow out of the well for extended periods, during which the engineers would measure the pressure, temperature, and mass flow rate. These data would enable them to estimate the well's generating capacity.

Environmental/Socioeconomic Program. During the grant period, the researchers on this program would complete the legal-regulatory and economic studies. They would also begin two new tasks, environmental monitoring and land-use studies. The environmental monitoring would include a baseline data collection of the chemical, biological, and physical characteristics of the area. This baseline would establish the standard against which to measure the impact of drilling. If the investigations indicated that the environment would be adversely affected, drilling plans would be altered. Finally, the fumes produced by the discharge of geothermal steam would contain gases such as ammonia and hydrogen sulfide. To measure the quantities of gas being releaseed into the atmosphere, a special team of scientists would conduct air quality studies. The land-use studies would provide two crucial bits of information. First, they would provide information on the zoning codes and the land-use laws that might restrict the well location and the drilling operation. Second, they would identify the owners of potential drill sites. Once this information was compiled, the team members would negotiate with the owners for the rights to enter their land and drill for geothermal resources.

The Drilling Program. This was the focal point of the proposal. Not only would drilling demonstrate the success of the HGP's initial research efforts, it would provide dramatic evidence of the HGP's progress toward generating geothermal power. Based on the work of each research program, as well as previous geological and groundwater surveys, the proposal envisioned drilling experimental holes in three general locations. The most favorable location, and the one where drilling would first take place, was along the east rift of Kilauea near Puna. In this area, three types of holes would be drilled:

1. Shallow holes (average depth—500 ft or 152 m) for water samples and temperature measurements.
2. Intermediate-depth holes (2000 ft or 610 m) for temperature measurements, rock alternation, and water chemistry.
3. Deep holes (6000 ft or 1829 m or more) to try to reach a potential geothermal source.

To manage all drilling operations, the Site Selection Committee would contract with an experienced geothermal engineering firm. This firm would be responsible for overall drilling management, including drawing up a drilling contract, subcontracting the drilling, managing the drilling operations, drawing up safety regulations, cleaning up the site, controlling the finances, and handling all other operational aspects. The Site Selection Committee would decide upon the location, number, diameter, and depth of all drill holes. Additionally, the committee—in conjunction with the engineering, geophysics, and environmental/socioeconomic programs—would determine the types of scientific measurements, when to take them, and how to assess the results. The Site Selection Committee would also hire the geothermal engineering firm.

In the description of the drilling plans, no specific drill sites were identified. Instead, the plans provided detailed maps of the general areas being considered for drilling and provided the geophysical data which indicated that geothermal resources existed in these areas. The Site Selection Committee would choose specific sites after the results of other geophysical surveys were received from the field and after the socioeconomic program indicated which areas were feasible.

The proposal was submitted to the NSF in July 1974 by the project director, John Shupe. The proposal established a one-year activity period, January–December 1975, and requested US$2,000,000, of which $1,200,000 would be allocated to the drilling program.

SELECTION, APPROVAL, AND ACTIVATION

Selection and Approval

In May 1974, formal notice was received that the Hawaii state legislature had approved the HGP's request for drilling funds; the HGP would be allocated US$500,000, provided that the project also received federal matching funds. Later in the month, the NSF approved the budget extension. The NSF would grant the project US$217,000 to enable the research teams to continue working through December 1974. The NSF program manager further informed the HGP that it would receive an additional US$118,000 in 1975 to complete the research.

In July 1974, as previously discussed, Shupe submitted the multi-million-dollar experimental drilling proposal to the NSF. Since the amount requested was so large, the proposal would take six months to review. While this was being done, each research team continued with its research tasks. Then in September 1974, Shupe conferred with the NSF program managers about the proposal. At this conference they informed him that the NSF would not fund such an expensive drilling program but that the HGP could expect to receive approximately US$500,000, which was enough to drill a single deep well. Moreover, the HGP should specify a drill site.

Shupe informed the HGP Executive Committee of the funding constraints and told the program coordinators that they would have to revise their programs. The revisions were to include the geophysical evidence and analysis that had been completed since the submission of the initial proposal, reductions in the level of spending and activity of each program, new drilling plans based upon the new budget constraints, and specific locations of each drill site. Each research team proceeded with the revisions; the bulk of the work, however, was to be done by the geophysics team and the drilling program team in conjunction with the Site Selection Committee.

The Site Selection Committee met in October 1974 to draw up new drilling plans. After discussing all options and reviewing all of the available data, they made three decisions. First, they decided that, rather than spend the funds on several shallow holes to gather more information, they would drill *one* deep hole to possibly tap a geothermal source. Second, because funds were so limited, the committee decided that no engineering firm would be hired to supervise drilling operations. Instead, a drilling consultant would be contracted and the drilling program team would manage the drilling. Third, the committee decided upon the single drill site.

The drill site decision was critical, and there was considerable pressure on the committee. Although the drill was explicitly intended to increase scientific knowledge, it was implicitly intended to tap a still hypothetical geothermal source. Thus, since only one hole would be drilled, the committee had to select a site that overlay a geothermal reservoir. Adding to the pressure on the committee was scientific uncertainty. The evidence from the geophysical surveys suggested underground hot water but was not definitive. Several exploratory holes are normally drilled because, as one expert had commented to the committee, "the odds of finding a usable steam reservoir in drilling are one in five, and geothermal search requires a good deal of luck."[8] Nonetheless, the committee had to select one site.

It considered two general locations: Area A, the Pahoa anomaly identified by the electrical resistivity survey, and Area B, the Opihikao anomaly, also identified by that survey. Both areas were situated along the east rift of Kilauea near Puna. Area A was about 1500 ft (457 m) north of the Puulena Crater; Area B was located approximately 3 mi (4.8 km) west (see Figure 6.7). After deliberating, the committee chose Area A and designated a drill site at the apex of the anomaly. An alternative site was also selected approximately 1500 ft (457 m) north of the apex.

In choosing Area A, the committee relied primarily on geologic conditions and the self-potential survey. The geological conditions of the region included a history of volcanic activity, an interesting offset in the formation of the rift that indicated the pathway for magma at depth, and groundwater with a chemical content that indicated a hot water source. The self- potential survey also pinpointed a definitive bull's eye on the site (see Figure 6.8); this indicated hot water trapped beneath the surface. Geochemical and geoelectrical surveys also tended to confirm the self-potential survey. The committee members thus assessed the possibility of finding a geothermal source at either site within Area A as very promising. Area B was also considered to be a site with high potential, but its geologic characteristics were not quite so promising. In sum, the Site Selection Committee was positive and optimistic about the chances of uncovering a geothermal reservoir.

In November 1974, the geophysics program team members met to revise their section of the proposal. They first reviewed all of the geophysical evidence that had been collected to date and then evaluated the selected drill

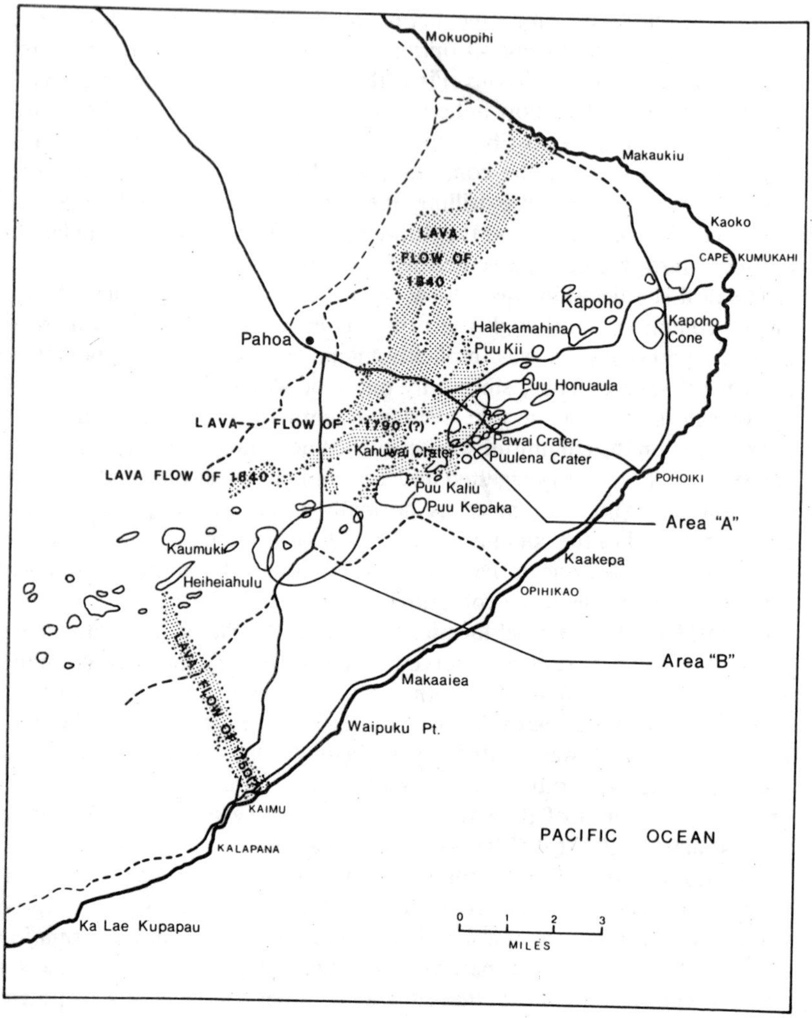

Figure 6.7. Location of Area A and Area B.

site. In reviewing the data, they examined the geoelectrical surveys, the magnetic surveys, the seismic surveys, the geochemical analyses, and the self-potential survey. After considerable debate, they concluded that the geophysical evidence required more study, and therefore they could not support the Site Selection Committee's optimism. Moreover, their interpretation of the data suggested that a drilling program to search for geothermal resources was unwarranted. The surveys, although indicating a high geo-

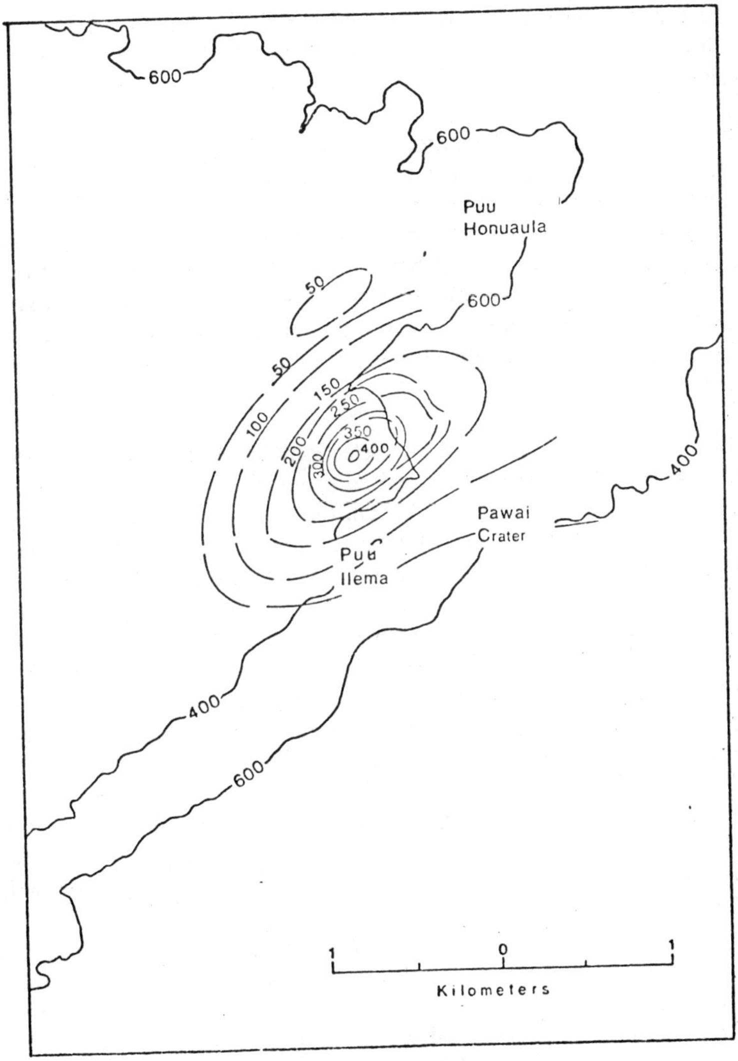

Figure 6.8. Self-potential map of Area A. (Source: Hawaii Geothermal Project, *Quarterly Progress Report,* No. 4, Honolulu: University of Hawaii, March–June 1974, pp. 5–25.)

thermal potential, could also reflect phenomena other than hot water or steam at depth. Thus, until the geophysics program completed a careful and comprehensive analysis of all data, they considered a drilling program to be premature.

The program team members also decided that if a drilling program were to be funded, despite their recommendations, they still could not support the location chosen by the Site Selection Committee. In elaborating on this position, the geophysics program coordinator wrote in a summary report.

> The Site Selection Committee for the drilling program, which is quite independent in organization from the geophysics program, met in November to select a drilling site for the renewal proposal. As far as the geophysics program is concerned, no special site can be recommended for geothermal exploration, but a hole could be recommended to check geophysical data. The committee chose a site based on self-potential data and geological formation. The geophysical program agreed to go along as a hole at that site will also have value in checking out gravity and magnetic data.[9]

Despite the optimism of the Site Selection Committee and the skepticism of the geophysics program, the revised proposal was written. As expected, it reflected the divergent outlooks. On the one hand, the geophysics team emphasized that the geophysical data were ambiguous and that further surveys should be undertaken. Moreover, they endorsed a drilling program, not because it had potential for uncovering a geothermal reservoir but because it could test geophysical interpretations.[10] On the other hand, the Site Selection Committee was positive about the site and about the potential of finding a reservoir. They stated in the proposal that "probing to depths where we now have no factual information would be most beneficial and we could conceivably arrive in the upper portion of a potential geothermal resource."[11]

The geophysics program coordinator was dismayed by the overall proposal. He later commented that "the fine distinction, exploratory hole to test data vs. exploratory hole for geothermal source, was lost in the writing of the proposal."[12]

The project director conferred with NSF officials early in 1975 about the revised proposal. He also met with officials from the Energy Research and Development Administration (ERDA). ERDA was the federal government agency responsible for the development of the nation's new energy sources; it would assume from the NSF the funding responsibility for an approved drilling program. Both agencies gave assurance that the proposal was high priority and that it certainly would be approved. The NSF even sent a staff worker to Hawaii to advise on preparing invitations to bid for the proposed drilling. Despite the assurances, however, the two agencies had not yet completed the proposal evaluations.

In early March, the evaluation concluded that the geophysical data and analysis were insufficient to justify a drilling program, especially since the implied intent of the drilling was to tap a geothermal source. The geophysics team thus concentrated on completing a thorough analysis. By the end of the month, a preliminary interpretation of the geophysical surveys was completed. Using the data from the gravity, magnetic, and microseismic surveys, the geophysics team projected the shape, width, and depth of the dike complex in the proposed drilling areas. The dike complex, or intrusive zone, was projected to begin about 2953 ft (900 m) below sea level. It was approximately 1.98 mi (3.2 km) wide, with a vertical extension of about 2.49 mi (4 km) and had the shape of a long, horizontal, rectangular prism with vertical walls. A complete interpretation of all the data was not made, but early interpretations tended to confirm that there was a possible geothermal resource at Area A.

More important, there were now adequate data and interpretation to justify an exploratory drilling program. The available data and the interpretations were sent to ERDA.

Then, in late April 1975, the ERDA approved the proposal. The HGP would receive US$1,064,000 for the period May 1975–April 1976. This amount, when added to the US$500,000 allocated to the project by the State of Hawaii and to the US$45,000 given to the project by the Hawaiian Electric Company, amounted to a total of US$1,609,000.

Activation

The project director had actually begun preparing for the drilling activities long before he knew whether the HGP would receive drilling funds. As early as October 1974, action was taken to acquire legal permission for the potential drilling. Robert Kamins, the coordinator of the environmental/socioeconomic program, had a University of Hawaii attorney prepare a model right-of-entry permit. The permit was a document granting the landowner's permission for the HGP to use his land for drilling. In November, after the Site Selection Committee had chosen the primary and an alternative drill site, Kamins identified the primary site owners as the Tokyu Land Corporation. He sent the corporation's managers a copy of the permit, but after reviewing it, they refused to grant HGP drilling permission. Kamins then began negotiations with the owners of the alternative site, the Kapoho Land Corporation. Since this corporation was not developing the site, it agreed to sign the right-of-entry permit. Specifically, the permit granted the HGP the right to enter, prepare, and drill the land for a fee of $1. Since the HGP was a research project, the question of ownership was not relevant. However, if a geothermal resource was discovered, ownership would have to be determined before it could be commercially exploited.

Fully expecting drilling funds to be approved, the project director and the program coordinators continued preparing for the drilling phase. In late January 1975, Abbott, along with the drilling program team and a consultant from the NSF, prepared invitations to bid on the proposed drilling. The invitations were sent to a number of firms in Hawaii and on the U.S. mainland. By March, however, drilling funds still had not been approved by the ERDA, so Shupe had to recall the invitations and wait for the funding decision.

An HGP Executive Committee meeting was held in late April. At the meeting it was announced, as has been noted, that the ERDA was satisfied with the information provided by the geophysics team in March and that firm assurances had been given to Shupe that the drilling would be funded. Official approval of the funds would be forthcoming before the end of the month. The geophysics program coordinator then commented on the selected drill site, Area A. He said that he had completed a more thorough interpretation of the geophysical data and now had serious doubts about the geothermal potential of Area A. He felt that Area B, which the committee had also considered, had greater geothermal potential. Because of these doubts, another Site Selection Committee meeting was scheduled for May 1975. It was also decided to invite George Keller to the meeting, since he had also expressed doubts about the site.

By May 1975 the ERDA had formally approved funds for the drilling; thus, the Site Selection Committee meeting took on added significance because it would provide the final opportunity to reconsider the drill site. To begin the meeting, the geophysics coordinator commented that Area B was more favorable than Area A because the area of anomalous low resistivity in Area B was considerably larger than that in Area A. More disturbing still was that Area A registered high magnetic readings. Since the Hawaiian basalt loses its magnetism above the Curie point, the high magnetism indicated that Area A might not supply enough heat for a geothermal reservoir. Adding support for Area B, George Keller noted that the seismic data indicated that rocks in this area had a Poisson ratio of 0.4. This indicated the presence of fractured rock, which might allow enough hydrothermal flow to create a reservoir.

In response to these comments, other committee members pointed out that when electrical data from several sources were analyzed, indications were that the anomalous resistivity lows were more definitive in Area A than in Area B. Moreover, the self-potential survey indicated an unambiguous bull's eye at Area A; and self-potential surveys were found by the U.S. Geological Survey to be the single most useful method for identifying anomalous thermal areas in Kilauea. Finally, there was a moderately high sound intensity of 9 dB in the vicinity of Area A, which indicated geothermal activity at depth. The high level of magnetism could not be explained, but the magnetic implications conflicted with the geochemical and temperature data. A previous geothermal test well located downslope from Area A had a temperature of 193°F (90°C), and the water in the well contained several times the normal levels of silica and chloride, all of which strongly suggested high temperatures at depth. Finally, the Curie point for theolitic basalt might be as high as 572°F (300°C), which was adequate for a geothermal reservoir.

A comparison of the data was then made between the two areas (see Table 6.2). It was concluded that the geophysical data were generally comparable, although the magnetic data favored Area B and the seismic data favored Area A.

The deciding factors would thus have to be geological and geology strongly favored Area A. First, Area A lay over the dike complex, while Area B was somewhat to one side of it. The dike complex was formed by the consolidation of magma in numerous fissures; thus, it formed a potential reservoir of heat. Second, Area A was located directly above an offset in the 1955 volcanic eruptions. These eruptions proceeded to the northeast, stopped, and then resumed in a significantly offset southwest direction. It was believed that a concentration of magma could be located in the vicinity of this offset. Third, Area A was coincident with the epicentral distribution of three separate episodes of shallow earthquake swarms in 1970. These episodes might have been caused by magmatic pressure. Fourth, Area A was located in the vicinity of both seismic activities that preceded the 1960 eruptions and the outbreak of the 1955 eruptions. It was thus believed that Area A was in a zone that had a recent heat source. Finally, there were a number of shallow wells downslope from Area A that were significantly hotter than normal. This supported the hypothesis that groundwater flowed downslope through a hot source near Area A.

After all of the evidence was again reviewed, unanimity could not be reached, so a vote was taken. All members of the Site Selection Committee, except for the geophysics coordinator, favored Area A. The geological evidence had been the determining factor.

Later in May, Abbott inserted a stake into the ground at the selected drill

TABLE 6.2. COMPARISON OF DATA ON AREA A AND AREA B.

SOURCE OF DATA	AREA A	AREA B
Loop-loop inductive soundings	3–5 ohm-m	5–8 ohm-m
Self-potential survey	450 mV	800 mV
Dipole resistivity mapping	8 ohm-m	5 ohm-m
Downslope well temperature	193°F (90°C)	73°F (23°C)
Downslope well chloride content	3410 mg/l	—
Downslope well silica content	174 ppm	1 ppm
Ground noise	4–9 dB	Background only
Magnetism	High	Low

TABLE 6.3. BUDGET ALLOCATIONS FOR THE HGP DRILLING PHASE (1975–1976).

Project director	$ 30,877
Geophysics	237,977
Engineering	155,972
Environmental/socioeconomic	59,412
Drilling, including:	
Subcontract	979,000
Consulting	40,000
Site preparation	35,000
Contingency, testing	50,000
Total	US$1,609,151

site within Area A. The overall HGP budget for the drilling phase of the project was then finalized. The allocations were as shown in Table 6.3.

The Consulting Firm and the Drilling and Testing Programs

Following the Site Selection Committee meeting, John Shupe met with Abbott and the other drilling program team members. They decided to hire a drilling consultant, since they had only limited experience in deep-hole geothermal drilling. The New Zealand firm of Kingston, Reynolds, Thoms, and Alardice (KRTA) had earlier been suggested by an NSF official, and thus Shupe began inquiring about the firm. At the May 1975 United Nations geothermal conference, Shupe learned that KRTA had extensive experience with geothermal drilling in New Zealand, the Philippines, and Central America. It was also one of the most respected geothermal consulting firms in the world. It was thus decided to contract KRTA's services, and an agreement was worked out with R. Kingston, the firm's managing director.

In June 1975, the coordinator of the drilling program, Agatin Abbott, temporarily withdrew from the project because of ill health, and his colleague, Dr. Gordon Macdonald, a University of Hawaii professor of geology and geophysics, assumed the coordinator's role. Later in June, invitations to bid for the drilling subcontract were sent to 28 firms. Most of the firms, however, were located on the U.S. mainland and would find it too costly to ship a rig to Hawaii. Thus, by July 1, the closing date for bids, only one bid had been submitted. It was from Water Resources International (WRI), the Hawaii-based company that had previously drilled Hawaii's only deep geothermal well. It was thus decided to negotiate a contract with WRI.

In July 1975, R. Kingston arrived in Hawaii for consultations with the HGP project team. He discussed the overall program with Shupe and held separate conferences with each of the program coordinators concerning the drilling and testing activities. He also spent a great deal of time discussing the drilling with WRI. He then returned to New Zealand and began preparing the drilling and testing plans.

During July and August, Kingston completed both the testing and drilling plans, which were based on the special conditions encountered in Hawaii, the needs of the HGP, and experience with geothermal projects in the rest of the world. The plans were crucial for HGP's success. They would be used not only as the basis for drawing up contracts between HGP and WRI but also to guide day-to-day operations. Consequently, the plans were comprehensive and detailed. The drilling plan was divided into three phases: predrilling site activities, the drilling program, and the site restoration. A brief description of each phase follows.

The predrilling site activities were intended to ensure that the site was adequately prepared and that the contractor had mobilized for a deep-hole drill. Specific responsibility for completing each activity was divided between HGP and WRI. Some of the more important tasks of the HGP included:

- Establishing rights of way and building adequate roads to the site.
- Clearing and grading the drilling area.
- Constructing an 8-ft (2.4-m)-deep drilling cellar large enough to support the drilling rig substructure.
- Implanting in the earth a 30-in. (50.8-cm) conductor pipe.

Important responsibilities of WRI included:

- Spreading over the drilling area crushed rock sufficiently fine to seal the surface from excessive rainwater percolation.
- Constructing on the site a 180,000-gal (684,000-l) water reservoir.
- Providing work offices with supply sheds, fences, fuel, and power.
- Obtaining necessary drilling supplies and equipment, such as liner and casing, cement, valves, hole openers, and various drilling bits.

The drilling phase was planned to be fairly conventional. In order to bore the well, the drilling contractor would use a rotary drilling rig, hole openers, various bits, and additional drill collars. As the drilling proceeded, fluid mud would be injected into the hole to cool and lubricate the bit and to remove the cuttings. It was anticipated that this process could penetrate the most difficult rock formations to a depth of 6000 ft (1829 m).

To encase the well, a series of steel tubes, called "casings," would be inserted into the hole. From the surface to a depth of 8 ft (2.4 m), a 30-in.

TABLE 6.4. HGP CASING PROGRAM FOR THE GEOTHERMALL WELL.

CASING	DIAMETER	DEPTH
Conductor pipe	30 in. (76 cm)	0–8 ft (0–2.4 m)
Surface casing	20 in. (51 cm)	3–400 ft (0.9–120 m)
Anchor casing	13 ⅜ in. (34 cm)	3–1000 ft (0.9–304 m)
Production casing	9 ⅝ in. (23 cm)	3–2500 ft (0.9–762 m)
Liner	7 ⅝ in. (18 cm)	2500–6000 ft (762–1829 m)

(76.2-cm)-diameter conductor pipe would be placed into and cemented to the sides of the bore. A 20-in. (50.8-cm)-diameter surface casing would then be inserted into and cemented to the sides of the conductor casing. This would extend from a depth of 3–400 ft (0.9–122 m), with the length of the casing below 8 ft (2.4 m) cemented to the sides of the hole. Another steel tube would then be inserted into and cemented to the surface casing. Into this steel tube another steel tube would be inserted; finally, if the drilling struck a geothermal reservoir, a slotted liner extending to a depth of 6000 ft (1829 m) would complete the well. Table 6.4 and Figure 6.9 elaborate on the planned well construction.

The final phase of the drilling program was site restoration. As planned, the contractor would have full responsibility for removing all equipment, disposing of all surplus supplies, and restoring the site.

The testing program, which Kingston completed in August 1975, was based on KRTA's experience in different settings throughout the world. It was intended to be cost effective while producing all of the necessary data. As stated in the testing program:

> The testing program which is recommended in this report is based on the experience which has been accumulated in the development of the geothermal fields in New Zealand. A similar program is now also being applied in many other countries including the Philippines, Indonesia, Chile, Kenya, Turkey and Nicaragua. The aim of the program is to produce the most useful and factual information which can be obtained from the well, in the most economical manner, and in the minimum time.[13]

The testing program was divided into three stages: (1) drilling tests, (2) drilling completion tests, and (3) output tests.

1. The drilling tests would be conducted during the actual drilling and would help determine how deep to drill and whether there was sufficient geothermal potential to complete the well. Two general types of data would

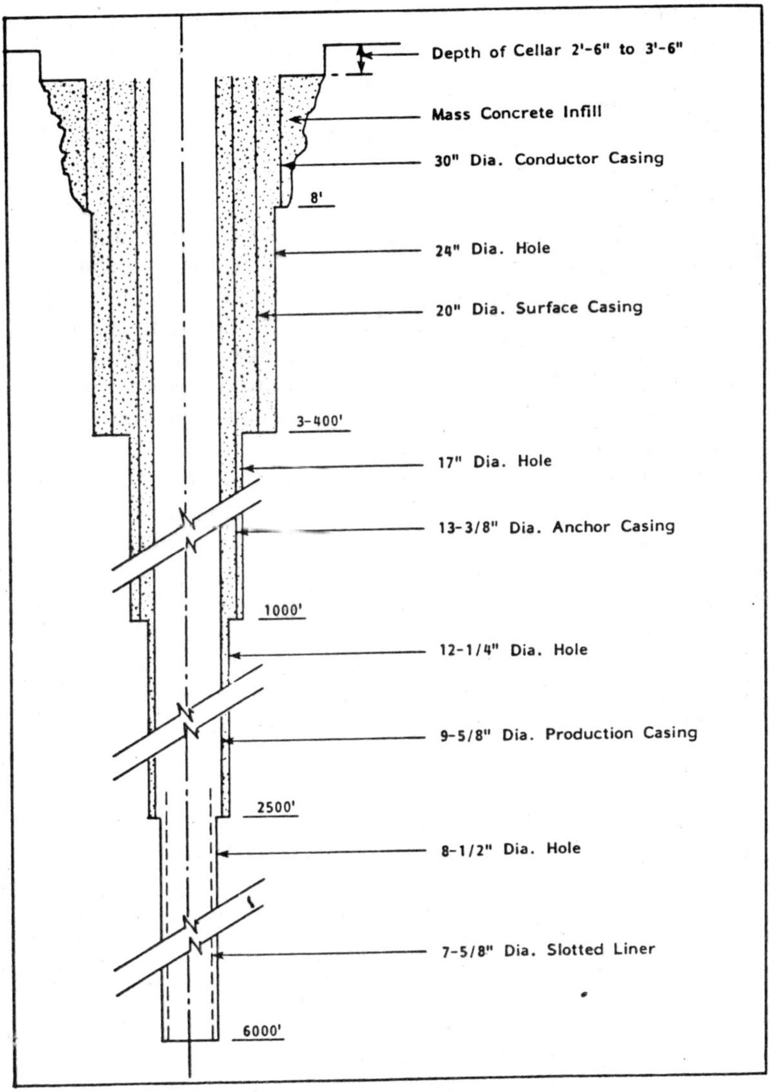

Figure 6.9. The well casing program.

be collected: lithologic data and drilling logs. To derive the area's lithology, geologists would take core samples from the well at approximately 700-ft (213-m) intervals and cuttings at 5–10 ft (1.5–3-m) intervals. These samples would then be used to complete petrographic and geochemical analyses, which would indicate the structure, composition, and sequence of the formation. The drilling logs, which included neutron, gamma, resistivity, and temperature surveys, would help determine the well's permeability, porosity, and temperatures at various depths. A cement bond log would also be taken to determine if the cement used for the casing was completely intact. Any flaws or gaps in the cement would have to be corrected with special equipment.

2. Drilling completion tests would be conducted after the well was drilled; they would consist of water loss tests, baseline temperature and pressure measurements, and well starting. The water loss tests were intended to determine the well's permeable zones. To locate these zones, researchers would pump water down the well and take a temperature profile. A gradual change in temperature would indicate uniform permeability, while a sudden change would indicate a major zone of permeability at or just above the depth of the temperature change.

After locating the possible zones of permeability, the HGP test researchers would try to determine the levels of permeability by pumping water into the well at rates of 100, 200, and 300 gal (380, 760, and 1140 l) per minute. If the rise in water pressure was high, this would mean that water in the permeable zones was unable to flow freely out of the well. This would imply low permeability, with the surrounding rock formation devoid of fissures, fractures, or cracks that would allow a constant flow of geothermal fluid. Lack of permeability would mean that the well was nonproductive.

The temperature and pressure of the well would be recorded at regular intervals. When these were stable, they would be the baseline against which all subsequent temperatures and pressures would be compared.

The final aspect of completion testing was to actually start the well. In this process, researchers would remove the top layers of water with compressed air. This would reduce the weight of the column of liquid in the well and enable the pressure from the steam and heat to force the bottom layers of geothermal fluid to flow out of the well naturally and continuously. Once the flow was established, the master valve would be closed and the flow would be shut off.

3. After pressure and temperature had stabilized following the initial well starting, output tests could begin. During output tests, the well would be allowed to flow continuously for periods varying between 7 and 90 days. During each of these periods, the temperature, pressure, mass flow rate, and heat flow rate of the geothermal discharge would be measured. These measurements over time would help indicate the well's electrical power potential and life expectancy. The researchers would also collect water and gas samples in order to monitor the chemical discharge of the well.

When Kingston submitted drilling and testing programs to the HGP in late August 1975, the drilling subcontract was still being negotiated. The major problem was that WRI was the only bidder, and thus there could be no competitive evaluation. Additionally, the project was jointly funded by the federal government and the State of Hawaii. The acting agencies, ERDA, and the University of Hawaii could not completely agree on what constituted acceptable criteria for evaluating a single source bid. Thus negotiations dragged on.

Meanwhile, John Shupe, HGP project director, decided to mobilize the project. He released available funds from the project budget to grade and compact the drill site, to construct the drill rig foundation, and to begin other site preparations. WRI similarly began mobilizing. They purchased a new drill rig and began moving it to the project site. By committing large sums prior to the conclusion of negotiations, Shupe and WRI assumed a substantial risk. If the negotiations failed, WRI could go bankrupt and HGP could face litigation. Both, however, were confident that points of contention would be resolved satisfactorily. Furthermore, the project was behind schedule, and if they did not begin mobilizing in September, the drilling could not begin until February 1976. It was thus decided to take the calculated risk.

Through September, contract negotiations dragged on. WRI continued to provide the information requested by the ERDA and the University of Hawaii; Shupe attempted to mediate and clarify the situation. But federal regulations concerning audit and review processes prevented a swift award of the contract to WRI. Later in the month, R. Kingston, the manager of KRTA, made another trip to Hawaii to help resolve the difficulties. He discussed the subject with the auditors and discovered that they needed more data concerning WRI's cost accounting and the estimated time needed to complete the drilling. The drilling time was particularly crucial because WRI charged—as was standard practice—by the drilling time expended rather than by the depth of penetration. The estimated drilling time was based on WRI's previous experience in drilling Hawaii's only deep geothermal well. For that well, drilling had averaged 100 ft (30 m) per day. Despite the fact that the HGP well required a hole of considerably greater diameter, WRI assumed that it could maintain that rate because it had purchased an improved drill rig that would increase efficiency.

The federal auditors, however, still could not approve the contract because they had difficulty in auditing WRI's records, upon which all costs were based. Finally, after correspondence between Shupe and the ERDA, the ERDA manager of geothermal development made a special trip to Hawaii to approve the contract. The contract was formally awarded to WRI in November 1975. A summary of the contract's financial accounting appears in Table 6.5.

In December 1975, just prior to beginning the drilling operation, the HGP was organized much as it had been in February 1974. John Shupe was the overall project director and director of the management program. Each

TABLE 6.5. SUBCONTRACT FOR DRILLING OPERATIONS.

	CONTRACT ESTIMATE
Mobilization	$120,192
Water reservoir	48,077
Casing (to 3500 ft) (1067 m)	100,000
Consumable materials (to 6000 ft) (1829 m) (bits, mud, cement, etc.)	202,431
Well-testing equipment and services	50,000
Well drilling, 0–3500 ft (1067 m)	199,185
Well drilling, 3500–6000 ft (1067–1829 m)	149,500
Demobilization	9,615
Contingency	100,000
Total	US$979,000

of the HGP's other programs continued to be guided by the original coordinators: Augustine Furumoto directed the geophysics program; Paul Yuen directed the engineering program; Robert Kamins directed the environmental/socioeconomic program; and Gordon Macdonald directed the drilling program. Each coordinator retained fiscal and operational autonomy for his program, and Shupe provided the overall coordination, direction, and leadership. Additionally, each of the program coordinators, along with the project director, shared responsibility as co-principal investigators of the grant.

Administrative responsibility for each of the programs was held by each of the coordinators. But since the drilling was subcontracted, authority over the drilling program was fragmented. Macdonald, as coordinator of the drilling program, was responsible for all scientific decisions, such as what tests to conduct and when. The drilling consulting firm, KRTA, was responsible for recommending specific technical decisions during the drilling; and KRTA provided one employee, Warwick Tracey, as the on-the-job drilling supervisor. The drilling contractor, WRI, was responsible for the daily operational activities of drilling, such as supervising the drilling crew, overseeing the equipment changes, and implementing the operational decisions. E. Craddick, president of WRI, would be at the drill site to oversee these duties.

Some of these responsibilities overlapped. For example, any scientific decision, such as when to take a core sample, impinged upon the drilling supervisor's ability to make technical drilling decisions. Sometimes it might be impractical to stop drilling in order to take a core sample. Thus, a technical decision would have to be made that might conflict with a scientific decision. Furthermore, KRTA's drilling supervisor could make recommendations to the contractor about the drilling process, but the contractor was directly responsible for the drilling crews and the operations. KRTA recognized these potential overlapping jurisdictions and, to some extent, tried to clarify them. In the testing program KRTA had stated:

> The University of Hawaii will appoint to the project a Drilling Manager and a Geologist who will supervise the drilling of the well through the Contractor. They will offer guidance and assistance to the Contractor, but in no way will this relieve the Contractor of the responsibility for the drilling operations. The Contractor is required to provide at all times supervision by a competent toolpusher, and skilled crews experienced in the operations of a drilling rig of this scale.[14]

Even with this clarification, the overlapping authority was bound to create some confusion. Thus, during the actual drilling, the HGP project director referred and resolved any differences among the drilling program team representative, the drilling supervisor, and the contractor. Figure 6.10 illustrates the HGP's organizational structure, as well as its major funding sources in 1975.

Another administrative difficulty concerning the drilling was that some of the key people would not be at the drill site. The project director had a dual appointment as the University of Hawaii's Dean of the School of Engineering; he would have to remain on the island of Oahu. Similarly, the

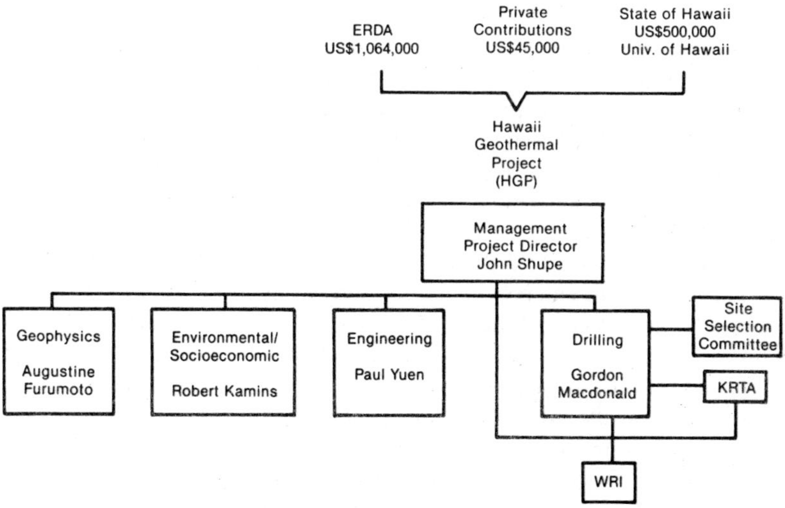

Figure 6.10. Funding for and Organization of HGP (1975).

coordinator of the drilling program would not be at the site after January 1976. He would have to return to his teaching duties at the University of Hawaii campus on Oahu. However, plans were worked out to alleviate this situation. Either the project director or the drilling program coordinator would visit the site once a week and would communicate with on-site personnel daily. Finally, other project staff would be at the site. D. Palmiter, a graduate assistant with Macdonald, would represent the drilling program, and HGP project members from the University of Hawaii campus on the island of Hawaii would help with the drilling. One person in particular, Bill Chen, a professor of engineering at the University of Hawaii's Hilo campus, was a key member of HGP's engineering program; he would help with the engineering aspects of the drilling.

OPERATION, CONTROL, AND HANDOVER

Operation: Drilling and Testing Program

The well site was dedicated on November 22, 1975, and final preparations were made for the drilling operation. WRI assembled the rig, completed installation of the plumbing, wired the electrical fixtures, lined the water reservoir, filled it with 180,000 gallons of water, finished constructing the mud pit, and transported to the site equipment such as drill bits, pipes, and casing materials.

Initial Drilling. Drilling commenced on December 10, 1975, but progress was slow because the 1955 lava flows had formed a hard basalt layer over the drill site. Drilling of the first 400 ft (122 m) was particularly time-consuming. Only limited weight could be placed on the bit, as it would not remain vertical. Further delays were caused by the high standards of the casing program, which stipulated that a 20-in. (51-cm)-diameter surface casing be installed from the surface to a depth of 400 ft (122 m). This meant that WRI initially had to drill into the lava with a 9-in. (23-cm) bit and then use hole openers to enlarge the bore progressively to 15, 20, and 26 in. (38, 51, and 66 cm). In early January 1976, the project director realized that this laborious process had put the drilling far behind schedule. He therefore conferred with the drilling supervisor from KRTA and then called Kingston, inquiring about the advisability of abandoning the 20-in. (51-cm) surface casing and proceeding directly to install and cement in the 13-in. (33-cm) anchor casing. Kingston consulted with his staff and with geothermal experts from the New Zealand government's Ministry of Works. Their consensus was that if a productive geothermal resource was discovered, the 20-in. (51-cm) surface casing would be necessary to prevent blowouts. Kingston thus strongly recommended that HGP adhere to the original casing program.

The project director thereupon decided to continue with the original plan. The hole was drilled to a depth of 400 ft (122m) and enlarged progressively with the 15-, 20-, and 26-in. (38-, 51-, and 66-cm) hole openers. Finally, the surface casing was inserted into the hole and cemented in. This time-consuming process lasted until early February; it had taken nearly two months to complete the first 400 ft (122 m) of the well.

Although the drilling proceeded much more quickly in March, it was still considerably behind schedule, as numerous operational difficulties were encountered. At one point, six bolts on the rig jack were sheared off and the rig had to be closed down; at another time, the chain drive linking two drawwork engines broke and had to be repaired; at still another time, the pump and generator engines had to be overhauled because of continuous usage; and, as a routine matter, the drill bits deteriorated rapidly in the dense lava. Additionally, numerous core samples and cuttings had to be taken. Although the coring was necessary and planned for, it was still time-consuming and added to the pressures of the drilling schedule.

From an administrative perspective, the drilling problems were handled within the overall framework of HGP's drilling supervision, which, as previously noted, was fragmented. For purely scientific decisions, such as when to take a core, Macdonald, the director of HGP's drilling program, made all decisions. After Macdonald returned to his teaching duties in January 1976, the scientific decisions were made by his on-the-job assistant, D. Palmiter, who called Macdonald daily concerning the scientific investigations.

For simple operational problems, E. Craddick, WRI president and the on-site drilling contractor, made the decisions. In complex and difficult drilling situations, Craddick consulted with Warwick Tracey, who was both the on-the-job KRTA consultant and the drilling supervisor. However, since the duties, responsibilities, and overall authority of the drilling supervisor and contractor were not absolutely defined, some conflicts arose when there was a difference of opinion. In one situation, for example, WRI's 20-in. (51-cm) hole opener had to be inserted into the same-sized surface casing in order to continue enlarging the hole for the anchor casing. The hole opener would not fit, so the drilling supervisor recommended that the contractor undercut the periphery of the cutters and then build them back up again with hard facing electrodes. The contractor, however, decided to simply cut off the periphery and remove the hard facing of the cutters.

Whenever there was a difference of opinion on critical activity, the drilling supervisor had to call Shupe and Kingston. For example, in February and March 1976, the drilling supervisor recommended that the contractor clean up the site and make adequate provisions for the disposal of reject mud and cuttings from the drilling. No site clean-up, however, was undertaken. This forced the drilling supervisor to write to Shupe and Kingston:

> Disposal of reject mud and cuttings is still a major problem, and as a result, the site is a mess. The contractor does not seem to appreciate the magnitude of the problem, and his disposal gear is primitive, if not inadequate.[15]

Shupe and Kingston then conferred with the contractor, who agreed to improve the disposal of reject mud and cuttings. If the problem was serious enough, an on-site conference would be held. In resolving the casing program, for example, Shupe contacted Kingston and arranged for him to fly in from New Zealand to meet at the drill site. Prior to the conference, Shupe conferred with the other HGP program coordinators.

During February and March 1976, two significant problems arose which went beyond the scope of the operational drilling management. First, on March 18, HGP project staff projected that an additional US$257,000 was required to complete drilling the well to the planned goal of 6400 ft (1951 m). The deficit had occurred because installing the surface casing had taken more drilling time than was originally estimated. Since payment to WRI was based on actual drilling time, the underestimate created a deficit that would force a halt to the drilling if additional funds were not secured.

The project director first contacted the ERDA and, after clarifying the situation through a letter and several phone conversations, received an additional US$150,000. The ERDA was extremely supportive because the well was so close to completion. WRI was also anxious to have a successful well, and agreed to donate US$60,000 of its time to finish the job. Finally, the project director met with the program coordinators. He had previously informed them of the drilling deficit and had discussed the possibility of reallocating funds. Now he stressed that the probability of encountering a productive geothermal resource would be increased if the well was drilled to its original target depth. Moreover, the ERDA, the funding agency, was extremely interested in completing the drill to the planned depth. The program coordinator thus agreed to shift US$47,000 from the research programs to the drilling.

The second significant problem centered on the differences of opinion within the HGP. As discussed earlier, there was a lack of unanimity on many of the HGP policy decisions. There had never been, for example, unanimous agreement on the decision to establish a drilling program or where to locate the drill site. Now, during the drilling, there was still some difference of opinion about the potential of the site. The geophysics program coordinator, after examining more data, believed that the drilling should be terminated at about 4000 ft (1200 m). His reasons included the fact (1) that if a geothermal reservoir existed, it should be located between the water table and the dike complex and (2) that gravity, magnetic, and deformation data now indicated that the top of the dike complex was situated at depths between 1640 and 4000 ft (500 and 1220 m).[16]

The drilling program coordinator had a different opinion. He believed that drilling only to 4000 ft (1220 m) was meaningless for the following reasons: (1) the purpose of drilling was to discover whether rocks or structures favorable to a geothermal reservoir existed at a depth of 6000 ft (1829 m), (2) there were many dikes in the rift zone, which could be located at any depth below the dike complex, and (3) there was a possibility of a geothermal reservoir in the interdike compartments below 4000 ft.[17]

The issue was resolved in a series of meetings and discussions among the project director and the program coordinators. It was decided that since there was enough money for only one deep drill, it would be counterproductive to stop just when the most difficult portions of the well had been completed.

Completing the Drilling. In early April 1976, after the production casing was installed to a depth of 2200 ft (671 m), the drilling proceeded rapidly. By April 27, the well was drilled to its target depth of 6400 ft (1951 m). The final 4200 ft (1200 m) of the well had been bored in less than three weeks, with no difficulties or significant problems. Since the temperature of the drilling mud at 6000 ft (1829 m) was about 145°F (63°C) and was increasing as time passed, it was known that the well was hot. However, it was not known how hot it was or whether it was productive.

The first measurements, the well logs, were conducted in late April, after the well had been drilled to its target depth. WRI used its own Gearhart-Owen equipment and hired an operator to conduct neutron, gamma, self-potential, and resistivity logs; these logs would provide indications of the formation's permeability and porosity. Temperature logs were also taken; they indicated that at a depth of 4000 ft (1220 m), the well temperature exceeded 300°F (135°C), the upper limit of the equipment. Thus, the precise temperatures were unknown, but it was certain that they were favorable.

The contractor then conducted a cement bond log, which determined the integrity of the concrete used to cement the casing. Any flaws in the concrete would have to be corrected before completion of the well. The cement bond log indicated a lack of bond, and, by implication, gaps in the cementing, from 40 to 220 ft (12 to 67 m) and from 320 to 868 ft (97 to 264 m).

Following the well logging, an HGP staff meeting was held and it was determined that three tasks would have to be undertaken. First, the gaps in the cementing of the casing would have to be filled; otherwise the well's steam pressure and thermal stresses could severely damage the casing. The gaps would have to be filled before proceeding further. Second, a slotted liner—a 7⅝-in. (18-cm)-diameter steel tube with eight slots per foot (0.3 m)—would have to be run into the well from a depth of 2200 to 6400 ft (670 to 1951 m). The slotted liner was essential. It would prevent the well's bottom uncased section from caving in, and its 2 × ¾ in. (5 × 1.9 cm) slots would allow steam or hot water to enter the tube from the side and be transported to the surface. Third, the drilling completion tests would have to be conducted.

These three tasks would require funds above and beyond the HGP's budget, since all funds had already been used to complete the drilling. It was estimated that an additional $248,000 would be needed. The project director therefore again contacted ERDA officials, and they invited him to present a progress report on the drilling at a meeting of the ERDA Geothermal Coordinating Group in late April. At the meeting, the progress of the drilling was reviewed and requests were made for additional funds to complete the well and to conduct tests. Additional funds were promised; the director then returned to Hawaii and ordered 4,500 ft (1,373 m) of slotted liner. Arrangements were also made to remedy the gaps in the casing.

Later that month, ERDA officials formally notified the HGP that they were releasing US$85,000 immediately, as well as an additional US$175,000 as soon as it could be transferred from the central office in Washington. They also mentioned that they would provide a further US$300,000 in 1977 to test the well comprehensively.

Completing the Well. After the money was secured in early May 1976, Gearhart-Owen perforating equipment and personnel were contracted to fill the gaps in the casing. Also purchased were the valves, gauges, and drilling rig time necessary to install the slotted liner and complete the wellhead plumbing. Finally, the project director arranged for KRTA to continue as consultants, and he released funds to purchase testing equipment such as separators and sampling bottles.

The special equipment and operators necessary to fill the voids in the cementing were not available until late May, so work on the well was halted for three weeks. Then, in late May, the special personnel and equipment arrived and the correcting of the casing gaps began. Within a four-day period, the special operators perforated the cement with controlled explosive charges and forced cement through the perforations into the cementing gaps. The contractor then ran a cement bond log and determined that the gaps were filled.

In early June, the slotted liner was inserted into the well without any problems. The contractor first used water to cool the hot mud, which had hardened in the bottom of the well, and then obtained circulation. Next, the bottom sections of the well were reamed out and the slotted liner was run into the well from 2200 to 6400 ft (671 to 1951 m). After the liner was installed, the mud in it was flushed out, and the wellhead plumbing, including the side and master valves, were installed.

While WRI was completing the well in June, the HGP project staff, aided by KRTA, conducted the drilling completion tests. HGP project staff, directed by Bill Chen, first did a survey of the well's baseline temperatures. The temperature at 4000 ft (1219 m) was about 338°F (170°C); between 4400 and 6000 ft (1341 to 1829 m) it remained constant, ranging between 464 and 482°F (240 and 250°C); and below 6000 ft (1829 m) it exceeded 500°F (260°C). Subsequent temperature surveys, conducted before and after the water pumpdown tests, indicated that the well was continually getting hotter as more and more of the drilling and mud cuttings were cleared from the liner. On June 15, eight days after the second pumpdown tests, the temperature at 4000 ft (1219 m) was nearly 572°F (300°C); and at 6400 ft (1951 m) it exceeded 608°F (320°C).

The other significant completion test was the water loss or pumpdown test, indicating the level of permeability. To conduct this test, HGP researchers pumped water into the well at rates of 0, 100, 200, and 300 gal (0, 380, 760, and 1140 l) per minute and simultaneously measured the back pressure with a Kuster pressure gauge. If the pressure increased over 150 psi, this would indicate very poor permeability and a nonproducing well.

The initial measurements indicated that the rise in pressure when water was pumped into the well between 0 and 300 gal (1140 l) per minute exceeded 700 psi. More pumpdown tests were conducted because the high back pressure could have been created by drilling mud or cuttings obstructing the slotted liner and preventing the inflow of geothermal fluid. However, subsequent tests also indicated high rises in pressure and relatively impermeable conditions (see Table 6.6).

Following these tests, WRI demobilized its part of HGP. Employees cleaned the site, removed excess material, removed drilling equipment, and dismantled the rig. However, the most dramatic aspect of the drilling completion test still remained to be done—starting the well.

On June 22, members of HGP's engineering program, who would conduct the output tests, attempted to start the well by airlifting. A hose attached to an air compressor was inserted into the well, and the compressor was started. The compressed air then evacuated the upper layers of cold liquid to lighten the well's liquid column, allowing it to be heated by the hot geothermal fluid and steam at the bottom. The first attempts to start the well were unsuccessful. Finally, on July 2, 1976, the well was flashed and allowed to flow for five minutes.

With the initial flashing of the well, the drilling completion tests were concluded. However, the HGP would still have to conduct the formal well tests to determine the well's potential and productivity.

TABLE 6.6. SUMMARY OF THE PUMPDOWN TEST.

DATE	GPM	TIME OF FLOW (min)	VOLUME (gal)	BACK PRESSURE (psig)
June 6	340	46	15,640	700+
June 6	108	105	11,340	500+
June 6	108	60	6,480	500+
June 6	200	55	11,000	600+
June 6	300	70	21,000	700+
June 6	530	10	5,300	750+
June 6	630	7	4,410	800+
June 6	300	8	2,400	700+
June 6	200	5	1,000	600+
June 6	100	6	600	500+
June 7	300	3	900	—
June 7	100	180	18,000	300
		Total	98,070 gal	

Source: "The Hawaii Geothermal Project," *HGP-A Reservoir Engineering*, September 1978, p. 7.

The Testing Period. The testing period of the HGP-A well lasted from July 1976 to June 1978 and was funded by the ERDA, which in 1977 was consolidated into the national Department of Energy (DOE), and the State of Hawaii.* The total funds that these sources awarded to the HGP amounted to US$439,000 during this time period.

The top priority during this period was, of course, well testing, and each of the programs was redirected accordingly. The project director, although still responsible for the overall management, coordination, and leadership of HGP, now increasingly concentrated on policy making, planning, and strategy for future geothermal power development in Hawaii. The HGP Executive Committee would also continue to play a large role in policy making for the future.

The engineering program, assigned the responsibility of conducting the well tests, became the most visible, as well as the most heavily funded, program. Consistent with previous policy, Paul Yuen, the engineering program director, had responsibility for allocating funds and making substantive program decisions. Bill Chen would be at the site to supervise the tests.

The geophysics program was consolidated into a geoscience program. Researchers for the new program would not only synthesize the geological, geophysical, and geochemical surveys into an integrated interpretation but would also oversee all new scientific inquiries, such as environmental monitoring and measuring physical samples from the well tests. The change in

*It was decided that if the well was successful it would be named in honor of Agatin Abbott, the initial drilling program coordinator, who died on July 31, 1975. Hence, the "A" in HGP-A stands for Abbott.

program designation thus reflected the program's broader and more encompassing scope. Named as coordinator of the new program was Charles Helsley. Helsley was a professor of geology and geophysics and was also the newly recruited director of the Hawaii Institute of Geophysics. Because he had worked previously with other deep drills, it was believed that he had the knowledge and experience necessary to synthesize all of the geological and geophysical data into an integrated interpretation. This was particularly important since there had been many conflicting interpretations and none were completely consistent with the actual findings from the drilling.

The environmental/socioeconomic program was nearing completion of its research activities and would be phased out by Robert Kamins, the director, after two crucial reports were finished. These reports were (1) an environmental baseline study of the Puna area and (2) an assessment of geothermal development in Puna. Kamins expected both reports to be completed by January 1977.

Initiating the Output Well Tests. In July 1976, after the well had stabilized, the engineering program's researchers prepared to conduct the output tests to determine the well's potential productivity and life span. As described by KRTA in the testing program, the well would be allowed to discharge continuously for extended periods, during which the temperature, volume, pressure, and chemical content of the discharge would be measured. After the discharge period the well would be shut down, and over the next few weeks researchers would record the well's temperature and pressure at various depths. If the well temperature and pressure recovered rapidly, this would indicate a potentially large reservoir.

The first extended discharge test was scheduled for July 22. Since a good deal of public enthusiasm and attention was now focused on the project, it was planned to be a four-hour public display. In this regard, the HGP had been primarily a research project, with no tangible product to capture the imagination. But now, there was more than an exciting idea: The HGP could actually display, for the first time in Hawaii, human-controlled geothermal energy. The public display was dramatic and impressive. Flowing continuously for four hours, the well sent geysers of steam and liquid over 100 ft (30.5 m) into the air. Because no muffling or silencer was installed for the first test, the noise exceeded 122 dB—the sound of a 747 at takeoff.

The test results themselves were very promising and even exceeded the expectations of the KRTA consultants. Lip temperature exceeded 302°F (150°C) for the entire four hours, and lip pressure from the 6-in. (15-cm) discharge pipe was 23 psig at the end of four hours. Subsequent temperature surveys indicated that the well recovered in about seven days and that the major production zones occurred between 3500 and 4500 ft (1067–1372 m) and at 6400 ft (1951m).

Based on the test results, the engineering program researchers were able to make some tentative conclusions. First, based on the data, they deduced that the well had a mass flow rate of 166,000 lb/hr. Assuming an enthalpy of 800 BTU/lb and 15 percent efficiency, the well could generate 5 MW of electricity. They also noted that fluid and steam were flowing naturally into the slotted liner, indicating that there was greater permeability than they had assumed from the water loss tests. Longer tests, however, would have to be conducted before any conclusions could be made about the well's productivity.

Before conducting such tests, however, the engineering researchers would have to construct more elaborate testing equipment. Thus, over the summer of 1976, the researchers added to the well a silencer-separator to muffle the loud noise of the discharge and to separate the water from the steam. Also added to the well were a twin cyclone sampler, which would obtain gas and water samples for chemical analysis, and a calorimeter to measure specific enthalpy. Figure 6.11 illustrates these instruments on the well.

Extended Flow Tests: Problems and Progress. In November 1977, with the new instruments and equipment installed, HGP researchers conducted a two-week test flow. The results were extremely encouraging, demonstrating that the well was capable of discharging continuously for a two-week period. Most prominently, well output stabilized after 25 hours. HGP researchers collected other data, such as noise level, temperature, steam quality, and water and gas samples; they also calculated the enthalpy of the discharge and its thermal power (see the Evaluation for complete data). By the end of 25 hours of continuous discharge, thermal power had stabilized at about 22 MW, and at the end of the test it was still at 20 MW. Thus, in terms of demonstrating the well's generating power, the November tests were a success.

However, since the tests were being conducted for the first time under real-world conditions, they also introduced a new issue—the well's impact on and interrelationship with the human community in Puna. This issue was underscored by the land use near the well. North and south of the well were undeveloped areas covered by recent lava flows and sparse vegetation. But to the east and west there were homes. Twelve families lived within 1 mi of the well, and within 2 mi there were several residential tracts that were being developed. The largest of these tracts was Leilani Estates, with a total of 2146 house lots.[18] Although only 50 families were then living there, they had formed an active community association that represented 2036 of the owners of the lots.[19] Two other residential tracts nearby included Lanipuna Gardens and Nanawele Estates; both had few actual residents but both were being planned for development. Within the immediate vicinity of the well there is also a state park and one paved road, usually with very light traffic

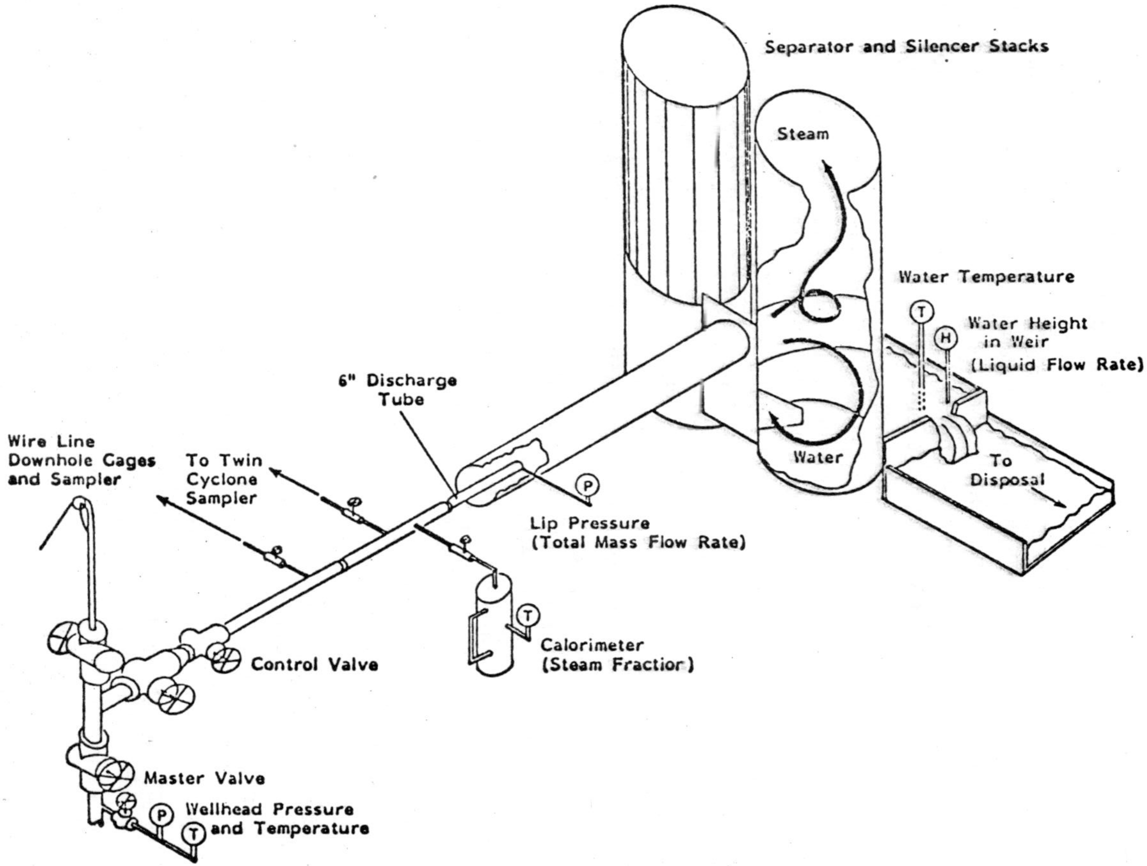

Figure 6.11. HGP-A wellhead testing equipment.

(see Figure 6.12). A statement from the environmental baseline study gives one an idea of the setting:

> In most hours of most days, the quiet of the roads in this portion of the Puna District is not much disturbed by passenger cars, or by an occasional truck or bus, most of them traversing the distance to beaches on the Puna Coast. (The well drilling itself generated a fair amount of traffic, not only from the dozen members of the drill crew and scientist observers, but also from some tour buses, whose operators were glad to find a drilling rig to add to the attractions of tourism in this outstandingly quiet corner of the Island of Hawaii.)[20]

Farther from the well site, but within a radius of several miles, are the communities of Pahoa, Kapoho, Opihikao, Kalapana, and Kaipu. Many of the residents of these communities are indigenous Hawaiians, who have lived in Puna for generations and who have adopted a rural agricultural lifestyle. The entire Puna District, in fact, is predominantly rural and agricultural. There are extensive cultivated fields of sugar cane and papaya, with smaller areas utilized for growing guavas, oranges, and macadamia nuts. Additionally, there are several small family enterprises growing tropical plants, such as anthuriums and orchids. Interspersed between the villages and the low-density residential tracts are areas of lush tropical vegetation, conservation zones, and several forest reserves (see Figure 6.13). In sum, the Puna District maintains a somewhat traditional rural Hawaiian setting. It is sparsely populated, little developed, primarily agricultural, and outstandingly quiet.

In this setting, the November flow tests began. And, within a few days, the Leilani Community Association objected vigorously to the noise from the well's discharge. The well had been muffled since the July test, which created a noise of 122 dB, but even with the muffler, the sound at the roadside was 87 dB, while 1 mi away it was projected to be 70 dB and at 2 mi, 40 dB. The Environmental Protection Agency (EPA) recommended 55 dB as a tolerable daytime level for residential areas, but the well discharged continuously and in an extremely quiet environment. At this point, the community association contacted their city council representative and state officials, demanding that the tests be halted. One resident stated that the noise was intolerable; he described the sound as a "bloodcurdling banshee howl." Other residents pointed out that the area was outstandingly quiet and that many of them had moved there for just that reason. Moreover, their whole way of life was being disrupted by the nuisance of the noise. The county officials responded that they would try to help. But after investigating the problem, they discovered that there were no noise standards governing residential areas on Hawaii. Thus, the county officials called the HGP and asked them to confer with the residents of the area.

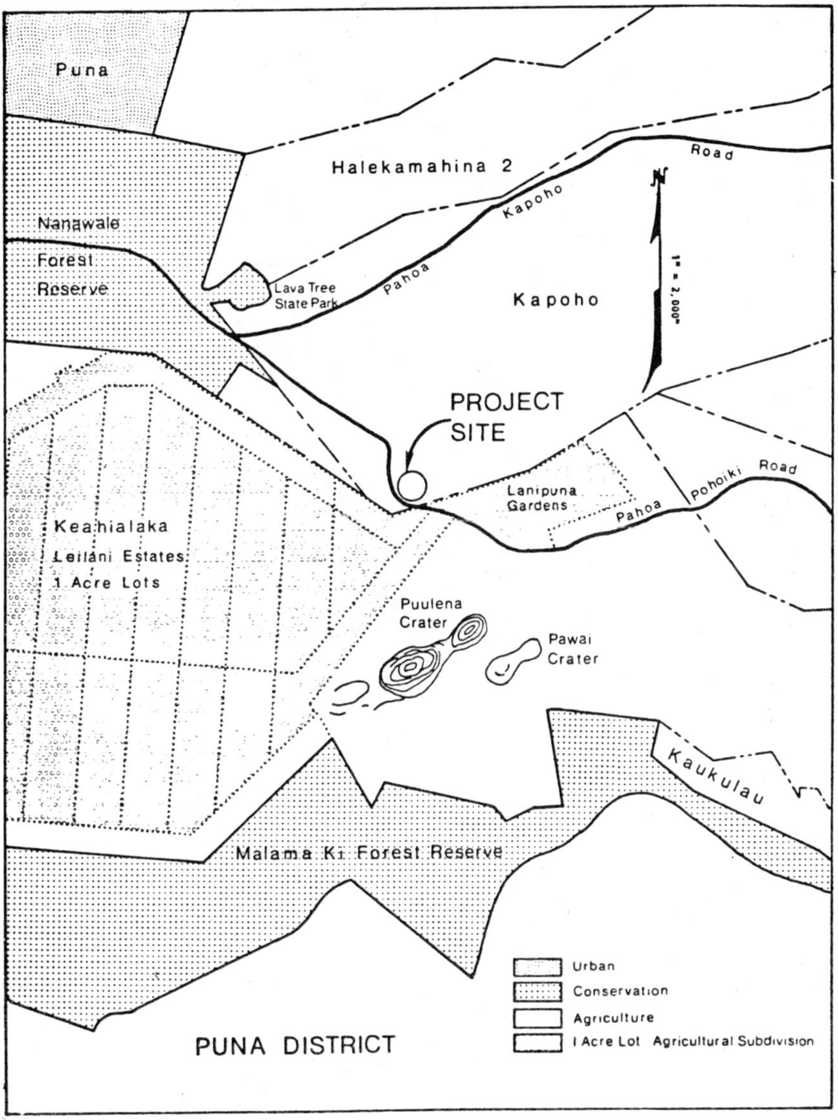

Figure 6.12. Land use within the immediate vicinity of HGP-A.

Eventually, the project director met with the residents and agreed to try to improve the muffling on the well. He pointed out, however, that the well was experimental and that the tests would be a nuisance for only a limited time. To cooperate further with the residents, Bill Chen, who lived on the

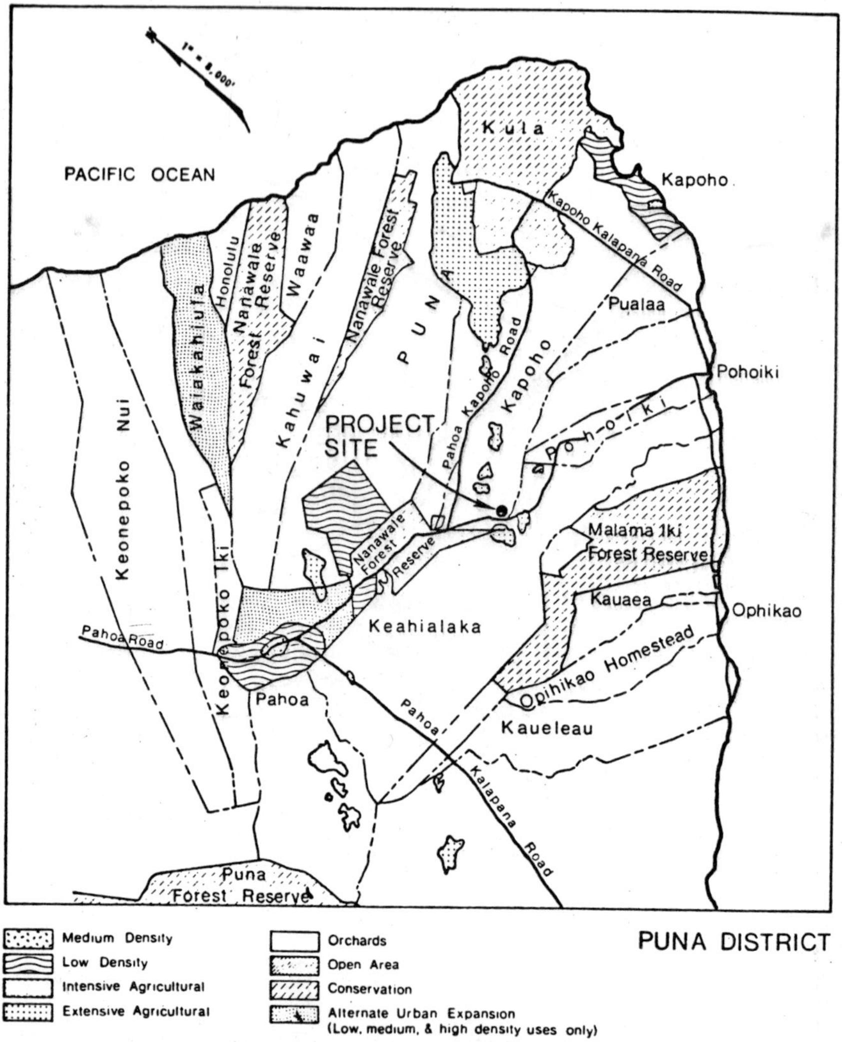

Figure 6.13. Puna District.

island and was helping to oversee the tests, agreed to confer with them before the tests and to meet with them when they so wished.

Well Tests in December 1976 and January–February 1977. In December 1976 the engineering program researchers conducted a flow test to obtain downhole temperature and pressure measurements while the well was discharging. The tests revealed that the downhole temperatures approached 662°F (350°C), one of the highest temperatures ever recorded in a geothermal well. Also encouraging were measurements showing that the well's temperature, pressure, and mass flow rate had increased significantly since the time of the November test.

During the December tests, residents again strenuously objected to the noise. Additional muffling was put on the well. This satisfied the residents, and they agreed to a two-week test in late January 1977.

The January tests were intended to determine the well's potential generating capacity, using orifice plates of different diameters. This would allow HGP researchers to determine which orifice was the optimum size to be used for generating electricity. The results of the test are presented in Table 6.7.

Following the above tests, Paul Yuen and Bill Chen decided that the well should be tested for a 90-day period in order to collect enough data to project the well's electrical generating capacity over a 30-year period. The test began on March 21, with the discharge line fully open; a few days later, a 3-in. (7.6-cm) orifice was placed into the line, since this was probably the discharge diameter that would be used to generate electricity.

Soon after the discharges began, residents of nearby Pahoa, Nanawele Estates, and Leilani Estates objected vigorously to the well's odor. The odor was caused by hydrogen sulfide, which was emitted into the air during discharge. In large amounts, it is lethal; in small amounts, it is obnoxious. It resembles the odor of rotten eggs, and the human nose is extremely sensitive to it—able to detect it in quantities as small as 3 ppb. The residents thus registered complaints with the Hawaii County Council, the State Department of Health, and directly with the project director. Some residents complained that the hydrogen sulfide fumes were environmentally dangerous and that the odor was a health hazard. Others complained of respiratory problems, while a doctor blamed the fumes for causing an increased incidence of sinus difficulties, asthma, bronchitis, diarrhea, and dermatitis.

A Department of Health representative met with the residents and explained that there were no ambient air quality regulations for hydrogen sulfide; there were, however, federal regulations for industry which specified 10 ppm for an eight-hour day. The HGP well was discharging about 3 ppm. The Department of Health official thus explained that the odor was a nuisance that would have to be controlled, but that he could not force the HGP to do anything.

After residents continued to protest, the project director met with the Leilani Community Association. At the meeting, he emphasized that the well was still experimental and that this was probably the last time any extended tests would be conducted before the HGP installed scrubbers to virtually eliminate the odor. He also noted that natural volcanic eruptions were

TABLE 6.7. THROTTLED FLOW DATA (JANUARY 26–FEBRUARY 10, 1977.)

ORIFICE SIZE (IN.)	TOTAL MASS FLOW RATE (klb/hr)[a]	STEAM FLOW RATE (klb/hr)	STEAM QUALITY (%)[b]	WELLHEAD PRESSURE (psig)	WELLHEAD TEMP. (°F)	POSSIBLE ELECTRICAL POWER OUTPUT(MWe)
8	101	64	64	51	295	3.3
6	99	65	66	54	300	3.4
4	93	57	64	100	338	3.5
3	89	54	60	165	372	3.5
2½	84	48	57	237	401	3.3
2	81	43	53	293	419	3.1
1¾	76	39	52	375	439	3.0

[a]klb = 1000 lb.
[b]Steam quality = fraction of steam in total flow.
Source: *Hawaii Geothermal Project, Phase III—Well Testing and Analysis,* Honolulu: University of Hawaii, April 1977, p. 19.

intensifying the fumes. However, he did acknowledge the nuisance factor and agreed that if there was any indication of a health hazard, he would stop the test immediately. In response, the residents cited numerous health problems and indicated that their water supply was largely from a rain catchment system; therefore, any fumes in the air were likely to endanger their water. After discussing the problems further, it was agreed to shorten the test period.

The test period was shortened to 42 days and ended on May 9. Although the full 90-day flow test would have provided considerably more information, the engineering program researchers had sufficient data to make some tentative conclusions about the electrical potential of the well. The most promising aspect of the data was that the well output had stabilized. Thus, extrapolations indicated that the well could continue to generate 3 MW of electricity over a 30-year period (see the Evaluation for complete well test results).

Completion and Handover

While the engineering program team was conducting the well tests during 1976 and 1977, John Shupe and other members of the HGP were formulating plans, policies, and strategies for promoting Hawaii's geothermal energy development. In mid-1976, in order to begin the planning activities, Shupe discussed with ERDA officials the possibility of their funding a long-term, large-scale geothermal program in the State of Hawaii. He discovered that the ERDA would be reluctant to support any such program for the following reasons:

1. The ERDA was doubtful that Hawaii's geothermal energy development had relevance and significance for the nation as a whole. In this respect, the HGP had emphasized the importance of obtaining geothermal knowledge of the island's volcanic regimes but had never emphasized the potential national spinoffs of such research. If Hawaii was to continue to receive federal funds, a strong case would have to be made for its contribution to the nation's geothermal energy development.
2. Since the ERDA was a national federal agency, it was concerned that the concentration of support—over US$2,000,000 thus far—to one geographical location was unbalanced. Requests for support of geothermal projects had been received from over 100 locations, and many would not be funded if Hawaii received a disproportionately large share of the national budget.
3. Finally, the ERDA was skeptical about funding development projects through universities because its objectives were application and utili-

> zation. The more practical and effective approach, which was normally ERDA policy, was to fund projects through industrial and other real-world organizations, such as utility companies and energy-related corporations.

Since ERDA funding was essential to future geothermal development efforts, Shupe prepared a number of recommendations that addressed these concerns. For the immediate future, he had two suggestions. First, he recommended that the HGP be dissolved at the end of 1977, following the completion of the final research reports. However, an essential corollary to HGP's dissolution would be the formation of a geothermal development consortium, composed of the Hawaii state government, the University of Hawaii, and the Hawaiian Electric Company. Second, he recommended that the consortium plan and implement a coordinated program of geothermal research and development for the state, with its first objective being the construction and operation of a small demonstration plant powered by the HGP-A well. These two recommendations were intended not only to satisfy ERDA's policy of funding real-world projects but also to achieve HGP's ultimate goal of generating geothermal electricity on a practical scale.

These two recommendations required immediate and vigorous action. Thus, in late 1976, Shupe asked Hideto Kono, the state energy resources coordinator, to assume the lead role in organizing and directing a geothermal consortium. Kono agreed and formally contacted officials from the Hawaiian Electric Company and the county of Hawaii. The state and county governments and the electric company were already cooperating in the development of geothermal power through their active participation in the HGP. These groups thus agreed to participate in the consortium, viewing it as a natural outgrowth of their cooperation with the HGP and as the appropriate organization for developing Hawaii's geothermal power. Also included in the consortium was the University of Hawaii, represented by the HGP.

Formally organized in early 1977, the consortium was named the HGP-A Development Group (HGP-A D/G). Kono was selected as the group's executive director, and Shupe was authorized to negotiate for the group in any dealings with the ERDA. The members of HGP-A D/G held several meetings early in 1977 and agreed that their immediate goal was to build a geothermal power facility to demonstrate the feasibility of generating geothermal energy from the HGP-A well. To achieve this goal, the group first prepared a funding proposal for the ERDA. Each consortium group contributed its special expertise and the state government provided the funds to contract TRW, Inc., a geothermal consulting firm, to aid in preparing the proposal. Completed in April 1977, the proposal was submitted to the ERDA.

The proposal requested funds to build an experimental geothermal facility at the site of the HGP well. The facility was envisioned to include three basic components: (1) the power generation system, (2) the experimental system, and (3) the support system.

The first component, the power generation system, was to be composed of a turbine generator, condenser, cooling power, antipollution devices, electrical conversion and distribution apparatus, and either percolation ponds or a reinjection well. It was envisioned that the steam and hot fluid from the well would be piped directly to a separator, where they would be separated. The hot fluid would then be piped to the reinjection well or to percolation ponds for disposal, while the steam would be routed to a demister. The demister would remove any remaining moisture in the steam and then allow the dry steam to exit into the turbine at 52 klb/hr at 160 psig. This would produce 3 MW of electricity.

The electricity would go to a specially constructed substation and would then be fed into the Hawaii Electric Light Company's (HELCO) power grid. However, since the grid at the substation could accept only 2 MW of electricity, the 1-MW surplus would either be fed into a load bank, where it would be dissipated, or used to supply the facility's electrical needs. Power plant operations were to be handled in a motor control and instrumentation center, where the turbine regulator, voltage regulator, voltmeters, ammeters, pressure meters, and other process control instruments would be contained.

The plant was intended to operate in an environmentally sound manner. The steam used to run the turbine was to be exhausted into a condensor, where cool water would condense the steam, leaving water for noncondensible gases. The gas would flow to a cooling tower and, after being cooled, it would either be piped to the reinjection well or recirculated to the condensor. The noncondensible gases, primarily hydrogen sulfide, would be treated in a pollution abatement system and, when safe, released into the atmosphere.

The second component of the facility was the experimental system, which was to consist of three test pads: one to conduct electrical geothermal experiments and two to conduct nonelectrical experiments. The nonelectrical experiments would include testing the environmental effects of geothermal fluid, developing a heat exchanger, and developing methods for sampling fluids and gases. The electrical experiments would include testing small geothermal generators, developing a total flow turbine, and evaluating corrosion and scaling problems.

The third component of the facility, the support system, was to include the supply buildings, the administration offices, the repair and maintenance areas, the buildings for the power station, the electrical substation, the instrumentation and equipment needed to monitor the facility, the electrical lighting, and all access and service roads. A detailed layout of all three components would later be integrated into a final design.

Management Plan. The proposal called for three stages of activity. The first stage was to be devoted to overall planning; specific activities would include devising a system of project management, drawing up a preliminary budget and work schedule, and establishing a monitoring program to control activities. Also during this period, an environmental impact statement (EIS) would be completed and a design contractor would be selected to draw up specifications for items such as the turbine generator and pollution control apparatus. The design contractor was then to integrate the power system, the research system, and the support system into the design for the total facility.

The second stage was to be the construction stage. During this stage the management would evaluate the bids and select an implementation contractor, who would handle all aspects of the construction. The contractor would be responsible for all subcontracting and for ensuring that construction meet design criteria.

The final stage was to be the operation and training phase. The plant would be operated by HELCO, which would contribute a geothermal engineer to train a staff of technicians and power operators. After the facility was completed, the staff would operate the station and HELCO would purchase the electricity at the commercial price. In the proposal, it was estimated that the plant would have a yearly income of US$260,000, which was enough to pay for all operational expenses while leaving a sizable surplus.

Cost Estimates of the Proposal. Four cost options were included in the proposal. The first option, costing US$6,447,000 was for the basic facility as described, using the most modern equipment. The second option, costing US$5,189,000, was for the basic facility, but using a surplus Westinghouse turbine generator adapted to geothermal requirements. The third option assumed the use of the surplus generator and deleted the reinjection well from the basic facility. It was estimated to cost US$4,655,000. The final option assumed the use of the surplus generator and deleted both the reinjection well and the research facilities. A summary of the costs for each option is presented in Table 6.8.

Project Completion

While the consortium was negotiating with the ERDA during 1977, the HGP continued with its own project responsibilities, which increasingly

TABLE 6.8. HAWAII GEOTHERMAL RESEARCH TEST FACILITY: ESTIMATED PLANT EQUIPMENT COSTS (US$1000).

ITEM	OPTION 1	2	3	4
1. Turbogenerator	1162.0	200.0	200.0	200.0
2a. Substation	445.7	445.7	445.7	445.7
2b. Instrumentation	126.2	126.2	126.2	126.2
2c. Load bank	54.6	54.6	54.6	54.6
3. Cooling water circulation system	54.3	54.3	54.3	54.3
4. Steam separator	71.3	71.3	71.3	71.3
5. Demister	16.0	16.0	16.0	16.0
6. H_2S abatement	150.0	150.0	150.0	150.0
7. Reinjection equipment	43.8	43.8	10.0	10.0
8. Trailers (two)	61.9	61.9	61.9	61.9
9. Condenser/eductors	61.5	61.5	61.5	61.5
10. Cooling tower	87.5	87.5	87.5	87.5
11. Site preparation	309.2	309.2	309.2	222.2
12. Foundations	128.4	128.4	128.4	105.0
13. Field piping	353.3	353.3	312.1	189.0
14. Remote instrumentation	—	—	—	—
15. Injection well	428.7	428.7	107.6	107.6
16. Research facility	866.7	866.7	866.7	0
17. Miscellaneous	226.6	177.3	156.9	100.6
Design costs	689	684	666	544
Construction costs	1111	869	770	493
Total	6447	5189	4655	3100

Source: HGP-A Development Group, *Proposal for A Geothermal Electric and Nonelectric Research Facility Utilizing the HGP-A Well on the Island of Hawaii,* Vol. II, Appendix A. Honolulu, 1977.

centered on the analysis of the data and the completion of final research reports. The environmental/socioeconomic program was the first to complete its research, formally concluding operations in January 1977 with the publication of a prototype EIS entitled "An Assessment of Geothermal Development in Puna, Hawaii." Although the assessment was not represented as an EIS, it did contain much of the information that would be required in a formal statement. It contained, for example, the environmental baseline measures of the chemicals in the Puna District's air, water, and soil. It also described the plants and animals indigenous to the area, noting especially the rare and endangered species. Also included in the assessment was a discussion of the socioeconomic conditions in Puna, including the residents' employment pattern, the housing situation, the lifestyle, and the distribution of the population. Finally, the assessment compared the potential benefits of geothermal development—such as implementation of an alternative form of energy, creation of more jobs in the area, and utilization of an indigenous source of energy—with the potential costs, such as the transformation of agriculturally zoned land to industrial land, an increase in the noise level, and an increase in the amount of airborne pollutants. Overall, it was estimated that the benefits of geothermal development were substantially greater than the costs.

As previously indicated, the engineering team completed the well testing in May 1977. During the remainder of 1977, the engineering team members analyzed the test results and then, in 1978, published a summary reservoir engineering report.

Researchers in the geosciences program continued to analyze data from the earlier geophysical surveys and completed two new research tasks. In January 1977 the researchers conducted seismic refraction surveys, and in June 1977 they completed preliminary geochemical and hydrological analyses of the samples from the well flow tests. During the rest of the year, analysis of all geophysical and geochemical data continued, and attempts were made to integrate all data into a unified interpretation. Although the synthesis could not be accomplished during 1977, several research reports were sent to the Department of Energy in 1978 to summarize the geosciences work. These summaries included reports of all of the geothermal explorations conducted from 1973 to 1977, including the electrical, magnetic, gravity, geochemical, seismic, and photogeologic surveys.

The initial plan had been to phase out the HGP upon submission of the research reports. However, the future of the HGP depended upon the HGP-A D/G proposal submitted to the ERDA in April 1977. The ERDA itself was being reorganized into the DOE during 1977, and after the transition was completed, a decision would be made. The ERDA formally became the DOE in October 1977, and in November, DOE officials notified the development group that the DOE would fund the proposal. Specific details of the proposal would have to be worked out in negotiations with the DOE.

Regardless of the future of the HGP, the responsibility for the development of geothermal energy in Hawaii was now transferred to the HGP-A D/G, which would accomplish the HGP's ultimate goal of utilizing geothermal energy in Hawaii.

EVALUATION AND REFINEMENT

No formal evaluation of the HGP was conducted. This was because the HGP was successfully integrated into the HGP-A D/G and therefore became part of the overall effort to develop geothermal power in Hawaii. From this perspective, the project is ongoing and cannot be evaluated independently of the larger development effort, which has yet to be completed. In this section, then, a summary of the major results of the HGP between 1973 and 1978 will be presented.

Well Test Results

In terms of accomplishing the goal of discovering an exploitable geothermal resource, the HGP was a success. The HGP-A well was discovered to be one of the hottest geothermal wells in the world, with downhole temperatures reaching 676°F (358°C) (see Figure 6.14 for a temperature profile of the well). There was a natural two-phase flow into the wellbore, with quality geothermal fluid and a substantial total flow rate. (See Table 6.9 for a complete statistical profile.)

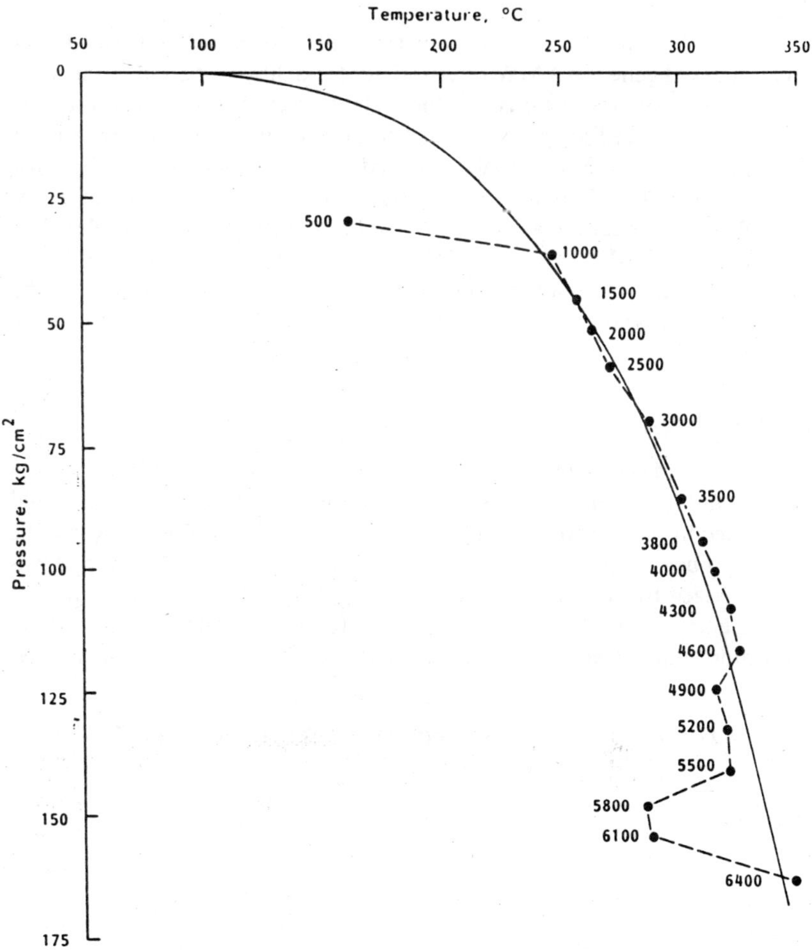

Figure 6.14. Temperature profile of the HGP-A well.

TABLE 6.9. HGP-A DISCHARGE RESULTS.

	NOVEMBER	DECEMBER	JANUARY	MARCH
Wellhead pressure (psig)	47	53	59	59
Wellhead temperature (°C)	146	150	151	153
Mass flow rate (klb/hr)	88	103	114	120
Steam flow rate (klb/hr)	60	64	72	75
Steam quality (%)[a]	68	62	63	62
Electric power potential (MWe)	3.4	3.8	4.3	4.5

[a]Steam fraction.

Based on the data collected from the well tests, it was estimated that HGP-A could generate 3 MW of electricity for a 30-year period. Table 6.10 shows the power projections for the well. It was also estimated that the entire reservoir feeding the well might be substantially larger. Estimates of the reservoir's generating capacity ranged up to 500 MW of electricity for the next 100 years. Compared to the island of Hawaii's total need of about 90 MW of electrical capacity and the state of Hawaii's present electrical capacity of 900 MW, this was quite substantial. However, estimates based on a single well were not sufficient to predict accurately the capacity of the geothermal reservoir; it would be necessary to drill other wells for more information.

Geological Results

Geologists and geochemists analyzed the cores and cuttings collected during drilling and found that the rock formation was tholeiitic basalt, which could be divided into three zones of alteration (see Table 6.11). Zone 1, where the alteration began, occurred between 2220 and 4265 ft (673–1300 m) and was characterized by montmorillonite, with minor calcite, quartz, and chlorite. Zone 2 occurred between 4455 and 6250 ft (1350–1894 m), with the principal alteration mineral being chlorite and accessories being quartz, actinolite,

TABLE 6.10. LONG-RANGE POWER PROJECTIONS FOR HGP-A.

TIME (YEARS)	TOTAL MASS FLOW RATE (klb/hr)	STEAM FLOW (klb/hr)	WELLHEAD PRESSURE (psig)	ENTHALPY (Btu/lb)	POWER (MWe)
1	81	59	153	900	3.2
15	78	58	142	904	3.0
30	77	57	140	906	3.0

Source: "Hawaii Geothermal Project," *HGP-A Reservoir Engineering*, September 1978, p. 42.

TABLE 6.11. GEOLOGICAL ANALYSIS AND INTERPRETATION OF POSSIBLE PRODUCTION ZONES.

DEPTH FROM WELLHEAD (FT)	MICROSCOPIC ANALYSIS	MEGASCOPIC ANALYSIS	BOUNDARY TEMPERATURE ZONES OF ALTERATION
0			
500	Unfilled	Generally high permeability	Little or no alteration
1000	Unfilled		
1500	Unfilled		
2000			
2500	Partially Filled	Higher Permeability	Zone 1: major mineral: montmorillonite; minor minerals: chlorite, quartz, calcite
3000	Partially Filled		
3500	Filled	Generally low permeability, but possibility of layers of medium permeability	320°C
4000			
4500	Filled		
5000		Varying but generally low permeability	Zone 2: major mineral: chlorite; minor minerals: quartz, actinolite, montmorillonite.
5500	Filled		
6000	Filled		340°C
6500	Partially Filled	High permeability	Zone 3: major mineral: actinolite; minor minerals: chlorite, quartz, pyrite, hematite

and montmorillonite. The boundary temperature between zones 1 and 2 was about 617°F (325°C). The third zone became dominant from about 6234 ft (1900 m) to the bottom of the well. Actinolite predominated in this zone, with chloride, quartz, pyrite, and hematite secondary. The boundary temperature between zones 2 and 3 was 644°F (340°C).

From the top of the well to a depth of about 3500 ft (1067 m) the lava was highly permeable, with excellent permeability between 2500 and 3000 ft (762–914 m). Then from about 3500 to 6200 ft (1067–1890 m), the permeability became poor, although layers of medium permeability existed throughout the dike, making possible geothermal production. At the bottom of the well, from 6200 to 6600 ft (1890–2012 m), the permeability was excellent. Figure 6.15 illustrates the zones of permeability as they relate to the HGP well.

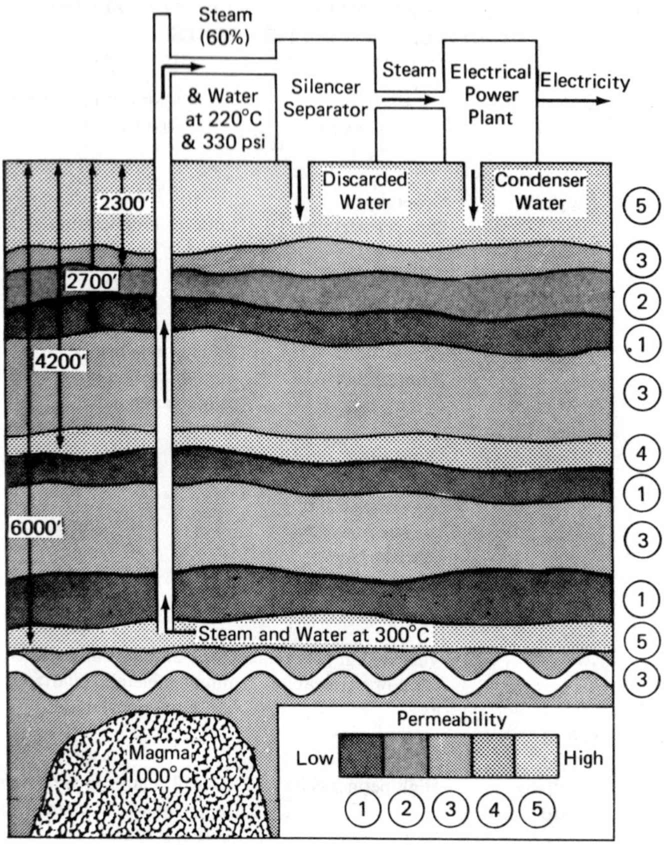

Figure 6.15. Layers of permeability in relation to HGP-A.

Based on this information, the HGP researchers derived several speculative models of the well's underground system. One of the most probable models depicted two production zones, one at about 4400 ft (1341 m) and the other at about 6400 ft (1951 m). Both zones were supplied by aquifers that were recharged by rainfall percolating into the ground. However, only high levels of rainfall could penetrate to these zones because of the alternating layers of poor permeability. The heat at these depths was sufficient to boil the water and produce steam.

Well Emissions

During the well testing, the HGP researchers collected atmospheric samples to determine the airborne chemicals emitted from the geothermal discharge;

they also collected downhole samples to analyze the chemicals in the geothermal fluid. With respect to airborne emissions, there was concern about sulfur dioxide (SO_2), hydrogen sulfide (H_2S), and mercury (H). Both SO_2 and H_2S were bothersome, but their levels were never dangerous. In fact, their levels in the atmosphere did not change during the well tests, indicating that the well was not adding significantly to the natural volcanic emissions of sulfide into the atmosphere (see Table 6.12). However, the odor of H_2S is particularly offensive to humans and, as previously noted, it can be detected in quantities as small as 3 ppb. Thus, although the flashing of the well did not significantly increase the atmospheric levels of H_2S, it did disturb nearby residents. This was especially true when there was no wind or when the prevailing wind blew toward nearby homes. The last bit of odor would have to be eliminated before further developments could take place.

Levels of mercury were another matter. Mercury is potentially dangerous at any level, and the provisional federal standard is no more than 0.1 $\mu g/m^3$ for continuous exposure. Mercury levels near the drill site were high, and during the July 1976 flashing they rose to 9.9 $\mu g/m^3$. Later analysis, however, revealed that the area naturally contained high levels of atmospheric mercury. Moreover, the high levels recorded in July were caused not by the well testing but by volcanic vents. Table 6.12 illustrates that even with the well shut, mercury in the air sometimes exceeded 0.1 $\mu g/m^3$. After monitoring the air for two years, researchers could find no evidence of a buildup of mercury.

The chemical content of the geothermal fluid was a cause of concern because any geothermal plant would have to dispose of or reinject the used geothermal fluid back into the earth. This could contaminate the groundwater. However, the chemical content of the HGP geothermal fluid did not differ significantly from that of the brackish water wells in the area (see Table 6.13). This suggested that the area's groundwater had been naturally contaminated due to the upward movement of heated salt water. Moreover, it appeared that no Ghyben-Herzberg lens existed in the area. In the event,

TABLE 6.12. AEROMETRIC DATA FOR HGP.

DATE	WELL STATUS	SO_2 (ppm)	H_2S (ppm)	HG ($\mu g/m^3$)
May 1975	Predrilling	0.5	0.5	1.1
May 1975	Predrilling	0.5	0.2	1.2
July 1976	Flashing	0.5	0.2	99.9
Nov. 1976	Well shutdown	—	—	10.0
July–August 1977	Well shutdown	0.3	0.2	0.8

Source: Adopted from Kamins, Robert M. *Revised Environmental Impact Statement for the Hawaii Geothermal Research Station Utilizing the HGP-A Well at Puna, Island of Hawaii.* Honolulu: State of Hawaii Department of Planning and Economic Development, March 1978.

TABLE 6.13. COMPARISON OF THE CHEMICAL CONTENT OF THE HGP-A WELL WITH THAT OF NEARBY WELLS AND SPRINGS (mg/l).

SITE	Cl	Ca	K	Mg	Na	SiO_2
HGP fluid (downhole)	925.0	84.2	135.0	2.1	830.0	440.0
Isaac Hole Spring	3534.0	32.4	86.0	200.0	2020.0	81.5
Airstrip Well	303.5	23.0	13.6	28.0	238.0	71.3
Allison Well	281.0	13.4	10.8	15.0	216.0	24.1
Malama Ri Well	3811.0	66.8	109.0	210.0	2105.0	81.5
Rainwater	7.2	0.25	0.25	0.75	4.5	0.0

Source: Adopted from Kamins, Robert M., et al. *Environmental Baseline Study for Geothermal Development in Puna, Hawaii.* Honolulu: University of Hawaii, Hawaii Geothermal Project, September 1976.

the residents used the local groundwater; they used water piped in from another source on the island. Only one potential hazard existed: silica. Because of the high downhole temperature, the level of silica in the HGP fluid was 440 mg/l, several times higher than normal. It would have to be filtered out before the well's geothermal fluid could be reinjected into the ground.

Noise

Despite constant improvements in the muffling of the well, noise continued to annoy residents throughout the testing period. Although the noise did not exceed EPA standards when measured at nearby houses, it was high-pitched and thus irritating. Moreover, many residents were accustomed to the quiet of the rural area, while others had moved to Puna specifically to get away from loud noise. (Table 6.14 provides data on the noise.) Thus, any subsequent developments would have to eliminate the noise problem.

TABLE 6.14. LEVEL OF NOISE NEAR THE HGP-A WELL SITE (dB).

LOCATION	7/19/76 (WITHOUT SILENCERS)	11/3/76	1/27/78	2/10/77 (3-IN. ORIFICE)	5/7/77 (3-IN. ORIFICE)
Corners of well					
40 ft away	113	100	96	98	—
40 ft away	113	98	93	95	91
70 ft away	94	98	89	91	—
70 ft away	94	98	91	91	89
At roadside					
200 feet away	122	87	80	80	75
Estimated					
1 mi away	—	—	—	—	70
2 mi away	—	—	—	—	49

However, the HGP was only an experimental program; the demonstration plant had not been built. When electricity was actually generated, the sound would be muffled by the generator, into which the steam would be fed, and by the cement building, which would house the generator and the operating facilities. It was anticipated that this would reduce the noise to an acceptable level.

Economic Aspects of the HGP

From the beginning, the HGP was a cooperative effort involving the federal, state, and county governments, the utility companies, and the University of Hawaii. Each contributed by giving the project expert advice and by providing their services when appropriate. In addition, each group supported the project financially. During the years 1973–1978, HGP's total allocation amounted to US$3,387,000. Table 6.15 presents a breakdown of the total funds granted to the project during this period.

Although this total amount was large, it must be put into perspective. First, it was spent over a period of five years, and it funded numerous activities ranging from geophysical surveys to socioeconomic assessments. Second, the project was intended to provide the basic research and development that would lead to the exploitation of geothermal resources in Hawaii. It was intended neither to be an exploration for geothermal resources nor to be an eventual profit-making venture. Finally, the project did discover a productive geothermal well and a potentially large geothermal reservoir. It is this well and potential reservoir that the 3.5-MW demonstration plant will utilize.

EPILOGUE (1980–1985)

The HGP-A demonstration plant came on line in 1981, generating 3 MW of electricity for the residents of the island of Hawaii. After three years of successful operation, the power plant has demonstrated the technical,

TABLE 6.15. FINANCIAL SUMMARY FOR HGP, 1973–1978 (US$1000).

FUNDING ENTITY	1973	1974	1975	1976	1977	1978	TOTAL
NSF	269	200					469
ERDA (1977)			119	1472	270	147	2008
State of Hawaii	100		500		66		666
County of Hawaii	100						100
WRI				60			60
Hawaiian Electric			45				45
Other			39				39
Total	469	200	703	1532	336	147	3387

economic, and environmental feasibility of geothermal energy development in Hawaii. As a result, there are now three private firms or consortia actively involved or interested in developing this indigenous energy resource.

Much of the material for the updated economic, environmental, and social impact analyses was obtained by the author as a result of meetings with key personnel in the Department of Land and Natural Resources (DLNR) and the Department of Planning and Economic Development (DPED), State of Hawaii, in 1982 and 1983. In particular, special acknowledgment is due Dr. Takeshi Yoshihara, Administrator, Energy Division, DPED, for his interest in and cooperation with the author's continued research and development of the IPPMC conceptual framework as an effective management methodology for the energy and other sectors.

The state adopted legislation in 1983 (Act 296–83) to establish geothermal resource subzones where geothermal activity may take place. Four subzones have since been established for continued geothermal exploration and development on both the island of Hawaii and the island of Maui.[21] Each geographical area identified as a designated geothermal subzone resulted from an assessment program using criteria provided by the DLNR.[22–26]

ECONOMIC IMPACT ANALYSIS

The economic assessment is based on two assumptions: (1) a 20- to 30-MW plant would be constructed and (2) application of the geothermal wells would be for the production of electricity for local consumption only.

As with any economic activity, the injection of funds into the economy will result in direct impacts through the purchase of various goods and services from other industries. In the case of a geothermal plant, the money added to the economy may be due to the inflow of investment capital or from the savings resulting from not having to import approximately 390,000 barrels of imported petroleum each year for conversion into electricity.[27] The additional purchases made will, in turn, cause these industries to purchase more goods and services from other industries. The result is a chain reaction of purchases or a multiplier effect produced by the original increase in purchases.

A 25-MW geothermal plant will require approximately 25 employees. As a result of this direct employment, an estimated 57 additional jobs will be created after all of the repercussions have taken place, both within the county and the State. Based on the available data, the wages to the 25 direct project employees will be about $560,000 per year. This direct income will stimulate a multiplier effect totaling an estimated $1.3 million.

For the production of electricity for local consumption only, the assumed 20- to 30-MW plant size being considered is reasonable. However, direct use and other applications would alter the plant size requirements. In addition, more significant impacts on the economy (both benefits and costs) would occur: more jobs, increased public revenue, increased housing and infrastructure demands, and so forth.

Regardless of the ultimate size of the geothermal plant decided upon, a more definitive assessment of the relative gain or loss to be realized by its existence must be made on a case-by-case basis.

ENVIRONMENTAL IMPACT ANALYSIS

Water Pollution

Groundwater in the various geothermal areas may occur as (1) perched water, (2) dike water, and (3) basal water. Basal water occurs most commonly in the islands. The basal groundwater body is the fresh water resting on salt water within the permeable rocks that make up most of the base of the islands. In the areas considered, groundwater resources will not be adversely affected because geothermal wells are drilled past the groundwater aquifer. In addition, surface casing will be set and cemented through a competent subsurface formation below the basal lens. The drilling, casing installation, maintenance, and abandonment of all geothermal wells, including reinjection wells, must be regulated and monitored to protect the groundwater aquifer.

Subsurface disposal of geothermal fluids by reinjection is permitted, provided that potentially dangerous contaminants in the fluids are first filtered out. The major potential hazard in this regard, as of 1984, is the high level of silica found in the HGP-A fluid (440 mg/l) (Table 6.13).

The presence of arsenic in geothermal fluids can cause health problems if concentrations reach 0.05 ppm. Monitoring to date has not found levels of concern.

Air Pollution

The DPED initiated a two-year environmental baseline survey of the Kilauea East Rift Zone in December 1982.[28] The principal parameters measured included atmospheric concentrations of particulate material, sulfur dioxide gas, hydrogen sulfide gas, chlorine gas, carbon monoxide gas, elemental mercury vapor, radon, elemental and organic contents of particulate material, rainwater pH, elemental and anionic content of rainwater, and wind speed and direction. In addition, a recent study of hydrogen sulfide and its impact on health was conducted in the Rotorua, New Zealand, Wairakei geothermal power plant, with comparisons made with the HGP-A project area.[29] The highlights of these studies are summarized below.

Hydrogen Sulfide. Hydrogen sulfide is found in nearly all high-temperature geothermal fluids. It also occurs naturally in coal, natural gas, and sulfide springs and lakes and is a product of anaerobic decomposition of sulfur-containing organic matter. Production of hydrogen sulfide from volcanic gases is the result of the action of steam on inorganic sulfides at high temperatures. The same reaction is responsible for the production of the gas in steam from geothermal wells.

Hydrogen sulfide is a colorless gas which has a characteristic obnoxious odor even at low concentrations (the odor threshold is measured in micrograms per cubic meter). At higher concentrations, the gas is toxic to humans and animals and is corrosive to many metals. In humans at low concentrations it can cause headache, conjunctivitis, sleeplessness, pain in the eyes, and similar symptoms. At high concentrations the gas can paralyze the olfactory nerve, and at higher concentrations it can result in rapid death.

Plant species differ widely in their response to hydrogen sulfide and to different concentrations of the gas. Long-term exposure to hydrogen sulfide results in damage to plants at concentrations between 0.042 and 0.42 mg/l (0.042–0.03 ppm). However, at 0.03 ppm, some types of plants exhibit growth stimulation, but at 0.3 ppm these species show damage.[28]

Permissible levels of hydrogen sulfide vary. The California State Department of Health has set an extremely strict maximum ambient air quality standard of 30 ppb (0.04 mg/m^3), which was once thought to correspond to the odor threshold. Other agencies have accepted higher levels. Of direct interest to geothermal development in Hawaii, the Rotorua, New Zealand, studies showed an average concentration of 100+ ppb more than 50 percent of the time, and concluded that the average level of ambient hydrogen sulfide in and around HGP-A could reach 30-fold higher levels without any hazard to human health, flora, and fauna.[29]

However, geothermal projects in Hawaii are required to have abatement systems that meet the proposed State Department of Health air quality standards. At present, the recommended hydrogen sulfide abatement system, the Stretford System, is capable of removing over 99 percent of the hydrogen sulfide in the noncondensable gases. Use of this system would enable facilities to comply with the proposed air quality standards that require 98 percent of the hydrogen sulfide present to be removed.

Sulfur Dioxide and Acid Rain. Hydrogen sulfide, released from geothermal facilities, will oxidize in the atmosphere to sulfur dioxide, which is then oxidized to sulfate aerosols. Sulfur dioxide is injurious to human health and the environment and is the principal precursor of acid rain. Studies dealing with acute inhalation of sulfur oxides generally indicate that health effects are unlikely at the ambient levels expected to occur as a result of atmospheric oxidation of hydrogen sulfide.

Acid rain usually originates with emissions of sulfur dioxide (SO_2), which can oxidize to SO_3 and eventually forms sulfuric acid (H_2SO_4), which falls as acid rain. Three potential sources of acid rain are (1) natural volcanic emissions, (2) geothermal emissions, and (3) emissions from oil-fired power plants. In the absence of volcanic activity, sulfur dioxide values are low. However, during an eruption, concentrations due to volcanic activity can exceed human health and plant impact values for days at a time.

Rainwater in the Puna and Ka'u districts in the vicinity of the Kilauea Rift Zone is slightly acidic due not only to acidification from local volcanic sources of sulfur dioxide but also to the long-range transport of pollutants across the Pacific.

At present, it is notable that no detectable sulfur dioxide is emitted from the Puna HGP-A facility's noncondensed gas stream. Hawaiian geothermal developments are expected to have abatement systems which can reduce hydrogen sulfide emissions by about 99 percent, which should meet proposed state Department of Health air quality standards for geothermal development of 98 percent hydrogen sulfide abatement during geothermal power plant operation in addition to an incremental standard. It is expected that the remaining unabated 1 percent of the hydrogen sulfide would take several days to become acidic and that, by that time, prevailing winds would take any pollutant remaining out to sea.

Mercury. The health effects of long-term exposure to airborne elemental mercury have been studied less than the effects of ingestion of foods contaminated with the methylated form of mercury. However, epidemiological studies indicate that persons exposed to mercury vapor in the work environment have shown mercury intoxication resulting in muscle tremors, psychosomatic disturbances, deterioration of intelligence, inflammation of the oral cavity, and lens discoloration (eye). Mercury emissions from geothermal facilities are not likely to cause acute health effects.

It should be noted that elemental mercury vapor levels and particulate mercury levels in the rift zone are well below ambient air quality and industrial standard levels but fall within the typical range of atmospheric concentrations. Mercury concentrations in the East Rift Zone are also regulated by the inflow of trade winds from the ocean, where mercury levels are extremely low.

Noise

During the initial phases of geothermal development, persons in the vicinity of a geothermal facility construction site will be exposed to noise levels varying from 40 to 120 dB, depending upon the distance from the site. High noise levels are produced by well drilling, production testing, and well bleeding before connection to the generator. Use of acoustical baffling and rock mufflers will effectively reduce noise level to 44 dB at the facility fence line.

Compliance with County of Hawaii noise guidelines will limit noise levels for geothermal activities to 45 dB at night and to 55 dB during the day.

Ground Subsidence

In Hawaii, subsidence from geothermal fluid withdrawal is not likely to be a problem, since the islands are generally composed of dense, yet porous, self-supporting basaltic rock. Of more concern is the volcanic or tectonic subsidence, which usually occurs on or about active rift zones, such as that of Kilauea. Subsidence and cracking may also be associated with tectonic earthquakes (subsiding slump blocks in a fault system at Kilauea, for example).

Collapsing pit craters and lava tubes can result in very severe localized subsidence. Pit craters usually occur within a summit or upper rift zone of a volcano and can result in subsidence of up to hundreds of feet. Fragile, near-surface lava tubes (usually found in pahoehoe flows) are subject to collapse from heavy surface activity. A geologic site survey could reveal these hazards.

Tsunamis

Tsunamis are large sea waves usually generated by the movement of large submarine rock masses, although some are caused by volcanic eruptions. These devastating waves can travel great distances at speeds of almost 500 mph and can move onshore turbulently or merely rise quietly. The highest reported wave, 60 ft above sea level, resulted from a local earthquake on the island of Hawaii in 1868. Much larger tsunamis have been reported elsewhere.

Tsunami hazards are probably localized to a zone of land at most 2 km wide around the coast and at elevations below about 75 ft. This should not pose a significant danger to geothermal developments, which are likely to be sited at higher elevations.

Earthquakes

Earthquake hazards include ground shaking, cracking, and subsidence. Several tectonic earthquakes above magnitude 6 have been reported on the island of Hawaii, particularly in the coastal and saddle areas. Less powerful volcanic earthquake swarms commonly occur in rift zone areas.

Geothermal developments near coastal areas should consider the possibility of damage from tsunami and ground subsidence.

SOCIAL IMPACT ANALYSIS

The social impact analyses of geothermal energy projects emphasize people's perceptions, attitudes, and concerns regarding geothermal resource development and operation. Considerations are based primarily on a 20- to 30-MW level of geothermal generation of electricity and are based on available public information.

Major social concerns considered were health aspects, noise aspects, lifestyle, culture and community setting, aesthetics, and community input. Also included was a review of the potential geothermal areas with respect to these factors of social concern. Two major communitywide survey studies produced information on perceptions and concerns about the effects of geothermal development. In addition, data were contributed by community and other organizations and individuals on various occasions.

Overall indications are that major social concerns and impacts could be minimized and preservation of a high-quality environment could be achieved by proper siting, landscaping, and design of plant facilities and by careful controls and monitoring of all operations. The necessity and desirability of increasing the participation of all sectors of the community should be emphasized.

The health aspects of geothermal resource development involve primarily the effects of chemical, particulate, and trace element emissions on the physical environment and on local residents. Hydrogen sulfide and sulfur dioxide are the major gaseous compounds of concern, but the naturally existing or ambient air of the volcanic regions also contains these compounds. The technical analyses of air and water quality are treated fully in the environment impact analysis report, but the concerns, perceptions, and attitudes of the residents regarding the health effects of geothermal emissions fall in the area of social concerns and sociological impact.

CONCLUDING REMARKS

The State of Hawaii has initiated a sound plan for the exploration, development, and production of geothermal resources as a viable alternative energy source. The plan resulted in legislation in 1983 (Act 296), amended by Act 151 in 1984, which provides criteria to ensure appropriate economic, environmental, and social impact studies. It is estimated that the geothermal potential in the Kilauea Rift Zone alone can produce as much as 500 MW of electrical energy for 100 years. To utilize this amount of power will necessitate laying over 160 mi of cable at depths of up to 7000 ft to tie into the Oahu grid system. Studies by the state's DPED indicate the feasibility of studying the technical problems involved in this type of engineering project.

Meanwhile, smaller-scale plans are moving ahead for the Island of Hawaii. In April 1986, HELCO signed a 30-year contract with Puna Geothermal Venture, a private group, for 25 MW of geothermal power by 1992, with 50 percent to be in production by 1989.

REFERENCES

1. City and County of Honolulu, *Report of the Mayor's Energy Resources Committee,* 1973, p. 1.
2. Kamins, Robert M. "An Assessment of Geothermal Development in Puna, Hawaii," Report prepared for Hawaii Geothermal Project (HGP). Honolulu: University of Hawaii, January 1977, pp. 4–5.
3. State of Hawaii, Department of Planning and Economic Development (DPED), "Energy Use in Hawaii," in *The Role of Alternative Energy Resources in Promoting Island Self-Sufficiency.* Hearings before the Subcommittee on Energy Research and Development. Washington, D.C.: U.S. Government Printing Office, 1979, pp. 110–111.
4. Kamins, *An Assessment of Geothermal Development,* p. 5.
5. University of Hawaii, Center for Engineering Research. *A Proposal to the Hawaii State Legislature in Response to House Resolution 351 Requesting a Study of New Energy Sources for the State of Hawaii.* Honolulu: 1971, p. 7.
6. Honolulu *Star-Bulletin,* March 5, 1973, p. A–20.
7. Hawaii Geothermal Project, *Summary Report for Phase I.* Honolulu: University of Hawaii, May 1975, p. 27.
8. Honolulu *Advertiser,* February 9, 1974.
9. Furumoto, A.S., Macdonald, G.A., Druecker, M., and Fan, P.F. *Preliminary Studies for Geothermal Exploration in Hawaii, 1973–1975.* Honolulu: University of Hawaii, Institute of Geophysics, December 1977, p. 140.
10. Hawaii Geothermal Project, *Phase II Revision to Proposal AER 7500285–000,* December 1974, pp. 2–51.
11. Ibid., pp. 5–6.
12. Hawaii Geothermal Project, *Summary Report for Phase I,* p. 27.
13. Kingston, Reynolds, Thom, and Allardice Limited. *Report on Geothermal Project Testing Program.* Honolulu: Hawaii Geothermal Project, August 1975, pp. 1–2.
14. Ibid., p. 2.
15. Entry in the drilling log of the Hawaii Geothermal Project, n.d.
16. Personal communication from John Shupe.
17. Ibid.
18. Honolulu *Advertiser,* April 22, 1977, B1.
19. Ibid.
20. Kamins, Robert M. et al. "Environmental Baseline Study for Geothermal Development in Puna, Hawaii." Honolulu: Hawaii Geothermal Project, University of Hawaii, September 1976.
21. Yoshihara, Takeshi. "The Designation of Geothermal Subzones in Hawaii," Department of Planning and Economic Development, State of Hawaii (Geothermal Resources Council Meeting), 1985.
22. State of Hawaii, DLNR. *Social Impact Analysis, Circular C–104.* Honolulu, 1984.

23. State of Hawaii, DLNR. *Economic Impact Analysis, Circular C–105.* Honolulu, 1984.
24. State of Hawaii, DLNR. *Environmental Impact Analysis, Circular C-106.* Honolulu, 1984.
25. State of Hawaii, DLNR. *Geological Hazards Impact Analysis of Potential Geothermal Resource Areas, Circular C–107.* Honolulu, 1984.
26. State of Hawaii, DLNR. *Geothermal Technology, Circular C–108.* Honolulu, 1984.
27. California Energy Commission. *Cumulative Impacts Study of the Geysers KGRA: Public Service Impacts of Geothermal Development, Final Staff Report.* Sacramento, July 1983.
28. Houck, James E., *Environmental Baseline Survey, Kilauea East Rift Zone.* Report. Prepared for State of Hawaii, Department of Planning and Economic Development. Honolulu, 1984.
29. Siegel, B.Z. "Hydrogen Sulfide and Health," Final Report. Prepared for Hawaii Natural Energy Institute, University of Hawaii, and Hawaiian Electric Industries. Honolulu: University of Hawaii, 1985.

CHAPTER 7

Hawaii Bagasse Pellets Project

This case history was researched in 1979–1980 and published in 1981.* The original case covers two bagasse projects: the Hilo Coast Processing Company (HCPC) and the Davies Hamakua Sugar Company, two of the largest producers of bagasse-generated power on the island of Hawaii and in the state. This chapter focuses on the latter project, which established the feasibility of designing, constructing, and operating the world's first bagasse pellet factory. The project was put into operation in 1981, generating approximately 15 MW of electricity, with 5 MW for internal use and 10 MW for the local utility. The section on evaluation covers both HCPC and Davies because of their joint concern for the future of the sugar industry in Hawaii.

The Epilogue contains a brief update from the period 1981–1985. It then examines and discusses planning efforts on the part of both the State of Hawaii and the sugar industry to increase the viability of biomass as an alternative renewable energy resource. Of interest to this discussion is the fact that most biomass projects can be environmentally benign with proper planning and management. Biomass energy is covered in Appendix D.

OVERVIEW OF BAGASSE ENERGY IN HAWAII

Upon his return from the 1979 Energy Summit Conference in Tokyo, United States President Jimmy Carter, meeting with nearly 300 Hawaii community leaders, stated: "There is no other place in our country which has best exemplified progress toward energy self-sufficiency than the State of Hawaii. On the big island, Hawaii, and on Kauai as well, almost 50 percent of all the energy used comes from biomass, primarily from sugarcane."[1] Delivered at a time when the combination of a dwindling oil supply and a rising demand for energy was creating strategic as well as economic problems, this statement gave national prominence to Hawaii's efforts to attain self-sufficiency in energy through the use of alternative sources. Inas-

*Castberg, A. Didrick, Miyabara, Tetsuo and Goodman, Louis J. in Goodman, L.J. and Love, R.N., eds. *Biomass Energy Projects: Planning and Management,* New York: Pergamon Press, 1981.

much as this achievement is largely due to the efforts of the sugar industry, this case history focuses on the biomass energy development program of the Davies Hamakua Sugar Company (Davies).

Before the program of this company is examined, however, it is necessary to see how biomass energy development fits into national energy policies. Energy policy in the United States is a combination of policies emanating from the federal government and from the numerous state and local governments. Overall energy policy is set by the federal government, but each state and county adapts its own modified strategy to achieve it. The federal government did not begin devising an energy policy until 1973, when the Arab oil embargo made it clear that the United States was economically and strategically dependent upon imported oil. This policy is now evolving; coherent and unified goals and priorities are being determined; specific mechanisms to achieve these goals, such as taxation, pricing, and direct support, are being deliberated. Nonetheless, there is general agreement that the United States should decrease its dependence on imported fuels by increasing domestic production. Thus, although tentative and not yet detailed and unified, a plan has begun to emerge. In 1979 it was articulated in the National Energy Plan (NEP) I and II. The plan breaks down energy policy into three periods: near-term: present—1985; mid-term: 1985–2000; long-term: 2000 and beyond.

The first period emphasizes conservation as a means of reducing dependence on foreign oil and thus reducing the vulnerability due to interruption of its supply. The second period will continue to emphasize conservation but will begin the development of higher-priced technologies (they are high-priced now but may well be competitive during this phase). Many of these technologies, however, would be petroleum based, such as the development of economical methods to extract oil from oil shale and tar sands, coal gasification, and extraction of heavy oil. Only in the long-term period does a substantial commitment to renewable alternative energy sources begin. Because this period is relatively distant, however, the commitment is vague; the federal government acknowledges that it cannot pursue the development of all technologies simultaneously; therefore, choices have to be made. These choices, the plan states, will be made by another generation, even though work must begin very soon if there are to be sufficient data by the year 2000 on which to base a decision. Three basic energy sources will be explored in the third phase: solar energy, nuclear fusion, and breeder reactors.[2]

Biomass conversion is included in the NEP under the overall rubric of solar energy. A total of US$597,000,000 is included in the fiscal year (FY) 1980 budget for solar energy projects, of which US$58,000,000, or almost 10 percent, is slated for biomass conversion.[3] Much of this sum will be used to support the development of liquid biofuels such as ethanol and methanol, but the development of biomass as a solid fuel for direct combustion will also be supported. In this context, the NEP recognizes the current energy role played by direct incineration of wood, and wood residues, a process which results in the production of 1.8 quads of energy per year, but notes that problems associated with emissions, collection, and transportation must be solved before such direct conversion can play a much larger role.[4] No specific mention is made of bagasse. As an energy source, biomass is noted as having two distinct advantages: (1) it is renewable and (2) the United States is the world's leader in crop production, thus making it possible to use a portion of these crops for fuel.

The NEP covers virtually all areas of conventional and alternative energy sources. Priorities can be determined from the budget authority for each source and potential source; biomass is allotted approximately 1.5 percent of the total amount allocated for FY 1980 in the NEP (see Table 7.1).[5]

Despite public controversy about nuclear power plants, the major government emphasis in the near term will be nuclear, while hydroelectricity will receive the least emphasis. The amounts listed in Table 7.1 are for development and deployment only; currently operational energy sources such as oil and coal are not included. There is no expectation that they will be displaced from their primary status until well into the second period, and even possibly into the third. Coal, in fact, will have an increasingly important role, the plan states, and industries will be encouraged to convert from oil to coal.[6] Given the emphasis on fossil fuels and nuclear energy, the importance of biomass lies not in its ability to replace conventional sources but in its ability in the long term to help provide an appropriate energy mix for the United States.

TABLE 7.1. DEPARTMENT OF ENERGY FUNDING FOR TECHNOLOGY AND DEVELOPMENT.

	FY 1980 (IN MILLIONS)	PERCENT
Fossil energy	US$ 796	22.0
Solar energy (including $58 for biomass)	597	17.0
Geothermal	111	3.0
Hydroelectric	18	0.5
Magnetic fusion	364	10.0
Nuclear fission	1037	29.0
Environment	278	8.0
Basic energy research	276	8.0
Other technology programs	106	3.0
	US$3583	100.5[a]

[a]Does not add up to 100 because of rounding.

Source: *National Energy Plan II* (Washington, D.C.: U.S. Government Printing Office, 1979), Appendix B, p. 3.

The NEP is, as the name implies, national in scope and therefore does not take up individual problems of specific regions of the country. These must be addressed by state and local governments, leading in some instances to a much more prominent role for biomass energy.

The State of Hawaii is one of, if not the most, isolated populated archipelagos in the world, located approximately 2400 mi from the continental U.S. mainland. The state has no fossil fuel reserves and thus must ship in all of its oil, an amount equal to about 31.5 million barrels in 1978 at a cost of over US$600 million.[7] Because of inadequate demand and waste disposal problems, nuclear power is not feasible. Coal is uneconomical because of the cost of shipping, as well as the cost of converting power plants. Thus, the state is almost totally dependent upon oil for energy, with 30 percent of this energy being in the form of electricity (the remainder being largely gasoline and jet fuel).[8]

This does not mean, however, that Hawaii does not have alternatives to oil as an energy source, especially for generating electricity. Extensive agriculture provides thc base material for biomass conversion. Over 220,000 acres are planted in sugarcane and over 60,000 in pineapple—the two main crops. The state is blessed with both substantial rainfall (average, 73 in./year) and sunshine, as well as wind.[9] Finally, the state possesses geothermal resources associated with its volcanic origins and is also situated near deep oceans, which can be used in thermal energy conversion. These resources make possible five alternatives to oil-based electrical power generation: biomass conversion, hydroelectric, geothermal power, wind power, and ocean thermal energy conversion (OTEC).

Of these alternatives, the greatest promise is shown by and the most development has been done in biomass conversion—specifically, the burning of bagasse, the fibrous waste remaining after sugarcane is milled. It has been used by Hawaiian sugar plantations for the past 40 years to produce steam and electricity. This form of biomass conversion plays a significant role because the technology is simple and well developed and the process is relatively efficient. Even more important, from an economic standpoint, is the fact that the fuel is a by-product of another valuable resource, sugar; therefore, the processing of sugar provides dividends in terms of the sale of power to public utilities. This form of biomass conversion accounts for approximately 14 percent of the electricity generated statewide and over 37 percent of the electricity generated on the island of Hawaii itself.[10]

In the United States, it should be noted, privately owned utility companies are responsible for generating, supplying, and developing electrical energy. These companies, commonly called "public utilities," own and operate large power plants that serve separate regions of the country through central transmission lines. Because electrical energy is vital to the nation, the government regulates the utilities' operations through public utilities commissions in each state. These commissions approve electricity rates and the building of new plants, ensure that utility companies meet the demand for electricity, and generally represent the public interest in decisions.

Despite its extensive resources and its great dependence on imported oil, the State of Hawaii does not have a comprehensive energy plan. The 1973 oil crisis did prompt the state to create the position of State Energy Resources Coordinator, the Hawaii Natural Energy Institute at the University of Hawaii, and the Natural Energy Laboratory of Hawaii, located at Keahole Point on the island of Hawaii.[11] The Energy Resources Coordinator issues annual reports on various aspects of the state's energy situation, including research and development, funding, and national policies that affect the state; however, no energy plan, as such, exists. The goal of the state is to be energy self-sufficient by the year 2000 (sooner for some islands), a goal that many energy planners feel is overly optimistic.

In the quest for energy self-sufficiency, biomass conversion seems to have a high priority, although investment is largely from the private sphere—if for no other reason than that it is the most developed and is associated with a major industry, sugar. Investment in other forms of biomass conversion, as well as in geothermal, solar, and wind projects, has been minimal, with the federal government providing a large proportion of the costs.

On the local level, counties are completing their own energy plans, which must be consistent in their goals with the national emphasis on reducing vulnerability and the state policy of increasing self-sufficiency. The county of Hawaii, encompassing that island, has taken the first steps toward its comprehensive energy plan by starting four years ago to plan toward self-sufficiency. The island of Hawaii, with perhaps the greatest potential energy resources, has the greatest need for an energy plan. It has a land area of 4,038 mi^2, or more than the total land area of the other islands combined, with two mountains reaching almost 14,000 ft (43,000 m).[12] Most of the tillable soil is devoted to sugar, with 92,629 acres under cultivation in 1978. These acres produced 387,459 tons of raw sugar in the same year; this production occurred on approximately one-half of the total acreage, since sugar is a two-year crop.[13]

Other resources of the island of Hawaii include a geothermal well, an OTEC site, wind generators, and hydroelectricity generators. A large proportion of the electricity generated on the island comes from alternative sources: bagasse, 37.6 percent; hydroelectric, 5.4 percent; and wind power soon to supply as small amount of electricity. The bagasse-generated power comes from various sugar mills, including the HCPC and Davies companies, with the former supplying the largest amount (22 percent of the island's total).[14]

Such an abundance of energy resources presents the Hawaii county government with a variety of difficult decisions, not the least of which is the direction in which the county is to go: maintenance of the status quo, agriculture, tourism, or industry (or the last three, in varying amounts, which would preclude the first). The county of Hawaii commissioned Stanford Research Institute (SRI) International to study the possibility of creating energy self-sufficiency in 1979. The report, published in two volumes, took an essentially conservative approach, recommending development of current sources of energy, especially the combustion of cane and wood.[15] A primary recommendation was the drying of bagasse, through the use of flue gases or other methods, to increase the heat value of the fiber (which would have the same effect as pelletizing).

This is not a new recommendation, of course, but it has not been implemented by sugar mills in Hawaii despite its effectiveness, probably because efficient generation of power did not have as much priority as it does at present. Wood has a marginally higher heat value, but more important, it can be grown in terrain incapable of supporting sugarcane and thus should be considered as a supplement, not a substitute, for bagasse. No boiler modifications would be necessary to burn a combination of bagasse and wood chips; and even macadamia nut shells have been burned successfully, despite their significantly higher burning temperature. SRI International noted that tree farming is only a pilot project at this point but is potentially a valuable source of fuel.

This study gives the County of Hawaii some justification to support conventional biomass conversion, especially since it has proven to be operational and would involve few or no county funds. Thus, for the State of Hawaii and especially the County of Hawaii, biomass energy provided by private sugar companies will be of high priority. A reinforcing factor was the added costs of meeting environmental standards set by the Environmental Protection Agency (EPA) to implement and enforce the federal legislation of the 1960s to prevent environmental pollution.

Two of the largest producers of biomass energy in the state are HCPC and Davies Hamakua Sugar Company (Davies), which produce large amounts of electricity and sell them to the local utility company. Located along the Hamakua coast on the island of Hawaii (see Figure 7.1), these companies use bagasse to fuel their power plants. Although similar in scope, their biomass energy programs have certain major differences. This chapter analyzes the biomass program of Davies because of its focus on pelletizing bagasse.

PROJECT BACKGROUND

The Davies Hamakua Sugar Company is owned by Theo H. Davies & Company Ltd., a wholly owned subsidiary of Jardine, Matheson & Company, a multinational conglomerate based in Hong Kong. Davies was formed in

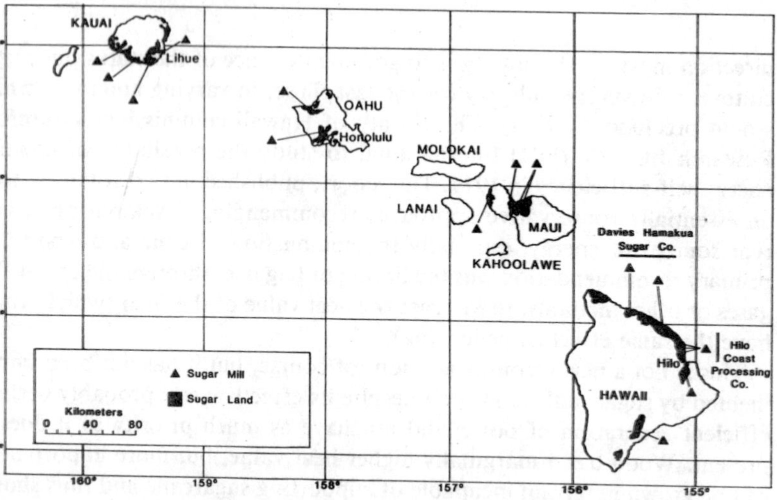

Figure 7.1. Map of Hawaii, showing location of sugar companies and areas of sugarcane cultivation. (Source: Adapted from Curt Beck, ed., *Biomass Energy for Hawaii:* Vol. II: *Sugar Operations* (Stanford, Calif.: Institute for Energy Studies, 1977, p. 4.)

1979 from the merger of two Davies plantations, the Laupahoehoe and Honokaa Sugar companies. These two sugar plantations, situated about 18 mi apart, have historically maintained independent operations with separate harvesting equipment, mills, and factories.[16]

During the 1960s and 1970s, the economics of these two plantations, like that of the sugar industry in general, underwent dramatic shifts. Rising labor costs, increasing operating expenses, and the uncertainty of market prices threatened the survival of many plantations. Additionally, the cost of meeting environmental standards had been rising steadily since the 1960s, when legislation such as the Solid Waste Disposal Act of 1965, the National Environmental Policy Act of 1969, and the Clean Air Act of 1970 were passed. Through these acts, the EPA, as mentioned earlier, adopted regulations requiring the sugar companies to install filters on their boilers, to construct water treatment systems for their effluents, and, most important, to halt the ocean dumping of sugarcane refuse. The refuse would therefore have to be incinerated or buried in a landfill, both of which were costly operations.[17]

In order to cope with these changes, the managers of Laupahoehoe and Honokaa, along with the agricultural group officers of Davies, planned a long-term program which included two basic actions. First, they would increase the economies of scale of their plantations by merging with other plantations and by consolidating factory operations. This strategy would not only reduce the costs associated with owning many small plantations, each of which required its own factories, shops, mills, and administrative services, but would also cut down on the amount of pollution control equipment that would have to be installed. Second, in the course of merging and consolidating plantations, they would modernize the operations. By installing technological improvements in the growing, harvesting, and processing facilities, productivity would be increased.[18]

As part of this overall strategy, Laupahoehoe first acquired other sugar plantations and in 1965 began to consolidate its two mills into a single large factory at Ookala. Construction of the new factory was completed in 1966, and the two other Laupahoehoe mills were closed. Continuing the long-range program in the early 1970s, the managers and executives of Davies merged another plantation, the Hamakua Mill Company, with Laupahoehoe. Simultaneously, they made plans to close the Hamakua factory and to further expand Laupahoehoe's factory.

A key element in the factory modernization and expansion in the 1970s was the installation of a larger boiler that would enable Laupahoehoe to burn its excess trash and bagasse, which previously would have been dumped in the ocean. The new boiler provided 312,000 pounds of steam per hour, twice the capacity of the old boiler. About 78 percent of the boiler's steam was routed to the sugar-processing facilities to power the cane shredder, trash shredder, cane mill, trash mill, and boiler auxiliaries. The remaining 22 percent was routed to a 5-MW turbogenerator that could produce electricity either for the plantation or for sale to the local utility company. It should be noted that the boiler had two primary functions. First, it had to supply steam both for sugar processing and for generating plantation electricity. In this regard, a 4-MW generator was added to the system in 1979. Second, because the EPA had ordered Laupahoehoe to halt the ocean dumping of cane trash, the boiler had to serve as an incinerator. (See Figure 7.2 for the layout of the energy generating system at Laupahoehoe.[19])

Another significant aspect of Laupahoehoe's factory modernization was the construction of a dual milling tandem that milled the trash and the sugarcane in two independent streams. In this milling process, the entire sugarcane plant was first brought to the factory cleaning facility, where it was washed to remove leaves, soil, and other debris from the stalk. After being removed from the stalk, this trash was conveyed to grinders, where it was milled, loaded into dump trucks, and discarded in a landfill, a process which was also designed to help comply with EPA requirements. In a separate operation, the stalk, after being washed and stripped of its leaves, was conveyed to a shredder, where it was milled and then squeezed on rollers to extract its cane syrup. The shredded remains of the stalk (bagasse) were conveyed to the boiler for fuel.

At Honokaa, the expansion and modernization program started later

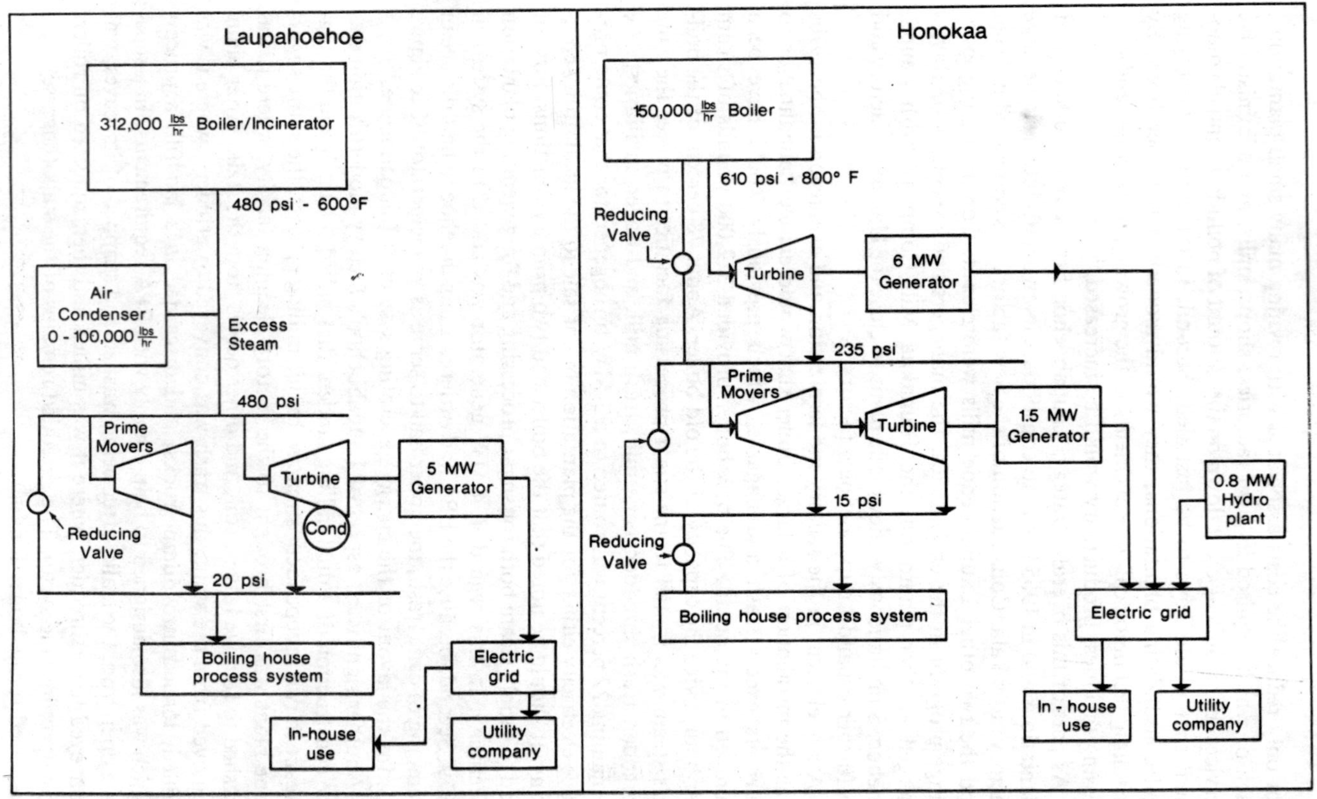

Figure 7.2. Generating facilities at the Honokaa and Laupahoehoe factories. (Source: Davies Hamakua Sugar Company.)

than at Laupahoehoe. It was not until 1972 that Honokaa was able to expand by purchasing the Paahau Sugar Company, located just to the south. Ironically, the owners of Paahau, C. Brewer and Co., had decided to sell the plantation because the EPA had required that nearly $4 million of pollution equipment be installed at the Paahau factory, and the investment was not deemed worthwhile. The EPA had thus given Honokaa the opportunity to purchase Paahau. Following its acquisition, the Paahau factory was shut down and its cane was processed at the Honokaa factory, which was forced to operate 24 hours a day, 7 days a week. To remedy this situation, it was decided to modernize and expand Honokaa's processing facilities.

In planning the modernization, a crucial factor was the dramatically rising cost of energy, a factor that had not affected the earlier program at Laupahoehoe. By 1973, the price of oil on the world market was controlled by the Organization of Petroleum Exporting Countries (OPEC), which were continuously raising their prices. This marked a significant transformation in the structure of energy pricing. Recognizing that this would mean long-term price increases for energy, Ernest Bouvet, the general manager of Honokaa, proposed that the factory's modernization be based on energy efficiency and conservation. In this view he was supported by Francis Morgan, the vice-president of the Davies agricultural group, and the president of the Davies plantations. Given this support, the management at Honokaa devised an overall policy of energy conservation and efficiency that was adopted in 1973. A report by the company provides a general explanation of the policy and its goals:

> Honokaa Sugar Company is committed to develop to the maximum its capabilities of biomass fueled electric power for its own needs and for export into the power system of Hawaii Electric Light Company (HELCO).
>
> HELCO's only fuel—apart from a very small hydroelectric plant—is fuel oil which has to be imported into Hawaii from foreign sources. It is therefore abundantly evident that any power derived from local biomass resources would help the state's economy and render Hawaii less vulnerable in case of international emergencies.
>
> With this purpose in mind, the management of Honokaa Sugar Company has deliberately followed a policy of energy conservation and development since 1973, when the steam generation and power complex was redesigned along lines novel in the sugar industry.[20]

The factory modernization at Honokaa thus proceeded with energy conservation as a primary goal. The first step was to increase the electrical generating capacity of the factory. This step would not only reduce Honokaa's purchases of electricity from the utility but would also make use of the existing boiler's surplus steam, which represented a large amount of wasted energy. The existing generating facility consisted only of a 1.5-MW condensing generator and a 0.8-MW hydroelectric unit. After careful consideration of various configurations, the general manager and his engineering staff decided to install a 6-MW topping turbogenerator, using the concept of cogeneration. They would link the new generator directly to the existing 166,000-lb/hr steam boiler, thus utilizing the initial outflow of steam. After being used to generate electricity, the steam would be routed to the milling operations and to the 1.5-MW condensing generator, where it would be reused (see Figure 7.2). This configuration of cogeneration was extremely efficient.

Another aspect of modernization at Honokaa involved an alteration of the milling process. As in Laupahoehoe's milling practice, cane trash was ground separately from bagasse and then dumped, resulting in the waste of a considerable volume of fiber which could have been converted to fuel. It was therefore decided to recover the trash and convert it to bagasse through a simultaneous milling process.

Experiments were run to determine the best design for simultaneous milling, and several problems arose. The cane trash contained mud and rocks that clogged the milling equipment, caused excessive wear on the grinders, and decreased the amount of recoverable cane syrup. Furthermore, because the cane leaves were so much lighter and more pliant than the stalks, they enveloped the cutting blades and prevented them from chopping the cane. To solve these problems, an additional washer and a new shredder were added. The washer would clean the mud and rocks from the cane, and the additional shredder would enable the leaves to be ground. Existing conveyors and shredders were relocated to allow for a more efficient flow of trash and cane. The shift to simultaneous milling allowed the recovery of an additional 86,000 tons of biomass fuel, increasing the total amount of bagasse from 196,000 to 275,000 tons. This additional amount was equivalent to 84,000 barrels of fuel oil. However, the existing boiler had a capacity of 166,000 pounds of steam per hour and could burn only about 68 percent of the total biomass made available.[21] The excess had to be dumped, resulting in the loss of all of the extra fuel.

Consequently, the next phase of the modernization plan was to purchase a larger, more efficient boiler. Capable of burning bagasse and fuel oil, as well as other fibrous materials such as wood chips and macadamia nut husks, the new boiler was rated at 288,000 lb/hr and could utilize all of the bagasse produced by the mill. Because the new boiler had a capacity 60 percent greater than that of the old boiler, the manager and the engineering staff at Honokaa recommended adding another generator to the power system to make use of the additional steam. The top managers at Davies agreed to this proposal, and a reconditioned 7.5-MW condensing turbogenerator was purchased as a complementary component to the new boiler.[22] The installed generating capacity at Honokaa would thus be 15.8 MW, with steam generators of 1.5, 6, and 7.5 MW and a hydroelectric unit of 0.8 MW.

In completing the new boiler-generator system, the management of Honokaa encountered substantial problems in dealing with the EPA. In 1977, plans for the boiler and its specially constructed filter to reduce the boiler's emissions were submitted to the State of Hawaii's Department of Health, which had been designated by the EPA to administer clean air standards. The boiler system was approved, but the EPA also requested the plans. No further communication came from the EPA, so the management assumed that the pollution equipment was satisfactory and construction of the system was begun. After construction was completed in September 1978, the EPA ruled that the boiler did not meet its emission standards and would have to be altered. The manager pointed out that approval had already been received, that the EPA had not communicated with the company for nearly one year, that the system had subsequently been built, and that it was now scheduled to be put into operation to power the entire processing operation. The EPA responded that initiating operations without further modifying the boiler's filter would result in a $1000/day fine. A satisfactory arrangement was eventually worked out, but only after considerable expense and negotiation.[23]

During modernization, other improvements to Honokaa's energy production system were made. These included the installation of an IBM computer to coordinate steam utilization with the demands for processing sugarcane and generating electricity, a 24,000-ft^2 preevaporator to replace the existing 10,000 ft^2 one, and a new bagasse sprinkler system to prevent fires in the bagasse storage facility. When all of these improvements were completed in 1979, the company was able to increase its power output from the 1975–1978 average of 3.3 MW to 12 MW. Expressed in other terms, Honokaa was generating the equivalent of 267,000 barrels of oil annually, compared to the 1975–1978 annual average of 169,000 barrels. Most important, the company had attained virtual self-sufficiency and had in fact become a net exporter of energy, selling electricity equivalent to 120,000 barrels of residual oil (see Table 7.2).

The modernization program had one other major component. In 1978, as part of their continuing efforts to increase the efficiency of all operations, the managers and executives of Davies decided to merge the Laupahoehoe and Honokaa sugar companies into a single entity, the Davies Hamakua Sugar Company. The amalgamation was decided upon for several reasons. First, it would centralize control of the two sugar operations, making it possible to coordinate and control a uniform company policy of energy efficiency. Second, it would minimize redundance. For example, with the merger, only one company manager would be required; the services of

TABLE 7.2. ENERGY PRODUCTION AT THE HONOKAA SUGAR COMPANY.

	1973–1975 (ANNUAL AVERAGE)	1975–1978 (ANNUAL AVERAGE)	1979	1980 (PROJECTED)
Bagasse production (tons)				
From cane	199,000	199,000	199,000	199,000
From trash	0	0	77,000	77,000
Total	199,000	199,000	276,000	276,000
Expressed in barrels of residual oil	193,000	193,000	267,000	267,000
Rate of power (MW)				
Produced	1.6	3.45	11.625	12.305
Required for processing	1.6	1.56	1.75	1.735
Required for pollution control	0	0.54	0.54	0.54
Available for export	0	1.35	9.335	10.03

other personnel would also be redundant, and their positions would be eliminated. Rather than lay off personnel, however, it was decided to eliminate their positions after they retired. Third, the merger would increase the flexibility of operations. If one factory was shut down for repairs or had more cane than it could process, the excess cane could be processed at the other factory. Finally, the merger would allow Honokaa and Laupahoehoe to integrate energy operations by linking their factories with power transmission lines. In this way, each power generation system would act as a backup for the other; if the power system at one factory broke down, that factory could tap into the electrical reserve of the other factory. This would eliminate the need to purchase electricity from the utility company.[24]

The cost of implementing the modernization program had been high, US$40 million in all. The cost of the energy-related improvements at Honokaa had been US$8 million (see Table 7.3). Still, the expenditures were

TABLE 7.3. CAPITAL EXPENDITURES FOR ENERGY IMPROVEMENTS AT THE HONOKAA SUGAR COMPANY.

Foster-Wheeler boiler	US$6,561,956
Simultaneous milling facility	408,000
7.5-MW turbogenerator	786,645
Preevaporator (24,000 ft^3)	225,000
Series 1 IBM computer	44,515
Exhaust steam line	63,895
Total	US$8,090,011

an investment for the future, and the merged company would continue periodically to modernize operations. Most significant, the company would improve its energy efficiency and energy conservation on an ongoing and continuous basis.

PHASE 1: PLANNING, APPRAISAL, AND DESIGN

Identification

Against the backdrop of the modernization program, the profitability of the sugar industry continued to decline for two reasons. First, the price of sugar on the world market had been falling steadily at about the same time that U.S. sugar price supports for domestic growers had expired. The result was that revenues could not keep up with operating costs. Second, the price of energy was rising rapidly in response to the escalating price of oil. The rising cost of energy, however, provided both a dilemma and an opportunity for Hawaii's sugar companies. On the one hand, the operating costs of any sugar plantation that was not largely self-sufficient in electricity would be unrealistically high. On the other hand, any company that produced surplus power now had the opportunity to sell electricity to the utility companies for a profit.

The combination of these factors was affecting the structure of Hawaii's sugar industry. Many plantations, unable to cope with declining prices and increasing energy costs, began operating at a net loss and had to consider ceasing operations. A number of companies did, in fact, go out of business. Other companies, such as the Hilo Coast Processing Cooperative, discussed in the first part of this chapter, had to consider energy production as a primary alternative to sugar production.

At Davies, the situation was not quite so gloomy. The sugar operations were still profitable; for several years in a row, Davies had been the most cost-effective sugar producer in the nation. The modernization program had enabled the company to resist the erosion of profits by increasing productivity. Consequently, no alternative to sugar production was considered. At the same time, however, there was a concerted effort to ensure the continuing profitability of sugar by making the best use of the energy situation. To this end, the energy efficiency of the company was improved by extending the policy of energy conservation from the Honokaa operations to the Laupahoehoe facilities. Additionally, it was decided to sell Honokaa's surplus power at a rate that would be equitable with the increasing cost of producing energy.

Thus, in 1978 the general manager of Honokaa, Ernest Bouvet, along with the special projects assistant, Norland Suzor, began negotiating a firm contract to sell HELCO their surplus power. Under the existing arrangement, the sugar company sold "dump" power to the utility. Dump power was the excess electricity generated by the sugar company, which was fed into the HELCO grid whenever it was available; no commitment was made by the sugar company to sell, or by HELCO to buy, a set amount of this power. Dump power was sold at a rate of about 4 mills (0.4 cent)/kWh, while electricity was purchased from the utility at the commercial rate of about 50 mills/kWh.[25]

In negotiating a firm contract, the objectives of Davies were to sell a fixed quantity of electricity to the utility at a rate higher than the dump price. The objectives of the utility were to purchase a set quantity of electricity in order to ensure that a minimum amount of power would be available on demand and to pay the lowest possible price for this power. During contract discussions in 1978, HELCO offered Davies a rate of about 20 mills/kWh to be adjusted annually, plus a demand fee for continuously maintaining 10 MW of power. They would purchase 87,000,000 kWh, and in return Davies would ensure that 10 MW was constantly on line to be fed into the grid.[26]

The manager of Honokaa and his special projects executive studied this offer. Since the Honokaa factory had a total installed capacity of about 15 MW and used only 3 MW for factory operations, they could easily generate the necessary 10 MW. There was a financial burden, however, in maintaining this power continuously. The supply of bagasse—the primary fuel source for the boiler—was intermittent, available only during the nine-month cane harvesting season. To generate a year-round, continuous 10 MW, then, the sugar company would have to burn fuel oil during the three months when bagasse was unavailable.

In examining the situation, the special projects assistant determined that 47,000 barrels of fuel oil would have to be purchased. Even with the price of oil at $18 per barrel, the contract would be profitable, and the manager decided to proceed with negotiations. Before terms could be agreed to, however, the price of oil jumped, with further price hikes certain to be imposed at unpredictable intervals. Because of this instability, the manager decided not to undertake a firm contract until the Honokaa operations could satisfy all power requirements without having to burn fuel oil.[27]

In trying to eliminate the need for an external fuel source, the bagasse supply was closely examined. It was found that the total amount of bagasse produced during the nine-month cane harvesting season provided sufficient fuel to maintain 10 MW continuously. Bagasse, however, could not be stored for long periods of time. Three problems prevented storage: (1) Since bagasse is organic, it would decompose quickly and therefore could be stored for only a limited time. (2) Even if the decomposition problem could be solved, bagasse had to be protected from rain and other elements to maintain its caloric value. Bagasse is, however, extremely bulky, with a density of only 7–10 lb/ft^3. Since 1 ton of bagasse is equivalent to about 1 barrel of oil, 47,000 tons would have to be stored, causing insurmountable problems in handling, loading, and conveying. (3) The combination of sugar and moisture contained in bagasse causes fermentation to take place, and this exothermal reaction results in stores of bagasse igniting by spontaneous combustion.[28]

In searching for a practical solution to these problems, the general manager of Honokaa learned of a potential process called Woodex that compressed wood waste into fuel pellets. These pellets provided a cost-effective substitute for fuel oil and coal, and their value had been proven through use. A brochure from the Bio-Solar Research and Development Corporation, the firm which held patent rights to the process, elaborated on pelletization:

> Woodex fuel pellets are refined from biomass wastes, which are available almost everywhere in some form. In this material is the energy stored and continuously renewed by the sun in all growing matter. After this raw material is pulverized to a desirable particle size, "free" water is extracted or added to give the fibers the correct moisture content. The unrefined fibers are then extruded under high pressures and temperatures. In the process, the cell structure of the fibers is changed; the lignins, waxes, sugars, and the cellulose they represent are separated. . . . Changing the cell structure of the cellulose material allows combustion air to unite with oxygen contained in the Woodex pellets and promotes rapid burning of the pellets' volatiles, which have separated from the remaining fiber and its carbon.[29]

On further inquiry, the general manager was told by the inventor of the process that no external chemical binders were used in production and that the pellets were about three to four times less expensive than fuel oil. Additionally, bagasse could easily be made into pellets through the Woodex process.

Feasibility Studies

The pelletizing process appeared to be a solution to the fuel supply problems of bagasse. The general manager of Honokaa thus asked his special projects assistant to prepare feasibility studies. Basically, two broad aspects of the feasibility of pelletizing bagasse were examined—technical and economic.

Technically, it was first determined that bagasse could indeed be transformed into pellets through the Woodex process. The Bio-Solar laboratory and experimental plant produced samples from bagasse and returned them

TABLE 7.4. COMPARISON OF BAGASSE AND BAGASSE PELLETS.

	BAGASSE	PELLETS
Density	7–10 lb/ft³	30–40 lb/ft³
Steam production per pound of fuel	2.5–2.8 lb	5.9–6.2 lb
Moisture content	45–50%	10–12%
Equivalence to oil	1 ton = 1 bbl	1 ton = 2–2.5 bbls

to Davies to analyze. The analysis indicated that the bagasse pellets had superior quality (see Table 7.4); their moisture content was about 10 percent, whereas that of raw bagasse was about 48 percent. Table 7.4 shows the caloric value of the pellets was considerably higher than that of bagasse; 1 lb of bagasse produced 2.5 to 2.8 lb of steam, while 1 lb of pellets produced 5.9 to 6.2 lb. The density of the pellets was approximately five times greater than that of bagasse, or 30–40 lb/ft³ compared to 7–10 lb/ft³. Finally, the pellets could be easily stored; they did not decompose and were extremely sturdy.[30]

In helping to solve the fuel supply problem, then, the feasibility study concluded that bagasse pellets (1) could be stored for long periods of time without deterioration; (2) could be stored, conveyed, and handled in a practical manner, since they were so much less bulky than bagasse; and (3) were not subject to spontaneous combustion because their moisture and alcohol were substantially removed. Additionally, the process of pelletizing transformed bagasse into a superior-quality fuel, thus providing more energy from the same amount of fiber.

The feasibility study also noted that the situation at Honokaa was eminently suited for pelletizing. There was ample space next to the factory for a pelletizing plant and a pellet storage warehouse. The supply of bagasse was adequate: moreover, unlike a typical wood pelletizing plant, which had to ship wood waste from various sources, the bagasse plant would have all of the fiber available on the site. Finally, and most obviously, the company's boilers had the capacity to use the pellets.

In examining the economics of the situation, the feasibility study linked the pelletizer with the overall modernization program. Capital improvements had been approved for upgrading the boilers, for installing more generators, and for simultaneous milling of trash and bagasse to increase fuel recovery. These improvements, as previously noted, resulted in greatly improved energy efficiency and greatly increased bagasse fuel production. Approximately 276,000 tons of bagasse would be available for fuel, yet only about 167,000 tons would actually be needed to meet the requirements of both an electrical contract and the sugar operations. This meant that approximately 100,000 tons of fiber fuel, equivalent to 100,000 barrels of fuel oil, would be excess.[31] This surplus could be used to generate electricity and sold to the utility as dump power. Selling dump power to the utility, however, was not profitable; it was a poor use of the excess bagasse. Moreover, since fuel oil would still have to be purchased, such a use was inconsistent with the overall investment in increasing energy efficiency and the policy of energy conservation.

Appraisal

After the feasibility study was completed, the special projects assistant went over the results with the general manager. It was agreed that the pelletizer suited the needs of the factory, and so the proposal to build the pelletizer was discussed with the Davies Agricultural Group vice-president. The general manager met with the group vice-president in Honolulu and reviewed the feasibility study. After some discussion and further study, it was decided to request the president to seek approval of the project from the head offices in Hong Kong and to commence the design.

The proposal for the pelletizer was sent to Jardine-Matheson for review. By the summer of 1979, written approval was received to conclude negotiations with Bio-Solar, which held the patent on the pelletizing process. Approval to proceed with the pelletizer was also granted. Although the precise funds for construction would not be formally committed until the Five-Year Expenditure Plan was decided upon at the Davies annual meeting in December, in-depth engineering studies could begin.

Design

The week after approval was received from the head offices in Hong Kong, intensive engineering studies began for the world's first bagasse pellet factory. The studies were conducted in-house by the manager of the factory division and his project design group. At the same time, there was a personnel reorganization resulting from the consolidation of the Laupahoehoe and Honokaa Sugar Companies into the Davies Hamakua Sugar Company. Under the reorganization, the manager of the Honokaa plantation, Ernest Bouvet, became the general manager and vice-president of the new company (see Figure 7.3). He was responsible for the administration of three separate divisions: (1) transportation, which included all of the trucks, vehicles, and operators; (2) agriculture, which included all sugarcane growing operations; and (3) factory, which handled all of the sugar processing operations, including energy production. Each division had one manager, who was responsible for the operations at both the Laupahoehoe and Honokaa facilities. Appointed as manager of the factory division was the former special project assistant at Honokaa, Norland Suzor. He would be responsible, along with his project design team, for completing the pelletizer's design.

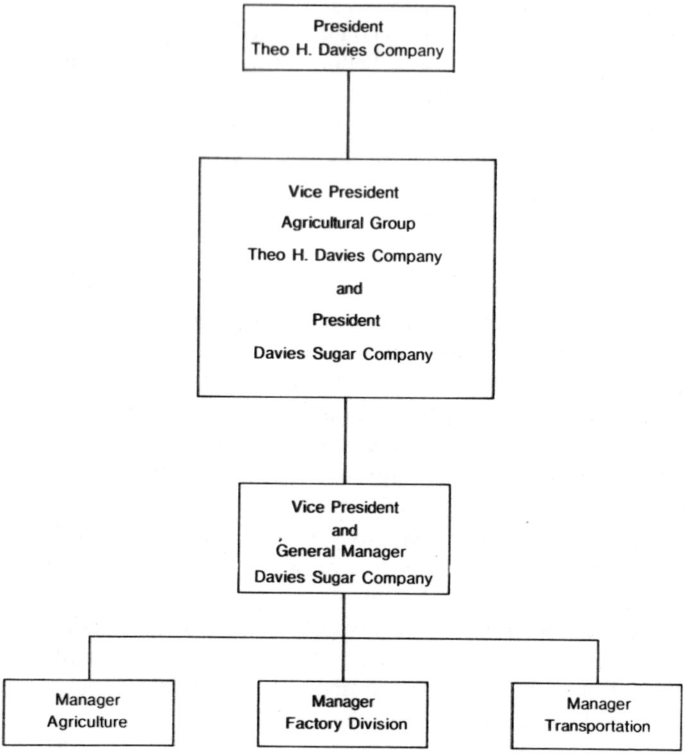

Figure 7.3. Davies Hamakua Sugar Company: Organization Chart.

To begin the design process, the factory manager studied the original plans and specifications of wood pelletizers that were currently in use. In the basic design of these pelletizers, wood waste was first brought to the pellet factory and conveyed to a grinder, which adjusted the wood to a particle size appropriate for pelletizing. The ground wood was then conveyed to a heater, where its moisture content was reduced to about 22 percent. The resulting wood fiber was then compressed under high temperature and pressure into pellets measuring 3⁄16 to ½ in. in diameter. Finally, the pellets were demoisturized to about 12 percent (see Figure 7.4).

Besides a review of the basic plans of existing pellet factories, two other key activities were involved in the design process. First, although the factory manager had the primary responsibility for completing the design, he consulted regularly with the general manager, the vice-president of the agricultural group, and the technical supervisor of sugar operations, who worked with the group vice-president in Honolulu. This consultation allowed a

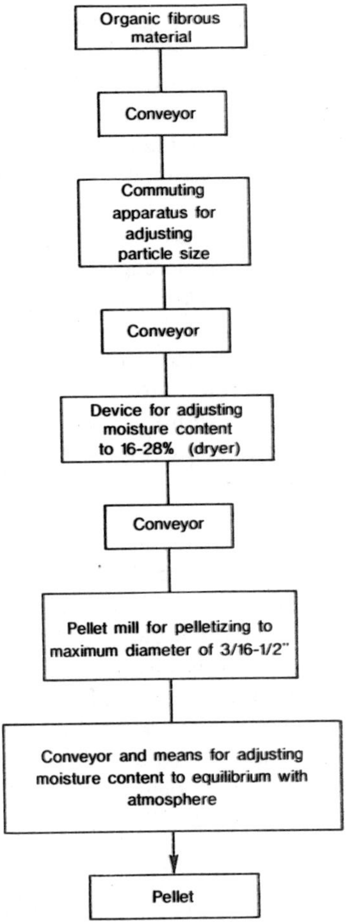

Figure 7.4. The Woodex process. (Source: "Woodex: The Refined Biomass Fuel," Bio-Solar Research and Development Corp., Eugene, Ore., n.d.)

broad range of expertise to be used in the design. Second, to obtain practical information on how a pelletizer performed in the real world, several trips were made to examine operating pellet factories. It was during these visits that a major shortcoming was reidentified: External fuel and power were required to operate the grinder, conveying system, demoisturizers, and pellet mill. For the demoisturizers, fuel oil or a portion of the manufactured pellets was used. For the grinder and other apparatus, electricity was purchased from local utilities. The overall energy gain from pelletizing was thus substantially reduced.

In visualizing the pelletizer and the generating-facilities of the sugar mill as an integrated system, however, it was determined that the need for external energy could be eliminated through two design modifications. First, upon close examination of the bagasse fuel source, it was discovered that about 50 percent of the bagasse contained enough fines, or finely ground fiber, to be pelletized without adjusting its particle size. There was thus no need for the particle adjuster. To take full advantage of this circumstance, it was decided to convey all the bagasse to a screen, which would separate coarse from fine bagasse. The coarse bagasse would be conveyed directly to the boiler for fuel; the fine bagasse would be used to make pellets. In addition to eliminating the grinder, there was another advantage to this separation: The boiler could be operated and controlled more efficiently because coarse bagasse tends to burn uniformly for a long period of time. In comparison, when using bagasse with fines, the boiler was difficult to control because the fines tended to ignite rapidly and sometimes exploded.

A second design improvement involved the dryer. After analyzing the pellet factory's requirements in relationship to the sugar factory's energy production system, it was realized that the dryer could be operated by using the exhaust flue gases. These gases ranged in temperature from 375 to 500°F (176 to 246°C) and constituted residual emissions from the boiler. Using the flue gases for the dryer would not only utilize wasted energy but would also eliminate the need for an independent fuel source.

In integrating the dryer into the system, a further way to increase energy efficiency was found. The large rotary dryer using flue gases was placed in front of the screens that divided the coarse bagasse from the fines, resulting in the drying of the entire volume of bagasse. The fuel quality of the coarse bagasse was thus improved, with a reduction in moisture from 48 to 35 percent and an increase in the bagasse's caloric value from 2290 to 2980 kcal/kg. The result was an increase in boiler efficiency from 62 to 78 percent. Essentially, a "virtuous," rather than a vicious, cycle was created. Wasted energy from the flues was used to dry the bagasse; because of this increase in fuel quality, less bagasse had to be used for fuel for the boilers; because less fuel was required, more bagasse would be available to make pellets. Consequently, wasted energy was transformed into fuel pellets—the virtuous cycle.[32]

After these improvements had been built into the design, computer simulations of the proposed pellet mill were run to estimate how the system would perform under real-world conditions. It was particularly important to see if the pellet mill could tolerate interruptions in the flow of bagasse, which would occur periodically during the milling of the sugarcane. Other important questions regarding the operation of the pellet mill included how well the system could cope with the large volume of flue gas required for the dryer and whether the screen system could adequately separate the total amount of bagasse. After running the simulations, it was seen that control of all operating systems would be critical. Coordination among boiler operations, the sugar mill, and the pellet factory required a precise and immediate response to changing situations. Because many variables such as mill speed, steam generation, steam distribution, and the supply of flue gas for the dryer had to be adjusted and coordinated simultaneously, a computerized control system was necessary. An IBM System 1 computer was thus installed to monitor the system. Another potential problem was the screens, which had to separate up to 60 tons of bagasse per hour. Because the screens could easily become clogged or jammed in dealing with such a large volume of fiber, a novel system of rotating and adjusting them was devised.

After all anticipated problems were resolved, the final design was completed. For this design, bagasse exited from the sugar mill at 50 percent moisture. It was then conveyed to a large dryer, which was powered by the boiler's exhaust flue gases, and demoisturized to 35 percent. This demoisturized bagasse was conveyed to the screen, which separated the coarse from the fines. The coarse bagasse was fed to the boilers and the fine bagasse was put into another dryer, where its moisture content was reduced to 12–16 percent. Using high temperature and pressure, the mill then compressed the fiber into small pellets with 10 percent moisture. These pellets were cooled and stored for future use (see Figure 7.5).

When the drawings and specifications were completed, the world's first bagasse pellet factory had been designed. Although the process of extracting fiber under controlled temperature, pressure, and moisture conditions was the same as in the original design, significant modifications had been made. In essence, a fusion of engineering had taken place and an original technique for pelletizing wood fiber had been placed within the framework of sugar technology. In this way, a new integrated energy system had been created.

PHASE 2: SELECTION, APPROVAL, AND ACTIVATION

Selection Confirmed

The fuel that would be used by each system was examined in relationship to its energy output to confirm the new design.[33,34] For the existing system, 275,000 tons of bagasse with 50 percent moisture would be burned. Additionally, since a major goal of the company was to conclude a firm electrical contract with the utility, it was assumed that 47,000 barrels of fuel oil would also be required. As previously discussed, the oil would ensure a continuous 10 MW of power and would be used primarily during the three months when bagasse was unavailable. The 275,000 tons of bagasse would have a

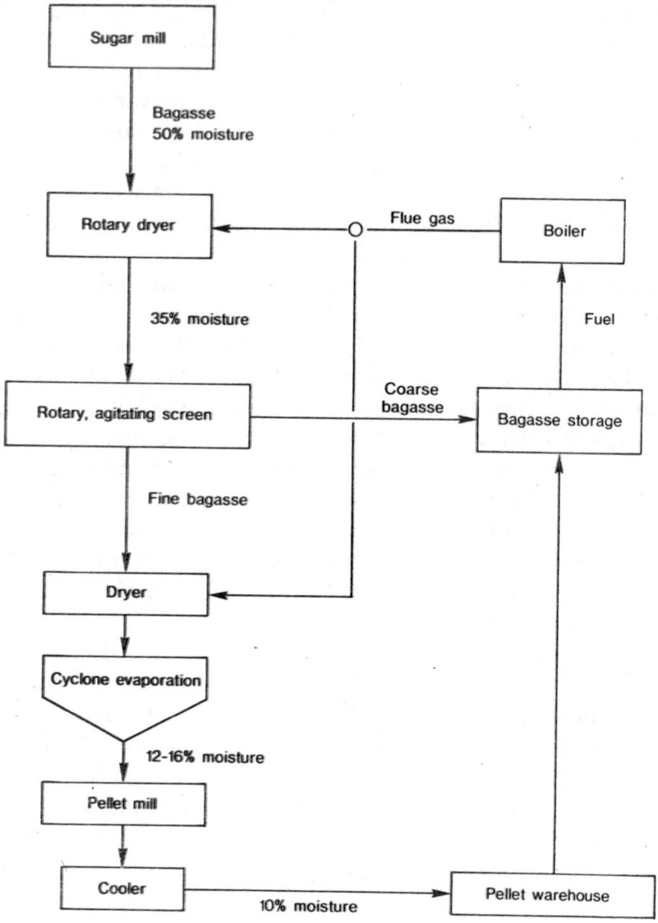

Figure 7.5. The bagasse pelletizing process. (Source: Davies Hamakua Sugar Company.)

heat value of 60 × 10^{10} Cal, and the fuel oil would have a value of 9 × 10^{10} Cal, for a combined total of about 69 × 10^{10} Cal.

The proposed system would also require 275,000 tons of bagasse but would use no fuel oil to fulfill the electrical contract. Instead, the new system would dry the 275,000 tons of bagasse with flue gases, leaving 234,000 tons with 35 percent moisture. Approximately 160,000 tons of this bagasse would be burned in the boiler, while the remaining 75,000 tons would be converted into 58,000 tons of pellets (only 54,000 tons of pellets would be burned). The heat value of the bagasse would be 44 × 10^{10} Cal, while that of the 54,000 tons of pellets would be 18 $\times$ 10^{10} Cal, for a combined total of 62 $\times$ 10^{10} Cal. It should be noted that the caloric value of bagasse increased by 30 percent when it was dried to 35 percent moisture. Consequently, although the 160,000 tons of bagasse represented only 58 percent of the initial total, it contained 75 percent of its energy.

The caloric value of the fuel for the existing system would still be higher than that for the proposed system. However, when actually used in the boiler, the combination of pellets and 35 percent moisture bagasse would produce more steam than the combination of fuel oil and 50 percent moisture bagasse. This would occur because the boiler would actually operate 10 percent more efficiently when burning the pellets and the 35 percent moisture bagasse. Boiler efficiency would increase from 71 to 81 percent.

When these factors were considered, the existing system, using 275,000 tons of bagasse and 47,000 barrels of fuel oil, would produce 49 $\times$ 10^{10} Cal of steam; the proposed system, using the same amount of bagasse but no fuel oil, would produce 50.49 $\times$ 10^{10} Cal of steam. In terms of electrical production, the existing system generated 104.59 million kWh/yr, while the proposed system generated 108.84 million kWh/yr. The additional electrical production would be used to power the pellet mill. In comparison to the existing system, then, the proposed system would eliminate the purchase of 47,000 barrels of fuel oil, produce more energy, and even create a surplus of pellets. Table 7.5 compares the two systems.

TABLE 7.5. NET ENERGY COMPARISON BETWEEN DAVIES' EXISTING SYSTEM AND PROPOSED SYSTEMS.

	EXISTING SYSTEM (WITHOUT PELLET MILL)	PROPOSED SYSTEM (WITH PELLET MILL)
Fuel requirement for operations		
Bagasse	275,000 tons at 50% moisture	165,000 tons at 35% moisture (100,000 tons for boiler; 65,000 tons for pellets)
Bagasse pellets	0	54,000 tons
Fuel oil	47,000 barrels	0
Total power generated		
Electricity	104.6 $\times$ 10^6 kWh	108.7 $\times$ 10^6 kWh
Steam	49.08 $\times$ 10^{10} Cal	50.49 $\times$ 10^{10} Cal
Power requirements		
For sugar processing	17.29 $\times$ 10^6 kWh	17.29 $\times$ 10^6 kWh
For pelletizing	0	4.15 $\times$ 10^6 kWh
For electric contract	87.3 $\times$ 10^6 kWh	87.3 $\times$ 10^6 kWh
Boiler efficiency	71.3%	80.9%

Approval

Approval to proceed with the pelletizer had been received from Davies' Hong Kong head offices in August 1979. Before funds were formally committed, however, the finances had to be coordinated within the company. Specifically, the cost of the pelletizer had to be put into the Davies capital expenditure plan for 1980 and formally reviewed at the Davies annual management meeting in December 1979. By the time of the meeting, fairly firm cost estimates for the pelletizer had been calculated. Based on the final design, the pellet mill would cost approximately US$1.9 million and the pellet warehouse would cost US$0.6 million, for a total of US$2.5 million.

Against this cost, the energy savings of the pelletizer to the entire system were projected to be 47,000 barrels of fuel oil annually, plus a surplus of 3200 tons of pellets. As of January 1980, the price of residual fuel was US$26 per barrel. A standardized corporate cash flow formula was used to determine the total savings of the system. When this calculation was completed, it was estimated that the pellet mill would have a payback period of three to four years. Based on the overall savings and the payback period, the pelletizer was incorporated into the capital expenditure plans of the company.

Another important development occurred during this period regarding the agreement between Bio-Solar and Davies. During the summer of 1979, Bio-Solar and Davies had negotiated an agreement whereby Davies received the master license for the Woodex process in the State of Hawaii. Any other company wishing to use the pelletizing process would have to work through Davies to build a pellet mill.

In late 1979, after examining the design for the bagasse pelletizer, the officials at Bio-Solar realized that the engineering was so different from the original wood pelletizer that it constituted a new technology, even though it used the same pelletizing principles. For this new generation of bagasse pelletizer, the personnel at Davies had the only real expertise. Bio-Solar thus decided to extend Davies' license to all areas in which Jardine-Matheson had offices, and also to use Davies personnel as consultants whenever a bagasse pelletizer was being considered.

PHASE 3: IMPLEMENTATION

By late 1979, the factory manager and general manager at Davies had completed their ordering for the pelletizing equipment, the screening system, and the dryer; by March 1980, construction of the pellet mill and installation of the equipment had begun. Like the design, all work in carrying out the project would be done in-house by Davies personnel. For example, the foundation work for the pellet factory and the warehouse would be done by Hilo Iron Works, a subsidiary of Davies; and the design, surveying, and all other engineering would be conducted by the sugar company's engineering group. The project would be coordinated by the factory manager and the general manager, while on-site supervision would be handled by the factory superintendant. Personnel required for the electrical work and other construction were recruited from the sugar company's factory division and constituted the project construction crew.

The use of company employees to carry out projects was a long-standing policy at Davies. In this regard, the management felt that they hired competent and capable people and that, as a routine matter, they should be used to modify or improve any of the existing operations. This policy was deemed especially appropriate for the pelletizer project. Company employees were well qualified; they were experts in sugar engineering and technology, as well as in power engineering as it related to the factory-generating system. Moreover, by building the pelletizer themselves, company personnel would strengthen their ability to repair, maintain, and modify the pellet system, which would be necessary in the future. Building the pelletizer with company personnel would thus be an investment in people. Finally, and most important, the pelletizer had been designed by company personnel especially for the situation in a sugar factory. Since no similar pelletizer had ever been designed, much less built, the management felt that company employees were most familiar with what had to be done and thus were most qualified to carry out the project.

Since construction of the pellet mill was still going on when this case was being written, it is possible only to describe the planned activities of the next two project phases according to the project schedule laid out by the factory manager and the general manager in early 1980. The pellet mill and warehouse would be built, installed, and fitted during the spring and summer of 1980. While construction was in progress, the personnel who would operate the mill were to be hired and trained. Three complete shifts, with three to a shift, were hired and began training in May 1980. By August, it was anticipated that all training would be completed and that the pelletizing system would be finished. During September, testing and debugging, as well as familiarization with the operation of the pellet factory, were scheduled. Finally, if all tasks were accomplished on schedule, the pellet factory would be in full operation by December 1980.

While project tasks were being accomplished, the general manager intended to complete negotiations with the utility company for a firm electrical contract. The management of the sugar company would guarantee to have 20 MW on line continuously from January through November; during December they would guarantee to have 8 MW on line. The sugar processing operations at the Honokaa factory would operate for nine months; during the three months when no bagasse would be available, the store of pellets would be used.

PHASE 4: EVALUATION

Both HCPC and Davies are major producers of electricity, with installed capacities of 23 and 15 MW, respectively. They became major energy producers at slightly different times and under different circumstances, which partly explains their different situations today. In concluding this case, it is useful to review some of the factors that led to their present situations.

HCPC arrived at its present position as a result of the need to replace aging equipment and to comply with pollution regulations, two events which occurred at about the same time and forced corporate officers to consider alternatives to their present operations. The policy decisions that brought the company to its present position were based on extensive and comprehensive studies that identified numerous options whose outcomes, though predicted, were still uncertain. The current situation, however, is at least as much the result of chance as it is of those decisions. There was, of course, no way to predict what pollution legislation would be passed in Congress or how it would be enforced by the EPA; nor could corporate decision makers predict the oil shortage and price increases resulting from OPEC policies or even that sugar prices would be so unstable during the mid-1970s. Thus, circumstances largely beyond the control of HCPC were responsible for the decision to produce power for sale, but that decision turned out to be a wise one.

The decision to produce and sell electricity was based on known and proven technology which the sugar companies had themselves developed over the years. As such, little or no research or development was necessary, and the only major technical questions that had to be answered dealt with the amount of bagasse available and the amount of power it would produce through various combinations of boilers and turbogenerators.

As for Davies, it is possible to say that, thus far, the modernization program is successful, having reduced the company's purchases of fuel oil while increasing its energy efficiency. It is not possible, however, to assess the program fully until the pelletizer is completed and the results of its operation are known. In conclusion, then, two factors stand out as the primary influences on Davies' present situation: the planning of energy improvements and the policy of relying on company personnel to execute all phases of the project.

The planning of energy improvements at Davies was guided by a policy of increasing energy conservation and energy efficiency for the sugar operations. This policy had two important effects in shaping the energy program. First, it maximized the energy potential of the plantation's existing resources. For example, the simultaneous milling process was instituted not so much because it increased commercial generating potential but because it made use of the plantation's trash, converting waste matter into fuel. Likewise, when it came time to select boilers and generators, the equipment chosen was matched to the amount of fiber the plantation actually produced. Only after energy conservation and efficiency were optimized at the plantation was the pelletizer built and a commercial electrical contract negotiated. The policy thus proved a reliable foundation of power operations that was appropriate to the sugar plantation's existing capabilities and resources.

The second major effect of Davies' energy conservation and efficiency policy was that it provided a long-range, systematic framework for analyzing the plantation's power operations. In essence, systematic, long-range planning was the only real way to increase energy conservation and efficiency. Given this framework, all energy-related activities had to demonstrate long-term benefits to the entire system. For example, when the pelletizer was analyzed, it was found acceptable because it increased the amount of net energy for the system by conserving fuel oil. Likewise, when an electrical contract was first considered, the necessity of importing oil to meet generating commitments was viewed as a long-term reduction in energy conservation. Although more power could be generated, the purchase of fuel oil would mean that energy was being wasted in transporting the fuel oil to the plantation. Additionally, with the long-term prospects of increasing oil prices, fuel oil would become an increasingly costly source of energy. Only after the pelletizer made it possible to eliminate imported fuel did negotiations for a firm electrical contract begin.

The use of company employees to design, plan, and carry out projects was also extremely influential in shaping the energy improvement program. By using their own personnel, the company was able to allow a fusion of ideas to take place in the projects. Whenever an energy project was planned, the employees were able to use their knowledge of the sugar process to integrate the new technology with existing operations. This resulted in an energy technology uniquely suited to sugar operations. In the pelletizer project, for example, company employees were able to eliminate the pellet mill's need for independent sources of heat and power by using flue gases from the boiler and electricity produced by plantation generators. Essential to this improvement was the employees' knowledge of sugar operations, which made it possible for them to take advantage of the sugar mill's existing resources.

The use of company employees also had the effect of making all energy improvements adjuncts of the sugar operations. Energy projects were designed not to produce the maximum amount of power with the highest efficiency but to optimize power production within the context of sugar operations. In essence, power generation was a component of the sugar process; as such, it had to be integrated into the factory system.

Several further points should be made concerning the use of company personnel and the planning process at Davies. First, Davies did take some risks in relying on company personnel to carry out projects. Their employees, although experts in sugar technology, would be adapting and modifying technologies with which they had limited experience. This was particularly true in expanding power operations, a process new to the employees. Nonetheless, Davies had enough confidence in the competence and ability of its employees to undertake the risks without the use of outside consultants. Second, the planning process at Davies benefitted from the experiences of HCPC. The problems HCPC encountered in generating electrical power and negotiating a contract did help Davies in their endeavors. Finally, Davies made many of their energy decisions after 1973. They were thus able to see the necessity for conserving energy and increasing self-sufficiency.

What lies in the future in energy production for the two companies? Their substantial capital investments in new equipment each year belie rumors that HCPC may close, as do the increasing prices of sugar and fuel oil on the world market. Brewer's* investment in the eucalyptus wood chip experiment, its proposal to produce ethanol from molasses, and the search for a cane variety that yields a higher Btu content all provide evidence that HCPC and Brewer are committed to biomass conversion.

Davies continues to be profitable as a sugar producer. It is, however, also continuing its policy of energy conservation and efficiency and is committed to maximizing its power-producing capabilities. One future plan being considered is to work out the problems of pelletizing at the Honokaa mill completely and then to build a pelletizer at the Laupahoehoe mill. When and if this plan succeeds, Davies will considerably increase its power capabilities, thus opening up the possibility of exploring biomass conversion as well.

EPILOGUE

The Davies Hamakua Sugar Company became the Hamakua Sugar Company, Inc., early in 1985. Linking the bagasse pelletizing process with the overall modernization program has resulted in a greatly improved energy efficiency and a greatly increased bagasse fuel production, with an anticipated dramatic reduction in the 47,000 barrels of imported oil deemed necessary during the nonharvesting period each year. The bagasse drying and pelletizing plant is functioning as an energy enhancing operation by absorbing flue or stack gases which were formerly lost to the atmosphere, and is thus also beneficial to environmental control.

---

*C. Brewer and Company, Ltd. is the largest producer of biomass energy in Hawaii, and HCPC is one of its sugar companies.

The plan to have 20 MW on line continuously for 10 to 11 months each year has not yet materialized. There are two reasons: (1) the failure of power-generating units in 1982 and 1983 and (2) the second driest year on record in 1984, resulting in a very light cane crop in 1985. However, expansion plans will approach the goal of 20 MW on line in the future, resulting in an increase of power sales of at least 50 percent. In addition, there is presently in construction an integrated system to produce a feedlot operation to fatten local ranchers' cattle, a slaughterhouse, and a rendering plant.

The diversification into cattle feed raises the universal issue of how to mix fuel and food as part of a company's decision to modernize in the interest of productivity in order to maintain or increase the level of employment. At this time, it is not known how this mix or integration will affect the production of electricity at Hamakua. The economics of biomass for cattle feed are becoming increasingly important in Hawaii. However, it is only one parameter in perhaps the most significant and controversial research issue to emerge from the cases and literature on biomass energy. That issue is the relationship between food and fuel—whether biomass should be directed into one of these channels or the other, or into an appropriate mix of both. Depending upon the complex set of variables present in each national or state setting, a series of arguments can be made both for and against either use of biomass resources. Some examples of statements in favor of biomass energy development over investment in food resources are the following:

1. A substantial amount of energy goes into food production—i.e., transportation, fertilizers, production equipment, and herbicides—all mainly petroleum based. Biomass would provide an energy tradeoff and replace much of the fossil fuels currently used, which have become increasingly costly since the 1973–1974 oil embargo.
2. Proper management of agricultural and silvicultural biomass production should and can occur to alleviate current use problems such as depletion of forests or leaching of soil nutrients. Double cropping, for example, can be applied to areas that are unproductive for parts of the year due to the seasonal character of the primary crop. Furthermore, existing technologies may be applied for increasing yields, superior genetic strains, and better fertilizers/irrigation.
3. Much of the feedstock used in many types of biomass production is total waste: i.e., human and animal excrement or agriwaste such as corn cobs, bagasse, and timber "slash." (The main issue of the food-versus-fuel debate, it should be noted, seems to be how biomass energy compares with food energy. The most questionable use of materials seems to be the use of high-quality grains such as wheat, corn, and others to produce alcohol fuels as a petroleum substitute.)

Equally persuasive statements have been made opposing the development of biomass energy at the expense of food products:

1. Heavy energy consumers such as the United States have high energy-per-capita consumption. Therefore, biomass energy production (specifically, alcohol fuels from grains) will "take food from the mouths of the hungry," with the need to fuel cars taking precedence over the export of grain to countries in need of aid.
2. In most countries, a general shift toward urbanization and increasing population has reduced the amount of timber and agricultural land available for large-scale biomass production.
3. Furthermore, most countries have exhausted their virgin land, and what now exists is suffering from nutrient depletion and erosion problems.
4. Marginal cropland (often suggested for biomass production) requires greater energy input than prime land, thereby making the concept of biomass fuel economically unfeasible.

These issues raise questions that defy simple answers and cannot be resolved here, but they must be seriously considered by policy makers and planners involved in making choices.

A recent workshop on biomass fuels, or biofuels,[35] in Honolulu recommends the establishment of an association (Hawaii Biomass Energy Association) to encourage or promote the use and development of biomass energy in the State of Hawaii. A basic element of the proposed research program is a biomass energy plantation development program. The author and his colleagues from the Asian-Pacific Region articulated the principle of "energy farming" in 1979–1980, the basic concept of which is covered in Appendix D.[36] With proper planning and management, an energy farm can be both productive and environmentally benign.

REFERENCES

1. *Weekly Compilation of Presidential Documents,* Vol. 15, No. 26, July 2, 1979, p. 1218.
2. *National Energy Plan II.* Washington, D.C.: U.S. Government Printing Office, 1979, pp. 7–9; II–30, 31.
3. Ibid., Appendix B, p. 3.
4. Ibid., p. VI–12. A quad is equal to 10^{15} Btu, or 1 quadrillion Btu.
5. Adapted from ibid., Appendix B, p. 3.
6. Ibid., p.5.
7. Energy Resources Coordinator, *1977 Annual Report.* Honolulu: Department of Planning and Economic Development, 1978, pp. 4–9.
8. *A Comprehensive Energy Program for Hawaii.* Honolulu: Senate Energy Natural Resource Committee, 1977, p. 2.

9. Department of Geography, University of Hawaii, *Atlas of Hawaii*. Honolulu: University of Hawaii Press, 1973, p. 143.
10. Vesy, Carl J. and Miller, Justus, *Energy Self-Sufficiency for the Island of Hawaii*. Honolulu: Hawaii Natural Energy Institute, 1979, p. 6.
11. Energy Resources Coordinator, *1978 Annual Report*. Honolulu: Department of Planning and Economic Development, 1979, p. 1.
12. *Atlas of Hawaii*, pp. 43, 18–19.
13. Vesy and Miller, *Energy Self-Sufficiency for the Island of Hawaii*, p. 6.
14. Inglett, Terris H., "Pepeekeo Sugar Factory Bagasse Used as Fuel in Boilers to Generate Electricity." Hilo Coast Processing Company, unpublished memo, November 1979, updated January 1980.
15. Stanford Research Institute International, *Energy Self-Sufficiency for the Big Island of Hawaii*, 2 vols. Menlo Park, Calif.: January 1980.
16. "Two Peas in a Pod," *Hawaii Business*, Vol. 21, January 1976, pp. 49–53.
17. "What's Hawaii's Ag Land Worth?" *Hawaii Business*, Vol. 22, March 1977, pp. 46–53.
18. "Big Isle Sugar Merger," *Honolulu Star Bulletin*, January 23, 1974, p. C10.
19. Bersch, John, personal communication, February 1980.
20. Bouvet, P. Ernest and Suzor, Norland L.C., "Biomass Conversion into Electrical Energy at Laupahoehoe and Honokaa Sugar Companies," unpublished paper, January 24, 1979, p. 1.
21. This figure is based on Bouvet and Suzor, "Biomass Conversion."
22. Suzor, Norland, personal communication, April 8, 1980.
23. "Ernest Bouvet's Lament," *Hawaii Business*, Vol. 24, November 1978, pp. 55–56.
24. Suzor, Norland, personal communication, April 8, 1980.
25. Public Utilities Commission data.
26. Hawaii Electric Light Company power engineer, personal communication, April 8, 1980.
27. Suzor, Norland, personal communication, April 8, 1980.
28. Bouvet, P. Ernest and Suzor, Norland L.C., "Pelletizing Bagasse for Fuel," paper presented at a meeting of the American Society of Agricultural Engineers, Hilo, Hawaii, March 19–29, 1980.
29. "Woodex: The Refined Biomass Fuel." Eugene, Ore.: Bio-Solar Research and Development Corp., n.d.
30. "Woodex," Theo H. Davies Co., Honolulu: mimeo, n.d., p.1.
31. Bouvet and Suzor, "Biomass Conversion," exhibits 1 and 2, pages unnumbered.
32. Bouvet and Suzor, "Pelletizing Bagasse," p. 10.
33. Calculations are based on ibid. and on Bio-Solar Research and Development Corp., "Woodex."
34. Suzor, Norland, personal communication, September 26, 1979.
35. Hawaii Natural Energy Institute, *Pacific Basin Biofuel Workshop Report*, Vol. 1. Honolulu: November 1984.
36. Goodman, Louis J. and Love, Ralph N., eds. *Biomass Energy Projects: Planning and Management*. New York: Pergamon Press, 1981.

CHAPTER 8

The Trans-Alaska Pipeline System

The Trans-Alaska Pipeline System case history* is one of 30 cases researched and published by the East-West Center during the period 1977–1982 with partial support from an Exxon Education Foundation grant. The sources used for this case are those generally available to the public, including special evaluative reports following completion of construction. TAPS is a complex project with many legal challenges that delayed the start of construction for over three years. The case provides many useful lessons, as analyzed in the Evaluation and in Chapter 9.

BACKGROUND OF THE PROJECT

The Trans-Alaska Pipeline System (TAPS) carries crude oil from Prudhoe Bay on the North Slope to Port Valdez on the Gulf of Alaska. Massive design and construction problems were encountered in all components of the system: the 800 mi of pipeline, the marine terminal, and the pump stations.

Had this project been undertaken in a more accessible location, the process of planning, design, construction, and implementation might have been far simpler.† The nature of Alaska itself—its location, difficult terrain, and harsh climate—created massive design and construction problems. Its fish, coastal mammals, and other wildlife represented unique commercial and ecological resources which, to some extent, would be threatened by oil development. The aesthetic values of Alaska and its virtually unspoiled natural environment focused the attention of environmentalists on the state. Other significant factors included the world's energy supply-and-demand relationships, the civil rights movement in the United States, a claims movement among indigenous groups in Alaska, and the socioeconomic characteristics of the state.

Of direct interest to this discussion is the project's environment—its physical, climatic, and natural resources.

---

*Adapted from *The Trans-Alaska Pipeline*, a case history by George Geistauts and Vern Hauck (edited by L.J. Goodman and R.N. Love), Honolulu: East-West Center, Resource Systems Institute, 1979.

†This does not suggest that later planning and design problems could have been eliminated.

Physical Environment

The State of Alaska includes 586,000 mi^2 (1,517,740 km^2)—over 375 million acres of land and inland water areas. Located in a semipolar region, 83 percent of it lying north of the 60th parallel and 27 percent north of the Arctic Circle, Alaska is far removed from the U.S. mainland.

Geographical features such as mountain ranges divide Alaska into several major regions, each with distinct geographic, climatological, and ecological features.

The region north of the Brooks Range (the North Slope) has a temperature range from 90°F to less than −60°F (32 to −51°C), with a mean annual temperature of 10–20°F (−12 to −7°C). Because of its very low precipitation, this area is referred to as an "arctic desert," even though the presence of permafrost (a condition in which, because of the short summer season, only the surface ground melts; underneath, the ground remains permanently frozen) prevents water from being absorbed into the ground and creates an ideal nesting area for waterfowl. The interior area south of the Brooks Range and north of the Alaska Range [which includes Mount McKinley—at 20,320 ft (6195 m) the highest point in North America] has greater temperature extremes, ranging from over 100°F to less than −70°F (38 to −57°C) and greater precipitation. The massive Yukon River winds its way through this region from its origins in Canada to the Bering Sea. This area includes Fairbanks, the state's second largest city.

The area south of the Alaska Range represents a transition to a maritime climate along the Gulf of Alaska's shoreline. Precipitation in this region is much higher and temperature changes are more moderate. All terminal sites which received serious consideration from TAPS were located in this maritime climate. Anchorage, the state's largest city, is located in this transition zone.

The state contains the 16 tallest mountains in the United States, more than 120 million acres of lakes, approximately 11 million acres of glaciers, and 10,000 streams and rivers. From 40 to 90 rivers are considered by different sources to have recreational and wilderness values of national interest. Alaska has over 47,000 mi (75,639 km) of tidal ocean shoreline.

Attracted by the scenery, camping, fishing, and hunting, visitors to Alaska enjoy the opportunity to experience the wilderness. The value of these resources cannot be measured solely in terms of revenue from this major industry in Alaska. The recreational opportunities and the wilderness experience are also very important to Alaskans themselves, since many moved to the state because of its wilderness character.

Alaska contains a number of minerals of national interest, including antimony, asbestos, chromium, copper, gold, iron, lead, and silver. Gold mining, an Alaska tradition, was responsible for the state's prosperity at the turn of the century, but gold now is produced on a relatively small scale.

Alaska's energy-related resources include coal, uranium, a large number of hydroelectric sites, and significant geothermal potential. The most commercially exploitable resources are oil and gas. The TAPS could ultimately be expected to serve not only the Prudhoe Bay field but other northern fields as well, including offshore fields in that region.

Timber is a major harvestable resource in southeast Alaska but has minor commercial significance elsewhere. Finally, Alaska has been estimated to have great agricultural potential, even though the infrastructure to exploit it is not present and agricultural activities are of minor importance.

Wildlife

Because Alaska is a vast storehouse of natural resources, the state became a focal point in the battle between a development-oriented industry and environmentalists. Of particular significance to environmentalists (as well as indigenous Alaskans, fishermen, and others who utilized them for profit or for recreation) are resources such as fish, birds, and marine as well as terrestrial mammals, and a number of rare or endangered species (see Figure 8.1). Both pipeline and tankers would pass close to or through the habitats of much of this wildlife. While the oil companies assured everyone that environmental damage would be minimal, many of those outside the industry remained skeptical.

Traditionally, the primary renewable resource in Alaska has been fish. The salmon fishery, for example, is the major source of employment for many coastal communities. Additional coastal fishing resources include halibut, king crab, and shrimp. Inland fisheries are primarily sport oriented, although a number of rural-area residents depend on inland fish stocks for subsistence. An oil spill accident along the coastline or a massive leak from a pipeline in the interior, then, could endanger a substantial economic and recreational resource.

Alaska provides 70 million acres (28,329,000 hectares) of the breeding habitat for 20 percent of all North American waterfowl (see Figure 8.1), which are an important source of food to Alaskans and an important game for recreational hunters throughout the United States. Alaska's coastline provides a feeding and breeding habitat for 27 species of marine mammals, including whales, walrus, seals, sea lions, and sea otters.

Alaska also is the home of polar bears, caribou, moose, black and brown bears, sheep, musk oxen, and many small fur bearers. Polar bears (which were declining alarmingly just a few years ago, but which have since recovered under a hunting prohibition) are found along the northern and northwestern Arctic coast. Caribou are found throughout most of the state, especially in the Arctic areas. It was felt that the caribou's migration pattern might be altered by the disruption caused by the pipeline construction or

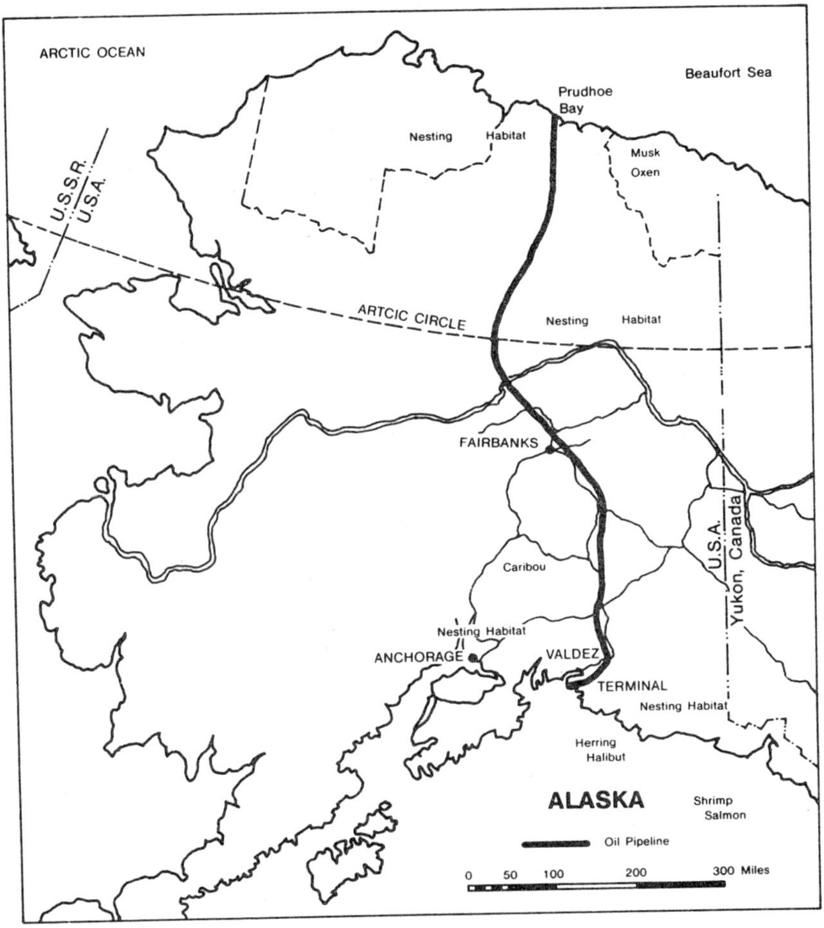

Figure 8.1. TAPS route, showing the physical environment and wildlife of Alaska. (Source: Compiled by the East-West Resource Systems Institute staff.)

even by its mere presence. Such a disruption might mean a drastic reduction in herd size.

PHASE 1: PLANNING, APPRAISAL AND DESIGN

Identification and Formulation

Early in 1968, the Atlantic-Richfield Company (ARCO), which had been engaged in exploratory drilling on Alaska's North Slope, announced that its well had encountered a substantial flow of gas at 8500 ft (2591 m). Further exploratory drilling confirmed that significant amounts of oil and gas were indeed present, and in a few months it became clear that reserves in the area represented the largest oil field ever discovered in the United States. The site of the discovery, the Prudhoe Bay region on Alaska's Arctic Ocean coastline, is a remote area which was then accessible year round only by air and only briefly during the summer by ships. The magnitude of the field clearly made it a priority for development to the production stage but, just as clearly, a major transportation system would have to be constructed before any oil could be sent to market.

The system ultimately chosen was a pipeline: an 800-mi (1287-km) link from the Arctic coast to the ice-free port of Valdez on the Gulf of Alaska. In Valdez, oil would be shipped by tankers to refineries or other pipelines on the U.S. West Coast. The oil industry companies* proudly proclaim that the Alaska Pipeline turned out to be "the most expensive privately-financed construction project in history," and for many, it represents a triumph of technology and engineering over a hostile environment.

The pipeline/tanker system decision resulted from experience with arctic climatic conditions and related problems such as the need for special reinforced tankers with icebreaking capabilities in the Northwest Passage—channels between the Canadian mainland and the large islands. Shipping west is also difficult and dangerous, and would only be feasible during a brief period in late summer. By comparison, a pipeline appeared to present fewer problems. In addition, Valdez is the most northerly ice-free port in Alaska, thereby providing the shortest possible pipeline route from the North Slope. Water depths within the port are more than adequate for the largest tankers afloat, and the port has good wind protection from surrounding mountain ranges. Furthermore, no native settlements exist within the area proposed for the terminal.[1] Figure 8.1 shows the pipeline route superimposed on a map illustrating the physical environment and wildlife habitats.

Preliminary Design: Feasibility Studies

The preliminary route selection was based on a combination of soil borings, soil temperature readings, air temperature data, geological studies, and aerial photographic interpretations. A right-of-way 100 ft in width was recommended for construction purposes for both pipeline excavation and haul road construction.

A formal application was filed by TAPS with the Office of the State Director, Bureau of Land Management, Anchorage, on June 6, 1969, for the

*In October 1968, ARCO, Humble, and British Petroleum formed the Trans-Alaska Pipeline System (TAPS) as an unincorporated joint venture.

pipeline right-of-way. The application included the need for 11 pumping station easements, each 1200 by 1600 ft. Air strips of approximately 200 by 5000 ft were requested for stations 3 and 4. The rationale for the preliminary design selection is best summarized in the following excerpts from the application:

> One of the prime considerations in selecting the route applied for herein was an in-depth analysis of soil conditions to insure a pipeline location providing maximum physical stability, maximum burial of the pipeline, and minimum disturbance of the natural environment. Extensive field examination in conjunction with ground-proofed aerial photographic interpretation was used in plotting the pipeline and construction road right-of-way alignment.[2]
>
> There are numerous special studies in progress to determine the best method of handling the Ecological, Archaeological and Conservation problems that will be encountered during and after the construction of the pipeline and road. Results of these studies will establish procedures to be used to meet all requirements of minimum changes to the terrain.[3]

In summary, the TAPS proposal was for a 48-in (122-cm) diameter hot-oil pipeline which would be buried for over 90 percent of its 800-mi (1287-km) length. The initial capacity would be 500,000 barrels a day, rising in stages to 2 million barrels a day. Approximately 641 mi (1031 km) of the line would be across federal lands, with completion expected sometime in 1972. The application also requested a right-of-way and permit to build a haul road of slightly less than 400 mi (644 km) to support construction.

At this time, a "land freeze" moratorium on the disposition of federal lands in Alaska pending resolution of indigenous Alaskans' claims was in effect, but the TAPS owners nevertheless hoped for quick approval. In their view, permits would be granted in July 1969, and construction would follow shortly thereafter. TAPS had already made a substantial financial commitment to the pipeline by ordering 500,000 tons of 48-in. (122-cm) pipe for US$100 million from three Japanese companies earlier in the year. An additional US$30 million order had also been placed for several of the giant pumps required to move the oil. ARCO's commitment already included a decision to build a new refinery at Cherry Point, Washington, to handle North Slope crude oil. (In September 1969, ARCO placed an order with the Bethlehem Steel Company for three new 120,000 dead weight ton tankers.)

Prior to approval of the pipeline system and route, a series of debates took place between supporters and opponents in 1968 and 1969. Those who supported the project included:

1. The oil industry, which had a resource but no way to reach a market.
2. The State of Alaska, particularly through its government, which

would derive substantial economic benefits from royal revenues and severance taxes (the state, in effect, owns 25 percent of Prudhoe Bay oil).
3. Local state businesses and governments, which would benefit from increased economic activity and an increased tax base.
4. Economically and defense-oriented federal government agencies, for whom economic growth, reduced balance-of-payments deficits, and energy independence were of prime importance.

Those who opposed the design choice included:

1. The environmentalists, who feared irreparable damage to the environment from both the TAPS project and subsequent development.
2. Federal agencies charged with preserving environmental quality.
3. Some members of Congress, who either supported environmentalists or who preferred to have the oil diverted to the interior United States, primarily the Midwest.
4. The indigenous Alaskans, who did not want to have land they were in the process of claiming crossed by a pipeline prior to the establishment of their claims.
5. Some Canadians, who either favored a Canadian route on economic grounds or felt that tankers posed a severe ecological hazard to Canada's western coastline.
6. Some Alaskan fishermen and a number of other residents who preferred a simple, nonindustrialized lifestyle.

These delineations are, of course, oversimplified: Some environmentally concerned individuals also work in the oil industry, and not everyone in Alaska's state government favored the pipeline. The desires of opponents also differed: Some extreme environmentalists wanted to stop the project totally, while most others wanted to impose environment-preserving modifications.

Essentially, five basic alternatives emerged, apart from not developing the oil field at all. The alternatives were:

1. The TAPS proposal of a combined system of pipeline and tankers, which would deliver oil to the U.S. West Coast.
2. A longer tanker route directly from Prudhoe, around Point Barrow, to the West Coast.
3. A sea route of almost 5,000 mi (8045 km) from Prudhoe through the Northwest Passage to the Northeast.
4. A railroad through Canada to the Midwest.
5. A trans-Canada pipeline to the Midwest.

The alternatives which received most attention were the one across the northern portion of Alaska to the Canadian border, and from there through Canada, to link up with existing pipelines leading into either the midwestern or western states (alternative 5) and the original TAPS proposal (alternative 1).

Additional environmental feasibility studies, debates, and delays resulted when the National Environmental Policy Act of 1969 (NEPA) was approved on January 1, 1970. NEPA declared a national policy of encouraging productive and enjoyable harmony between man and his environment by promoting efforts to prevent or eliminate damage to the environment, as well as stimulating the health and welfare of man. An Environmental Quality Council was created to analyze environmental trends, appraise programs, and recommend national policies promoting improvement in the quality of the environment. Section 102 of the act outlined the specific requirements that any proposed action, including the pipeline project, would have to meet in terms delineating the environmental impact and providing for public comment. The act imposed environmental impact statement (EIS) requirements on all agencies and departments, including the Department of the Interior. Part C of Section 102 specifically required identification of adverse environmental impacts, consideration of alternatives, and public distribution of these documents.

Pipeline System Design

To ensure that TAPS did comply with the new standards of environmental integrity and to ensure that the project could cope with the arctic environment, technical solutions representing new pipeline technology had to be developed. The principal technical problems to be overcome were:

1. Insulating the permafrost from the hot oil in order to keep the permafrost stable so that the pipeline would not settle or sink and rupture.
2. Providing enough flexibility in the line to handle thermal expansion as the hot oil started to move.
3. Providing a design to resist rupture in case of a severe earthquake.
4. Providing rupture detection systems so that, in case of rupture, the line could be shut down before much oil spilled.
5. Providing rupture control by means of oil containment provisions at the pump stations and the terminal.
6. Reducing air emissions of hydrocarbons at the terminal to preserve ambient air quality.
7. Preventing minor oil leaks or spills in the waters of Port Valdez and providing rapid cleanup capability if such spills occurred.

8. Providing collision avoidance systems in Port Valdez, particularly in the approaches to Valdez Narrows, to prevent tanker collisions.
9. Providing game crossings along the pipeline route without disrupting traditional game migration patterns.

Figures 8.2 through 8.4 summarize the essential features of technical design. The solutions to technical design problems include the following:

1. Where the pipeline is buried in permafrost, the line is insulated and the permafrost is refrigerated by pumping cold brine through buried pipes (Figure 8.2).
2. Approximately half of the pipeline is buried in stable soils, with no refrigeration required (Figure 8.2).
3. Expansion due to the passage of heated oil through aboveground pipe is compensated for by building the pipe in a zigzag configuration. This converts expansion into sideways movement (Figure 8.3).
4. With the exception of strategically placed fixed anchor supports (Figures 8.2 and 8.3), the aboveground portion of the pipe is attached to a sliding shoe, which is free to move over a limited horizontal range. This allows adjustment both for thermal expansion and for movement due to earthquake activity (Figure 8.2).
5. Where required, aboveground vertical support members (VSM) are designed with thermal radiation devices to prevent heat transfer to the permafrost (Figure 8.2).
6. All tanks where bulk oil is stored are surrounded by dikes to contain any spills in case of rupture.
7. Ballast water is pumped to a settling and filtration system for purification before being discharged into the sea.
8. A vapor recovery system at the terminal prevents oil vapors from escaping into the atmosphere (Figure 8.4).
9. Computer-aided centralized control of the system is provided by a master control station in Valdez.
10. Pressure deviations and flow variations are monitored to detect any ruptures or leaks in the line. Valve shutdown will contain most of the oil within the pipeline, and cleanup crews are on standby to deal with spills. The whole line can be shut down in 10 minutes. Check valves prevent reverse flow.
11. The terminal facility is designed to withstand an earthquake registering 8.5 on the Richter scale. Storage tanks are surrounded by dikes.
12. Stringent enforcement of the "rules of the road" by the Coast Guard in the Valdez Narrows and its approaches, utilizing control concepts analogous to air traffic control, is designed to minimize the possibility of grounding or collision.

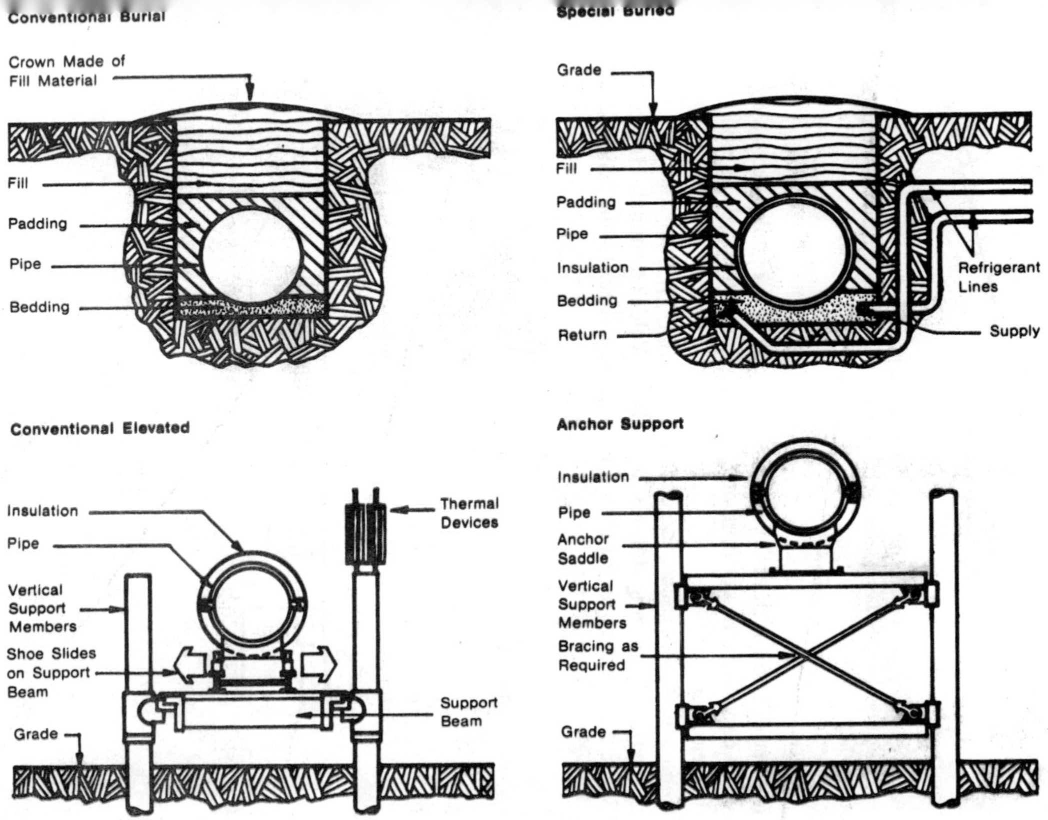

Figure 8.2. Construction modes. (Source: Alyeska Pipeline Service Company, *Summary Project Description of the Trans Alaska Pipeline System,* Anchorage, September 1974.)

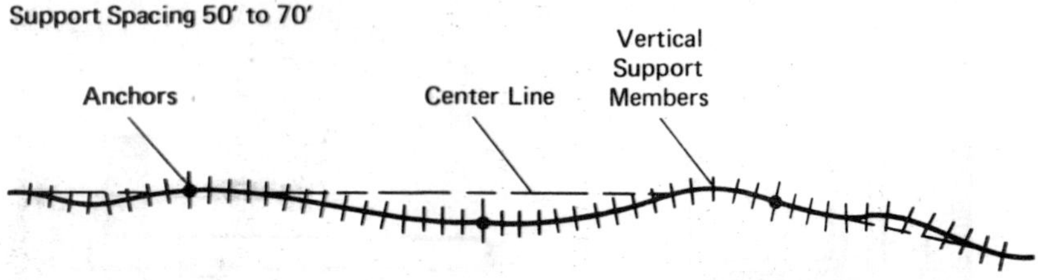

Figure 8.3. Typical zigzag configuration of the pipeline. (Source: Alyeska Pipeline Service Company, *Summary Project Description of the Trans Alaska Pipeline System,* Anchorage, September 1974.)

A number of these technical solutions represent new pipeline technology required to cope with the arctic environment and new standards of environmental integrity.

In summary, TAPS called for construction of (1) a haul road, (2) the pipeline itself, (3) pumping stations, and (4) the Valdez terminal. However, was this the total system required to transport oil and gas to markets? Actu-

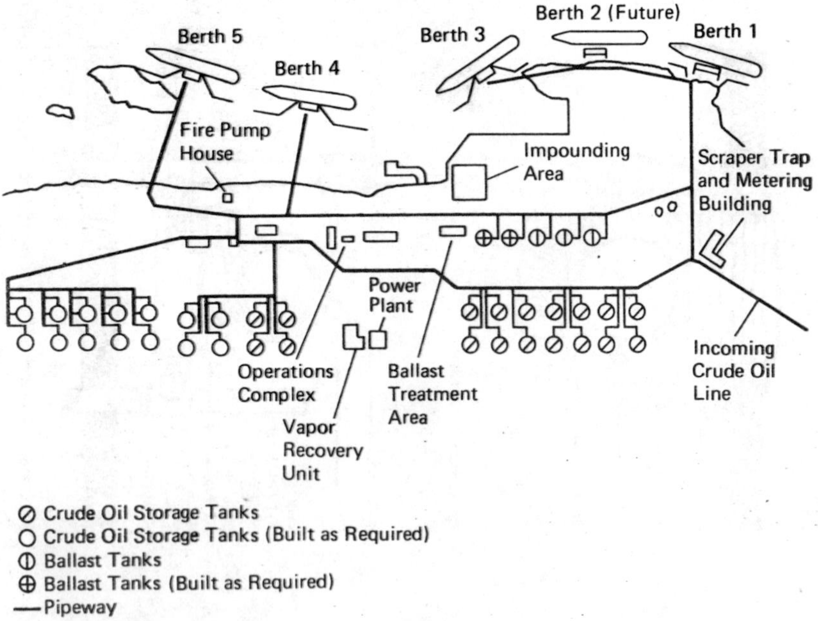

Figure 8.4. Valdez terminal, maximum development. (Source: Alyeska Pipeline Service Company, *Summary Project Description of the Trans Alaska Pipeline System*, Anchorage, September 1974.)

ally, only part of the problem was solved. The West Coast could only absorb a limited amount of Alaskan crude oil for its own use, and the high sulfur content of Alaskan oil made it difficult to refine in the facilities existing in that region. But shipping oil east from the West Coast would require connections to the pipeline systems in the interior of the United States.

PHASE 2: SELECTION, APPROVAL, AND ACTIVATION

Selection

Evaluation of the alternatives and final selection did not take place as an orderly sequence of analysis and review under the supervision of any single agency or individual. The process that took place is best described as adversary rather than as analytic. Each group attempted to advance its views through a combination of purportedly objective studies designed to reinforce its arguments, public relations efforts, congressional lobbying, and legal test actions.

The actions of the Interior Department, which apparently favored the TAPS concept throughout the process, were designed to issue a permit as soon as possible, provided that the permit could be linked to a framework which would ensure a certain amount of protection for both the environment and the claims of indigenous Alaskans. The latter objective was met by passage of the Alaska Native Claims Settlement Act (ANCSA) in 1971. The Interior Department's way of ensuring environmental protection was to link the permit to a set of contractual stipulations which would govern construction, and adherence to which would be enforced by an on-the-scene "authorized officer" representing the department. The department also started to study a 12-mi-wide transportation corridor along the proposed route, which would allow for some flexibility in response to conditions encountered during actual construction.

Despite the favorable attitude of the Interior Department, officially authorized construction in 1969 was relatively minor. Preliminary work on ground clearing at the Valdez terminal site was authorized by the Forest Service (the site lay in the Chugach National Forest). A short segment of the haul road connecting the south bank of the Yukon River to the end of the state highway system was authorized by the Interior Department.

The environmentalists adopted a number of tactics designed to prevent or slow down approval. Public relations tactics depended primarily on the use of the media to acquaint Americans with the potential dangers of the project and to mobilize citizen pressure on Congress. Lobbying and direct testimony at each of the several congressional hearings was used to try to influence members of Congress directly. However, the most effective delaying tactic for the environmentalists turned out to be the court suit.

In January 1970, the Secretary of the Interior issued a Public Land Order establishing a transportation corridor, which would presumably have been followed by the appropriate permits for the pipeline itself. Opponents and critics of the pipeline turned to the courts. In March and April 1970, several suits were filed in the federal courts by both indigenous Alaskan groups and environmental organizations. The three basic sources of legal grounds for challenging the TAPS plan were:

1. The 1920 Mineral Leasing Act, which specified that a pipeline right-of-way should consist of the ground necessary for the width of the pipe plus 25 ft (8 m) on either side. TAPS required a 100-ft (30-m) right-of-way. The Mineral Leasing Act provided a legal basis for those opposed to the pipeline to delay it through court challenge. (In reality, the extra width presented no problem in terms of land availability, but it did provide the technical grounds for challenge.)
2. The Alaska land freeze brought about by the claims of indigenous residents. Resolution of those claims was required before a permit would be granted.
3. NEPA, which became the primary basis for legal challenge to TAPS plans.

In April 1970, three environmentalist groups (the Wilderness Society, the Environmental Defense Fund, and the Friends of the Earth) petitioned in court to bar issuance of permits under provisions of NEPA and the Mineral Leasing Act. Initial arguments based on NEPA contended that an EIS had not been prepared, as required by law, and that opportunities for public input had not been sufficient. When the courts finally refused to accept the environmentalists' contention of noncompliance with NEPA, the environmentalists returned to the right-of-way width issue as a legal basis of argument. On this issue the courts upheld their position, and the Interior Department was not allowed to issue the requisite permits. The Trans-Alaska Pipeline Authorization Act finally removed this barrier.

Indigenous Alaskan groups at first had thought that the TAPS project would offer them jobs, and several villages had signed waivers allowing TAPS to cross the lands they were in the process of claiming in return for a promise of jobs on the project. However, when TAPS announced the first awards of contracts, indigenous businesses failed to get even a single contract and disillusionment set in. The villages withdrew the waivers and instituted a law suit. For a period of time the environmentalists and indigenous residents were allies, but as the oil company lobbyists interceded on behalf of interests in Congress, the alliance weakened. The passage of ANCSA destroyed the basis for large-scale indigenous opposition, while the provision of the act which created profit-seeking indigenous regional corporations also created a powerful incentive for indigenous residents to support economic growth and development in Alaska. Over a period of time, local residents would assume ownership of 44 million acres of land, some of which would have oil and gas potential. A pipeline would also be required to transport their oil. ANCSA also removed the original basis for the land freeze in Alaska.

During this period of opposition and debate, TAPS [which was reorganized and incorporated as the Alyeska Pipeline Service Company (Alyeska) in 1970] had relatively little control of events and was forced into essentially a position of reaction. *The original design plan had to be modified from one in which about 95 percent of the pipeline would be buried to one in which only about half would be buried.* Increasingly tighter stipulations proposed by the Interior Department further restricted Alyeska's freedom of choice in design and construction practices.

The State of Alaska suggested its own solutions: first, by proposing to build the haul road itself, and second, by suggesting that the state take over the pipeline's financing in an effort to increase the state's own assets. Both concepts were rejected by Alyeska, which was now estimating project costs at US$3 billion or more.

Major discussion about basic alternatives quickly began to focus on the two fundamental possibilities: the TAPS proposal and the trans-Canada alternative. Although a complete tanker system and a railroad system continued to be advocated by some, these systems never generated sufficient support to become serious contenders. Transportation of oil directly by tanker from the North Slope presented the massive problems previously outlined. Although a basic decision to build a pipeline had already been reached by the oil companies, the experimental voyages of the specially constructed *S.S. Manhattan* are illustrative of the problems with a tanker system. The *Manhattan* was a reinforced tanker which Humble leased for a test voyage from the East Coast to Prudhoe Bay through the Northwest Passage. Accompanied by an icebreaker, the *Manhattan* experienced much difficulty with the ice. Despite its special construction, it had to be freed from the ice on several occasions, and on the voyage back from Prudhoe, a projection of ice ripped a long gash in the hull.

Transportation by railroad would involve immense construction expense, with many of the environmental problems associated with a pipeline, as well as significant operating costs. The oil companies had briefly considered a railroad but quickly rejected this concept. (An Interstate Commerce Commission report in 1969 showed that the average railroad charge per ton-mile was five times as high as that for pipelines.) A variety of studies examined the cost and environmental characteristics of most major alternatives. Because each had to make economic and other assumptions in the analysis, the results were often contradictory and open to criticism.

Environmental Concerns

The oil companies were surprised that permits were not granted rapidly. After all, the economic benefits to the nation and to Alaska of developing the North Slope oil were obvious. While there would be some environmental damage as a result of construction, the oil companies were prepared to take steps they considered reasonable to minimize it. Besides, the damage would be limited to a very tiny proportion (about 0.01 percent) of Alaska. Hardly anyone lived there. In many of the foreign countries where oil companies operated, the authority for making this kind of decision would be clear and a rapid response could be expected. Even in the United States, such decisions in the past had been made in a relatively straightforward manner.

TAPS, however, had underestimated the complexity of the situation. Environmentalists and many others were not ready to accept TAPS' assurances that good pipeline design would automatically mean minimum environmental damage or to agree that all questions surrounding the TAPS project should be project specific. The TAPS proposal would be attacked as bad design, as environmentally undesirable, and as socially disruptive. The resulting debate would take four years.[4]

Opposition from the environmental movement became especially strong when those who placed a high value on environmental protection and preservation became aware of the proposed pipeline and its basic design.

In the view of environmentalists, major damage to the environment (both an aesthetic heritage and the basis for subsistence economy for rural people) could occur through at least four distinct scenarios. *First*, poor construction practices and carelessness could pollute and scar the environment along the pipeline corridor. Because of Alaska's short growing season and the delicate character of the tundra in permafrost areas, recovery from local environmental damage would be a slow process at best. Stream siltation during construction and any oil spills that might occur could destroy the spawning grounds of anadromous fish. *Second*, since the proposed design called for burying the hot oil line in most areas where it crossed permafrost, the line would then be inadequately supported and subject to buckling or rupture. *Third*, the route of the line crossed areas of severe earthquake activity, and the terminus would be located in an area which had experienced a massive earthquake (8.5 on the Richter scale) in 1964. Thus, a severe earthquake which could rupture the line and the storage tanks could cause a massive oil spill. *Finally*, the oil would be transported from the terminal at Valdez to the U.S. West Coast in large supertankers. En route the tankers would have to pass through several narrow channels where the possibility of grounding or collision, again in the view of the environmentalists, would be great.

Prediction of impacts, however, requires both an adequate data base and appropriate evaluative methodology to apply to that data base. Figure 8.5 is a schema of a partial indication of the complexity of impact analysis. For a system large enough to deliver North Alaskan oil, and for one which would operate in the difficult but fragile arctic environment, proper impact evaluation would apparently be a lengthy process. Yet by late summer 1968—only a few weeks after the full extent of the Prudhoe Bay field could be estimated—oil men were already engaged in defining specifics for a pipeline across Alaska to a tidewater port on its coast.

To critics, it appeared that the TAPS concept had been chosen prematurely, without adequate consideration of alternatives, and that no permit should be granted until all alternatives had been fully investigated. The answers to the North Slope Task Force seemed to confirm that the design was based on partial data and that the design was itself incomplete. TAPS executives, however, pointed out that pipelines (unlike most projects) could be designed and built sequentially. Despite criticism from environmentalists, economists, and others concerned with both oil and impact, the oil companies (which could finance such a massive project) held unflinchingly to their first choice.

Approval

Over a period of time, the courts had considered the arguments of those opposing the pipeline and the counterarguments of those favoring it. On August 15, 1972, District Court Judge George L. Hart ruled that the legal requirements of NEPA had been met and that the Interior Department could deal with the right-of-way width problem by issuing special land use permits. However, an appeals court reversed that ruling because of the Interior Department's lack of authority to issue special permits. The U.S. Supreme Court then refused to review the appeals court decision. Thus, in 1973, the issue was back in Congress, which now alone had the power, in effect, to authorize the pipeline through special legislation.

Indications of an energy crisis were by now apparent to many in Congress. A number of bills were introduced by members, and the hearings process started once again. As an acceptable bill began to evolve, events in the Mideast dramatized the seriousness of the energy problem for the United States. The Trans-Alaska Pipeline Authorization Act of 1973 passed overwhelmingly in both houses of Congress. The way was clear for the issuance of the required permits, but the estimated cost of the pipeline had now climbed past $4 billion. In addition, the act provided for formal public agency involvement which would influence project construction, as noted in the Supervision and Control Task.

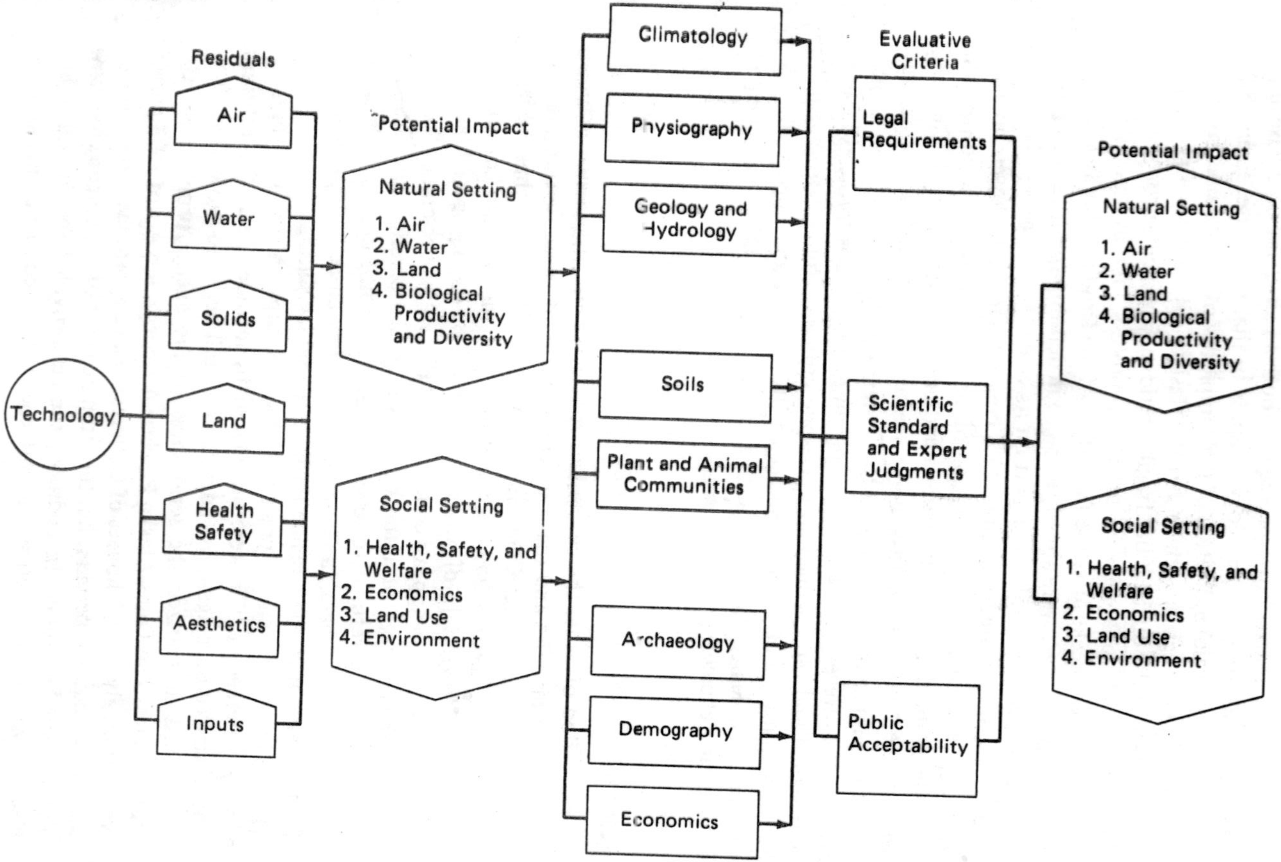

Figure 8.5. Conceptual diagram of impact analysis. (Source: Adapted from *Energy Alternatives: A Comparative Analysis*, prepared for the Council on Environmental Quality by the Science and Public Policy Program, University of Oklahoma, Norman, 1975.)

The Trans-Alaska Pipeline Authorization Act effectively settled the issue of legal authority for granting the required construction permits. It also defined the authority of the Interior Department regarding oversight and imposed certain requirements and limitations upon the owner companies and Alyeska.

The act set a 60-day limitation for legal challenges to be made in court following the granting of a right-of-way permit; as it turned out, no new challenges were filed. The act also required oil transported through the pipeline to be shipped to the rest of the United States, and any foreign shipments allowed only if the President designated them in the national interest.

Results of the Trans-Alaska Pipeline Authorization Act

1. Congress found the trans-Alaska pipeline to be the most viable alternative and its earliest possible construction to be in the national interest.
2. Congress authorized prompt construction of the pipeline and directed the Secretary of the Interior and other appropriate federal agencies to administer various authorizations; the secretary also was given power to provide greater environmental protection by modifying the route during construction.
3. Limits on further legal challenge were indicated; construction and operating activities could not be challenged under NEPA.
4. Liability for damages
   a) Holders of the right-of-way would be liable, on a no-fault basis, for damages along or near the right-of-way except for damages caused by an act of war or by U.S. government negligence or by the damaged party. No-fault liability would be limited to US$50 million for any one incident and would be in proportion to ownership interest; liability for damages beyond this amount could be pursued under the ordinary rules of negligence.
   b) Polluting activities by or on behalf of the holder of the right-of-way would have to be controlled and stopped at the holder's expense.
   c) The owner and operator of each vessel used to transport oil from the pipeline would be liable without regard to fault for all damages resulting from discharges of oil from each vessel.
5. Negotiations with Canada by the President of the United States would be held regarding various aspects of any trans-Canada route.
6. The civil rights section of the act guaranteed all persons equal rights for receiving or participating in any activity conducted under various authorizations of that section.

7. A width of right-of-way provision (from an amendment of the Mineral Leasing Act of 1920) extended the Secretary of the Interior's authority to set right-of-way widths in accordance with construction and safety needs.
8. The President would use his authority to ensure that all regions of the United States would benefit indirectly or directly from the North Slope oil.

Activation

In planning for implementation of the TAPS project, attention had to focus on the Alaskan construction cycle. The traditional construction cycle in Alaska begins in winter, when temperatures drop to −75°F (−59°C). In this viciously cold portion of the year, the Arctic tundra is frozen and its delicate surface is less likely to be damaged by the movement of equipment. During the dead of winter, heavy equipment and materials are moved to construction sites across temporary snow roads and ice bridges made by compacting several layers of snow and ice on the top of frozen ground, river, and lake surfaces. The next step in the construction cycle begins in early spring. Warm weather by late March or early April allows workers to achieve normal productivity levels. Once begun in spring, work often continues around the clock either until the project is completed or the weather cools in the fall. Most construction not completed by late September or early October is abandoned until the following spring; winter construction normally is too costly. Significantly, projects that are even one month off schedule in October are potentially months behind. Work not finished by October must wait up to seven months, until the following April, to be completed.

Decision making on project organization, bidding and contracting, information and control systems, and resource procurement and allocation was handled by the Alyeska owner companies. The eight firms that controlled the pipeline venture comprised the owners' committee. The owners retained direct responsibility for setting overall project policy, acquiring capital, and sharing profits or losses. Agreement on project policy by the owners was a common prerequisite for major construction decisions and actions. For example, agreement between the owners was necessary before major contractual arrangements could be formalized by Alyeska, such as which construction management contractor (CMC) to hire. Contractual arrangements, however, were just one of hundreds of necessary policymaking decisions, since almost every aspect of construction was touched by the owners. In short, since each owner company was a massively large employer in its own right (ARCO, for example, has about 55,000 employees), it was able to use some of its own employees at every stage of the project to gain valuable information for decision making. One of the more efficient information-gathering structures for owner decision making was the ad hoc subcommittee system, by which technical and expert advice flowed up the chain of command from the subcommittees and Alyeska. Then, once policy was made, the owners controlled the implementation process down the chain of command by allowing the ad hoc subcommittees to work with all levels of the organization.

PHASE 3: OPERATION, CONTROL, AND HANDOVER

Implementation

Brief Overview. The builders of the Trans-Alaska pipeline tried to follow Alaska's traditional construction cycle. Snow roads and ice bridges were built following construction permit authorization in December 1973. Heavier equipment and materials were moved across the frozen arctic surface to construction camps between January and April 1974. Official construction commenced on April 29, 1974, in warmer weather. Figure 8.6 shows the six sections assigned to major contractors. Workers and remaining materials were airlifted to construction zones after the snow and ice bridges had melted. The entire first portion of the construction plan—the haul road—was completed during the first construction season. Most of the other portions of the construction plan—the 800 mi (1287 km) of pipe, the pump stations, and the marine terminal in Valdez—were completed during the 1975 and 1976 construction seasons. Some final construction was accomplished early in the 1977 season. Oil was introduced into the pipeline at Prudhoe Bay as scheduled on June 20, 1977.

The project's organization structure and manpower level tended to change with the flow of construction activity. In July 1974, the proportionate ownership of the pipeline changed; Sohio, ARCO, Exxon, and British Petroleum now owned 90 percent. During that same summer, the highest number of administrative and craft workers—approximately 3400—were employed. Major portions of actual construction were completed during the 1975 and 1976 construction seasons. Employment levels reached 21,000 during the summers of 1975 and 1976, with approximately 26 million employee-hours totaled by craft workers in each construction season. In 1977, Alyeska began to demobilize itself as a construction company and shifted its organizational structure to that of an operating company. The level of construction tapered off in 1977 to a total of less than 11,000 workers.

An example of the project's organizational structure in 1974 is shown in Figure 8.7. Responsibility and authority for all construction rested at the top of the management pyramid. This meant that the relatively few firms at the head of the organization, such as Alyeska, supervised all portions of

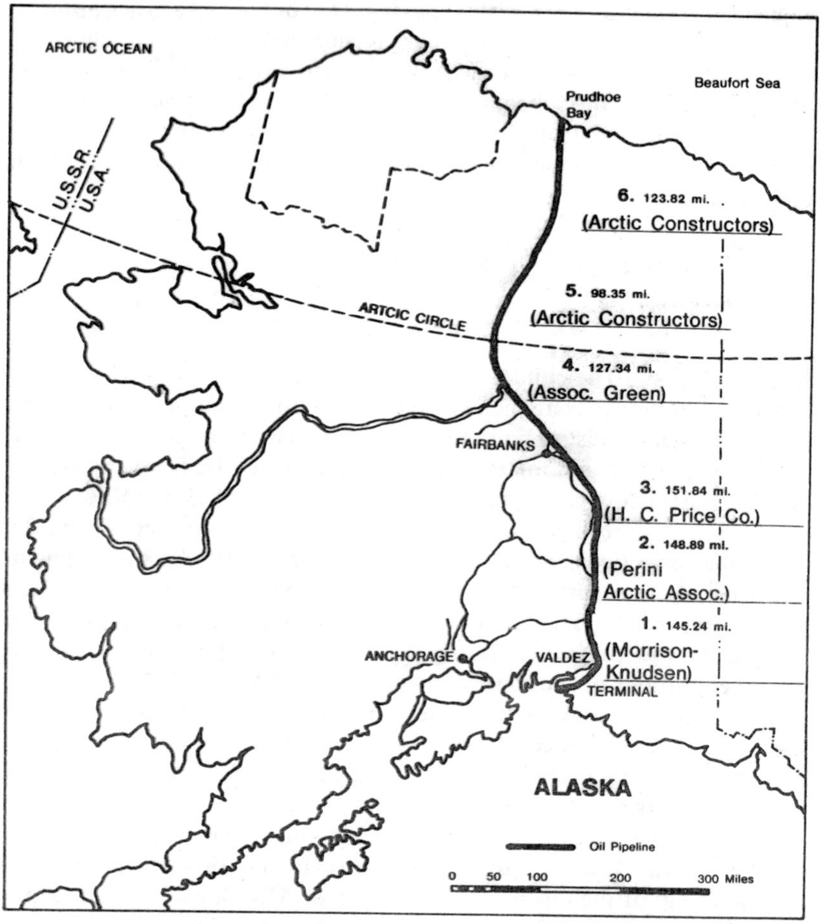

Figure 8.6. The Trans-Alaska Pipeline route, showing ECs.

construction simultaneously. In contrast, each of the many firms at the middle and bottom levels of the organization had only limited responsibility and authority by contract for a portion of the haul road, the pipeline, the marine terminal, or the pump stations.

Construction of Haul Road. Private management's coordinated effort to build the haul road is indicative of the massive scale of the entire project (see Table 8.1). Some 358 mi (576 km) of highly compacted and graded gravel surface road were constructed in the arctic wilderness, along with 39

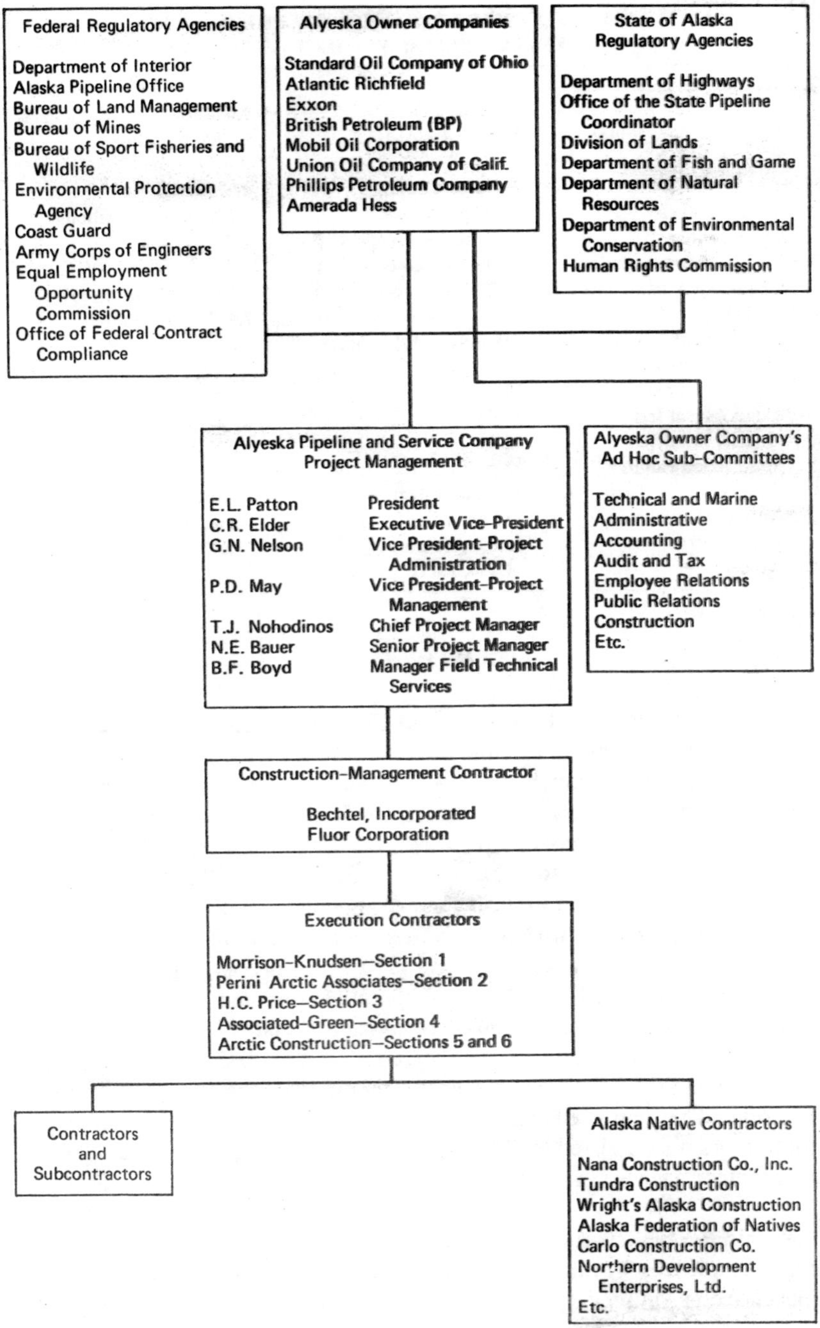

Figure 8.7. TAPS: Project organizational structure (Summer 1974).

TABLE 8.1. DEVELOPMENT STATISTICS OF THE HAUL ROAD, ALYESKA PIPELINE PROJECT (1977)

1. Pieces of vehicular equipment	716 heavy	2,054 total
Yukon River ice bridge	1,074 truckloads	24,700 total tons
Hercules air cargo transport	2,448 planeloads	47,736 total tons
Consumed fuel	1,171 planeloads	8,530,110 total gallons
Air operations	708 per day (ave.)	127,440 total
2. Lodging accommodations	3,600 road const.	
Accumulated man-hours	3,077,000 to date	4,391,000 (projected)
Employees	3,596 north of the Yukon	7,447 at orientation
3. Miles of road	358 north of the Yukon	
Bridges, permanent	20	
Bridges, temporary	19	
Bridges, lineal feet	3,462	32,457 pilings
Culverts, lineal feet	83,417	1,029 total
Construction camps	12 north of the Yukon	
Airports	7 cargo, 4 light	11 total
Mineral material sites	135 open sites	
Mineral extractions	22,636,000 cu yd gravel 1,754,000 cu yd rock	31,612,000 tons (projected)

bridges, 1029 culverts, 11 airports, and 135 mineral acquisition sites. Over 7000 employees attended the one-day orientation necessary for authorization to pass north through the Yukon River checkpoint; 3596 employees (including cooks, drivers, and janitors) made up the on-site support force for the equally large construction crews (tradesmen and supervisors), all of whom were warned not to disturb any of the area's wildlife.[4]

Although Alyeska had exclusive use of the highway during pipeline construction, its ultimate ownership reverted to the State of Alaska. The haul road was begun at Livengood in May 1970 and was completed at Prudhoe Bay in September 1974. Because of complications and delays caused by competing interest groups (similar to those associated with all phases of construction), more than five years were required to design, gain approvals for, and complete a road that required only nine months of actual construction time. The road itself was divided into eight sections. Five construction contractors were assisted by 7 local contractors and regulated by at least 14 government agencies, including 8 federal agencies and 6 from the State of Alaska.

Within the first six-month period allowed by the traditional construction cycle, employees working on the haul road had to learn how to use the special arctic equipment, to understand the constantly changing land forms of Alaska (from arctic desert to the highest mountains in North America) and soil characteristics, and to construct the road across pristine wilderness.

Coordinating construction was complicated because Alyeska's corporate headquarters was maintained in Anchorage, but actual haul road construction headquarters were 355 mi (571 km) to the north, in Fairbanks. In addition, no connecting roads or normal communication links existed. Coordinating haul road construction was further complicated by arctic weather and atmospheric conditions. Specifically, changing arctic weather patterns often delayed the delivery of airlifted workers, supplies, and equipment to construction points. Arctic atmospheric conditions are among the strangest in the world. Communication by voice radio is unreliable at best. In sum, the normal supervision and control methods for building the haul road, indeed all portions of the project upon which management relied, were thwarted by the size, geographic location, uniqueness, and complexity of the project.

Pipeline Construction. The scope of the Trans-Alaska pipeline project is massive by any standard. It is often described as the largest construction project undertaken by private industry in history. While such a claim is difficult to prove, it is probably fair to say that it is the largest construction project undertaken by contemporary private industry. The scope is vast for each of the four parts of the project's construction plan. In comparison, the work associated with the pipeline itself was probably greater than that of the other three parts of the project (haul road, pump stations, and marine terminal). Nearly 15,000 workers were assigned to pipe installation and related tasks during the summer peak in 1975 and 1976. The workers assigned to lay pipe worked on clearing the right-of-way, laying a gravel pad to protect the environment from damage by heavy equipment, or installing the pipe itself.

The first 1900 ft (579 m) of pipeline was buried beneath the Tonsina River on March 27, 1975. Tractor-backhoes ditched the Tonsina to depths of 18 ft (5 m) below the stream bed and up to 10 ft (3 m) below the maximum scour depth of the river channel. Each 300-ft (9-m) section of pipe was precoated with 9 in. (0.229 m) of concrete to combat the buoyancy of the empty line. The cement coating, which weighed 80,000 lb/40 ft (12 m) of pipe, anchored the pipe in its burial ditch. Tractors with side-mounted booms picked up the sections of pipe in webbed slings, holding the pipe for welding of additional sections to each end until the 1900-ft (579-m) span was completed. As more pipe installation continued along the right-of-way, the realities of the Alaskan terrain began to cause engineering and design modifications. Alyeska engineers had detailed the pipe-laying work on a mile-by-mile basis from Prudhoe Bay to Valdez before construction began, but these plans had to be constantly changed. When crews drilled holes for vertical support members (VSM), for example, subsurface soil conditions often caused the pipeline to be moved from one side of the right-of-way to the other; or, more expensively for Alyeska, portions of the pipeline planned for burial had to be elevated to avoid harm to the permafrost. But despite design changes, actual pipe laying moved quickly.

Pipe-laying activities forged ahead of other portions of the project during 1975 because pipe burial and installation did not require the extensive site preparation common to terminal and pump station construction. By 1977, however, pipe laying had slowed; three sections of the line were part of the last construction completed on the entire project. First, glacial soils in the original burial route and avalanche danger at the 4790-ft (1460-m) Atigun Pass in the Brooks Range led to several route and design changes. An 8-ft^2 (2-m^2), 6000-ft-long (1829-m-long) concrete box with the pipe inside in a 21-in. (53-cm) thickness of Styrofoam was built. This entire unit was then placed at a steep vertical angle along the side of the right-of-way crossing Atigun Pass.

At Keystone Canyon, Section 1, the pipeline had to be rerouted along the canyon's 4-mi (6-km) lip because the highway prevented the laying of pipe on the canyon floor. At first, tracked vehicles such as bulldozers pulled materials and equipment up the canyon walls, but the rock faces proved too steep for drilling crews. Heavy equipment and materials were disassembled, flown to the top of the canyon, and reassembled above the rock face. Helicopters airlifted crews and materials to one of four canyon-top staging areas where, when work resumed, portions of the pipe were laid along a 60 percent grade. At the 2500-ft (762-m) Thompson Pass, Section 1, crews were faced with several miles with 45° slopes. Since the pipeline route followed an almost vertical grade, heavy equipment was anchored to the slopes by cables; in fact, the pipe itself was winched up the side of the pass with a cable tramway system. Welders lashed to the pipe to keep their footing worked the entire 1976 construction season to complete the job. Not surprisingly, the last portion of pipe to be laid was at Thompson Pass.

Construction of the Marine Terminal and Pump Stations. Responsibility for the marine terminal in Valdez and the initial eight pump stations was contracted to the Fluor Corporation on December 21, 1972. Fluor completed most of the major planning and design work for its two portions of the project by July 1974, although some engineering changes occurred as late as the summer of 1977. Fluor's management activities are distinguished from those of the rest of the pipeline project by a number of important characteristics. First, since much of Fluor's work was performed indoors, crews worked all winter. Also, because the crews worked year round, workforce levels tended to remain relatively small. Fluor used 5000 to 6000 workers during the construction peak in the summers of 1975 and 1976. The construction crews at Pump Section 1, Prudhoe Bay, fluctuated between 270 and 430 workers between January and August 1976. Fluor's management, however, did find its tasks to be more complicated than those on previous pipeline construction projects. Welding required extra ability because of the special chemistry of the low-temperature metallurgy. Unusual stress, snow loads, permafrost, earthquake safety requirements, and government monitoring stipulations combined to make the Alaska terminal facility and pump stations unique. Fluor supervised the terminal construction separately from the pump station construction.

Supervision and Control

Figure 8.7 shows the Alyeska Pipeline and Service Company to be responsible for overall project management, with Bechtel, Incorporated, and the Fluor Corporation as CMCs. Since the Alyeska Project Management (Alyeska) had responsibility and authority for construction, it implemented the policies set by the owners. Specific tasks performed by Alyeska to meet its responsibilities depended upon the stage of construction—from planning and engineering to building. When during planning, for example, several companies were interested in becoming CMCs, Alyeska reviewed their initial proposals and recommended to the owners which firms should be awarded contracts.

Alyeska's engineering tasks included the design of the pipeline (originally planned for burial over 90 percent of its length). The engineering team revised this original design almost continuously throughout the project, so that at completion approximately 52 percent of the pipeline was buried. Alyeska's building task was to supervise the firms doing the actual construction. As project manager, Alyeska did not wish to supervise on-site construction; it intended to audit and ensure fulfillment of contractual obligations by the CMCs.

Among the other responsibilities delegated to Alyeska were preparation, revision, and control of the project budget. Constant revisions were necessary in order to maintain control of the budget because it escalated from US$900 million initially to US$4.5 billion in 1974, to US$6.5 billion in 1975, to US$7 billion in 1976, and to US$8 billion in 1977. Estimates attribute approximately 50 percent of these budget revisions to inflationary pressure, 30 percent to environment requirements, and 20 percent to other items such as design changes or changes in engineering standards imposed by reviewing government agencies.

In addition to these more usual management duties, Alyeska provided a focal point for extensive government regulatory activity. Government agencies found it easier to go directly to Alyeska rather than to deal with each owner individually. Acting in this capacity, Alyeska satisfied environmental protection regulations by providing a steady stream of reports concerning the impact on the approximately 30,000 acres (12,141 hectares) of land disturbed by construction. Government agencies required Alyeska to make reports regarding erosion control, construction-related oil spillage, sewage treatment standards at the construction camps, fair employment commitments, and damage to wildlife, for example. Alyeska was also responsible for public relations, including hosting government officials inspecting pipeline progress.

The CMC duties were divided. Bechtel was responsible for construction of the haul road and pipeline, and Fluor for the pump stations and marine terminal. Each CMC was given decision-making latitude within the boundaries of its specific tasks. However, Alyeska and the owners expected the CMCs to develop transportation plans for equipment to the job site, to plan construction camps, to set up policies and procedures to be followed by the execution contractors (ECs), to establish an organization for on-site quality inspection, to determine a method for strengthening control over the ECs, and to set up a procurement organization to achieve cost savings by buying needed supplies and equipment in bulk.[5]

The relationship between the CMCs and other members of the organization differed. On the one hand, Fluor worked in conjunction with Alyeska to design the pump stations and marine terminal. Accordingly, Fluor was intimately familiar with the engineering aspects of its tasks. Since much of the engineering design directly supervised by Fluor was then built by its own subsidiary, the Fluor Construction Company, rather than another EC, the transfer from design to finished product was much simpler on the Fluor-supervised portion of the project. In addition, Fluor's supervisory communication links were relatively simple because each of its tasks was centrally located. On the other hand, Bechtel did not work in conjunction with Alyeska to design the pipeline and haul road. Alyeska's engineering of both left Bechtel to manage the actual building through a multitude of ECs. Since it was responsible for building the pipeline and haul road according to Alyeska's specifications, Bechtel, unlike Fluor, began its duties without intimate familiarity with the engineering aspects of its tasks. Thus, at first, Bechtel could not supervise as closely the work being done by its ECs. Also, unlike Fluor, Bechtel's supervisory communication links were relatively complex because its two tasks were spread out over 800 mi (1,287 km) of Alaskan wilderness. Bechtel's ability to supervise and control its portions of the project, therefore, was somewhat reduced.

Unfortunately, the formal organizational structure as it was conceived when construction began in the summer of 1974 was strongly affected by both internal and external stresses caused by policymaking, financial, and risk distribution decisions made by the owners. Even before the 1974 construction startup, the eight owners disagreed about basic policy. For example, Bechtel, Arctic Contractors (Arctic), and Morrison-Knudsen Company, Inc. (Morrison-Knudsen), were being considered for the general project planning contract. ARCO supported Bechtel, but the other owners favored Arctic. Eventually, the general planning contract was modified and awarded to Arctic in August 1972. Because of this particular conflict (refusal to authorize formal arrangements with Bechtel), Bechtel would later find that it did not have adequate project planning time.

Policy disagreements sometimes led to insightful solutions to project problems. In many cases, if individual owners and their subcommittees felt that on a particular problem they had more expertise than Alyeska, Alyeska was bypassed first by one and then another member of top management. For instance, top management took over much of the procurement function originally assigned to the CMCs. Alyeska was directed to purchase directly for the ECs, buying supplies and equipment at substantially reduced bulk rates.

Alyeska's management role was modified greatly by top-level management decisions. In practice, Alyeska's role became that of mediator among the various management levels in the organization. As already suggested, the opinions of the owners, their ad hoc subcommittees, and Alyeska differed.

Alyeska's project management team, as well as most of its internal organization, consisted of employees on loan from the owner companies. These employees had the management philosophy and style associated with their own companies. Consequently, Alyeska's organization encompassed every management approach from democratic to authoritarian; no particular management philosophy prevailed. In addition, Alyeska's employees generally did not have a career-oriented commitment to the firm.

In summary, supervision and control left much to be desired because of lack of coordination and cooperation in a complex project plagued by inadequate planning and a duplicative four-tiered management structure established by the owner companies: (1) the owners' committee, (2) Alyeska, (3) Bechtel (pipeline and haul road) and Fluor (pump stations and terminal), and (4) ECs (see Figure 8.7).[6] The owners terminated Bechtel's employment in 1975, with Alyeska assuming responsibility as CMC. A revised organizational structure is shown in Figure 8.8.

Superimposed on this cumbersome and inefficient management structure was the public agency involvement at both federal and state levels. Public management was formally organized so that the federal authorizing officer, the state pipeline coordinator, and the Joint Fish and Wildlife Advisory Team did most of the monitoring. These three agents, along with several others, had the power to halt the project if construction activities violated the law. The staff of the public organization is shown statistically in Table 8.2. The largest number of employees overseeing construction worked for

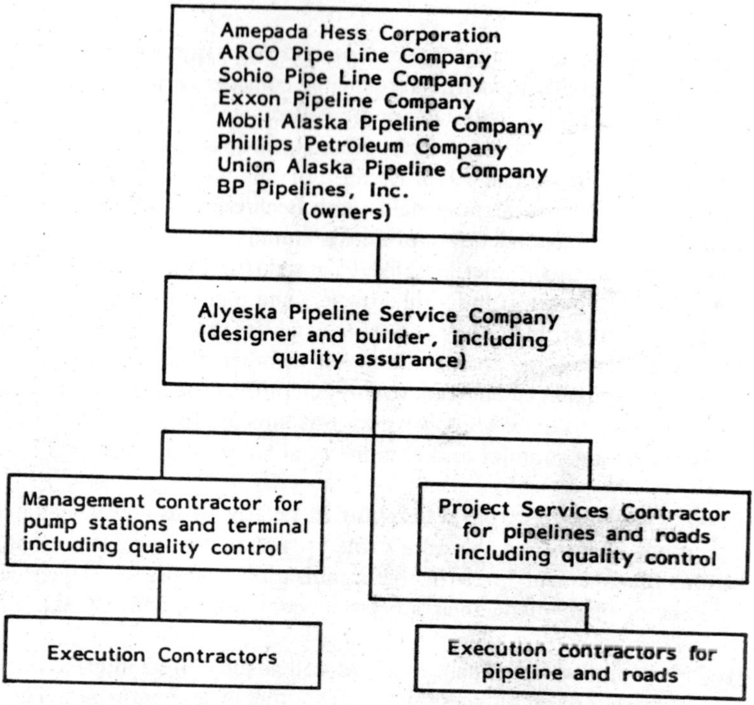

Figure 8.8. TAPS Project: Revised Organization Structure (Summer 1975). (Source: *Trans-Alaska Oil Pipeline—Progress of Construction Through November 1975*, Report to Congress by the U.S. Comptroller General, February 1976.)

private industry because the authorized officer contracted with private industry for expertise regarding compliance with environmental and technical stipulations. According to the table, the project staff consisted of 64 management and administrative employees, 37 technical employees, and 83 field surveillance employees.

TABLE 8.2. STAFF OF PUBLIC AGENCIES SUPERVISING TAPS.

	FEDERAL			
	AUTHORIZED OFFICER	CONTRACTOR	STATE	FISH AND WILDLIFE
Management and administration	23	19	13	9
Technical	9	13	4	11
Field surveillance	16	39	15	13
Total	48	71	32	33

Source: *Trans-Alaska Oil Pipeline—Progress of Construction Through November 1975*, Report to Congress by the U.S. Comptroller General, February 1976.

The impact of the various government agencies on construction was profound. A case in point is the gravel pit at scenic Sukakpak Mountain in the Brooks Mountain Range. A.P. Rollins, the authorized officer, gave permission for construction crews to quarry rock from a gravel site on the lower slopes of the mountain before the Bureau of Land Management had approved the action. The gravel was extracted and used for construction of the haul road. After the pit had been opened and the road completed, the Bureau of Land Management rejected the permit because Sukakpak Mountain is considered to be one of the most scenic vistas along the pipeline route. Alyeska and the contractors were required to return the gravel pit to its natural state—at great expense.[7]

In the summer of 1975, another setback occurred when, for the first time since 1897, the ice pack in the Arctic Ocean scarcely moved from the shoreline. A fleet of 47 barges and 23 tugs was stalled nearly 300 mi (483 km) from Prudhoe Bay, waiting for the ice to recede during July and August. Ten barges and several tugs finally got to Prudhoe Bay in early September, despite hull damage. Seventeen more barges were able to reach Prudhoe Bay on October 5. Nineteen barges had to return to Seward and Anchorage. Because the CMCs and other contractors had to reorganize to have the 19 barges unloaded and their needed cargo shipped to Prudhoe Bay via rail and truck, the trucking fleet was expanded and shipping costs increased.

The failure of the ice pack to recede was just one of many events which put the CMCs' construction plan off schedule. By November 30, 1975, the pipeline system was scheduled to be 43 percent completed, but according to Figure 8.9, the entire project was only 37.6 percent completed. Only the pipeline itself was considered on schedule. The contractors in charge of camp housing, camp sewage facilities, and delivery of equipment or supplies were most seriously affected, which changed the construction timetable. For example, difficulties occurred for contractors drilling the holes for pipeline support members when the contractors supplying the drilling equipment were unable to meet their delivery dates.[8]

Private management organized its quality control checking activity into two functional areas. The CMCs were responsible for day-to-day field inspection of all work. Alyeska monitored and evaluated the CMCs' quality inspection efforts by random spot checks and audits designed to ensure overall project quality. Alyeska instituted a bonus plan tied to quality and cost savings as an incentive for contractors to comply with project quality standards as well as to hold down costs. Private management had sole responsibility for checking and meeting construction quality standards, but not the sole charge of administering the quality control program. Public management assumed the right to approve the quality of construction. Public inspectors reviewed everything, looking for substandard construction quality that might hurt the environment. One troubling concern was the

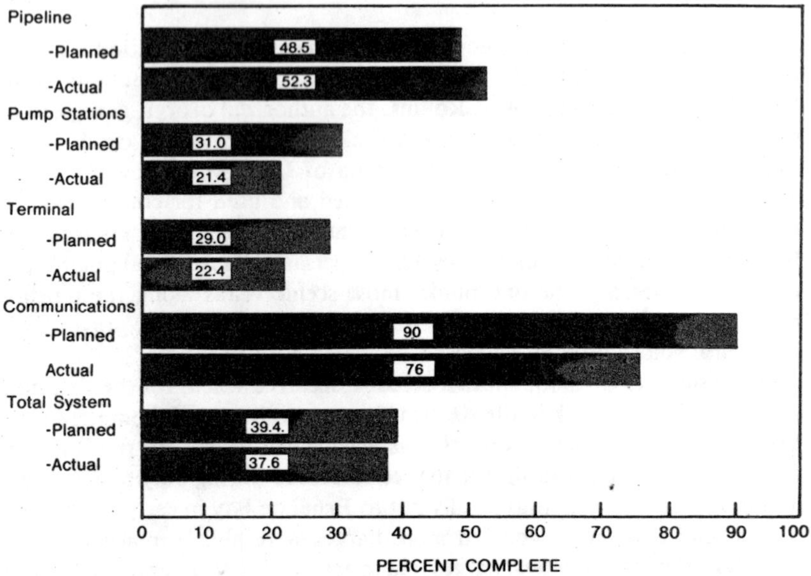

Figure 8.9. Percentage of construction completed on TAPS as of November 30, 1975. (Source: *Trans-Alaska Oil Pipeline—Progress of Construction through November 1975*, Report to Congress by the U.S. Comptroller General, February 1976.)

report of the staff of the Energy and Power Subcommittee of the House Interstate and Foreign Commerce Committee, which stated that once oil began to flow, Alyeska's detection system was so unsophisticated that up to 500 barrels of oil per day could leak unnoticed. Other evaluations of the detection system alleged that faulty welds would allow up to 1700 barrels a day to leak undetected.[9]

Completion and Handover

To Alyeska, perhaps the final measure of the success of the project was the call for "oil in" at Prudhoe Bay in 1977. Start-up of Alaska's oil pipeline presented unique technical problems. The oil was hot and the pipeline was cold. The pipeline heated while the air cooled until the two reached the same temperature. The temperature difference at the beginning was great; the oil reached the pipeline at a temperature as high as 160°F (71°C); the pipeline's average temperature was 20°F (−7°C). The conventional method of starting a pipeline is to fill it with water in order to remove oxygen that could explode when mixed with hydrocarbons, place a separator called a "pig" in the line, and remove the water by moving crude oil through the line behind the separator. In Alaska, however, this method could not be used because the water would freeze. Rather than using water, the Alaska pipeline used nitrogen, which is an inert gas that cannot support combustion. The oil was put in the line and a ground party moved southward from Prudhoe Bay. The ground party inspected for oil leaks, checked clearances between shifting pipe and pipe supports, and looked to see that the vertical support members were able to accommodate the weight of the filled pipeline. For several weeks, crews continued to check and double-check for oil leaks and weight distortion.[4]

Oil spills along the pipeline are not desirable for anyone. Nonetheless, they are almost inevitable. The pipeline design included highly sensitive oil leak detection devices. Public management required workers to report all oil spills regardless of size. When oil leaked, Alyeska would advise the proper government regulatory agency. Apparently, four major oil spills occurred during construction.[10] First, an estimated 60,000 gallons of fuel leaked from a buried pipeline at Galbraith Lake. This was not discovered immediately because the holding tanks feeding the line were filled on a routine schedule and no control existed over the amount of fuel being consumed. Second, an explosion at Isabel Pass caused havoc in a fuel yard. Barrels of fuel were crushed by falling rock, and workers spent two days cleaning the areas, as well as bringing in new dirt to cover the spill. Third, a tanker truck overturned at Chandalar, spilling 8500 gallons of fuel. A fourth spill of about 70,000 gallons occurred at Prudhoe Bay in January 1976. Fuel tanks were mistakenly topped off when the temperature was −50°F (−46°C). When the temperature rose to 60°F (15.5°C) in 12 hours, a valve burst and oil spilled on the tundra. The cause of the spill appears to have been a lack of understanding about the special weather conditions of the far north. Because so many possibilities exist for oil spills unrelated to the actual movement of oil through the pipeline, Alyeska trained and equipped an oil spill cleanup crew, which was kept on immediate standby.

For the most part, the pipeline start-up process was relatively smooth, with only a few minor problems typical of those encountered in the early stages of any massive system. There was one major exception, however. At Pump Station 8, a relatively minor problem of cleaning a strainer was compounded by human error (which itself may have been made possible by an inadequate fail-safe feature in design). The result was an explosion and a fire which destroyed the station, killed one man, and injured several others. The damage was estimated at tens of millions of dollars, and without the pressure of Station 8's pumps, the pipeline had to be operated for months at a flow rate of 800,000 barrels per day—two-thirds of the initial expected operating rate. The owner companies thus experienced a consequent loss of revenue.

Alyeska found itself with huge amounts of surplus construction equipment that had to be sold at the completion of the project. This sale, which took approximately two years to complete, was perhaps one of the largest surplus equipment sales ever recorded, save after major wars. Alyeska's list of over 20,000 items of used equipment had cost US$800 million to purchase and included 240 cranes, 119 backhoes, 719 bulldozers, pipe layers and loaders, 1340 generators, 1357 trucks, 3315 other vehicles, and 1637 welding machines, as well as 1500 gas-heated outhouses, originally priced at $10,000 each. Aside from its size, this surplus sale is significant for the several hundred million dollars in revenue that it generated, which had to be deducted from the total construction costs. The owner companies were guaranteed a reasonable rate of return on their investments based on the cost of building the pipeline. Similarly, the State of Alaska was to receive a royalty that could be affected by the cost of building the pipeline. Thus, both private and public management were concerned with the surplus-sale dollars. Private industry needed to dispose of the extra equipment. Public management needed to ensure that the surplus equipment brought a reasonable price because Alaska's royalties on Prudhoe Bay production could be reduced for years to come if the equipment was sold for too little.

The organization and construction work described previously evolved to build the Alaska pipeline. When construction of the project was completed during the summer of 1977, Alyeska was demobilized. In simplistic terms, Alyeska's construction company was dissolved and replaced by its operating company. All employment contracts were officially terminated, so that employees could return to their parent company or elect to stay in Alaska as part of Alyeska's operating company. The responsibility of the Alyeska construction company had been to build the Trans-Alaska pipeline. The responsibility of the Alyeska operating company is to operate and maintain the pipeline.

PHASE 4: EVALUATION AND REFINEMENT

Evaluation

The Alyeska pipeline project has had a major impact on the owner oil companies, the State of Alaska, and the nation, as well as a secondary international impact. The full effects are difficult to determine for several reasons, especially since the process of adjustment to this major social, economic, and environmental disturbance is not yet complete, or, where it is apparently complete, it is either poorly documented or obscured by the effects of other disturbances.

The following discussion summarizes the specific impacts of TAPS upon the various groups and special interests involved. It concludes with an evaluation of the project planning, design, construction, and management system utilized, as analyzed by the general editors for the series of case histories (Goodman and Love). Included are references to a report to the Alaska Pipeline Commission by the commission's special counsel.[5]

Impact on the Oil Companies. The pipeline must be considered a technical success; once authorization had been received, construction was completed on schedule. Instead of weeks, however, years were spent obtaining authorization, and the final costs were many times higher than originally estimated. While such costs would normally be recovered through tariffs, the owners' proposed tariffs have been contested on the grounds that a substantial amount of the cost overrun was due to poor planning and management. Thus, full costs may not be recovered by the owner companies through tariffs. The owners, as producers of Prudhoe Bay oil, also face a possibly reduced profit as long as the West Coast oil glut continues. On the other hand, the owner companies are now assured substantial access to domestic oil, and British Petroleum has obtained an effective entry into the U.S. oil market.

Impact on the Alaskan Communities. All Alaskan communities have been affected to some extent by the pipeline's development. The effects on the smaller rural communities not on the pipeline's route have been mostly indirect. Many rural residents who worked on the pipeline's construction earned high wages, if only briefly, and thus increased the cash income of their community. When the workers returned to these communities, they brought not just more money but undoubtedly new values. These communities also benefit from increased state oil taxes and royalty payments—for example, a 1978 legislative provision to spend over US$100 million on rural school construction. Some communities lost residents to the urban centers or larger communities. The pipeline's impact on rural communities is difficult to separate from the impacts of the Native Claims Settlement Act and the 200-mi (322-km) U.S. fishery jurisdiction zone established in 1977.

Communities directly affected by the pipeline either exist directly on the pipeline's route or provide important support and coordinating services. The first category includes Valdez, Glennallen, Delta, and Fairbanks. The other category includes Anchorage (the state's major commercial and transportation center and the headquarters of the Alyeska Pipeline Service Company, as well as the location of many government offices), Seward (which was a major supply port for construction), and the state capital of Juneau. Many of these communities experienced a similar short-term impact: rapid increases in the cost of living, improved economic conditions, physical expansion, increased crime, greater demand for government services, and temporarily reduced unemployment. Valdez appears to have attained a permanent and substantial economic base. Fairbanks is experiencing the consequences of overexpansion, including a much higher than normal level of unemployment. The effects of the end of the boom period in Anchorage to date have been relatively mild, since secondary business expansion (including a large amount of building construction) has maintained a viable level of economic activity.

Effect on Alaskan Values. In Alaska, urban concepts of economic interdependence clash with rural concepts of self-sufficiency and subsistence from the land. Environmentalists predict ecological disaster from development, while growth advocates predict economic disaster and criticize environmentalists' adamant convictions regarding land use. Local leaders of regional corporations must balance a congressional mandate, with emphasis on profit seeking expressed in the Native Claims Settlement Act, against claims for social action or immediate distribution of all corporate assets to maintain the traditional subsistence lifestyle. Alaska is clearly a pluralistic society, with differences in opinion as great in magnitude as the differences in geography. The pipeline appears to have sharpened this conflict and created (although indirectly) the basis for increased polarization.

Effect on Alaska's Government. The oil tax and royalty revenues have substantially increased state government tax receipts. Many citizens have thus increased their demand for services, since they believe that the state government is in a better financial position to deliver them. However, because of the higher than expected pipeline completion costs and the West Coast oil glut (which together have significantly increased transportation costs for North Slope oil and thus have reduced the wellhead value, on which taxes and royalties are based), the state is actually receiving far less oil income than had been predicted. This smaller than expected revenue, combined with increased expectations of services, has paradoxically placed the state government of oil-rich Alaska in a fiscal squeeze, necessitating curtailment in the growth of services. As of January 1979, state officials were actively seeking federal permission for oil exchanges in which Alaskan oil would be shipped to Japan in return for increased oil shipments to the Gulf Coast or eastern United States from the Mideast or Mexico. The sale of Alaskan oil in Japan would increase its wellhead value substantially. For the same reason, Alaskans are probably the only people in the United States who benefited from OPEC price increases. In the context of decades rather than years, many Alaskans (and particularly Governor Jay Hammond) worried about how to sustain state government at a high level of services when the oil resources were used up. Alaskans voted to establish a permanent fund in which at least 25 percent of oil revenues would be invested in order to preserve at least a portion of the revenues for the future.

Effect on the Environment. Because of the slow rate of ecological adjustment in Alaska, the full environmental effects of TAPS probably will not be apparent for years. As of January 1979, system (pipeline and tanker) failure had not caused an oil spill of crisis proportions. This does not conclusively prove that such a spill could not happen in the future. During the process of construction and start-up, numerous smaller fuel spills occurred, but their damage was localized and Alyeska attempted to minimize the damage by using cleanup measures. A certain amount of local damage was also due to siltation and erosion, although the stipulations required Alyeska to minimize these problems. During construction, wildlife was disturbed along the route and some species (particularly bears) became nuisances. Longer-run effects on wildlife must still be evaluated.

Effect on the National Energy Situation. Although there is no doubt that the development of North Slope oil reserves is a major addition to domestic oil resources, the full benefits of this addition have not yet been realized. The reluctance of the federal government to authorize an exchange involving oil shipments to Japan has reduced the net benefit to the U.S. balance of payments. In addition, the oil companies apparently do not have a sufficient incentive to expand the pipeline capacity to the full design potential of 2 million barrels per day. Furthermore, the natural gas pipeline (although authorized) has yet to be supported by investors, and some doubt exists that it will be built anytime in the near future. Therefore, the natural gas resources of the North Slope may remain unavailable for some time.

Impact on Alaska's Businesses. The boom period in many cases exceeded expectations. Many individual Alaskans and Alaska businesses experienced a temporary sharp increase in income. Others not employed either on the project or in a secondary supporting organization faced higher costs from pipeline-generated local inflation.

During the construction period, government agencies and many businesses found it difficult to retain employees when they could not match the salaries or wages paid for working on the pipeline. Employees on the line were often earning $50,000 or more per year, although many of these were outsiders whose pay left the state. With increased population came increased demand. The resultant seller's market for many businesses then generated a secondary business expansion, which differed in intensity with the community and the business sector. The end of the pipeline construction has forced upon many businesses the unpleasant task of contraction. For those who overexpanded unwisely, the ultimate prospect may be bankruptcy.

Refinement

The final task in the IPPMC is an evaluation of the three previous phases or the lessons learned from each completed project to provide a basis for refinement of the integrated project cycle. This task should provide useful insights for improving policy decisions, planning, design, and management of future projects. This is the subject of Chapter 9, which evaluates four projects, including the three presented in Chapters 6–8. Hauck and Geistauts also provide an interesting summary discussion of a retrospective analysis of TAPS in the IPPMC conceptual framework.[11]

REFERENCES

1. Hearings, United States Senate Committee on Interior and Insular Affairs, Fall 1979.
2. Trans-Alaska Pipeline Application, June 6, 1969.
3. TAPS to Russell Train, Interior Department, June 10, 1969.
4. Roscow, James P. *800 Miles to Valdez, the Building of the Alaska Pipeline.* Englewood Cliffs, N.J.: Prentice-Hall, Inc., 1977.
5. Lenzner, Terry F. *The Management, Planning and Construction of the Trans-Alaska Pipeline System.* Washington, D.C.: Wald, Harkrader and Ross, August 1977.
6. Ibid.
7. *Trans-Alaska Oil Pipeline—Progress of Construction Through November 1975.* Report to Congress by the U.S. Comptroller General, February 1976.
8. United States Department of the Interior, *Summary of Trans-Alaska Pipeline System Critique Session.* Washington, D.C.: Alaska Pipeline Office, October 1977.
9. Hanrahan, John and Gruenstein, Peter. *Lost Frontier: The Marketing of Alaska.* New York: W.W. Norton and Co., 1977, p. 182.
10. McGrath, Edward. *Inside the Alaska Pipeline.* Millbrae, Calif.: Celestial Arts, 1977.
11. Hauck, V. and Geistauts, G. "Construction of the Trans-Alaska Oil Pipeline." *Omega,* Vol. 10, No. 3, pp. 259–265, 1982.

CHAPTER 9

Lessons Learned from Selected IPPMC Case Histories

As the IPPMC model clearly indicates, *policy* occupies a central position in the management cycle. It has become increasingly evident over the past three decades that the success or failure of any project is directly linked to the policymaking process. Without adequate communications or feedback channels, projects either become divorced from policymaking or are doomed to be replicated uncritically without the benefit of policy refinement. Although refinement of policy and planning occurs in the IPPMC model as a discrete task in phase 4 (evaluation and refinement), it is important to note that this model presents the ideal situation. The cycle proposes that continuous feedback occur between each major phase/task and that continuous linkages be formed during each phase with the central hub of the cycle, *policy*.

With the central function of policymaking providing focus and direction for each task, it is imperative to determine and analyze the lessons and insights gained from each project. Then we must respond to the question, how can these lessons be applied to refine and improve future policy decisions on project planning and management?

Policy refinement is an area of great complexity and one that has not been well researched. Many agencies recognize the importance of this process but fail to discuss it adequately. The World Bank, for example, utilizes a fairly autonomous organization called the Operations Evaluation Department (OED) to provide its policy makers with the data deemed necessary for refinement of policy. In their project cycle, however, evaluation is the final task of project management, and is handled in that manner (with no ongoing evaluation in the earlier tasks). It is stated that evaluations are "proving [to be] a goldmine of information" but that, nevertheless, over 91 percent of all projects audited in terms of investments have proven to be worthwhile and not in need of even minor policy refinements.[1] This kind of statement raises questions about the importance of policy refinement as a major task in the project management cycle.

While the problem is recognized as important, there is little evidence that a strategy or structured mechanism exists for implementing a policy refinement process. For example, a Ford Foundation report containing an extensive review of development policy and project management stressed that a major problem for development agencies (the World Bank in particular) is the need to successfully "evaluate and explore generic issues of importance for policy and practice."[2] The importance of the role of policy refinement in project development, then, is well recognized. What are some of the more critical elements of the policymaking process? The IPPMC model illustrates the complexity of the refinement process. In addition, in-depth analysis of 30 projects, coupled with the use of the 30 IPPMC cases in both education and training, confirm the need for a new project management team to assume responsibility and control of all tasks in the project cycle.

Thus, the most important factor in the integrated project cycle concept is the relationship between project managers and central policy makers. Both parties have the responsibility for making decisions and providing one another with information about such decisions; the daily decisions the project manager must make in implementing project activities are closely linked to the overall policy laid down by central policy makers. Thus, besides their interdependency within the project cycle, all tasks within the four phases of the project cycle are further linked by the larger set of policies guiding the project.[3] A project should be viewed as a learning experience from which to review planning and policy decisions, updating and modifying them according to the new information the project provides. Lessons learned from the project are the foundation upon which new projects are planned and implemented. This information for the future, whether the project has been judged a success or a failure, is an important contribution that every project can make to the betterment of the economy and the enhancement of the individual.

This chapter will examine and analyze the three IPPMC case histories presented in Chapters 6, 7, and 8 to illustrate the lessons learned and to show how these lessons can be applied to improve the policymaking process. A brief examination of the complete process is first discussed from an IPPMC case on a small paper mill project in India.[4]

KABINI PAPERS, LTD.*

Appendix B demonstrates the significance of national or federal government policy reinforcement of state policy in encouraging the creation of jobs through small-scale industrial development by providing incentives. The feasibility studies, including the impact of the effluent on the environment, were thorough, as confirmed by the results and impact of the project.

*An executive summary is presented in Appendix B for project background.

Refinement of Policy and Planning

This case has many lessons that are relevant for policy formulation, project planning and management, and their interrelationships for successful projects. The success of the initial mini-paper plant project is due to the combination of a viable industrial policy of the Indian government and the ability of an indigenous consulting firm to develop and effectively implement appropriate technologies for manufacturing paper from agricultural waste. In the process, technical expertise from a local university was retained to develop an inexpensive method of treating the plant's effluent to eliminate damage to the environment. Indeed, the treatment created an irrigant which would augment agricultural production in the area. The consulting firm had extensive experience with research, management, and "turnkey operations"—responsibility for a project from identification through completion, including handover to operations, and sufficient follow-up to ensure satisfactory production. Many turnkey projects by multinational firms created future problems because of lack of attention to maintenance needs. Increasing experience with turnkey projects by local firms promises a higher rate of success.

In particular, the Kabini case demonstrates the benefits of integrated planning and management to ensure the success of a project that capitalizes on the identification of opportunities to optimize raw material resources through the development and implementation of a new technology: one that results in the establishment of mini-paper plants in rural areas utilizing agricultural waste materials in place of the conventional but more expensive raw material, wood pulp. The problem is complicated when the development project seeks to satisfy a variety of basic needs in backward areas of developing countries, including creation of jobs and improvement of food production, in addition to the primary objective of meeting the demand for paper in the area.

The case illustrates the importance of managerial capability to put into effect and sustain viable policies, innovative social and technological plans, and resource development programs. It is especially significant in light of India's official policy, which discourages the importation of paper products through the imposition of heavy import duties. This policy, in turn, has created a paper shortfall, and for this reason the government has supported efforts by individual entrepreneurs to develop paper plants. Government support for small and medium-scale paper plants has resulted in widely dispersed enterprises throughout India, which not only contribute paper products but also facilitate employment, especially in rural areas. For areas that have been designated "backward," the government has offered incentives in the forms of cash subsidies, income tax deductions, low interest rates, reduced electrical power rates, and interest-free sales tax loans. Small and medium-sized industrial units, including paper plants, have thus been encouraged to locate their operations in these regions and have contributed to India's overall development plan.

The Kabini Papers, Ltd., project was successful in achieving its objective: promoting an attractive development-oriented industrial venture in a backward area of India, utilizing agricultural raw waste materials. This was a breakthrough in the use of indigenously developed appropriate technology for the manufacture of paper. It conformed to the government's industrial policy objectives of creating jobs, developing raw material resources, and increasing the standard of living in a developing economy. The project employed an appropriate method of effluent treatment which provided a desirable use for it as an irrigant in augmenting agricultural production. Finally, a conceptually clear project management approach was used, helping the project to overcome serious problems to reach a successful conclusion.

A government agency called the Karnataka State Industrial Investment and Development Corporation (KSIIDC) also refined its policy toward small to medium-sized paper projects. The successful experience of Kabini Papers, Ltd., resulted in a project for manufacturing 8 tons of kraft paper a day in the Nanjangud District and promoted a project for manufacturing 20 tons per day in another backward area in the State of Karnataka. With their apprehensions about small paper projects dispelled, KSIIDC planners were able to clarify and reinforce a policy of action promoting such projects.

Provided that such projects are properly conceived and implemented, the future of paper projects based on agricultural wastes looks promising for developing countries with an agrarian base, since utilization of agricultural wastes provides an inexpensive raw material system. In the future, such plants could also be planned to include their own power generation from such agrarian resources as farm animal dung. Gas produced from this source provides an inexpensive method of running generating sets to provide power. Plants of Kabini's size require only about 1000 kW, which can be generated inexpensively from farm animal wastes; in India, power from biogas produced from dung is already being used to run large farms.[5] Thus, the future may see paper plants based on agricultural wastes powered, as a public policy, by their own captive biogas generating system.

THE TRANS-ALASKA PIPELINE SYSTEM (TAPS)

The details of the various tasks undertaken to plan, design, and construct this large, complex project in arctic weather were presented in Chapter 8. It is clear from the IPPMC documentation and analyses that many factors contributed to the enormous cost overruns. Indeed, the Alaska Pipeline Commission retained a special counsel to investigate the excessive costs and charges incurred by the Alyeska Pipeline Service Company.[6] This discussion covers major problem areas ranging from feasibility through completion, concluding with lessons learned.

IPPMC Phase 1

Phase 1 commenced in July 1968 with pipeline feasibility studies and continued through November 1973 with passage of the Trans-Alaska Pipeline Authorization Act. This formative or preconstruction phase was plagued by many legal challenges which delayed the start of construction. Unfortunately, the owners failed to take advantage of the lengthy delay to plan and design the pipeline, the pump stations, and the marine station in a systematic and thorough manner. The basic problem inherent in phase 1 and subsequent phases was one of mismanagement and indifference to project costs. The lack of adequate planning by the owners was exacerbated by their lack of understanding of the need for a *single* project management team to oversee the entire integrated project cycle.

Of particular concern in the feasibility studies was (1) the inadequate geotechnical studies for later design and construction of the various structures, including the pipeline, and (2) lack of understanding of worker productivity, material procurement, and communication problems in the arctic environment. Indeed, there is no evidence that the feasibility studies seriously considered personnel needs to properly control and direct the project.

Inadequate design data were prepared for all components of TAPS. The consequent need to constantly revise designs during construction contributed greatly to the cost overruns. This was especially serious in the construction of the pipeline, pump stations, and marine terminal. The two major reasons for design problems were (1) Alyeska's deficient geotechnical planning and (2) the lack of concern for escalating construction costs by the owners. Alyeska's president, E.L. Patton, confirmed a major mistake made by his firm in planning for design and construction in the difficult and diverse soil conditions in Alaska.[7]

IPPMC Phase 2

One of the crucial problems of the TAPS project was that its organizational hierarchy and management structure were poorly conceived from the outset and were only marginally improved as the project progressed. Despite the ample time available to Alyeska and the owner companies prior to the start of construction, the available evidence shows inadequate planning and preparation for construction, as well as an ineffective management structure characterized by duplication and unclear lines of responsibility and authority. In 1972 the owners rejected Alyeska's recommendation to retain

Bechtel for planning and construction management. Bechtel was finally retained late in 1973, four months prior to the start of construction, and only for construction of the pipeline and haul roads.

Because of the confusing lines of management authority, the owners and Alyeska failed to establish (1) a project cost estimate plan and related control systems for implementation/expenditures and (2) viable contractor incentive plans for work in a difficult environment.

In addition, TAPS' management failed to develop systems and procedures to ensure that construction equipment, material, and spare parts were purchased, delivered, and inventoried in a cost-effective manner. The result was an often chaotic situation. Execution contractors (ECs) desperately sought to requisition spare parts which were already located in their own warehouses. Because of inadequate warehouse space, equipment and material were often stored outdoors and became lost after the first snowfall. By the time the spring thaw came, much material had either been ruined by the weather or stolen.

Equally serious was the failure to provide sufficient labor camp facilities, a cost-effective food catering service, and an adequate communications system. Again, as a result of late planning, TAPS construction began without adequate housing, catering control, or communication facilities in place. As a result, not only did expenditures for these vital support functions far exceed expectations, but the housing and communications problems delayed construction. They also caused numerous adverse ripple effects.

In sum, making policy decisions critical to the success of phase 2 was clearly influenced by self-interest on the part of the owners, compounded by lack of understanding of the project's needs. Indeed, this attitude prevailed in all of the phases, and was especially influenced by pressure from the environmentalists.[8]

IPPMC Phase 3

It is readily apparent from the previous discussions that there were serious disputes among the owners, Alyeska, and Bechtel concerning the appropriate scheduling of design and manpower, as well as the basic contracting strategy to be pursued with the pipeline's ECs. For example, Bechtel strongly recommended negotiating of contracts with ECs at the earliest possible time to allow their involvement in planning for the road and pipeline construction schedule for 1974. When this strategy was arbitrarily rejected, Bechtel correctly predicted that the resulting loss of construction and planning time would produce substantial cost overruns.

The Bechtel–Alyeska–owners dispute reflects a more profound problem. The duplicative management structure developed by the owners led not only to excessive administrative costs but also to paralysis of management's decision-making process. Confusion pervaded all levels of the project while the ECs, labor, Bechtel, Alyeska, and the owners attempted unsuccessfully to sort out their relationships and responsibilities. There is irony in Alyeska's and Bechtel's assessment of the same problems and their diametrically opposed solutions. For example, while Bechtel was demanding increased compensation for additional personnel to correct alleged Alyeska errors, Alyeska was criticizing Bechtel for utilizing unnecessary personnel in handling contractual duties.

Thus, implementation was constantly plagued by lack of direction and construction control. An example of costly and persistent quality control and quality assurance problems related to welding. One of the most serious welding problems experienced in all pipeline sections was the unreasonably high weld reject rate, which averaged 30 percent and reached as high as 80 percent. The slow pace of x-ray crews, which lagged several miles behind welding crews, perpetuated faulty welding techniques and production of welds suspected of having a high percentage of defects. As early as May 1975, owner company representatives observed firsthand the poor x-ray productivity and inefficient quality control which led to a high percentage of weld rejects.

Another serious and highly publicized implementation problem was that of workers frequently idle at the job site (including sleeping on buses and sunbathing along the right-of-way). Alyeska's own documents show that the principal responsibility for idleness rested with management's poor supervision and utilization of the work force. Most of the workers were willing to work but lacked "adequate direction and support" from a disorganized project management.

In addition to poor supervision and utilization of labor, Alyeska failed to implement adequate systems and policies to ensure control over man-hour expenditures. Alyeska only belatedly established adequate records to measure and monitor productivity and man-hours. Moreover, Alyeska failed to take corrective action, which these records showed to be necessary. Thus, such situations as the nonenforcement of essential work rules, payment for grossly excessive overtime, and rampant time card abuse (including a number of workers who were paid for successive 24-hour days) remained largely uncontrolled throughout the project.

Another implementation problem concerned those portions of the pipeline constructed aboveground. The aboveground mode required the main-line pipe to be supported on a crossbeam installed between two vertical support members (VSMs) embedded in the ground. The VSM construction operation suffered from a profusion of difficulties, all of which were marked by mismanagement and inadequate supervision.

The impact of late and inadequate design work affected all ECs. The three major components of construction—the pipeline, marine terminal, and pump stations—were adversely impacted.

In sum, the effects of incomplete and inadequate design extended well beyond the start-up of construction. Indeed, the ECs complained of insufficient engineering support throughout the 1976 construction season. The evidence shows that the contractors faced a particularly consistent problem in obtaining adequate construction drawings promptly from Alyeska. In addition, due to a lack of engineering authority in the field and a cumbersome bureaucracy in the home office, Alyeska failed to ensure the timely resolution of engineering problems encountered during construction. The results of these deficiencies included (1) numerous and costly delays as men and equipment awaited overdue engineering decisions, (2) problems with efficient work rescheduling as contractors tried to build around those areas for which they lacked sufficient engineering, and (3) in some instances, work that had to be redone because of inadequate engineering studies and deficient designs.

Lessons Learned

Many of the TAPS construction problems could have been avoided if the owners and their project management group (the Alyeska Pipeline Service Company) had recognized the importance of teamwork among owners, planners, designers, constructors, and managers of projects during the preconstruction period (1968–1973). As discussed in Chapter 1, this basic need relates directly to the priorities of the construction industry in particular[9] and to all projects in all sectors in general.[10] Thus, this need becomes the basic lesson, which can be applied to all problem areas ranging from the TAPS project to the Challenger rocket disaster on January 28, 1986.

The second major lesson is the need for a detailed checklist of questions to be prepared by the owners and their representative, Alyeska, preparatory to commencing the feasibility studies. The checklist could be adapted from the guidelines for case writers presented in Chapter 5, and would provide the owners with an appreciation of the number and complexity of the issues and factors affecting a proposed project such as TAPS. Equally important, the checklist would ensure proper attention to the feasibility studies, which should become the basis for preliminary designs, technical and environmental alternatives, and the subsequent tasks in the IPPMC.

The third major lesson is the overdue need for a data base for planning, designing, and constructing a variety of public works and private sector projects in different environments. For example, a data base containing case histories of projects such as the Distant Early Warning (DEW Line) System would have been invaluable for the owners and Alyeska in planning

TAPS. Indeed, the development of a data base for public works projects that would include case histories of a representative cross section of projects, both successes and failures, would provide valuable lessons and insights for the planning and management of future projects in the dual interest of safety and cost effectiveness.

A fourth major lesson is the need for detailed feasibility studies, which serve a multitude of purposes ranging from preliminary design refinement (for cost estimates and manpower/equipment needs) to development of necessary baseline data for ongoing evaluation of subsequent tasks and environmental impact (both short- and long-term). The details of project feasibility studies are covered in Chapter 3, and it is clear that such detailed information would have avoided the majority of design and construction problems encountered with TAPS.

Related to the first four lessons are the lessons learned regarding the need for project responsibility and accountability, which cut across proper planning and implementation of communications systems, material and equipment procurement systems, construction control systems (including management of labor/worker productivity), cost control systems, and so on.

In sum, the lessons learned from the TAPS project are profound and have many implications for both educators and practitioners—for educators because of the overdue need to include public policy, project planning, and project evaluation in engineering curriculum, and for practitioners (consulting firms, for example) who must interact with educators in developing the badly needed data bases discussed earlier. The TAPS experience confirms repeatedly the need for engineers to have a better understanding of the role of policy and evaluation in the integrated project cycle, and thus the importance of IPPMC case histories for both educators and practitioners. It also confirms the inseparable process of going from planning to design and through completion.

HAWAII GEOTHERMAL PROJECT (HGP)

The previous discussion clearly provides a positive response to the question: "Can learning from the past yield useful lessons for policy officials, planners, designers, and managers for the future?" The lessons drawn from the TAPS experience are multiple, cutting across each of the 10 tasks in the IPPMC and relating directly to all projects in all sectors.

The HGP provides a number of useful lessons in the dual context of (1) research and development of a viable alternative energy source and (2) the need to fully comprehend the potential conflicts between and among a natural resource development/utilization project, protection of the environment, and maintenance of stable societal conditions. Because of the nature of the HGP-A project, a demonstration or pilot research and development project, this discussion will not follow the four IPPMC phases. Rather, it will focus on two outstanding problem areas: (1) cooperation between and among the university, government, and industry and (2) development of a data base (case history library) for land-based alternative energy projects such as geothermal and biomass projects. A common denominator in each of these two problem areas is the need to understand the environmental impacts of alternative energy development on people, property, wildlife, and plant life. As noted in earlier chapters, baseline data are required first to estimate and later to measure the project's impacts on the environment.

The successful completion and operation of the HGP-A demonstration or pilot geothermal power plant is related directly to the interaction and cooperation among the University of Hawaii, the County of Hawaii, the State of Hawaii, the Hawaii Electric Light Company (private sector), and the federal government. The details of the creation and development of this vital cooperation are presented in Chapter 6. The success of this project was aided in large measure by the project director's efforts in forming the Hawaii Advisory Committee (HAC) and the National Liaison Board (NLB). The HAC was composed of leaders such as the president of Hawaii's electric company, the director of the state Department of Planning and Economic Development, the director of a leading environmental group, the president of the Congress of Hawaiian People, and officials from the County of Hawaii. These people represented the groups that formulated Hawaii's energy policy, so their support was critical. The NLB was composed of geologists, geophysicists, and engineers—experts in geothermal power development. Besides representing a core of the nation's geothermal experts, they worked for key agencies such as the National Science Foundation (NSF) and the U.S. Geological Survey. Thus, they were very influential in ensuring federal funding for the project. The importance of HAC and NLB to the success of the HGP illustrates the necessity of enlisting the support of key figures for policy making and funding. Of course, the key ingredient was the foresight and ability of the project director to both orchestrate the necessary teamwork and provide follow-up.

A long overdue case history library of a representative cross section of land-based alternative energy projects has been initiated for geothermal and biomass energy.[5,11] These case histories provide lessons and insights of benefit to policy makers, planners, designers, and managers of future geothermal and biomass energy projects. For example, HGP-A in Hawaii and Tiwi in the Philippines[11] greatly benefited from the earlier economic, environmental, managerial, scientific/technical, and social/political problems and experiences analyzed from the Wairakei project in New Zealand.[11] Indeed, the government of New Zealand has adopted the refreshing policy of providing free access to the information compiled over the years from Wairakei, in addition to giving technical assistance to other countries.

Again, Hawaii and the Philippines are excellent examples of applications of lessons learned from a carefully documented case history elsewhere.

An analysis of the case histories of three geothermal projects[11] provides useful insights demonstrating that the planning, design, and management of such projects must be capable of the following tasks: (1) coordinating resource exploration and evaluation activities and selecting an optimum plant location; (2) establishing the size of the resource and its hydrothermal and chemical characteristics; (3) designing the site's infrastructure improvements and plant module foundations; (4) designing the collection and reinjection system pipelines; (5) managing the procurement and detailed design of all modules; (6) designing and procuring the environmental monitoring equipment; (7) specifying and procuring appropriate alternative or optional units; and (8) managing the construction, activation, and training activities associated with full implementation of a geothermal power plant.

The method by which these eight activities were achieved differed in the three projects. Each project, however, had to utilize the same planning, technical, and managerial skills to bring their operations to the point where power was actually produced. Future geothermal projects will follow the same path, but the advances in these skills should be available to ensure that project objectives are met in the most effective way.

Beyond these considerations, the cases demonstrate that geothermal power development involves numerous separate but interrelated tasks. These tasks are accomplished by the combined actions of government policy makers, government departments, private organizations, universities, and specialist consultants. Working together, they must establish firm legal guidelines for utilizing and developing the geothermal resource and provide the organization, manpower, and other resources necessary to implement the project.

In sum, site-specific baseline data on environmental concerns must be established, with provision for monitoring critical areas of air and water pollution, land subsidence, noise, blowouts, and weather modification. Environmental data and experience with ongoing geothermal projects can be transferred and adapted to new project locations. Thus, the need for a case history library or data bank is reinforced by (1) the lessons derived from the initial three case histories and their parallels with one another, (2) the geothermal potential throughout the world (80 countries in 1975), and (3) the need to understand cultural, economic, environmental, political, social, and technological areas of special concern *and* their interrelationships in each project location. In Hawaii, some of these issues are as follows:[11,12]

1. Land ownership and geothermal rights in Hawaii are volatile issues in which tourist-oriented businesses and their employees, banks and

financial investors, the construction industry, real estate developers, agribusiness, and native-rights *huis* (associations) are often in conflict.

2. Hawaii has pluralistic lifestyles which are the result of ethnic diversity and an uneven distribution of population and economic activity. Current geothermal resources on the island of Hawaii exist in a highly rural setting, whereas the city of Honolulu, the state's population center on the island of Oahu, dominates the social, economic, and political life of the state.
3. Because of the single-wall construction used in building homes in Hawaii, noises from a geothermal source have similar intensities both indoors and outdoors. The nearest residences are located about 4000–5000 ft from the present well, and it is likely that about 1 in every 10 persons will become irritated by the noise at this distance. Residences and future well sites will be approximately the same distance from each other.
4. Subsidence due to removal of geothermal fluids is not considered a problem, but the collapse of lava tubes due to altered seismicity or water table modification is of major concern. However, the self-supporting nature of the rocks in the region of fluid withdrawal and the high rate of water recharge indicate that there is little geological evidence in Hawaii to support these concerns. This conclusion is based on experience with wells in California and New Zealand.
5. Accidents caused by geological events, such as lava flows or earthquakes, which would drastically change the operation of a geothermal facility are of concern to nearby residents and farmers.
6. Because of high natural environmental baselines, any major additions of SO_2, H_2S, mercury, or arsenic must be carefully monitored locally and regionally during any geothermal development. The one extant well, HGP-A, causes little or no deterioration of ambient air or water quality (while scrubbers are operational), but extrapolation of performance data from a single well must be done cautiously.
7. Hawaii has more unique endemic species than any other state—approximately 2000. Extreme care must be taken in geothermal site selection, and assurances must be provided that no degradation of unique habitats will occur.
8. Appropriate technologies have been developed to produce electricity from geothermal resources.[11] However, site-specific technologies must be thoroughly studied and documented to mitigate geologic hazards such as earthquakes, lava flows, and subsidence. In addition, more experience with environmental control systems must be documented in case history form to better understand the risk factors involved with long-term impacts on health, climate, and flora and fauna.
9. Although the amount of radioactivity released by HGP-A operations

from the Kapoho reservoir probably falls below hazardous levels in open-air conditions, there are two situations that have not been adequately examined with respect to radon in geothermal effluents: (a) will radon daughter radionuclides accumulate in confined spaces in hazardous amounts, and (b) can radionuclides be introduced into the food chain in hazardous amounts by uptake and concentration in plants?

HAWAII BAGASSE PELLETS PROJECT

Appendix D states that there are thousands of terrestrial and aquatic plants (solar energy–fixing systems), any one of which could be the ideal choice for a given application in a given set of circumstances. Learning to understand the growth characteristics of a particular plant, however, can take years—decades in the case of trees—and millions of dollars in research costs. Research work undertaken now will probably not be significant before the next century.

The biomass resource, therefore, should be one which is already well known and which producers know how to manage under different climatic and soil conditions. Even the reorientation of the end-product objective from traditional food or fiber to biomass energy may involve research. For any project to proceed, however, there must be no question about the supply of the essential feedstock. Then, if the feedstock can be fully utilized, the end result is a waste-free operation which will benefit both economic and environmental concerns.

It is in this context that extremely useful lessons and insights can be drawn from the bagasse pellets case history. Sugar companies in Hawaii have had extensive experience with bagasse as a source of steam and electricity. Lacking was an understanding of how to optimize the total use of bagasse throughout the year. This knowledge gap, coupled with the combination of rising labor costs, the high cost of meeting environmental (EPA) standards after 1970, and the dramatic increase in the cost of imported oil after the Arab oil embargo, plagued the sugar industry. A brief discussion of useful lessons for each of the IPPMC phases of the Davies Hamakua Sugar Company's bagasse pellets project to address these problem areas follows.

IPPMC Phase 1

The major lesson in this phase was the management decision to plan a long-term integrated program, commencing in the mid-1960s, to consolidate and modernize all factory operations for cost effectiveness. In 1973, this plan resulted in a new policy of energy conservation and development to improve productivity. A key factor in this process was the move to conduct feasibility studies on pelleting bagasse during the harvesting season, storing it for fuel purposes when it was not available during the year. A second major lesson was the decision to use company personnel for the feasibility studies and subsequent design. Technical personnel with extensive experience in sugar technology were instrumental in designing the world's first bagasse pellet factory, creating a new integrated energy system. This resulted in an energy technology uniquely suited to sugar company operations.

IPPMC Phases 2 and 3

Continuity to ensure successful activation and implementation was provided by utilizing the same managerial and technical personnel involved in phase 1. This integrated approach also resulted in a number of energy improvement adjuncts of the sugar operations. One example was the elimination of the pellet mill's need for independent sources of heat and power by the use of fuel or stack gases from the boiler and electricity produced by plantation generators.

Summary of Lessons Learned and Issues

Energy and environmental benefits resulted from a sound policy of increasing energy conservation and efficiency by optimizing bagasse utilization. This could only be accomplished by adapting a pelletizing process to bagasse, with improvements of the technology to eliminate waste. This accomplishment clearly resulted from the use of company personnel experienced in sugar resources and sugar technology. The significant lesson for other sugar companies still plagued by high operating costs and environmental concerns with surplus bagasse during the harvest season is to adopt a policy that will provide the necessary focus and direction—a policy that would enable the Hamakua Sugar Company to transfer their long-range program leading to a cost-effective, integrated bagasse/bagasse pellet energy system. This would include training programs to provide necessary manpower skills for planning, design, construction, management, and operation of the new facilities.

Experience demonstrates that an ideal starting point in this transfer of technology and skills is the availability of a data base or case history library that documents similar problem situations and describes how they were addressed in practice. Appendix D notes that many resources are required to generate biomass, which is then converted by various technological processes to different forms of energy. The establishment of biomass energy projects therefore requires attention to a wide range of necessary inputs, such as land, labor, capital, and energy, in addition to the technology and special skills highlighted in the bagasse pellets case. Some of these issues have been analyzed and discussed in the context of the individual case histories.[5] Unfortunately, at this time, biomass energy research and development is too embryonic to permit detailed analyses and discussions that might set forth the prerequisites for the planning and management of successful biomass energy projects in different socioeconomic and political settings. Available literature in the field is inconclusive and at times contradictory. This fact alone reinforces the need for a data base or case history library covering a variety of biomass energy projects. However, experience also confirms the significance of lessons learned from individual IPPMC case histories in improving the policy making, planning, implementation, and management of similar and new projects. Importantly, the IPPMC conceptual framework, complemented by IPPMC cases, provides the necessary guidelines and checklists to ensure success.

REFERENCES

1. Baum, Warren C. "The World Bank Project Cycle." *Finance and Development*, Washington, D.C., 1978.
2. The Ford Foundation, *Report on the External Advisory Panel on Education*. Washington, D.C.: Ford Foundation, 1978.
3. Goodman, Louis J. and Love, Ralph N., eds. *Project Planning and Management: An Integrated Approach*. New York: Pergamon Press, 1980.
4. Goodman, Louis J., Hawkins, John N., and Miyabara, T. *Food and Agricultural Waste Development Projects: Planning and Management*. New York: Pergamon Press, 1982.
5. Goodman, Louis J. and Love, Ralph N., eds. *Biomass Energy Projects: Planning and Management*. New York: Pergamon Press, 1981.
6. Lenzner, T.F. *The Management, Planning and Construction of the Trans-Alaska Pipeline System*. Washington, D.C.: Wald, Harkrader & Ross, 1977.
7. *U.S. News and World Report*. Washington, D.C., June 20, 1977, p. 37.
8. Geistauts, G. and Hauck, V. *The Trans-Alaska Pipeline*. (Goodman, Louis J. and Love, Ralph N., eds.). Honolulu: East-West Center, Resource Systems Institute, 1979.
9. The Business Roundtable. *More Construction for the Money*. New York: The Business Roundtable, 1983.
10. Goodman, Louis J. "Integrated Project Planning and Management: A New Approach." Drexel Hill, PA: Project Management Institute, Vol. 15, No. 4, 1984.
11. Goodman, Louis J. and Love, Ralph N., eds. *Geothermal Energy Projects: Planning and Management*. New York: Pergamon Press, 1980.
12. Siegel, Barbara Z. *The Impact of Geothermal Development on the State of Hawaii*. Honolulu: University of Hawaii, 1980.

CHAPTER 10

Summary and Conclusions

We have come a long way from the initial articulation of ongoing serious problems with wastage and mismanagement in many project areas despite increasing attention to engineering management education. It is therefore useful to refocus on the last paragraph in Chapter 1 as a lead-in for a summary of the many lessons derived from Chapter 9. Attention is then focused on specific projects and programs in both government and industry that could benefit from the IPPMC conceptual framework and IPPMC case histories.

In Chapter 1, four sorely neglected areas were highlighted as being instrumental in ensuring both environmental quality and project productivity.

- Encouraging long overdue teamwork among planners, designers, contractors, and owners of projects.
- Satisfying the need for accurate information flows between and among the aforementioned personnel to ensure safe, cost-effective projects.
- Creation of data bases in each sector through carefully researched and documented case histories of projects to provide useful lessons and insights for both current project troubleshooting and future projects.
- Application of the lessons learned from the case histories to refinement of policies and planning of new projects.

Examples of project problems have been examined and discussed, ranging from the multiple problems in the Trans-Alaska Pipeline System (TAPS) to the financial and environmental problems encountered in the research and development of the Hawaii pilot geothermal project (HGP). In the first case, there was complete lack of understanding of how to plan, design, and manage a large, complex project effectively. The fragmented approach adopted for the project was compounded by lack of teamwork and information flows. As discussed in Chapter 9, this combination resulted in inadequate feasibility studies and analyses. Without the benefit of a built-in mechanism for evaluation of each task in the project cycle, the inevitable occurred:

- Inadequate preliminary design and cost estimates.
- An inadequate final design.
- Inadequate attention to planning and scheduling of construction in the arctic environment.
- Inadequate attention to personnel needs in order to direct and control the project properly.

The lessons and insights learned from the TAPS case history are many, and are useful to all project areas—especially in public works—and to the construction industry. Indeed, the lessons from the case conclusively focus on *feasibility analysis and appraisal* as the critical steps in the project cycle *in all sectors* (Chapter 3). It was emphasized in Chapter 3 that comprehensive feasibility studies are vital to many decisions and policies affecting the problem areas encountered by TAPS and by many other projects, ranging from costly overruns to structural collapses. A set of guidelines and checklists must be developed from the feasibility studies to ensure that the final design and implementation result in both environmental quality and project productivity.

Project productivity is measurable in terms of cost effectiveness and safety. Environmental quality may take years to measure, especially in the case of TAPS, because of the slow rate of ecological adjustment in Alaska. As of early 1985, system (pipeline and tanker) failure has not caused an oil spill of crisis proportions. During the process of construction and start-up, numerous smaller fuel spills occurred, but their damage was localized and Alyeska attempted to minimize the damage by using cleanup measures. A certain amount of local damage was also due to siltation and erosion.

In the HGP, financial problems were resolved by sound planning, management, *and follow-up*. Importantly, lessons learned from initial well testing in both Hawaii and the Wairakei geothermal project in New Zealand led to the establishment of environmental baseline data and a follow-up monitoring system.[1]

The Hawaii bagasse pellets case history also vividly demonstrates the value of IPPMC cases in providing guidelines and checklists to assist owners, planners, and designers to anticipate potential problems *and* to adopt a policy for their solution if these problems occur. This approach applies to any industry or public works agency. Again, the value of the IPPMC framework, as documented in Chapter 7 and analyzed in Chapter 9, is demonstrated in its applicability to a variety of project areas other than those in the sugar industry.

The four sorely neglected areas highlighted in Chapter 1 and mentioned again here are common problems in many projects in all sectors, and in both developed and developing countries. Of imminent concern to both civil and environmental engineers is the long overdue need to utilize a model such as the IPPMC *and* to identify key personnel to implement the model in (1) eliminating hazardous wastes altogether and (2) cleaning up the thousands of existing toxic waste dumps in the United States alone. The EPA continues to work on risk-based guidelines for maximum allowable contaminant concentrations, using different approaches in its attempts to clean up specific sites. A scientific approach could be developed by researching and documenting IPPMC case histories of past cleanups, both successes and failures, in order to provide the necessary data base. Every Superfund cleanup is an experiment, and some EPA professional staff now understand the desirability of developing a scientific data base by research and publication of case histories for each site cleaned to date. Training programs could then be offered based on the lessons learned from each case, and guidelines/checklists prepared to assist in dealing with hazardous waste problem areas.

There are many other programs/projects in the federal government that could benefit greatly from an integrated project planning and management systems approach. The general examples presented below are taken from a report commissioned by President Ronald Reagan in June 1982 and published in January 1984.[2] These examples are deemed appropriate here because of their impact on the economic and social well-being of the United States (in 1985 we joined Argentina, Brazil, Mexico, and other developing nations in the debtor class, and on April 4, 1986, the national debt reached a mind-boggling $2.0 trillion—an increase of $1.0 trillion in a mere five years). One of the most serious problems reported by the Grace Commission[2] is the "information gap." No one knows (1) how much money is actually being spent for defense; (2) how many consultants are hired by the government; (3) the number of federal employees, by department and agency, in each state; (4) an inventory of consultants' reports on priority problem areas *and* an inventory of available spare parts within the government; and so on. The results of this information gap are duplication and waste. (Author's note: the Business Roundtable, in New York City, reported in January 1983 on the results of a Construction Industry Cost Effectiveness Study. One of the major problems is "a bizarre lack of accurate information" from federal government statistics).[3] Indeed, as a consultant for the U.S. Agency for International Development (USAID), the author has encountered lack of cooperation and communication among various USAID programs. In addition, the duplication of management training programs in the federal government is mind-boggling, and the results are ineffective.

In the private sector, the construction industry is the nation's largest industry, as well as the most fragmented and one of the least productive. In recent years, it has been required to build facilities which are more and more complex, utilizing a fragmented approach rooted in the education system (see Chapters 1 and 2). The results are reflected in a marked decline in the efficiency and productivity of the industry. The resulting increase in the cost of every power plant, office building, hotel, and factory built raises the price that must be charged for the goods or services produced in those facilities.

One major reason that construction is comparatively inefficient is its lack of teamwork, as demonstrated in Chapter 8. Construction is a US$300 billion-a-year activity involving close to 1 million contractors, over 70 national contractor associations, more than 10,000 local and national labor organizations, about 5 million workers, and many customers. Despite the capabilities of the larger and more progressive contractors, and despite the sophistication of many clients regarding construction, too much of the industry remains mired in the past. Construction effectiveness starts with the owners, and they, along with governmental regulators of the construction industry, are part of the problem. An adversarial relationship often exists, breeding suspicion and lack of cooperation among the participants.[4]

The keys to upgrading the construction industry are cooperation and communication between and among the principal parties—owners, planners, designers, builders, managers, and educators. There is a great need for organized knowledge and exchange of information. Meaningful research must involve realistic data gathered from both past projects and current practice. This can be best accomplished by developing an IPPMC case history data base.

In summary, there are many problems with both public and private sector projects. As noted in this chapter, the approach needed to solve the problems is threefold: (1) an integrated approach to project planning and management, (2) complementary case history libraries, and (3) a comprehensive checklist of questions adapted from Chapter 5 and relevant cases to serve as the basis for improving the cost effectiveness and performance of all projects. Schools of architecture and engineering, and practitioners (architects/engineers, planners, contractors, and managers), must collaborate to meet this need. There is also great need for formal courses in universities in both project planning and evaluation. Ideally, these courses should be interdisciplinary, and should include a team building focus. Unfortunately, these courses will take time to develop because of the slow pace of change in curricular matters.

The conclusions drawn from 10 years of experience (1977–1986) with the IPPMC curriculum and case histories clearly demonstrate its versatility in providing the necessary coordination and control of the various tasks in the project cycle. Specific examples of applications are as follows:

1. The IPPMC curriculum is useful for project management education and training, both formal and informal.
   a) It can be adapted for one or two three-hour courses at the graduate school level.
   b) It can be adapted for seminars, workshops, and training programs ranging from 2 to 16 weeks.
2. IPPMC case histories are extremely useful to both educators and practitioners
   a) As resource material for class assignments.
   b) As reference material for both educators and practitioners who seek past project autopsies or postmortems as a basis for developing guidelines and checklists for planning, design, and management of new projects.
3. The IPPMC model provides the necessary framework for researching and publishing additional case histories to develop badly needed data bases for
   a) public works project areas such as hazardous waste disposal.
   b) the construction industry.
   c) the manufacturing industry.
   d) the agricultural sector.
   e) the social sector such as education and public health.
4. The IPPMC cases can be used for the development of checklists of potential problem areas to anticipate in the design and implementation of specific projects, ensuring prompt remedial action.
5. The IPPMC model provides a framework for both the private and public sector to organize project teams with leadership requirements for overall control: teamwork, continuous performance review, and accountability, thereby satisfying project objectives in all categories (purpose, time table, and budget).

In conclusion, the IPPMC fills a long overdue need to integrate project planning, design, implementation, and management in order to achieve unified control of all projects. This will improve the quality, efficiency, and cost effectivenss of projects, resulting in annual savings of US$30 billion in the construction industry alone. It will halt the design and construction of multiple nuclear power plants (such as the five recommended for the State of Washington) during the feasibility studies, saving $20 billion in public (municipal) bond default, waste, mismanagement, and litigation in one state alone.[5] It will ensure that final designs of all projects satisfy relevant building codes, thereby preventing structural collapses such as the Kansas City Hyatt Regency hotel atrium walkways in 1981 which killed 114 persons.[5] It will provide a sound basis for preparing guidelines and checklists for all future programs/projects in order to fulfill goals and objectives on budget and on schedule in a wide variety of fields. This includes EPA's Superfund Program No. 2 (US$8.5 billion to clean up more than 300 toxic waste sites, 1986–1991) and the programs of other federal agencies.

The conclusions presented and discussed in this chapter clearly demonstrate the urgent and long overdue need for both educators and practitioners to interact and collaborate in adopting the IPPMC model as the framework and methodology for future projects. Educators must include it in one or two courses to commence the learning process. Practitioners must utilize a framework based on the IPPMC to provide the necessary quality for both projects and the environment. This can be accomplished by preparing a checklist of guidelines and questions necessary for unified control of each task. The checklist can be drawn from Chapter 5, and a small sampling is shown in Appendix E.

REFERENCES

1. Goodman, Louis J. and Love, Ralph N., eds. *Geothermal Energy Projects: Planning and Management.* New York: Pergamon Press, 1980.
2. Summary Report of the President's Private Sector Survey on Cost Control. *War on Waste.* New York: Macmillan Publishing Co., 1984.
3. The Business Roundtable. *More Construction for the Money.* New York: The Business Roundtable, 1983.
4. Aquino, Rosemary, Goodman, Louis J., and Hawkins, John N. "Summary Report: Planning Conference on Management Training for Public Works Projects." Honolulu: East-West Center, Centerwide Programs, 1982.
5. Goodman, Louis J. "Integrated Project Planning and Management: A New Approach." Drexel Hill, PA: Project Management Institute, Vol. 15, No. 4, 1984.

APPENDIX A

Prototype Curriculum Outline for a Course in Project Planning and Management*

INTRODUCTION

WEEK 1

Day 1 Project Planning and Management
1. Course orientation
2. Integrated project cycle: An overview

Days 2 and 3 Case History Method
1. Use of the case history approach
2. Lessons from case histories of development projects in different socio-economic settings
3. Examples of successes and failures

Day 4 Development Planning: Structural Elements and Comparative Analysis
1. Methods and organizations involved in planning and implementing programs at various levels
2. Role of organizations concerned with projects, including vertical and horizontal linkages between organizations
3. Various frameworks for development planning and implementation

Day 5 Focus on the Role of Programs/Projects
1. Problems in project planning
2. Lessons in development planning
3. Planning in relation to national and state goals

WEEK 2

Day 1 Focus on Project Planning
1. National, sectoral, and state plans
2. Problems with and constraints on project plan implementation
3. Analysis of country and state strengths and weaknesses in relation to project planning

*The prototype curriculum was designed and developed by an international team of scholars and practitioners during the period 1975–1977. It is intended for an intensive 16-week training program for project managers in all sectors. It is also flexible enough to be adapted to either a shorter training program or an academic course. It was implemented in seven countries in 1978, with favorable results.

Day 2 Management of Projects
1. The management process: An overview of concepts and issues
2. Problem areas in project planning, implementation, and evaluation
3. The role of the project manager in the management process

Day 3 Project Management Environment
1. Environmental factors affecting projects and project management: political, administrative, social, economic, technological, and ecological factors
2. Factors facilitating and/or constraining project management

Day 4 Overview of Strategies for Effective Project Management
1. Administrative capability: concepts and issues
2. Enhancing administrative capability: leadership role in resource generation and management, problem solving, and motivation

Day 5 Promoting Interorganizational and Individual Cooperation
1. The rationale for interagency involvement in project planning, implementation, and evaluation
2. The structural, legal, and behavioral dimensions of interagency, intersectoral, and intergovernmental relationships and project management
3. Strategies and techniques to ensure inter- and multilevel cooperation

WEEK 3

Day 1 Conflict Identification and Resolution
1. Understanding and identifying conflict in the organization
2. Strategies and techniques for resolving conflict using creativity in organizations

Day 2 Generating Environmental Support
1. Concepts and issues in establishing institutional linkages
2. Techniques in building support for the project in the environment

Day 3 Systems Approach in Project Management
1. Introduction to the systems approach
2. Systemic nature of projects
3. The systems approach and project management

Day 4 The Integrated Project Management Cycle
1. Basic tasks
2. The role of project managers

Day 5 Management Tools and Techniques Essential to Project Management
1. Theory and practice of management: administrative planning, programming, and organizing
2. Other essential management skills: controlling, budgeting, communicating, and organizing
3. Project management methods, tools, and techniques, including bar charting, network analysis, and case analysis

4. Other methods, tools, and techniques useful to the project manager: systems analysis, analysis simulation models, linear programming, management games, and management information systems (MIS)

PHASE 1: PROJECT PLANNING, APPRAISAL, AND DESIGN

WEEK 4

Days 1 and 2 Project Identification

1. Initiating the project plan
2. Guidelines for project identification: macro- and micro-analysis
3. Nature of projects: to determine whether a project is related to other projects
4. Strategies, priorities, and sequencing of projects
5. Awarcness of available resources, instruments, and time constraints
6. Identification of political and administrative support

Day 3 Project Formulation

1. Process of project formulation
2. Factors and elements to be considered in project designs and alternatives
3. Preliminary feasibility studies of projects and project designs
4. Selection from among design alternatives
5. Supportive systems design
6. Seeking initial political and administrative support

Day 4 Preliminary Project Design

1. Objectives of project design
2. Communications requirements in project design
3. Procedures and steps in design
4. Obtaining sufficient data for design

Day 5 Project Resources

1. Identification of critical resources
2. Estimating and scheduling resources
3. Planning procurement of resource needs
4. Coordinating with resource sources and authorities

WEEK 5

Day 1 Project Feasibility: Overview

1. Concepts and components of feasibility studies
2. Procedures and organization of feasibility studies

Day 2 Project Feasibility: Technical Aspects

1. Project location and layout
2. Required technologies
3. Physical facilities needed
4. Manpower: skills, competence, and experience
5. Training and development requirements

Day 3 Project Feasibility: Economic, Social, and Political Aspects
1. The concepts of opportunity cost, cost/benefit analysis, and spinoff benefits
2. Variables of national economic impact analysis
3. Limits of required resources
4. Financial analysis of project parameters
5. Marketing and commercial analysis
6. Social/political factors and issues

Day 4 Cost/Benefit Analysis
1. Economy-analysis methods and their application
2. Time value of money, equivalence, and depreciation
3. Various costs and their evaluation
4. Estimate of benefits
5. Value theory
6. How to handle intangibles
7. Estimation of input values
8. Methods of choosing among technical alternatives

Day 5 Project Feasibility: Environmental Aspects
1. Environmental baseline studies
2. Guidelines for preparing environmental impact studies

WEEK 6

Day 1 Project Feasibility: Managerial/Administrative Aspects
1. Defining the components of administrative feasibility
2. Approaches to administrative feasibility analysis
3. Organization and procedures of feasibility analysis

Day 2 Project Appraisal
1. Purpose of project appraisal
2. Procedures and criteria for project appraisal
3. Examination of procedural documents for project appraisal currently used by the World Bank, national funding sources, and other funding agencies

PHASE 2: SELECTION, APPROVAL, AND ACTIVATION

Day 3 Project Selection
1. Understanding the project selection process of:
   a. Local government
   b. International agencies
2. Identifying selection criteria
   a. Economic: net social return on investment
   b. Financial: availability of funds
   c. Technical: availability of required technology and manpower
   d. Sequential: to decide which projects are to be implemented first (ir-

rigation and transportation projects are requisites for agricultural projects—water needs and transport of produce to markets)
   - e. Political
3. Applying selection criteria

Day 4 Project Negotiation
1. Identifying items to be negotiated
   - a. Funds: sources, amounts, terms
   - b. Market and management arrangements
   - c. Technology arrangements
   - d. Necessary budget and personnel arrangements
   - e. Necessary cooperation with related agencies
2. Establishing the negotiating team
3. Establishing the negotiation position
4. Establishing the negotation strategy

Day 5 Project Approval
1. Obtaining legislative authorization (if required)
2. Obtaining executive approval (if required)
3. Confirming procedures for budget operations
4. Confirming procedures for personnel operations
5. Confirming procedures for interagency cooperation

WEEK 7

Days 1 and 2 Project Design Refinement
1. Preparation of working contract drawings and other documents such as specifications
2. Discussion of the various problems connected with:
   - a. In-house designs
   - b. Designs contracted to outside firms
3. Design data input from the project manager
4. Design fee and designer's responsibility
5. Establishment of a design timetable
6. Interagency and intersectoral inputs and coordination
7. Project timetable and control:
   - a. Project inspectors
   - b. Preparation of the critical path method (CPM) or another network model (see WEEK 9)
   - c. Management information systems

Days 3 and 4 Tenders and Contracts
1. Project drawings and specifications
2. Definition of contracts
3. Establishment of a committee on bids and awards to advertise, accept, and evaluate proposals
4. Prequalifications of bidders
5. Comparison of the various types of contracts:
   - a. Lump sum

b. Cost plus
c. Unit price
d. Man-hours and others

6. Establishment of procedures for change orders and extension of contract time
7. Evaluation of bids

Day 5 Project Organization

1. Concepts needed in handling complex organizations
2. Skills needed in setting up the operational framework of an organization for project implementation

WEEK 8

Day 1

3. Systems and human dimensions in the context of project management organization
4. Planning the appropriate organization and operations activities
5. Setting up implementation units, recruitment, and selection
6. Establishing a work plan, a budget, and a communication system within the organization
7. Recognizing interdependencies (external)
8. Creating linkages with other organizations (setting up a communication system)
9. Interface with project beneficiaries

PHASE 3: OPERATION, CONTROL, AND HANDOVER

Day 1 and 2 Project Administration/Management

1. Management process
2. Hierarchy and levels
3. Project manager
   a. Qualities of leadership
   b. Management of conflict in project teams
   c. Authority and responsibility

Day 3 Systems Modeling

1. Modeling/various types of models
2. Application of models in project management and various phases of the project cycle

Day 4 Bar Charting

1. Bar chart models
2. Application, virtues, and limitations of bar chart models
3. Network-based model

Day 5 Network Modeling—critical path method (CPM)

1. Network planning and scheduling with CPM
2. Critical path analysis

WEEK 9

Day 1 Network Modeling: Other Techniques

1. Precedence network
2. Program evaluation and review techniques (PERT)

Day 2 Simulation Models

1. Simulation concepts, models, and techniques
2. Application of simulation techniques to typical problems in project management
3. Limitations of simulation

Days 3 and 4 Management Information Systems (MIS)

1. Concepts of MIS
2. Definition of information requirements
3. Sources of information
4. Organization and procedures of MIS
5. Criteria for relevance of management information
6. Techniques of MIS
7. Design of MIS for projects

Day 5 Monitoring of Projects

1. Concepts and objectives of monitoring projects
2. Management-by-exception principle
3. Monitoring techniques
4. Establishing and using performance criteria as a basis for information collection

WEEK 10

Day 1 Project Feedback and Control Systems Approach (Closed-Loop System)

1. Identification of critical feedback elements
2. Identification of feedback channels
3. The use of feedback information

Day 2 Coordination and Control Procedures

1. Selection of coordination and control procedures for management, administration, and organization of project needs
2. Procedures to coordinate internal and external project activities

Day 3 Financial Control

1. Project budgets: preparation and review
2. Forecasting and monitoring financial aspects of project activities
3. Framework control, reporting, and feedback systems

Day 4 Materials Control

1. Procurement procedures for materials and services
2. Techniques for achieving optimum inventory levels
3. Monitoring of materials usage and comparison with budget

Day 5 Computer Applications

1. Computer capabilities for project management
2. Computer software and its uses in project management

WEEK 11

Day 1 Project Termination or Assimilation

1. Making the decision to continue, terminate, or "fold into" the activity of an ongoing agency
2. Restructuring the ongoing agency (via legislation, organizational decisions, budgets) to review continuing activities
3. Problems of transfer
   a. If the project is a pilot or demonstration program, difficulties related to movement to full-scale operations
   b. Difficulties related to meaningful transfer of project expertise ("as built" into), contracts, etc.
   c. Related to the termination or transfer of project employees
   d. Related to the transfer of capital assets
4. Formal transfer procedures
5. Problems of supporting receiving organizations

PHASE 4: PROJECT EVALUATION AND REFINEMENT

Days 2 and 3 Project Evaluation

1. Need for and role of evaluation
2. Objectives, scope, and types of project evaluation
3. Tools for efficient evaluation. Postevaluation as the summary and completion of MIS-type ongoing evaluation
4. Tools for effectiveness evaluation of project results measured against criteria established in the feasibility study
5. Comparison between projected and actual project results: variance analysis and cost/benefit analysis
6. Tools for evaluation of project impact
   a. Measuring effects on local or sectoral settings
   b. Unforeseen effects or spinoffs
7. Tools for evaluation of project benefits
   a. Assessment of medium- and long-term benefits
   b. Planning for long-term evaluation benefit studies
8. Administrative support for evaluation. The formation of evaluation teams
9. External audit methods
10. The role of evaluation by external or funding agencies
11. Writing the project evaluation report
12. Indicating alternatives for termination or assimilation
13. Recommending follow-up action and the magnitude of future resource requirements

Day 4 Project Follow-Up

1. Developing a report: What has been learned by each stage of the project cycle?
2. Identification of unmet needs
3. Identification of potential projects emerging during project implementation
4. Developing proposals for follow-up projects
5. Can we have a case history?

Day 5 Review and Refinement

1. Review of management functions and actions in managing projects
2. Phase-by-phase analysis of the project cycle to identify important management activities based on case history discussions and shared experiences
3. Preparation of group reports on critical aspects of the management of projects
4. Preparation of guidelines and checklists to improve the planning and management of future projects

PRACTICUM

WEEKS 12–15

1. Reading and analysis of selected cases
2. Group reports on lessons learned
3. Fieldwork (at discretion of instructor)

WEEK 16

1. Presentation of group reports
2. Use of checklist of IPPMC questions/issues
3. Summary of course

APPENDIX B

Executive Summaries of Six Cases

BANGKOK METROPOLITAN IMMEDIATE WATER IMPROVEMENT PROGRAM*

Abstract

This case history documents the interim program initiated by the Bangkok Metropolitan Administration to cope with the water supply needs of the city of Bangkok, Thailand, until a long-term plan could be implemented. It illustrates the consequences and high cost of expediency planning and implementation. It provides useful lessons for future public works programs in both developing and developed countries.

Program† Background

The provision of water to any highly urbanized area needs careful planning and effective administration because it involves the design, construction, and maintenance of extensive water works, integration of several technical systems, accommodation to different categories of users, and an effective distribution system. To ensure an acceptable, sufficient, and timely output requires considerable engineering and public health skills in addition to complex organizational and procedural arrangements.

The case of Bangkok's water supply from 1960 to 1970 presents a dramatic example of the difficulties noted above. The city's inhabitants suffered from chronic shortages and service inadequacies, which were due to faulty administration and to delays in enlarging the water supply sufficiently to cope with rapid urban growth and increasing demands.

The Bangkok water supply administration was first set up as a Water Works Unit in the Sanitation Department of the Ministry of Metropolitan

---

*Adapted from a case history by Chakrit Noranitipadungkarn, published in *Management of Development Projects,* Louis J. Goodman and Ralph H. Love, eds. (New York: Pergamon Press, 1979).

†Here a program is considered as comprising several interrelated projects. Each project may consist of one or more activities.

Administration. When the ministry was abolished four decades ago, Bangkok Water Works became a division of the Public and Municipal Works Department (PMWD) of the Ministry of the Interior. Later the Bangkok Municipality, established in 1939, assumed supervision of that division. In 1952 the Ministry of the Interior, considering the administration of the water supply to be unsatisfactory, requested the return of the division to the PMWD. It remained there for the next 15 years until it was transformed into a public enterprise. In 1967 the four water works systems then serving the four contiguous cities and the greater Bangkok area—Bangkok, Thonburi, Nonthaburi, and Samutprakan—were consolidated to reduce costs and to increase the efficiency of the operation. The reorganized agency was named the Bangkok Metropolitan Water Works Authority (MWWA) and continued to be attached to the Ministry of the Interior.

At the height of the water crisis in 1967, consumers were compelled to scramble for whatever water was available. Because only a few drops of water ordinarily reached the end of the service lines in the daytime due to heavier use, many residents would awaken during the night to draw off enough water for the next day's use. At commercial places and some residences, it was not uncommon for owners to install water pumps illegally in their bid for a greater and more regular supply of water. Although the MWWA continued to approve the installation of water pipes to new buildings, some new housing areas were left without service because development funds were not sufficient to complete the job. Complaints from users and nonusers alike were voiced constantly in the city's daily and weekly newspapers, demanding either new services or a cleaner, more dependable, and sufficient water supply.

Earlier in 1966, the cabinet decided to take steps toward certain reforms in the capital city. The initiative to do something about the water supply came from the National Economic Development Board (NEDB), a central planning agency of the government. NEDB members were convinced that no more time should be lost in expanding and improving the several water systems in the metropolitan area. An ad hoc Committee on Bangkok Water Works Improvement was proposed, and this action was endorsed by the Cabinet, the highest decision-making group in the nation. The committee was composed of the deputy secretary-general of the NEDB, as chairman, and representatives from the Bangkok Water Works Authority, the PMWD, the Ministry of the Interior, the Budget Bureau, and the NEDB. Its purpose was to suggest improvements and to plan for the future.

The committee's first recommendation was to reorganize the agencies that were providing water to the metropolitan area. Another assignment was to determine the types of studies necessary to formulate specific recommendations for improving the water supply itself. Committee members, lacking the requisite knowledge and expertise themselves, agreed to recruit the engineering firm judged to be most suitable for conducting a thorough survey and preparing a master plan for both management and technical improvements in the MWWA's operation. It was the committee's firm conviction that only by this strategy would supplies of water to the metropolitan area in the future be sufficient and uninterrupted.

The U.S. firm of Camp, Dresser, and McKee was selected, based on the facts that its time and cost estimates were the most reasonable and that it had the best experience and past performance. After the necessary negotiations, the committee signed a contract with the company to carry out its assignment. This process of evaluation and approval took several months, however, and many more months would be needed to get the project moving. This greatly aggravated situation forced the committee members to realize that some *intermediate* plan was needed to provide the maximum amount of water in the shortest time possible. Such an intermediate proposal would have to be consistent with the more fundamental long-range plan.

Camp, Dresser, and McKee began work in June 1968. After seven months spent in an extensive study of various possibilities, the firm presented a preliminary report that included a series of recommendations as emergency measures to meet the minimum water requirements for the metropolitan area projected to the year 1975. This was a proposal for a so-called Immediate Water Improvement Program, whose work would be completed in fiscal years 1969 and 1970. The criteria used in formulating these recommendations were that a maximum increase in the water supply must be developed in the shortest possible time, with the least investment cost, and with minimum disruption of existing operations.

The Immediate Water Improvement Program consisted of four major projects designed to meet the stated goal. For each project, specific targets were identified, costs were estimated, time schedules were set, and needed improvements were detailed. The MWWA would bear responsibility for working out further details and procedures as the projects were implemented. The four major projects were as follows:

Project 1: Improvement of the surface water transmission canal and water treatment plants. Both banks of the main canal would be raised 1 m. In each of the 10 existing treatment plants in Bangkok, a new, larger water tank would be constructed, and pipelines, valves, and other accessories would be replaced as needed.

Project 2: Increase of groundwater production by additional deep wells and shallow aquifers. The latter would cost less than the deep wells, but the quality of the water would not be as good, although it would meet the standards for treatment at the Thonburi plant, then operating at only half of its capacity.

Project 3: Repair of leaking pipelines for water conservation. New work units would have to be organized to survey the full extent and nature of the leakage. Necessary equipment would be purchased and personnel would be recruited and trained to carry out this work for the entire metropolitan area. This activity would be critical in remedying the existing situation, but it would also have to be continued on a permanent basis as part of the long-range master plan.

Project 4: Repair or replacement of the large number of nonfunctioning water meters discovered in the firm's preliminary survey. A problem-oriented task unit would have to be created to complete this work within the two-year duration of the improvement program. The existing Water Meter Division would bear responsibility only for the installation of new meters.

Results and Impacts

The project on the detection and repair of leaky pipelines was the only one completed on schedule (September 1970). The remaining three projects overran their schedules by one to five years because of unanticipated difficulties, including a much longer period to reorganize MWWA and a variety of meter repair and replacement problems. However, the program did raise the total capacity of water production and distribution in the Bangkok metropolitan area to a new high of 1,200,000 m^3/day.

The following observations drawn from the experience of the Bangkok Immediate Water Improvement Program highlight certain critical factors in project planning and management that may occur elsewhere in the conduct of similar programs of planned change.

1. *An Interim Program to Gain Time.* The Immediate Water Improvement Program consisted of four projects, devised for implementation by the MWWA to alleviate as quickly as possible the very serious water shortage in the greater Bangkok area. Under the circumstances, it was not intended to, nor could it, solve the whole problem of water supply faced by the people and their government. Rather, it was designed to be an interim effort for the purpose of gaining time while the large-scale, long-term development program was being prepared.

2. *A Program of Separate Projects.* Instead of a situation in which a professional authority forecasts that a crisis will occur sometime in the future and recommends measures to cope with it, the concept of the Immediate Water Improvement Program emerged only in response to extraordinary public pressure. The MWWA, the organization responsible for the program, was poorly prepared to take up the challenge. The severe time limits understandably contributed to an implementation plan in which the four projects were carried out independently instead of being coordinated.

3. *A Test of Management Capacity.* Originally, the consulting firm attempted to formulate its recommendations into a single program, that is, to integrate several activities or projects that would serve the single overriding objective and that could, or should, be carried out simultaneously. This strategy was based on the firm's feasibility study of the water service system, taking into account factors of demand and supply judged to be crucial in determining the scope of the remedial program and the engineering capacity to cope with the problem. At the same time, potential sources of additional water were extensively explored. But the planning consultants sorely underestimated the time required to complete all of the projects.

Perhaps most important of all, they failed to gauge correctly the organizational capacity of the MWWA to implement the whole program. The consulting firm had recommended specific courses of action based on accepted project management principles and practices. However, MWWA administrators were not familiar with or experienced in these concepts and their ramifications. Therefore, when the Water Improvement Program was finally launched, the MWWA was still in the midst of a reorganization aimed at modernizing its management structure and procedures. The result was that an unexpectedly long time was needed for total implementation of the program and its affiliate projects.

4. *Benefits of Strong Government Support.* The MWWA was unable to operate solely with its own financial resources. It was fortunate, therefore, in having strong moral and fiscal backing from the government. The support from the NEDB, as well as the powerful personality of the board chairman, who was at the same time deputy prime minister, contributed significantly to the receipt of the necessary funding from government sources. With such direct support, the MWWA was not compelled to seek loan funds, either internal or external. That would have meant many months of negotiation and execution of loan agreements, forcing undue postponement of the Water Improvement Program.

5. *Emphasis on Physical, Rather Than Social, Development.* The kinds of work called for in the Bangkok program posed fewer problems than might be expected in other types of development projects. The principal reason for this was that the program was almost entirely limited to new construction or repair work, both of which were primarily physical. No far-reaching changes in either the attitudes or the behavior of the city's population were contemplated, except for a limited reorganization of personnel and responsibilities in relevant MWWA work units. Any attempted major alteration of Bangkok society or culture would have been very difficult to introduce or maintain. Innovative elements in the water improvement projects, both physical and organizational, were to a large extent simply added to what the MWWA already had or was accustomed to, and this made the task somewhat easier. It may be noted, however, that in the meter repair and replacement project, some client users of water were delinquent, break-

ing meters and otherwise circumventing the system by illegal means; they would have to be educated to a more cooperative behavior in the future.

Conclusions

This case study has demonstrated how organizations may be modified or created to cope with the problems arising in project implementation. Certain permanent units within the MWWA were able to serve project demands with only minor adaptations. In other instances, ad hoc temporary units had to be established to accomplish a given task. Another lesson learned was that organizational change proceeded more smoothly when it was carried out one step at a time, at a pace that was not unduly disruptive, building on what was familiar and well established. A third innovation, which promised gains for the MWWA both then and in the future, was a double-check system whereby one work unit regularly reviewed the work of another to achieve greater efficiency and integrity in services offered to the public.

The case also demonstrates the need for better planning with respect to possible implementation problems that result in costly overruns. It further shows the need to integrate planning and management.

THE PEOPLE'S REPUBLIC OF CHINA: ENERGY FOR RURAL DEVELOPMENT—THE YAOCUN PROJECT*

Abstract

This case history describes a small-scale hydroelectric project in rural northern China. The project site was in the county of Linxian, located in the northernmost point of Henan Province. This area consists of an extensive canal system from which numerous small hydroelectric stations operate. The 80 or more small hydroelectric stations in the country were designed and constructed in integrated clusters. This case focuses on one such cluster of two stations, constructed during the period 1973–1977 and known as the "Yaocun Project." Many problems in the management of such projects were documented: the political-economic environment; planning and management in a state socialist system; rural farmer participation; the multiple uses of water control projects; and the process of establishing an informal technical training program. This case is a good example of the variety of problems that emerge in project management when lines of authority are not clear and governmental decisions and messages are inconsistent.

---

*Prepared by John Hawkins, published in *Small Hydroelectric Projects for Rural Development,* Louis J. Goodman, John Hawkins, and Ralph H. Love, eds. (New York: Pergamon Press, 1981).

Project Background

Efforts to transform rural China into a more productive, modern, and integrated sector of the Chinese economy have been a major priority of the Chinese government for the past 30 years. This has been the case despite the many factional disputes that have emerged among the leadership since 1949. Regardless of which administration exists in Beijing, broad economic policy guidelines have consistently reinforced the need to promote rural development through a policy of "walking on two legs" or giving equal attention to transforming indigenous, small-scale technology and to introducing (or transferring) more modern techniques and technologies.

More relevant to this case are government policies regarding small-scale enterprises in general and small-scale hydroelectric plants in particular. Especially since 1958, the government has promoted the development of intermediate and small-scale enterprises and has generated, at different times, criteria that must be met before an enterprise can qualify as a small-scale plant. In summary form, the following profile emerges of a typical small-scale plant in rural China: First, it must be located in the rural sector, most often in association with a rural commune or county seat. Second, the technology selected to operate the plant must be as uncomplicated as possible, utilizing discarded machinery as appropriate and dependent upon indigenous resources. The emphasis must be on supporting the development of agriculture, which means that most enterprises fall into the category of supplying agricultural inputs of various sorts (fertilizer, electricity, cement, irrigation, etc.).

The primary goal of this project, then, was to follow the executive order of the Ministry of Water Conservancy and Electricity that counties increase their generation of electricity for rural development. Linked to this demand was a request that hydroelectric power become a priority, together with sideline utilization of this power—for example, canal systems, water conservancy, irrigation, and small-scale industries (fertilizer plants, raw materials extraction, etc.). These were the objectives of the Yaocun Project.

Results and Impact

The Yaocun Project had five basic areas of impact on the county of Linxian. First, since it was related to a large-scale canal development system, its primary result was to increase the irrigation facilities of the entire county. This resulted in increased agricultural yields and, therefore, more income for the villages in the area. Second, since the region was drought prone, the canal system solved the problem of water starvation and shielded the residents from a historical pattern of water deprivation and hardship. Third, and more directly related to the Yaocun Project, was the increased electricity generated for the county as a whole, which allowed residents more electricity for household use, village use, and overall economic development purposes. Fourth, the increased electricity generation resulted in an expansion of sideline production in such areas as small-scale industries, fertilizer inputs, and raw materials processing.

Finally, the project initiated an informal education training program to upgrade the skills and techniques of rural farmers so that manpower could be shifted from traditional agricultural practices to semi-industrialized skills associated with low-head hydroelectric plants. Labor was thus released from traditional farming practices to assist in rural modernization while not being displaced to the ranks of the under- or unemployed. This informal training component was utilized as a model for other rural areas throughout north-central China.

Conclusions

Six major lessons emerged from the Yaocun Project. While they were specific to this particular case, some of them are applicable to similar small-scale projects in other settings:

1. A structural problem affected all small-scale hydroelectric plant construction projects on the canal. Since the canal was originally designed for water management and irrigation, rather than to generate hydroelectric power, planning for this capacity was absent. The subbranches of the canal were not structurally suited to hydroelectric power plants; therefore, considerable reconstruction was necessary to make this adaptation. Each time a plant was built, a slightly different technique was used to cope with this problem, and each time the adaptation process became more efficient. These experiences were recorded and made available to future project leaders developing small-scale hydroelectric stations.
2. The project met initial opposition from the residents. Local farmers associated with the three production brigades and their leaders were reluctant to engage in a new and possibly costly enterprise. Specifically, they did not want to divert human resources from agriculture to the hydroelectric construction crew and were reluctant to sink what amounted to venture capital into the initial project—the construction of the physical plant.
3. In view of the political events of the time, arbitrary orders were given by politically motivated cadres with little technical expertise who were working on the project. The project manager and other technicians, who had to take several political risks to protect the technical quality of the project, might have been in serious trouble if the political environment had not changed in late 1976.

4. Some administrators associated with the Yaocun Project (at the county level) were themselves politicians, having been promoted because of their support of the dominant political group at that time. They had little administrative experience and occasionally compromised the efficiency of the project by creating bottlenecks in supply procurement and other areas.
5. It was concluded that the time spent to complete the project (four years) was too long. A project of this scale should have been completed in less than three years. The reason given for the delay was the tense political situation, which on one occasion halted construction while numerous political discussions were held regarding a local investigation that was underway.
6. Finally, there were several efforts on the part of enthusiastic cadres to implement overzealously the principle of "design while constructing." This is actually a formative evaluation technique that can be used to great advantage. Mechanically following design plans that reflect only the advice and expertise of provincial and county authorities can cause as much difficulty as constantly changing the plan. It was recommended that some balance be found between these two extremes.

In sum, the Yaocun Project provided a certain amount of security to the region in at least two ways: The supply of electricity was clearly increased to consumers who were too distant from Anyang to benefit from the larger source of electricity, and the contribution of the small plants to the Anyang network helped to provide an overall saving, especially during the peak demand periods. Given China's extensive water resources and the current problems associated with fossil fuels, it is likely that both large- and small-scale hydroelectric projects will remain a high priority within its overall energy policy.

BALIGUIAN RIVER MINI-HYDROELECTRIC PROJECT*

Abstract

This case history documents the planning and implementation of a 100-kW hydroelectric project in an isolated rural area in southern Luzon (Province of Camarines Sur), the Philippines. The project represents a new policy by the Philippine government to accelerate its energy program, with special emphasis on mini-hydroelectric projects for rural development—providing

*Adapted from a case history by Rosemary Aquino, published in *Small Hydroelectric Projects for Rural Development,* Louis J. Goodman, John Hawkins, and Ralph H. Love, eds. (New York: Pergamon Press, 1981).

inexpensive and dependable power to create new jobs, in addition to creating multipurpose water supply systems and flood control. The case demonstrates the significance of electric cooperatives in rural areas. It further illustrates the strength of well-planned and coordinated projects, which range from indigenous manpower skills to the development of the necessary technologies.

Project Background

During the 1960s, many rural areas in the Philippines had little or no power. Some rural cities had small generators capable of supplying only lighting. Because one government priority was to develop rural areas, and in recognition of the fact that electrification played a very important role in rural development and industrialization, a government agency was set up to undertake rural electrification. The Electrification Administration was created in 1962 under Republic Act No. 2717. In 1969 this agency became the National Electrification Administration (NEA), when President Ferdinand Marcos signed Republic Act No. 6083, abolishing the Electrification Administration and creating this agency in its place.

The primary objective of the NEA is to undertake the rural electrification program on an area coverage basis, with electric cooperatives as the primary medium. The electric coop is the organization that sells energy to the community. Generally, an electric coop covers 9 to 10 municipalities with a total population of 100,000 to 500,000 people. The electrification program aims to bring the benefits of electricity to the rural areas by providing needed power for income-generating industries and irrigation systems for increased agricultural production. The long-range objective of the NEA is to attain the total electrification of the country by 1990 and to provide electrification to all *barrios* (small villages or communities) by 1984.

The NEA also planned to develop local expertise in the technology of mini-hydroelectric plants. Aside from encouraging local innovation and design, in 1979 the agency negotiated with the People's Republic of China (PRC) for the transfer of technology in building generators and hydraulic turbines. In April 1980, President Marcos approved a licensing agreement between the Atlantic, Gulf & Pacific Company of Manila, Inc., and the China National Machinery and Equipment Import and Export Corporation to transfer technology for manufacturing mini-hydraulic turbines; a cooperative production agreement between the Philippine Electric Corporation and the China National Machinery and Equipment Import and Export Corporation to transfer technical knowledge of mini-hydraulic generators; and an agreement of cooperation between the China National Machinery and Equipment Import and Export Corporation and the NEA on the financing and supply of mini-hydroelectric generating units.

Meanwhile, the general manager of the Camarines Sur IV Electric Cooperative, Inc. (CASURECO IV), Engineer Percival Favoreal, undertook a study on the feasibility of constructing a mini-hydroelectric plant to reduce the cost of power. In early 1978, he and his staff made on-the-spot inspections in the Caramoan Peninsula and found a waterfall in the municipality of Presentacion on the Baliguian River. Their investigations revealed that the measured flow of the river was 5.7 m^3/sec, with a head of 27 m. The height of the waterfall was 28.66 m. Computations showed that the potential of the river was 200 kW. Favoreal then proceeded to plan how to harness this waterfall for generating to electric power to serve the surrounding municipalities. He obtained a small budget from the coop for research and development, and by mid-June 1978 had completed the design for a mini-hydroelectric plant.

In January 1979, after satisfactory testing of the mini-hydroelectric model he had built, Favoreal informed the board of CASURECO IV of the need to build the actual mini-hydroelectric plant. When the board granted approval, negotiations were conducted with a local machine shop that supplied spare parts to the coop to fabricate the turbine, payable in three months' time.

The NEA approved a loan request for the project, and construction commenced in May 1979. All building and civil works were done by the CASURECO IV administration. A local firm, the DCCD Engineering Company, was hired to supervise the civil works. Reinforced concrete for the culverts which make the penstock were precast at the CASURECO IV headquarters in Tigaon. The generators were purchased from the municipal electric plant at Ragay. These generators were then out of order and not in use, as the municipality was supplied with power by another electric coop.

The project was built mainly by people from the area. Seventy workers were involved in the construction of the plant and other related structures. Eighty percent of them were from the *barangay* of Presentacion; the rest consisted mostly of technical personnel employed by the coop.

Results and Impact

The project overran its budget by more than 40 percent, primarily because of the need to transport all materials and equipment by boat to the site. However, the gift of electricity to a community spells opportunity and hope for development. For a community like the Baliguian *barangay,* an underdeveloped fishing village once part of a logging concession, the chance for development is even more significant. The area to be served by the hydroelectric project is mountainous, but the mountainsides have been denuded by past logging operations. The people plant *camote* (sweet potatoes) as their staple food. No paved roads exist in the *barrios,* and travel to places outside the peninsula is difficult and expensive for the townspeople.

The mini-hydroelectric plant has been operating since its inauguration in late 1979. Three local people operate it on a three-shift basis, one person per shift. The municipalities of Presentacion and Caramoan now benefit from the steady supply of electric power. As of early 1980, the coop had built power lines extending 9 km to Presentacion, benefiting 300 families, and 16 km to Caramoan, benefiting 400 families. The plant provides the coop with a monthly savings of ₱30,000 (approx. US$3,000 in 1979), equivalent to 15,000 liters of diesel fuel.

The NEA is monitoring the operation of the mini-hydroelectric project. Teams of consultants and foreign visitors have already been brought to the site. Through the NEA newspaper, *SINAG,* information about the project has been disseminated to other cooperatives and interested parties.

The mini-hydroelectric program will provide additional employment in the rural areas. The initial Baliguian project resulted in employment for some 70 workers from the project area and the area covered by the coop. It has stimulated equipment and parts fabrication for the coop's technical staff and an engineering shop in a rural city. Its impact on indirect employment generated through industrialization cannot yet be measured. This effect, however, is probable and will be felt in the coming years.

Conclusions

This case demonstrates the viability of well-planned and implemented mini-hydroelectric projects in furthering the growth of rural areas. A number of useful lessons can be learned from experience gained with the Baliguian project. The outstanding lesson is to locate and train the skilled manpower needed to plan, design, build, and operate small hydroelectric facilities. A second lesson concerns coordination and support. Much coordination is necessary within and among the various government agencies for a program such as the mini-hydroelectric program to be successful. Outside the Ministry of Energy, however, government agencies such as those involved in irrigation programs, local government, community development, and the provision of basic services to communities all engaged in development projects for rural communities. For hydroelectric projects, which are usually complex undertakings, to have maximum impact on the rural areas, coordination among these agencies is necessary.

The Baliguian project is a remarkable example of a project initiated at a level close to that of the users, with full support from the central planners. The board of the coop is composed of representatives from each of the municipalities in its coverage area. The unique needs of each municipality can, therefore, be readily recognized and considered. The NEA, on the other hand, has been able to respond equally well to the needs of the coop for funding—cutting through bureaucratic red tape—so that project approval to completion took less than one year. The NEA has proved that it can manage a centralized program of mini-hydroelectric development and yet build in the flexibility to respond to requests from coops for support in innovative projects—a centralized-decentralized approach that may prove effective in the mini-hydroelectric program.

TALOMO RIVER MINI-HYDROELECTRIC PROJECT*

Abstract

This case history examines a cluster of three small hydroelectric projects with installed capacities ranging from 300 to 600 kW near Davao City in Mindanao (Province of Davao del Sur), the Philippines. The first project consisted of the repair and rehabilitation of a power plant constructed by the Japanese before World War II, with subsequent destruction of all equipment by the Japanese army. In addition, a fourth related project of 1.6 MW is documented. The case demonstrates the ability to repair and renovate an existing dam and powerhouse, along with the development of indigenous expertise for the design and implementation of later projects. Another highlight is the leasing of government power projects to the privately owned Davao Light and Power Company.

Project Background

A program to develop small hydroelectric power projects was pursued by the National Power Corporation (NPC), a government agency created on November 3, 1936, to create hydroelectric and other natural sources of power. This program was started in 1947 and continued during the 1950s.

From the start of its operations in 1936, the NPC conducted surveys, investigations, and hydrologic and hydrographic studies of river systems in the country and compiled all existing data on locally available power. The corporation initiated the construction of its first major hydroelectric power project in 1939—the Caliraya River Hydroelectric Project, with an initial 27-MW capacity.

After World War II, with the country devastated, all economic development plans for the Philippines advocated a shift of the national economy from purely agricultural to semi-industrial. Industrialization necessitated power development, hence the urgent need to tap a known and abundant power resource—hydroelectric power. The government was interested in developing power not only for industry but also to improve the quality of life.

---

*Adapted from a case history of Rosemary Aquino, published in *Small Hydroelectric Projects for Rural Development,* Louis J. Goodman, John Hawkins, and Ralph H. Love, eds. (New York: Pergamon Press, 1981).

A Philippine Power Program was prepared as a result of an agreement made in March 1947 between the Philippine government and the Westinghouse Electric International Company. The agreement commissioned Westinghouse to undertake, with the NPC, the preparation of a power program for the Philippines, as well as to provide the data necessary for securing loans to fund the recommended projects.

Because there was an immediate need for power in areas other than those specified for development in the Philippine Power Program of 1947, the National Power Board of the NPC approved a complementary program of small hydroelectric power projects scattered throughout the Philippines. Funding for the project would come mainly from the NPC. This program was expected to be operational in 1948, simultaneously with the major hydroelectric power program, with a wide distribution of the benefits of electricity among the population.

Ten sites were initially identified in the six-year program of small hydroelectric power projects: six in Luzon, two in the Visayas, and two in Mindanao. A total 8-MW capacity was expected to be developed, requiring a financial outlay of P10 million (approx. US$2.5 million in 1950s). Thirty-eight towns and cities were expected to benefit from this program. Of the initial sites, four were planned for the Talomo River, including the reconstruction of the extensively damaged Japanese power plant previously mentioned.

The Talomo River, located in Davao City, is well suited to hydroelectric power development. The river bed has a good shape. River discharge in this area of well-distributed annual rainfall is very steady. The river drains the northeastern slope of Talomo Peak, an extinct volcano, with a drainage area of about 175 km^2 of sloping land. It flows into Davao Gulf a few kilometers west of the center of Davao City.

During World War II, the more than 22,000 Japanese planters and workers who lived in Davao joined the Japanese Imperial Army and became the occupation units controlling the city. Before American liberation, the Japanese army destroyed structures in the city, including the hydroelectric plant of the Ohta Development Company on the Talomo River. All the equipment in the powerhouse was destroyed, as was the superstructure. The dam, forebay, penstock, and powerhouse substructure were usable, however, although in need of minor repairs. This hydroelectric power plant was designated "Talomo No. 2," with reconstruction providing an installed capacity of 400 kW.

No feasibility study was prepared for the rehabilitation of the original Talomo hydroelectric power plant, designated "Talomo River No. 2." Since this was considered a repair and rehabilitation project, only engineering drawings were prepared. Feasibility studies, however, were prepared for subsequent plants on the river.

These studies proposed a plant installation of 300 kW for Talomo No.

2B, 400 kW for Talomo No. 2A, and 1600 kW for Talomo No. 3. Plants 2A and 2B would be clustered with No. 2, whereas No. 3 would be downstream. The studies considered growth factors in agricultural and industrial areas in Davao City and the surrounding areas. They also considered the need to increase the capacity of Plants 2 and 2A in the future by adding a third 200-kW unit to each.

Results and Impact

Shortly after the Talomo No. 2 plant became operational, pollution problems were encountered. The canal system of the plant was 4 km from the dam, passing through cultivated areas also used by the area's inhabitants to dispose of grass cuttings, banana stalks, tree branches, garbage, and other refuse. Some of this matter was caught in the forebay of the plant, where it clogged the trash racks and sometimes penetrated to endanger the turbines. In 1952 a chicken wire screen was used to solve this problem, but it required continued vigilance to keep it clean. Three maintenance men were employed—one on each shift—to clean and watch this screen, and frequently they became ill from a combination of pollution and chill. As a solution, NPC engineers designed and constructed a motor-operated revolving screen to use in place of the chicken wire screen.

Delays were encountered in the operation of Talomo No. 2A because of the late delivery of machinery and equipment ordered from U.S. manufacturers. The project was scheduled for completion in January 1952, but although the civil and hydraulic structures were completed by 1952, the project was finally completed and commissioned into service on April 14, 1953.

Reports on the progress of each project were included in the NPC's annual reports during the 1950s. Progress reports included the status of the projects, costs incurred, and problems encountered. Once a project was operational, monthly energy generation and income received were presented in the reports. This NPC monitoring system was effective in keeping department and project managers up-to-date on the performance of each hydroelectric power project. Targets set for the hydroelectric power programs were reviewed and accomplishments noted, as were delays and their causes. As a result of these reports, policy refinements or changes in procedure were undertaken. For example, in the early 1950s, delays in delivery of equipment from the United States (as a result of the accelerated U.S. defense effort) were noted. This caused delays in NPC project schedules, and the NPC general manager urged the government to secure defense priorities for these orders.

The Talomo hydroelectric project was built by a government agency, and the power generated was sold to the Davao Light and Power Company (DLPC), a private utility franchise holder. The relationship between the public and private sectors in the development and distribution of power proved beneficial. In this instance, the Talomo hydroelectric plants were operated by the NPC and eventually leased to the DLPC in the 1970s. In a position paper dated July 1977, the DLPC indicated that it had been able to increase the efficiency of the plants significantly through careful supervision and monitoring of operations and the improvement of plant equipment and facilities. It has since included several rural municipalities in its franchise area coverage. This sizable investment and efficiency of operation—accomplished without government subsidy—have resulted in expanded operations for the hydroelectric projects.

In recent years, more private participation in mini-hydroelectric power projects has been encouraged. The Center for Nonconventional Energy Development of the Ministry of Energy supports research projects by private groups in water power technology. In 1979, President Marcos issued Letter of Instruction No. 933, setting up an Energy Priorities Program under the Board of Investments to encourage the local manufacture of mini-hydroelectric equipment. Other suggestions coming from the private sector include participation in the implementation of actual projects: simplified guidelines and procedures for a private enterprise to set up a mini-hydroelectric project and the possibility of a "wheeling" arrangement whereby a private company sets up the mini-hydroelectric plant at a feasible site for use by nearby communities in exchange for power at the site of the company from the NPC grid.

The initial six-year program of small hydroelectric projects produced two significant results. First, the use of project teams by the NPC provided invaluable training for indigenous engineers who would be responsible for future small hydroelectric project planning, design, and implementation. Second, the delays in delivery of equipment from abroad provided the impetus to develop local expertise for the design and manufacture of all equipment.

Conclusions

The Talomo hydroelectric project contained a number of positive factors. This project graphically demonstrated the ability to repair and renovate an existing dam and powerhouse in order to make a significant contribution to the energy needs of several rural municipalities. Of equal importance was the fact that the NPC used this project to train young engineers in the management of hydroelectric projects, thereby developing a pool of experts for future projects. A third factor was the leasing of the Talomo power plants to the DLPC in the late 1970s. This transfer from the public to the private sector shows how the efficiency of a badly needed water power system can be improved without the need for any additional government subsidy.

KABINI PAPERS LTD.: A DEVELOPMENT PROJECT UTILIZING AGRICULTURAL RAW MATERIALS*

Abstract

This case history describes the development and implementation of a mini-paper plant in a rural area of India designed to meet a paper shortage and to create jobs involving both professional and technical personnel. Using local available but unutilized agricultural resources, such as rice straw and elephant grass, the plant was designed to produce 10 metric tons of kraft paper (industrial paper) per day. Highlights of the case study include the project's organizational and funding complexities, the design problems, the technical solutions, and the overall impact on rural development efforts. The case clearly demonstrates the significance of the ways in which meaningful employment can affect people's lives. It further illustrates how an integrated approach to project planning and management overcomes problems and produces beneficial results.

Project Background

The term "kraft paper" covers a range of industrial papers of high strength which have found increasing use in wrapping, flexible packaging, and other types of packaging materials. The strategic role played by kraft paper in a developing country like India is well established, as it is useful in packaging a wide variety of consumer goods for shipment, in addition to meeting the needs of local industries for the storage and protection of various items, including foodstuffs. Production projections at the end of the Fifth Five-Year Plan (1974–1979) were of the order of 1,200,000 metric tons of paper and paperboard. The demand projections for kraft paper were on the order of 350,000 to 450,000 metric tons per year, whereas the expected production capacity was only 250,000 metric tons per year. Moreover, the quality of the kraft paper hitherto produced in India had not been very satisfactory. There appeared to be no quality standards, supplies were irregular, and prices were exorbitant because of the ever-increasing gap between demand and supply.

---

*Adapted from a case history by Arvinder Brara, published in *Food and Agricultural Waste Development Projects,* Louis J. Goodman, John Hawkins, and Tetsuo Miyabara, eds. (New York: Pergamon Press, 1982).

The Indian government's industrial policy has been to encourage the setting up of small- to medium-scale industrial units throughout the country to generate additional employment and development opportunities, particularly in the underdeveloped rural areas. To motivate industrial units to locate in these areas, the government has declared a number of such regions to be "backward areas." Attractive incentives have been offered for the relocation of industries from overstrained urban areas to rural areas, where traditionally about 80 percent of the 623 million Indians live. Historically, from the time of Mahatma Gandhi, the Indian government has continually attempted to move labor-intensive industries to undeveloped rural areas in order to increase employment, development, and social stability. The incentives offered include a cash subsidy from the government in proportion to 15 percent of the fixed assets employed, income tax deductions for up to 10 years, lower rates of interest for loans, cheaper electrical power rates, and interest-free sales tax loans. This policy has resulted in an opening up of the Indian rural areas to private, joint sector, and public sector industries.

It is in this context that the paper industry offers good entrepreneurial opportunities in India. An experienced administrator, A. Basu, joined forces with a well-known Indian consulting organization, M.M. Suri and Associates PVT, Ltd. (MMSA), in 1974 to formulate plans to design, construct, and operate a mini-paper plant (Kabini Papers, Ltd.). MMSA was especially experienced in paper technology, including research and development in both the process and utilization of agro-waste materials.

MMSA suggested a 10-metric-ton-per-day plant as the smallest economical unit, considering the limited resources for investment by the promoters. Such a project would cost approximately 10.3 million rupees (Rs.), (approx. US$1.35 million in 1974), generating a sales turnover of Rs.16.5 million. MMSA also recommended that, in keeping with the Indian government's policy of developing industries in backward areas and to take advantage of the attractive incentives offered, the project should be set up in a rural area. The following features were identified as important in deciding on a suitable plant location, based on the various factors MMSA used in identifying small-industry locations.

1. Availability of raw materials—rice straw or other agricultural straws and sources of longer fibers such as cotton rags, jute, and banana fiber.
2. Proximity to consumer centers of the product (in this case, kraft paper).
3. Availability of continued and uninterrupted supplies of water, coal for steam generation, and electrical power in adequate quantities.
4. Transport facilities by road, rail, and air.

5. Effluent disposal facilities.
6. Acceptability and availability of technical personnel, including skilled and semiskilled industrial workers.
7. Availability of incentives to locate in backward areas.
8. Proximity to academic and research organizations.

Among the various sites considered, the area of Nanjangud in the Mysore district of Karnataka State appeared to be the most suitable.

Result and Impact

The evaluation done by MMSA in conjunction with Kabini Papers, Ltd., showed that the project had been successfully established. The capacity tests had shown that the plant could indeed make 10 metric tons per day of high-quality kraft paper. Indigenous technology had been successfully used to promote a development-oriented project. A major breakthrough had been achieved in designing and introducing a machine-glazing (MG) cylinder, which could be manufactured locally at a considerable saving over the conventional cast-iron version.

The impact of the project in various areas was evaluated as follows:

1. *Political:* The project contributed to the government's policy of promoting employment-oriented, agro-based, small- to medium-scale industries in backward areas using indigenous resources as much as possible. The doubts of some financial organizations about the viability of small- to medium-scale paper units were successfully overcome, and the project was accepted both politically and financially.

2. *Social:* The Nanjangud area benefited from the project because it provided a source of income to the farmers; it created a demand for agricultural waste, which previously had had no market. In addition, the Kabini project improved employment in the area by providing both direct and indirect employment opportunities. The influx of professional, technical, and financial executives helped to improve the social environment, and the income potential and earnings of the local people improved, thereby helping to raise their standard of living. The project was fully accepted by the local Nanjangud society as one that would help to improve their economic situation.

3. *Cultural:* Because of the influx of about 170 well-paid employees of the paper plant, most of whom lived locally, the cultural environment of Nanjangud was given a boost. With increased recreation demands, local cultural institutions became more active. The plant also helped to activate a local club which served as a meeting place for a variety of people, thereby

increasing communication and cultural interchange among the residents of Nanjangud.

4. *Environmental:* The impact of the paper plant on the natural environment was favorable. Previously, some of the rice straw had been used as cattle feed, but most of it was burned or thrown away. This practice added to the pollution and litter in the area. With a new local market for rice straw, the major agricultural waste of the area, the environment benefited. Moreover, the effluent was not pumped out directly, which would have polluted the neighboring areas or the nearby local river. Instead, it was treated to serve as an irrigant. A number of local farmers welcomed the treated effluent of the paper plant for use in their fields in this capacity.

5. *Refinement of Policy and Planning:* Based on the experience gained in completing the Kabini project, the MMSA reviewed its policy on the management of turnkey projects. The considerable delay in getting the MG cylinder from the supplier showed that this situation would have to be avoided in the future. The policy to spread out the orders of fabricated equipment would have to be adapted to fit the country's developing industrial environment. This was necessary because delivery schedules from vendors were usually affected by raw material shortages, occasional power disruptions, and working capital constraints. It was therefore imperative not to order most of the fabricated items from one vendor, however competitive and capable he might appear to be. Also, vendor follow-up would need to be done more effectively from the start.

The Karnataka State Industrial Investment and Development Corporation (KSIIDC) and the consortium of banks also evaluated the project upon its completion. Its cost had escalated, mainly due to delays in gaining financial approval and to the vendors' failure to supply the vital MG cyclinder on time. Nevertheless, the project's viability had not been impaired, both because of its inherent strengths and because of the favorable increase in the market price of paper. KSIIDC was so impressed with the developmental benefits provided by such a paper project based on agricultural wastes that they initiated two similar projects in the State of Karnataka.

The MMSA also decided to promote and pursue the construction of further small- to medium-scale projects based on agricultural wastes in order to manufacture kraft paper, writing paper, and specialty papers.

KSIIDC also refined its policy regarding small- to medium-size paper projects. Based on the successful experience of Kabini Papers, Ltd., it helped to promote a project for manufacturing 8 tons of kraft paper per day in the Nanjangud district and a project for manufacturing 20 tons per day in another backward area of the State of Karnataka. With their apprehensions about small paper projects dispelled, KSIIDC planners were able to clarify and reinforce their policy on promoting such projects.

Conclusions

The Kabini Papers, Ltd., project was successful in promoting an attractive development-oriented industrial venture in a backward rural area of India, utilizing agricultural raw material wastes. This project was a breakthrough in the use of indigenously developed appropriate technology for the manufacture of paper. It conformed to the government's policy objectives of employment generation, raw material resource development, and increasing the standards of living in a developing economy. The project used an appropriate method of effluent treatment to help provide a desirable use for it as an irrigant in augmenting agricultural production. Finally, a conceptually clear project management approach was used, thus helping the project to overcome serious problems to reach a successful conclusion.

Provided that they are properly conceived and implemented, the future of paper projects based on agricultural wastes is good for developing countries with an agrarian base, because utilization of agricultural wastes provides an inexpensive raw material system. In the future, such plants could also be planned to include their own power generation from such agrarian resources as farm animal dung. Utilizing gas produced from this source is an inexpensive method of running generating sets to provide power. Plants of Kabini's size require only about 1000 kW, which can be generated inexpensively from farm animal wastes. In India, the generation of power from biogas produced from dung has been used to run large farms. Thus, the future may see paper plants based on agricultural wastes powered as a public policy by their own captive biogas power generating system.

MALIA COAST COMPREHENSIVE HEALTH CENTER*

Abstract

This case history describes the interaction of cultural, social, economic, and political factors in the planning, design, and management of a health center to deliver health care services to a rural area on Oahu over a 10-year period. The case analyzes the many problems associated with a low-income community's struggle to organize and mobilize resources to provide an urgently needed health center, with complications arising from the lack of a competent project administrator or manager who was familiar with each task from

*Adapted from a case history by Nancy Crocco and Tetsuo Miyabara, published in *Management of Development Projects: An International Case Study Approach,* Louis J. Goodman and Ralph H. Love, eds. (New York: Pergamon Press, 1979). Malia is the fictitious name of a coastal area in rural Oahu, Hawaii; it is used because of the personally and politically sensitive issues involved.

inception to completion and sensitive to the cultures of a multiethnic population.

Project Background

Situated on Oahu's western shore is the Malia Coast, which is isolated from the rest of Oahu by the ocean to the west, the Malia mountain range to the east, and the nearly impassable jeep trail to the north. To the south lies the only road to urban Honolulu, which is about 30 mi away. The habitable land occupies a narrow corridor situated between the ocean and the mountain range. Along this 7-mi corridor are several closely grouped residential areas whose inhabitants identify themselves collectively as the community of Malia. Malia has a multiethnic population of approximately 27,000 people. Hawaiians or part Hawaiians make up 36 percent of the population, Caucasians 27 percent, Filipinos 14 percent, and Japanese 5 percent. Compared with the rest of Oahu, Malia suffers from high unemployment, lack of local employment opportunities, low family income, low educational levels, substandard housing, and poor health.

A major problem facing Malia was the lack of health services. One health facility, the Plantation Medical Center, served the area. But this had closed in 1946 when the plantation was shut down. Between 1946 and 1964, Malia's medical services were limited to two physicians who worked in the area. Then, in 1964, the Kaiser Foundation Health Plan began operating a Malia clinic. However, it did not meet the residents' needs. The clinic was open only during weekdays from 8 A.M. to 4:30 P.M., with no emergency service at other times. It was staffed only by one full-time physician, a laboratory technician, and a nurse. Most significantly, the clinic limited its services to members of the Kaiser Prepaid Health Plan, which few residents could afford. In 1964 the medical needs of Malia's residents were served essentially by two private physicians, a city and county ambulance station, and one dentist.

In 1966 the Community Action Program (CAP), a federal government program that assisted poverty-designated communities to organize and solve their problems, assigned representatives to Malia. The representatives helped to unify Malia's efforts by serving as a means by which the community could articulate its health care needs. They also coordinated the residents' activities through CAP committees. Representing a good balance of the residents, the CAP committees were assigned the vital task of formulating a unified health proposal for Malia. This proposal was rejected by the federal government's Office of Economic Opportunity (OEO) in 1967 since it lacked implementation plans and had been criticized by the Honolulu County Medical Society because the health center's range of services was too broad and its cost unjustified. The Medical Society also objected to medical facilities and services financed by public funds. The Kaiser Foundation Research Institute developed a second proposal and submitted it to the OEO. It was also rejected for the same reasons.

In 1968, Model Cities, a federal antipoverty program that provided "model neighborhoods" with funds to plan and operate development projects, designated Malia as a model neighborhood. At the same time, the Regional Medical Program (RMP), a federal program that gave development funds to health projects, was directed to coordinate funding with Model Cities. To receive Model Cities funds, residents would first have to organize a neighborhood planning committee, as required by the funding provisions. The planning committee would have two purposes. First, by placing a priority on the neighborhood's development efforts, it would act as the community's policymaking body. Second, by requiring a majority of the committee members to be local residents, it would guarantee residents' participation in neighborhood planning.

Using the organizational structure of the old CAP committees, residents quickly organized a neighborhood committee and named it the Malia District Neighborhood Planning Committee (MDNPC). Like the grass-roots organizations and the CAP committees, the MDNPC was democratically organized and relied on active community participation to plan and make decisions. A health task force was organized, and with support from the governor's office and the School of Public Health, University of Hawaii, it formulated a health center program in 1968–1969. The guiding principles were based on the following recommendations:

1. A community organization would develop policies and provide guidelines for all health services.
2. The community organization would fully coordinate its efforts and cooperate with all professional health care providers.
3. All ancillary health activities—social, welfare, and referral—would be integrated into a single system.
4. Services would be provided rapidly *and* the client's personal dignity would be maintained.
5. Community resources and manpower would be trained, developed, and used whenever possible in staffing the health center.

The overall health program would consist of three component projects, with a board of directors providing policies and guidelines for the program administrator and staff. Reflecting Malia's urgent need for a general health facility, the first component would be a comprehensive health center. In addition to providing 24-hour emergency service, the center would offer clinic services, special diagnosis, medical treatment, and education and training programs. The second component would be home care, consisting of home health care and outreach workers. To be organized soon after the health center began operating, this component would emphasize preventive medicine, hygiene in the home, and patient rehabilitation at home. The third component would be a hospital, to be built at a later date. Funding would be sought from the federal government through Model Cities, RMP, the Department of Health, Education, and Welfare (HEW), and local governments (state and city/county of Honolulu.

In essence, the health program concept was an overall health master plan. It recommended general guidelines, identified health projects, established a schedule for implementing these projects, and suggested ways to fund them. It did not, however, provide specific project plans. Nor did it outline administrative and medical guidelines and procedures. Initial funding was received from the Honolulu City Council in 1970 to pay for a project director, some staff, an office, and a one-year planning period (June 1970–June 1971) to develop more precise project plans, designs, and budgets.

Federal funding began to come in late 1971, and construction of the health center commenced early in 1972, in spite of staffing problems at the center and criticism from Model Cities regarding the administrative staff and from the Honolulu County Medical Society regarding the health program. RMP and HEW approved funding, with stipulations on annual reviews and on the development of a *Board of Directors Procedure and Policy Manual* to describe the rules, duties, and accountability of all administrative staff by February 1, 1973.

The health center began operating in a temporary facility in October 1972. Management problems created a crisis in 1973, with HEW informing the center that funding would cease in September of that year unless the center's board did the following:

1. Recruited a qualified project director acceptable to HEW.
2. Recruited three physicians, with one as the medical director.
3. Completed the prepaid health plan and a marketing strategy.
4. Developed policies and procedures to expand board participation, including other representatives of affected health interests.

HEW finally terminated funding as of December 10, 1973, because the health center had not satisfied these requirements. Indeed, the administrator continued to function with (1) lack of policies and procedures, (2) lack of physicians, and (3) lack of a prepaid health plan.

The city and county of Honolulu took over administration of the center immediately, organizing a temporary project team of physicians and support personnel. Reorganization along the lines stipulated by HEW took place between February and June 1974 with support and cooperation from various health agencies at the local and federal levels. In June 1974 the health center was operating under a new and permanent administrator, a nonresident of Malia.

Results and Impact

The project cycle formally spanned five years—from March 1969, when the health program concept was formulated, to June 1974, when the health center was transferred to permanent administration. From beginning to end, the project failed to meet major deadlines in all tasks ranging from policy and procedure formulation to personnel and physical facilities. No project phase was finished on schedule, and cumulative time overruns so exceeded the deadlines that the board of directors decided to open the center before completing the prerequisite activation tasks. This decision eventually culminated in the temporary shutdown and reorganization of the center. As a result, the center was handed over to the permanent administration about a year late, without the specific goals and objectives having been achieved.

Because it was both a community facility intended to serve residents and a professional clinic expected to conform to national medical standards, the health center created tension between residents and health professionals. The residents demanded that the center be managed in accordance with local needs; the health professionals stressed compliance with national guidelines. The basic philosophy of the health center, then—a facility intended to serve the community and, at the same time, to stand above it—established the potential for a conflict over control.

Exacerbating this tension was the intense feeling of community within Malia, which made residents antagonistic toward outsiders who tried to exercise authority over Malia's affairs. The sense of community was especially applicable to the health center because the residents had actively participated in identifying and gaining support for it through their grass-roots initiatives and through the CAP and Model Cities efforts. Residents looked upon the health center as *their* project. Thus, before the project began, they were committed to local control.

Another problem was the complexity of multiple funding. The health center had to obtain funding from numerous sources to become a viable organization. This meant that many conditions would be imposed upon the project, inevitably creating conflicting priorities. For example, contention occurred because Model Cities gave top priority to hiring Malia residents, whereas HEW required the use of highly qualified professional administrators. The lack of professional health administrators in Malia, combined with residents' dislike of outsiders, made the conflict inevitable.

The major flaw in the design, stemming partly from its lack of emphasis on the inherent problems of the health center, was inadequacy. Three major areas of the design were suboptimal. First, the board and the project director never anticipated the complexity of multiple funding and the related detailed administrative requirements or conditions necessary for approval. Second, they did not anticipate the complexity of operating the health center. Thus, they prepared no detailed plans and procedures for conducting statistical research, for providing an integrated system of health delivery, or for establishing the requirements for special training programs. Third, the board and the project team omitted the major objective of developing a community organization capable of guiding the policy of the health center and articulating sound goals and objectives.

Without formal policies and procedures, the project could not be effectively organized since (1) no dependable mechanisms for resolving problems existed; (2) no operational continuity and clarity could be established; (3) no clear-cut assignment of responsibilities could be made; and (4) no clear authority for project decisions could be determined. From this perspective, the dramatic events of December 1973 reflect the consequences of problems that were never resolved throughout the project's life cycle.

The overall objective of the project was to make adequate medical care available to all residents. During the course of the project, administrative problems, such as the inability to recruit physicians and the unwillingness to cooperate with support groups, interfered with the availability of medical services and led to the temporary closing of the health center. Moreover, the administrative problems reduced the quality of medical services by weakening the support of allied health care providers and by preventing the expansion of services. Nonetheless, some primary medical care was provided throughout most of the project's life; over 5000 patient visits were made to the health center before the transition to the permanent administration.

Conclusions

Although this case history had raised many health-related issues, the problems in implementing the health center were created not by substantive health problems but by basic managerial oversights which could have hindered any project. These oversights can be generalized as the following four policy issues for management, all of which were missing in the Malia project.

1. *Project management must be comprehensive.* The project manager must be familiar with the project in its entirety. He must know enough of the technical details of all project tasks to make knowledgeable decisions, such as when and how to use temporary experts. He must also be familiar with enough of the administrative aspects of the project to deal effectively with personnel problems, organizational complexity, and conflicting priorities. This requires familiarity with every project phase and task. The project

manager must completely prepare the project for implementation. Some procedures must be worked out to deal with special situations that may arise during activation and implementation. These factors stress the importance of feasibility studies and analyses.

2. *Project management must be integrated.* During the course of the project many different groups perform various tasks, and these groups and tasks may appear to be independent. However, they are all interrelated. It is the job of the project manager to bring together, coordinate, and fit together the work of all of these groups in a manner that ensures a coherent and unified project. To accomplish this, the project manager must open channels of communication between himself and each group. This involves cooperating willingly with designers, funding agencies, technical specialists, and all other support groups involved in the project.

3. *Project management must be flexible.* The project manager will face many situations in which he must make tradeoffs. Often he must compromise and negotiate in order to ensure the completion of the project's most important goals. In this respect, planning is continuous, and project managers must not become intransigent.

4. *Project management demands leadership.* The project manager must deal with a broad range of issues: the needs of the many support groups, the demands of the funding agencies, the sudden unforeseeable obstacles, and the changing situations. All of these issues, and many more, become critical during implementation. The project manager must make crucial decisions. This requires strong and insightful leadership.

APPENDIX C

Geothermal Energy

For centuries, man has been both fascinated by and fearful of the volcanoes, geysers, fumaroles, hot springs, and pools of boiling mud that are the dramatic visual manifestations of the immense reservoir of the earth's heat. This heat originates beneath the earth's crust, where a vast storehouse of energy waits to be harnesssd by human technological ingenuity.[1] At present, however, less is known about the interior of the earth and its storehouse of energy than about the deep oceans and outer space.[2] This illustrates the complexities of environmental issues and impacts on geothermal energy projects.

What information we have about the inner earth is largely indirect. The structure of the earth consists of three concentric spheres, which are illustrated in Figure C.1.

Life on the crust of the earth is dependent upon the atmosphere which surrounds the earth and the heat from beneath the crust. Directly under the crust lies the mantle, toward the center of the earth is the liquid core, and at the earth's center is the inner core. The earth's heat comes from deep within; the closer one gets to the center, the higher the temperature and the density become.

The emergence of heat in one of its various forms occurs when the crust of the earth is penetrated by the heat source from within. The crust is made up of six major and a few smaller discrete plates. These plates are continually in motion relative to each other. Where they spread apart, molten rock underlying the crust flows upward; where they move together, one plate goes up and the other goes under it and melts into the interior. It is at these points, the junction of the plates, that heat travels from the hot interior of the earth to the surface, where it may appear as a volcano. Cold surface water may go down to great depths and may be heated by high-temperature zones within the crust. The heated water then flows upward by convection, giving rise to spectacular geysers and hot springs.

At the earliest sites where geothermal energy was used by mankind—Italy, New Zealand, Japan, and Iceland—surface manifestations such as volcanoes, geysers, and hot pools occurred. These early sites, along with other areas in which the earth's heat is now being considered as a potential

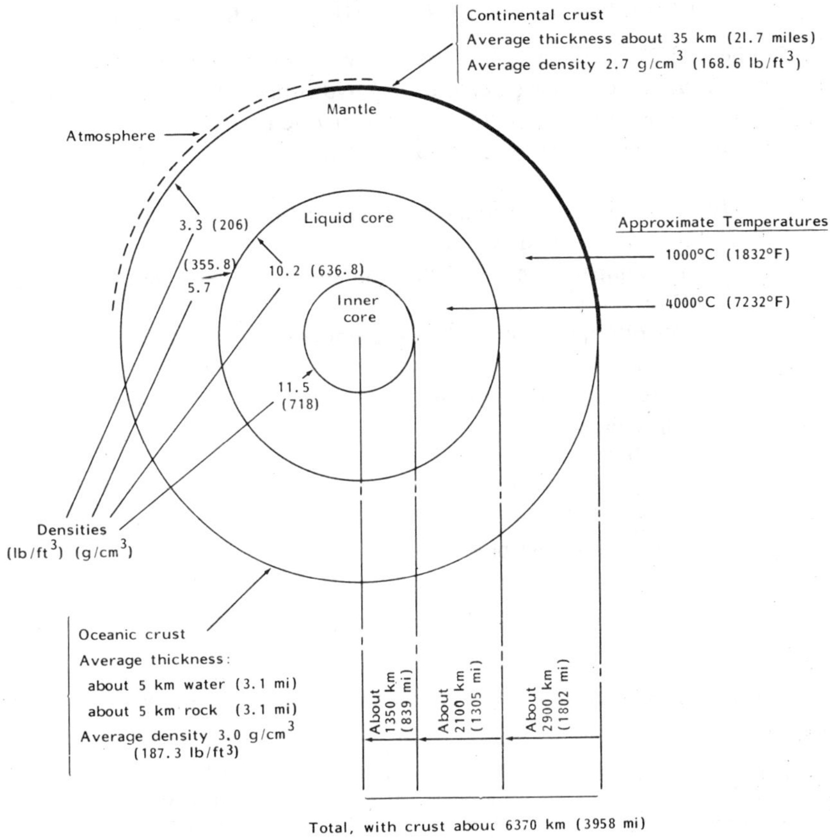

Figure C.1. Concentric layers of the earth. (Reprinted by permission of E. & F.N. Spon, Ltd., from *Geothermal Energy,* by Armstead, H.C.H. (London, 1978, p. 19.)

energy source, fall mainly but not exclusively within the so-called seismic regions, which coincide with the margins of active tectonic plate boundaries.

Over 80 countries are listed as having geothermal potential. For some of them, such as New Zealand and the Philippines, this resource has become an indispensable part of their total energy supply. Other countries, such as Saudi Arabia, with its supply of oil, have little interest in developing their geothermal potential. The countries and regions which have known and theoretically probable geothermal potential are listed in Table C.1.

CLASSIFICATION OF GEOTHERMAL RESOURCES

Geothermal resources may be classified in a number of ways, but basically they fall into three main categories: (1) hydrothermal convection systems, (2) hot igneous systems, and (3) regional conductive environments. Each of these three areas can be classified as follows:

1. Hydrothermal convection systems can be identified in three areas:
   a. Vapor-dominated systems
   b. High-temperature, liquid-dominated systems (above 150°C; 302°F)
   c. Moderate-temperature, liquid-dominated systems (90–150°C; 194–302°F)
2. Hot igneous systems have two main parts:
   a. Molten part
   b. Crystallized part (hot dry rock)
3. Regional conductive environments consist of two systems:[3]
   a. Geopressured part
   b. Normal pressured part

TABLE C.1. AREAS OF KNOWN OR PROBABLE GEOTHERMAL POTENTIAL.

Africa (North)		*America* (North)		Texas	C
Algeria	B, C	(Including Canada, Arctic)		Gulf of Mexico	C
Morocco	B, C	Christian Island	C	Rainbow Lake	
United Arab		Melville Island	C	(Canada)	C
Republic	B, C	Alaska Gulf	A, B	Hawaii	A, B
Africa (Central)		Wrangell		*America* (Central)	
Cameroon	B	Mountains	A, B	Mexico	A, B,
Chad	B	Northern Andes	A	Guatemala	A
Nigeria	B, C	California	B, C	El Salvador	A
Virunga volcanoes	A	Nevada	A	Honduras	A
Africa (East)		Oregon	A	Nicaragua	A
Ethiopia	B, C	Washington	A	Costa Rica	A
Somali Republic	B	Wyoming	A, C	Panama	A
Kenya	B	Utah	A	British Honduras	A
Uganda	B	Arizona	A	*America* (South)	
Rwanda	B	New Mexico	A	Colombia	A, C
Congo (east)	B	Colorado	A	Venezuela	C
Zambia	B	Idaho	A	Trinidad	C
Mozambique	B, C	Dakotas	A	Ecuador	A
Rhodesia	B	Arkansas	C	Peru	A, B
Malagasy		Louisiana	C	Chile	A, B
Republic	B	Oklahoma	C	Brazil (Andean)	A

Region/Country	Class
Bolivia	A
Paraguay	A
Argentina	A
Galapagos Islands	A
Antarctica	
South Shetlands	A
Graham Land	A
Europe	
Austria	C
France	C
Germany	C
Great Britain (offshore)	C
Holland	C
Hungary	C
Italy	A, B, C
Poland	C
Romania	C
Spain (south coast Canary Islands)	A, B
Far East	
Australia	C
Burma	C
China (eastern provinces)	A, B
China Sea (south)	A, B, C
Bengal (east)	C
India	B, C
Indonesia	A, C
Japan	A, C
New Guinea	A, C
Timor	A, C
Middle East	
Afghanistan	A, B, C
Baluchistan	A, B, C
Pakistan	A, B, C
Persian Gulf	A, B, C
Iran	A, B, C
Israel	B
Jordan	B
Lebanon	B
Saudi Arabia	B, C
Syria	B
Tibetan highlands	B
Turkey	A, B
Island Arcs	
(1) Pacific	
Aleutians	A
Fuji-Bonin Zone	A
Halmahera	A
Japan (north and west)	A
Indonesia (Sumatra and Java	A
Marianas	A
Kamchatka	A
New Britian	A
New Hebrides	A
New Zealand	A
Northern Celebeses	A
Philippines	A
Ryukyu Islands	A
Solomon Islands	A
Tonga Kermadec Islands	A
(2) Caribbean	
Lesser Antilles	A
Puerto Rico	A
(3) Eastern Mediterranean	
Aegean Islands	A
Greece	A
Northern Crete	A
Mid-Atlantic Ridge	
Iceland	A
Jan Mayen	A
Spitzbergen	A
Soviet Union	
Aspheron Peninsula	C
Azerbaidzhan	C
Ciscaucasia	C
Turkmeniya	C
Ukraine (east and west)	C
Urals	C
Uzbekistan	C
Volga	C

Classification of fields
A: Acid volcanic association
B: High-temperature zones
C: High-pressure reservoirs
Source: C.J. Banwell, "Geothermal Energy and Its Uses: Technical, Economic, Environmental, and Legal Aspects," *Proceedings of the Second United Nations Symposium on the Development and Use of Geothermal Resources,* San Francisco, May 20–29, 1975, p. 2265.

The development of geothermal resources for electrification first occurred in Italy in 1904. Prince Piero Ginori Conti first promoted electric power generation using earth heat from the dry steam fields in Larderello. By 1913, a 250-kW power station was in service in Larderello. Today this geothermal resource complex has a capacity of more than 400 MW. Following this pioneering effort, many other geothermal power projects were developed.

IPPMC case histories have been researched and published on the Wairakei power project in New Zealand,[4] the second geothermal project in the world; Tiwi in the Philippines[4]; and a pilot project in Hawaii (HGP, Chapter 6).

REFERENCES

1. Armstead, H.C.H. *Geothermal Energy.* London: E. and F.N. Spon, 1978.
2. Barnea, Joseph. "The Earth and Its Unknown Interior," *Geothermal Energy* 5, February 1977, p. 22.
3. White, D.E. and Williams, D.O. "Assessment of the Geothermal Resources of the United States: 1975," United States Geological Survey, Circular no. 276, 1975.
4. Goodman, Louis J. and Love, Ralph N., eds. *Geothermal Energy Projects: Planning and Management.* New York: Pergamon Press, Inc., 1980.

APPENDIX D

Biomass Energy

Another energy area of great interest and concern to environmental engineers is biomass. From biomass—plant matter available for processing into food, fiber, and chemical products—comes mankind's oldest and most fundamental source of renewable energy. Until the use of fossil fuels became widespread, biomass in the form of wood was the main energy source for most countries; for some it remains the only source. In the broadest terms, however, biomass resources for energy include not only wood but also microbes, plants, animals, animal and vegetable oils, and organic wastes.

Figure D.1 shows how the natural forces of photosynthesis work in plant systems to produce biomass energy. Photosynthesis is the biological process by which plants and algae convert sunlight, water, and carbon dioxide into carbohydrates and oxygen. The carbohydrates are then used as energy sources and raw materials for all other synthetic reactions in the plant. When the plants are harvested (or the organic wastes are processed), the solar energy they have stored can be converted to a variety of biomass fuels: solids such as wood and charcoal, liquids such as oils and alcohols, gases such as methane and hydrogen, or electricity. The exploitation of these photosynthetic by-products represents a long-established technology for energy conversion and storage.

The production of a biomass fuel, once photosynthesis has taken place, can be summarized as follows (see Figure D.1): A *plant system,* whether crops, forests, exotic species, or an energy farm, is harvested, producing a wide range of *biomass resources*, including crop and forest residues, energy crops, and animal and urban wastes. These resources may then be *pretreated* in several ways, including drying, separation, hydrolysis, densification, and pelletization; ideally, in an integrated management system, some type of biomass energy can itself be used as the processing energy. At a center producing ethanol from sugarcane, for example, part of the refuse can be converted into bagasse to fuel the ethanol production process.

The *conversion* process that turns a biomass resource into a *fuel* can be either biological or thermochemical. Besides fuels, biomass resources produce electricity in the forms of steam and chemicals such as feedstocks and fertilizers. All of these products have diverse domestic, commercial, industrial, and transport uses. With proper planning and management, a number of the by-products of the conversion process, such as fertilizers made of

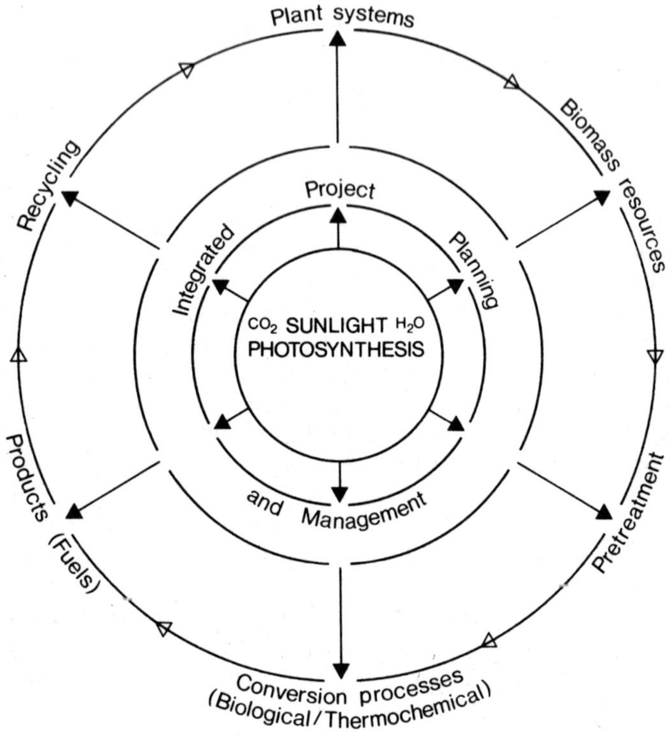

Figure D.1. The biomass energy production process.

compost from bagasse or sludge from biogas digesters, can be *recycled* into the plant system, recharging the land and creating a closed energy cycle.

Until recently, scientists have paid little attention to biomass conversion technologies. The reasons for this neglect are many. First and foremost, with cheap supplies of fossil fuels until 1973–1974, there was little incentive to explore renewable resources of any sort. Second, biomass fuels (often referred to as "biofuels") are in many ways more difficult to study than their fossil fuel counterparts. While it is easy to determine the energy content of oil, or even to obtain reliable values for the various grades of coal, it is difficult to obtain similar values for raw biomass resources. The complexity of the subject matter is largely due to the interrelationships of the dynamics of biology, photosynthesis, ecosystems, and bioconversion methods.

Third, biomass is considered an inconvenient material to process industrially. It is not as easy to handle as fossil fuel materials; it tends to be highly nonstandardized in shape and density and is frequently bulky; and it often requires tedious collection methods and pretreatment such as drying, chipping, pelletizing, and other transformations. Finally, biomass energy resources require flexible management if they are to be reliable. Whereas the rate of extraction of coal or oil is fairly simply fixed by policy and technology, biomass resources—like any other agri- or silvicultural resources—are subject to the vagaries of weather, pests, and disease.

Despite these limitations, there is little doubt that biomass fuels will become increasingly attractive in the future. The most important factor in the renaissance of biomass research is, of course, the high cost and foreseeable depletion of oil. As biomass is a form of solar energy, its renewability makes it appealing. Here it should be noted that estimates of current biomass use, as quoted earlier, tend to mask some of the major factors involved—the most important of which is the efficiency of energy use in the developing countries. For example, because of lack of capital and information, much of the biomass presently burned is used in combustion equipment whose form has remained unchanged for hundreds of years. It is therefore likely that, on the average, less than 15 percent of the energy in biomass fuel goes into useful work. With the application of appropriate technologies, this efficiency could probably be doubled.

With certain important limitations and modifications, therefore, biomass conversion does represent a flexible and widely available solution to the severe problem of dependence on imported fossil fuels. The development of a diversity of technologies can offset some of the difficulties involved in biomass processing. Unlike the fossil fuel industries, which tend to be similar in structure and management from place to place, biomass energy systems may possess the flexibility to be either high or low in technology, capital or labor intensive, and large- or small-scale in management and organization. Therefore, it is important to explore the technological potential of biomass projects, as well as their present status.

Furthermore, with proper planning and management, most biomass projects can be environmentally benign. For example, the drastic shrinkage of natural forests, harvested to meet mankind's ever-increasing demand for timber products, can be countered by the introduction of man-made forests in an energy farming concept. If the amount of biomass harvested is in balance with the amount planted, combustion of fuels made from biomass resources will not contribute to an increase in atmospheric carbon dioxide.

The goal of a traditional biomass production cycle, whether farming or forestry, is to produce a high-value product such as sugar, sawn timber, or corn; the residues, normally left in the field, can be collected and used for fuel. But the recent interest in providing high-yield, energy-efficient feedstocks for biomass production has resulted in the concept of energy farms where one or more plant species are grown specifically for the purpose of

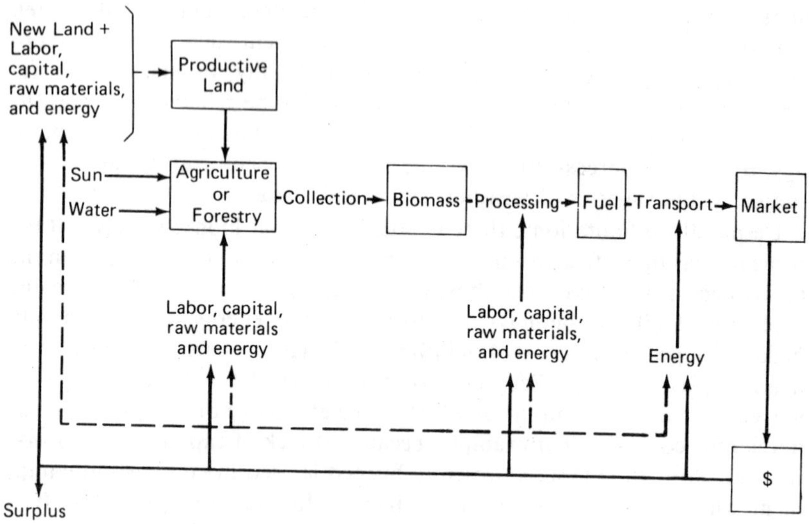

Figure D.2. The energy farming process.

fuel production. Such energy crops include a wide range of possibilities, from conventional crops such as sugarcane or beet or corn to man-made forests of short-rotation trees.

The energy farming cycle shown in Figure D.2 closely resembles a biomass production cycle, with one important exception: No distinction is made between high-value and low-value products. In the sugarcane industry, for example, this means omitting the production of crystal sugar and directing all sugar toward ethanol production, using the bagasse, or waste, to fuel this process. Energy farming projects are now being developed throughout the world as the concept of biomass energy production as a renewable closed system gains increasing status.

Biomass energy fuels may be classified in a number of ways, but basically they fall into three main categories: (1) solid fuels, (2) liquid fuels, and (3) gaseous fuels. The wide range of fuels available indicates the great advantage of biomass over other less versatile natural energy resources—its ability to produce liquid fuels as well as solid and gaseous fuels on a renewable basis.[1]

Bagasse is an example of a solid fuel obtained from sugarcane and is the subject matter of an IPPMC case history in Chapter 7.

REFERENCE

1. Goodman, Louis J. and Love, Ralph H., eds., *Biomass Energy Projects: Planning and Management*. New York: Pergamon Press, 1981.

APPENDIX E

Sample IPPMC Checklist*

A. Phase 1: Planning, Appraisal, and Design
   1. Prepare purposes and goals of project
      a) clarity of project statement
      b) identification of potential problem areas in design, manpower needs, and timetables.
   2. Extent of preliminary design
      a) manpower needs for preparation
      b) reliability of design data and assumptions.
   3. Selection of overall project manager (or project management team) who will have responsibility *and* accountability for entire project.
   4. Detailed layout of feasibility studies and analyses to determine if available resources (financial, manpower, materials, technological) are adequate to ensure a successful project
      a) the technical feasibility studies (project location and layout, subsurface conditions and problem areas, technology needs, availability of construction materials, training of technical personnel, labor market, water supply needs, waste-treatment requirements)
      b) the financial feasibility analysis (investment analysis, projected capital needs at various stages)
      c) the economic feasibility analysis (local economic benefits, cost-benefit studies of alternative designs, effect on employment)
      d) the market and commercial feasibility studies (as appropriate)
      e) the administrative, organizational, and managerial studies
      f) the environmental baseline studies
      g) the environmental impact studies (estimate impact of proposed project)
      h) the social and political impact studies.
   5. Outline procedures to be used for the appraisal process
      a) determine how many stages the process should go through
      b) have the appraisal team make necessary on-site inspections.
   6. The final design should clearly and explicitly satisfy the purposes and goals of the project
      a) alternative designs should be considered as appropriate
   7. The final design must include measurable targets for attaining purposes and goals (measuring the project's outputs)
      a) relevant building codes must be satisfied
      b) provisions must be made for environmental impact assessments.

*Adapted from the 248 questions contained in Chapter 5.

8. Plans, specifications, job descriptions, and work schedules must be prepared in detail.
9. Provisions must be made for continuous evaluation of each task, also serving as the basis for a post-evaluation plan.

B. Phase 2: Selection, Approval, and Activation
1. The final selection and approval of the project design must include a final financial plan for funding of the project, with assurances that budgets and timetables are coordinated.
2. Outline the necessary linkages with the various agencies and civic groups interested in, and concerned with, the project.
3. The overall project manager must carefully review all project tasks in light of personnel needs, position descriptions, and budgets to organize the project internally.
4. A preliminary control system such as CPM or PERT is now prepared and approved by the overall project manager. This must include:
   a) work/activity scheduling
   b) authority, responsibility, and supervision
   c) communication channels among divisions and with supporting organizations
   d) relationships between technical and administrative divisions
   e) resource procurement and allocation
   f) monitoring and reporting
   g) public participation, as appropriate.
5. Anticipate the possible need for on-the-job training for a select number of persons, who will assume more responsibility on future projects.

C. Phase 3: Operation, Control, and Handover
1. Be prepared for intense activities as the various tasks and functions become operational in the start-up of the project.
2. The overall project manager must review the control system (CPM or PERT) and adjust if necessary to optimize coordination and control of the many diverse operations
   a) the flow of necessary resources
   b) the viability of information flows and feedback systems
   c) the ability to trouble shoot any problems that might arise: personnel, technical, or financial.
3. Responsibility for on-going evaluation of each task with weekly (or daily if necessary) meetings with the overall project manager to assure smooth operations. Any request for changes in construction must be carefully checked to ensure safety and timetables are maintained.
4. Have a plan for a smooth handover of the project to its owner or administrator, with arrangements to transfer unutilized or excess resources to other projects or organizations.
5. Project completion report.

D. Phase 4: Evaluation and Refinement
1. Prepare an Evaluation Report consisting of the on-going evaluations in Phases 1–3, and a post-completion evaluation
   a) include evaluation parameters developed from the feasibility studies (Phase 1)

b) measure and analyze the difference between projected and actual results.

2. Will the evaluation results lead to the formulation of proposals for further projects?
3. What lessons and insights were learned from the project?
   a) was there an analysis of the reasons for deviations in implementation from the operating plan?
   b) did the analysis reveal both long- and short-term lessons?
4. How can these lessons be applied to refine future projects?
5. How can these lessons be applied to future policy decisions on project management?

SELECTED BIBLIOGRAPHY

Phase 1: Planning, Appraisal, and Design

Archibald, Russell. *Managing High-Technology Programs and Projects.* New York: Wiley, 1976.

Clifton, David S., and Fyffe, David E. *Project Feasibility Analysis.* New York: Wiley, 1977.

Lal, Deepak. *Methods of Project Analysis: A Review.* Baltimore: Johns Hopkins University Press, 1974.

McColl, G.D., and Throsby, C.D. "Multiple Object Benefit-Cost Analysis and Regional Development." *The Economic Record,* Vol. 48, No. 122, June 1972.

Merrett, A.J., and Sykes, Allen. *The Finance and Analysis of Capital Projects,* 2nd ed. New York: Halsted Press, 1974.

Ostrofsky, B. *Design, Planning, and Development Methodology,* Englewood Cliffs, N.J.: Prentice-Hall, 1977.

Phase 2: Selection, Approval, and Activation

Srinivasan, V. "Project Reshaping." Washington, D.C.: World Bank, Economic Development Institute, 1976.

Thamain, Hans J., and Wilemon, David L. "Conflict Management in Project Life Cycles." *Sloan Management Review,* Vol. 16, No. 3, Spring 1975.

United Nations Industrial Development Organization. *Contract Planning and Organization.* New York: United Nations, 1974.

United Nations Industrial Development Organization. "The Initiation and Implementation of Industrial Projects in Developing Countries: A Systematic Approach." New York: United Nations, 1975.

Phase 3: Operation, Control, and Handover

Holden, Ian R., and McIlroy, P.K. *Network Planning in Management Control Systems.* London: Hutchinson, 1970.

Johnson, R.A. *Operations Management: A Systems Control.* Boston: Houghton Mifflin, 1972.

Lock, Dennis. *Project Management.* London: Gower Press, 1968.

Martino, R. *Project Management and Control.* New York: American Management Association, 1965.

Staffurth, C. (ed.). *Project Cost Control Using Networks.* London: Operational Research Society and Institute of Cost and Work Accountants, 1969.

Phase 4: Evaluation and Refinement

Berger, Michael. "Divesting Project Resources." Vanderbilt University: Graduate School of Management, 1974.

Hansen, John. "Summary of the Principal Methods of Economic Industrial Project Evaluation." Washington, D.C.: World Bank, Economic Development Institute, July 1971.

Weiss, Carol H. *Evaluation Research: Methods of Assessing Program Effectiveness.* Englewood Cliffs, N.J.: Prentice-Hall, 1972.

Index